Llewe 2

Moon Sign Book

Copyright © 1991 Llewellyn Publications
All rights reserved.

Printed in the United States of America
Typography property of Llewellyn Worldwide, Ltd.
ISBN: 0-87542-467-8

Edited by Terry Buske and Trish Finley
Cover Painting by Lisa Iris

**Contributing Writers: Carl Llewellyn Weschcke, Terry
Buske, Louise Riotte, Ralph Jordan Pestka, Bruce
Scofield, Carly Wall, Bill Tuma, Gavin Kent McClung,
Noel Tyl, Nancy Soller, Pat Esclavon Hardy, Anne
Lyddane**

Published by
LLEWELLYN PUBLICATIONS
P.O. Box 64383-467
St. Paul, MN 55164-0383, U.S.A.

DECEMBER 1991	JANUARY 1992	FEBRUARY 1992
S M T W T F S	S M T W T F S	S M T W T F S
1 2 3 4 5 6 7	1 2 3 4	1
8 9 10 11 12 13 14	5 6 7 8 9 10 11	2 3 4 5 6 7 8
15 16 17 18 19 20 21	12 13 14 15 16 17 18	9 10 11 12 13 14 15
22 23 24 25 26 27 28	19 20 21 22 23 24 25	16 17 18 19 20 21 22
29 30 31	26 27 28 29 30 31	23 24 25 26 27 28 29

MARCH 1992	APRIL 1992	MAY 1992
S M T W T F S	S M T W T F S	S M T W T F S
1 2 3 4 5 6 7	1 2 3 4	1 2
8 9 10 11 12 13 14	5 6 7 8 9 10 11	3 4 5 6 7 8 9
15 16 17 18 19 20 21	12 13 14 15 16 17 18	10 11 12 13 14 15 16
22 23 24 25 26 27 28	19 20 21 22 23 24 25	17 18 19 20 21 22 23
29 30 31	26 27 28 29 30	24 25 26 27 28 29 30
		31

JUNE 1992	JULY 1992	AUGUST 1992
S M T W T F S	S M T W T F S	S M T W T F S
1 2 3 4 5 6	1 2 3 4	1
7 8 9 10 11 12 13	5 6 7 8 9 10 11	2 3 4 5 6 7 8
14 15 16 17 18 19 20	12 13 14 15 16 17 18	9 10 11 12 13 14 15
21 22 23 24 25 26 27	19 20 21 22 23 24 25	16 17 18 19 20 21 22
28 29 30	26 27 28 29 30 31	23 24 25 26 27 28 29
		30 31

SEPTEMBER 1992	OCTOBER 1992	NOVEMBER 1992
S M T W T F S	S M T W T F S	S M T W T F S
1 2 3 4 5	1 2 3	1 2 3 4 5 6 7
6 7 8 9 10 11 12	4 5 6 7 8 9 10	8 9 10 11 12 13 14
13 14 15 16 17 18 19	11 12 13 14 15 16 17	15 16 17 18 19 20 21
20 21 22 23 24 25 26	18 19 20 21 22 23 24	22 23 24 25 26 27 28
27 28 29 30	25 26 27 28 29 30 31	29 30

DECEMBER 1992	JANUARY 1993	FEBRUARY 1993
S M T W T F S	S M T W T F S	S M T W T F S
1 2 3 4 5	1 2	1 2 3 4 5 6
6 7 8 9 10 11 12	3 4 5 6 7 8 9	7 8 9 10 11 12 13
13 14 15 16 17 18 19	10 11 12 13 14 15 16	14 15 16 17 18 19 20
20 21 22 23 24 25 26	17 18 19 20 21 22 23	21 22 23 24 25 26 27
27 28 29 30 31	24 25 26 27 28 29 30	28
	31	

Contents

FROM THE
PUBLISHER

**CARL
LLEWELLYN
WESCHCKE**

ONE WORLD!

Gaia

In the morning we watch the national weather forecasts that show us satellite views of the United States, and then of the Persian Gulf area, and then other areas that may be of current interest. We gain a global perspective in just this, so simple, exercise. We are lifted beyond our most narrow horizons and shown that our true home is Earth.

In the evening we watch the international news, often with live clips from around the globe. We learn of major events as they are happening. We are given impressions from the people living where these events are happening. We are given background information about the events, the area, the people, and told how such events effect the American economy, the flow of illegal drugs, our security interests, etc. We discover that American and German business firms have been supplying weapons and the ingredients for more destructive weapons to the Iraqi military machine that (at this writing) are likely to soon be used against our own people.

Weekly we read the news magazines that give us still more detail, and show not only how international events effect us, but how they effect the other people of the world. We find Japanese and Europeans buying American businesses and properties, and know that Americans have been investing in Europe and elsewhere ever since World War II. We learn that interest rates in the United States influence the flow of money throughout the world. Decisions made in European trade talks affect the health of American and Third World agriculture. The decline in real estate values in Tokyo and New England change lending policies in Latin America and Asia.

More. We read books and see television specials that give us yet more information, in depth, showing how the burning of the rain forests in Brazil will effect world climate, and the growth of food all over the planet. We learn from Carl Sagan how even 100 nuclear weapons could bring on "Nuclear Winter" and massive crop failures that would result in billions of people starving to death. We understand how a changed weather pattern in the southern Pacific Ocean leads to years of drought in the western United States and other major food producing areas.

More. Some of us are thinking. We propose wide-scale plantings of trees to replenish the soil and compensate for the destruction of forests elsewhere. We turn to organic farming methods to revitalize the soil and the food we consume, and to reduce the use of chemical fertilizers and pesticides that not only rob the soil of life, rob the food of life, but slowly poison our drinking water. We see that simple solar cookers can be sent to Haiti to replace the people's dependence on the wasteful use of charcoal for fuel that has left the nation barren.

Our thoughts get bigger. We begin to question the views of our political leaders based on the information we study for ourselves. Should we (as tax payers) support tobacco farmers with subsidy payments while at the same time we (paying taxes and insurance premiums) pay the medical costs wrought by cigarette smoking? Should we (as tax payers and potential military victims) unilaterally (or nearly so) undertake to preserve world order?

No matter one's political disposition or philosophical

outlook, we cannot escape the fact that we do live in a "global village"—where the simple decisions of a mother to hoard food in Moscow or of Berliners to donate a million tons of stockpiled food to help the USSR through the winter may determine the outcome of political events around the world. We see entertainment originating in London, and the French see entertainment that originated in New York; we click cameras made in Japan and the Japanese drink $100 whiskey from America; we export "legal" drugs to Latin America, and Columbia exports "illegal" drugs to us.

One World. Yes, we are learning to recognize our ties to one another, and we may soon decide that education is the cheapest and most profitable investment that can be made. We may soon agree that the treatment of symptoms—whether medical or social—is wasteful in comparison with changes that root out the causes. We just might decide to invest in longevity research rather than merely prolonging life. As we move into a service and information economy, with the accompanying transformation of industry and agriculture, we find that "capital" is humanized, and that as such we are all richer to the extent that it can be managed by each person for him or herself. And to this end, *Self-Knowledge and Self-Understanding* become the most important subjects of our education.

Awareness of the global village is but a small step towards realization of, and *conscious participation in,* the Living, Evolving Organism that is the Earth as a Whole, of which we are a part: *GAIA.*

Dr. Rupert Sheldrake has demonstrated that humans and other creatures all participate in a vast collective mind that transcends time and space such that one individual can learn from others without direct contact. Birds in the south of England learned to peck off milk bottle caps to get at the cream beneath—suddenly other birds of the same species, far beyond contact with the first group, do the same thing. Two separate groups of humans are given the same crossword puzzle to solve in a 10-minute span—one works the puzzle two days after the first *with 20% better results* even though there was no contact between the groups.

In his book *The Rebirth of Nature*, Sheldrake proposes

that this same "morphic resonance" extends throughout
the planet and the solar system, and beyond and within—
from atoms to galaxies. Through reverence, and prayer
and ritual, we can connect our mind to nature, experience
the world as alive, and learn to intuitively respond to the
needs of the Earth at our feet. Such mysticism has become a
necessity for survival, and for peace.

Such mysticism is becoming more common place—in
part because the need is so great, and in part because we
have extended our awareness so far beyond the immediate confines of the personal and group environment. As
mystics we intuitively know what we have to do, and we
invent new products and processes that enhance life. And
we know what we must not do—but we still flounder in
finding out how not to do these things.

For thousands of years, we intuitively worked with the
phases and signs of the Moon and the seasons of the Sun
and Earth to plant and harvest, to nurture and preserve, to
heal and care for; we intuitively returned compost to the
soil; and together, WoMan and Nature, selected and bred
crops that were larger and better suited to human use.

Organic and lunar farming techniques are not just for
the "amateur": today large scale farms of 600 to 3000 acres
are producing more profits than the same farms did with
chemical dependency. A fellow named Terry Holsapple
in Greenup, Illinois converted his 600 acres to organic
methods, and saw his profits increase more than 50 percent. Instead of chemical fertilizer, he grows green cover
crops rich in nitrogen after the fall harvest and then in the
spring tills them back into the soil—cutting winter erosion
and adding health to the soil. Terry has learned how not to
pollute the ground water and poison the foods he grows.
And he has learned how to live better doing better.

Dan Carlson, at his Hazel Hills Research Farm near
River Falls, Wisconsin, employs only organic methods
with his tree crops—fruit and nut—and intuitively has invented what he calls "Sonic Bloom" (special recorded
sounds broadcast on large speakers to the fields and orchards combined with a spray of naturally produced mi-
cro nutrients) to increase crop production as much as 100
times greater than can be produced by old fashioned
chemical dependent methods!

Less land, no chemicals, less water for irrigation, more food and better food, *produced without harm to the land!* Chemicals used on so much of the farmland is responsible for most of the water pollution in the United States. Both the National Research Council and the Environmental Protection Agency agree on this.

People—farmers and scientists—come from all over the world to see what Dan Carlson is doing. People from Africa to California, from Iowa to the USSR have come to Hazel Hills to learn the harm of chemical dependent farming methods and how to move on to new methods that work in harmony with the Earth Herself. While writing this article, I called Dan and found he had visitors today from Papua New Guinea who want to apply his methods on 10,000 acres of teak and 10,000 acres of coffee. Another large project under consideration involves 20 square miles of vegetables in Africa.

Back here in the U.S., he has produced 145 bushels of barley per acre, 7.9 tons of alfalfa to the acre, 35 to 50 large bell peppers per plant, cauliflowers three times larger than average, 860 tomatoes per plant, avocado trees with 18 to 20 avocados in place of the average one to two, soybeans with 300 pods per plant, tomato plants 16 feet tall—crops that are healthy and rich tasting, strong and resistant. And how about a 410-pound 1st, 2nd and 3rd-prize winning pumpkin at the Sonoma County (California) Fair. But that wasn't the largest: another "Sonic Bloom" grown pumpkin weighed 527 pounds.

You can write to Dan Carlson for information at his business address: #708—119th Lane N.E., Blaine, MN, phone 612/757-8274. He makes his technology available in both inexpensive small kits for the gardener and for large scale crop application and plantation sized reforestation projects.

Dan Carlson, Terry Holsapple, and thousands of others are making a planetary difference just by doing what is good for the Earth. *Gaia.* Our Mother, our Home. We live within Her being. We had better learn to live right.

FROM THE EDITOR

Welcome back! I want to thank all of you who sent in the survey from last year's *Moon Sign Book*. Your suggestions were excellent.

We were able to incorporate some of your ideas this year. Others will have to wait until next year. You will find a list of retrograde planet dates in the first section of the book. Many of you requested this information for your planning needs. Unfortunately we cannot accommodate those of you who wanted a list of Moon void dates and times. There are so many during the year (one about every 2 days) that we could not possibly list them all. We do not have a computer program that provides just this information. Maybe in the future we can supply these times as well. It would certainly be in keeping with what the *Moon Sign Book* is all about—everything you need for Moon planning! You CAN find Moon void of course times in either *Llewellyn's Daily Planetary Guide* or our *Astrological Calendar*.

You will also notice that there are quite a few articles on healing and herbs in this edition. It was one of the biggest requests for subject matter that we had. We will continue to present this kind of information in future editions.

Many of you commented on the size of the *Moon Sign Book*. Most of you liked it's compact size. Some of you felt that it would be better to have it spiral bound. The reason that we cannot do this is that the stores want a spine (with the title showing) on the book. It is difficult for them to display and sell spiral bound books.

We are going to try to keep the book from "growing" every year. We have cut down on the space for horoscopes (please pick up *Llewellyn's Sun Sign Book* for those) and brought back the material on finding your personal Moon sign (a heavily requested item). We want the *Moon Sign Book* to remain usable (easy to open and read). Having a "not so fat" book will help in that area. The saved space will be filled with all of the topics that you, the readers, have asked for. I would appreciate getting more comments and suggestions. They really do help!

We have an old friend with us this year. Many of you will remember Noel Tyl from the *Astrology Now* magazine days of Llewellyn. He has written an incredible new book entitled *Prediction In Astrology* to be published by Llewellyn this year. The *1992 Moon Sign Book* includes Noel's excellent article on what's ahead for the world in the coming years. Keep in mind that this article was written in early 1991—watch as situations unfold!

We also have another old friend with us—Anne Lyddane. Anne has written the horoscopes this year as she does for the *Astrological Calendar* and for *Fate Magazine* every year. She is also one of our professional astrologers for Llewellyn's Personal Astrological Services (see the resource section in the back of this book for more information).

Of course the *Moon Sign Book* would not be complete without contributions from Louise Riotte, Nancy Soller and Pat Esclavon Hardy. As always, their articles are top-notch. If you would like to see any special focus in the areas of gardening, medicine, herbs, weather, or market forecasting, please let me know.

We also have other great contributors this year. I would like to thank the following people for their work and wisdom: Carly Wall, Bill Tuma, Gavin McClung, Ralph Pestka, Vince Ploscik, Bruce Scofield, Lisa Iris, Trish Finley, Carol Maki, Jack Adair, Chris Wells and Carl Llewellyn Weschcke.

I hope that this year brings you much peace and prosperity. Please be kind to our planet. Recycle, use organic methods, conserve oil and water, plant more green things, compost, and USE YOUR MOON SIGNS!

On a personal note, I just bought my first house and can't wait to dig in and get that dream garden going! This year I will only be moving perennials, but next year I hope to build some raised beds and start experimenting with all of the latest methods. I'll keep you posted.

Terry Buske

HOW TO USE YOUR MOON SIGN BOOK

We get a number of letters and phone calls every year from readers asking the same types of questions. Most of these have to do with how to find certain information in the *Moon Sign Book* and how to use this information.

The best advice we can give is to read the entire introduction, in particular the section on how to use the tables. We provide examples, using the current Moon and Aspect Tables, so that you can follow along and easily figure out the best dates for all of your important activities.

The information in the remaining part of the book is divided into categories. If you want to find out when to cut your hair, look in the Health & Beauty section. Sections are listed in the Table of Contents for your convenience.

The Moon Tables do *not* take into account the Moon void of course. Just before the Moon enters a new sign it will have one last aspect to a planet; its entrance into the next sign is void of course. It is said that decisions made while the Moon is void never come to fruition in the way intended, and sometimes not at all. Sometimes purchases made during a Moon void turn out to be poorly made or a bad investment. If you want to avoid making your decisions during a void of course Moon, please refer to either *Llewellyn's Daily Planetary Guide* or *Llewellyn's Astrological Calendar*. Many people do not pay attention to the voids; it is virtually impossible to avoid all of them when making decisions or purchases.

Although we have included a list of retrograde planets in this year's *Moon Sign Book,* the Moon Tables do *not* take into account planetary retrogrades. For more information on these see *Llewellyn's Astrological Calendar*.

All times given the the *Moon Sign Book* are set in Central Standard Time. You must adjust for your time zone and for daylight-saving time.

THE MOON'S PHASES

Everyone has seen the Moon wax and wane, growing progressively larger and smaller through a period of approximately 29 1/2 days. This circuit from New Moon, when the surface of the Moon is completely dark, to Full Moon, when it is totally lit, and back again, is called the "lunation cycle." It is the result of a relationship between the Sun, Moon and Earth. As the Moon makes one entire trip around the Earth, it reflects the light of the Sun in varying degrees, depending on the angle between the Sun and Moon as viewed from Earth. During the year, the Moon will make thirteen such trips, each called a lunation.

This cycle is divided into parts called "phases." There are several methods by which this can be done, and the system used in the *Moon Sign Book* will not necessarily correspond to those used in other almanacs and calendars. It is important, when using the Moon as a guide, to use Llewellyn's *Astrological Calendar* or *Moon Sign Book*, as these books have been designed for astrological use.

The method of division used by Llewellyn divides the lunation cycle into **four** phases or quarters. These are measured as follows.

The **first quarter** begins when the Sun and Moon are in the same place, or *conjunct* (the New Moon). The Moon is not visible at first, since it rises at the same time as the Sun. But toward the end of this phase, a silver thread can be seen just after sunset as the Moon follows the Sun over the western horizon.

The **second quarter** begins halfway between the New Moon and Full Moon, when the Sun and Moon are at right angles, or a 90° *square* to each other. This half-moon rises around noon, and sets around midnight, so it can be seen in the western sky during the first half of the night.

The **third quarter** begins with the Full Moon, when the Sun and Moon are *opposite* one another and the full light of the Sun can shine on the full sphere of the Moon. The

13

round Moon can be seen rising in the east at sunset, and then rising progressively a little later each evening.

The **fourth quarter** begins about halfway between the Full Moon and New Moon, when the Sun and Moon are again at 90°, or *square*. This decreasing Moon rises at midnight, and can be seen in the east during the last half of the night, reaching the overhead position just about as the Sun rises.

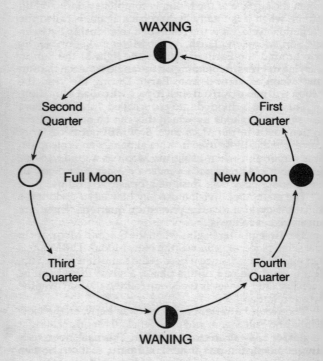

THE PHASES & SIGNS OF THE MOON

New Moon: Finalization, rest, hidden reorganizations, incipient beginnings, or chaos, disorganization, confusion, regret, stagnation, covert revenge.

Full Moon: Fulfillment, culmination, completion, activity, social awareness, or unfulfilled longing, unrest, fretfulness, sentimentality, and overt revenge.

First Quarter: Germination, emergence, beginningness, outwardly directed activity.

Second Quarter: Growth, development and articulation of things which already exist.

Third Quarter: Maturity, fruition, assumption of full form of expression.

Fourth Quarter: Disintegration, drawing back for reorganization, rest, reflection.

Moon in Aries: Good for starting things, but lacking in staying power. Things occur rapidly, but also quickly pass away.

Moon in Taurus: Things begun now last the longest and tend to increase in value. Things begun now become habitual and hard to alter.

Moon in Gemini: An inconstant and fickle position for the Moon. Things begun now are easily moved by outside influences.

Moon in Cancer: Stimulates emotional rapport between people. Pinpoints need, supports growth and nurturance.

Moon in Leo: Draws emphasis to the self, to central ideas or institutions, away from connections with others and emotional needs.

Moon in Virgo: Favors accomplishment of details and commands from higher up, while discouraging independent thinking and enterprise.

Moon in Libra: Increases self-awareness, favors self-examination and interaction with others but discourages spontaneous initiative.

Moon in Scorpio: Increases awareness of psychic power. Precipitates psychic crises and ends connections thoroughly.

Moon in Sagittarius: Encourages expansionary flights of the imagination and confidence in the flow of life.

Moon in Capricorn: Artificial, disciplined, controlled and institutional activities are favored. Develops strong structure.

Moon in Aquarius: Idealized conditions lead to the potential for emotional disappointment and disruption in the natural flow of life.

Moon in Pisces: Energy withdraws from the surface of life, hibernates within, secretly reorganized and realigning for a new day.

ALL TIMES GIVEN IN THE MOON SIGN BOOK ARE IN CENTRAL STANDARD TIME. YOU NEED TO ADJUST THEM TO YOUR TIME ZONE AND TO DAYLIGHT-SAVING TIME.

HOW TO USE THE MOON SIGN BOOK TABLES AND ACTIVITY INFORMATION

Timing your activities is one of the most important things you can do to ensure success. In many Eastern countries, timing by the planets is so important that practically no event takes place without first setting up a chart for it. Many times weddings take place in the middle of the night because that is when the influences are the best. You may not want to take it that far, and you don't really need to set up a chart for each activity, but you may as well make use of the influences of the Moon whenever possible. It's easy and it works!

In the *Moon Sign Book* you will find all of the information you need to plan just about any important activity: weddings, fishing, buying a car or house, cutting your hair, traveling and more. Not all of the things you need to do will fall on particularly favorable days, but we give you the guidelines you need to pick the best day out of the several you have to choose from.

Let's run through some examples. Say you need to set up an appointment to have your hair cut. You have thin hair and would like to have it look thicker. Look in the Health & Beauty section under Hair Care. You will see that you should cut it during a Full Moon (marked FM in the Moon Tables or O under the Sun in the Lunar Aspectarian). You should, however, avoid the Moon in Virgo. We'll say that it is the month of March. Look up March in the Moon Tables section. The Full Moon falls on March 18th at 12:19 p.m. It is in the sign of Libra, which is good for beauty treatments. Because the Full Moon occurs around Noon, the entire day is good for cutting hair. If the Full Moon happened late in the evening, the next day would be just as good. The times are fairly flexible; you do not have to use the exact time of the Moon change.

That was an easy example. Let's move on to a more difficult example that uses the phase and sign of the Moon.

You want to buy a house for a permanent home. Look in the Home, Family & Pets section under House. It says that you should buy a home when the Moon is in Taurus, Leo, Scorpio or Aquarius (fixed signs). You need to get a loan so you should look in the Business and Legal section under Loans. Here it says that the 3rd and 4th quarters favor the borrower (you.) You are going to buy the house in April. Look up April in the Moon Tables section. The Moon is in the 3rd and 4th quarters from April 17th through the 30th. These dates are good for getting a loan. Now look at the signs. The Moon is in Scorpio (good) on the 17th and 18th. It is in Aquarius (good) on the 24th, 25th and part of the 26th. It is in Leo and Taurus (the other good signs) in the 1st and 2nd quarters—not good quarters for getting a loan. So, the best dates are the 17th, 18th, 24th, 25th and the morning of the 26th. You just match the best signs and phases (quarters) to come up with the best dates.

With all activities, be sure to check the Favorable and Unfavorable Dates for your Sun Sign in the table next to the Lunar Aspectarian. If there is a choice between several dates, pick the one most favorable for you (marked F).

OK. Now you have mastered these examples. Let's go to an example that uses signs, phases and *aspects*. You will find the lunar aspects listed in the Lunar Aspectarian on the page facing the Moon Tables. The letters listed under the planets stand for specific aspects—C=conjunct, Sx=sextile, Sq=square, T=trine and O=opposition. You will be using the squares and oppositions more than the other aspects as these are considered negative.

Our example this time is fixing your car. We will use June as the sample month. Look in the Home, Family & Pets section under Automobile Repair. It says that the Moon should be in a fixed sign (Leo, Taurus, Scorpio, Aquarius) in the 1st or 2nd quarter and well-aspected to the Sun. (Good aspects are sextiles and trines, marked Sx and T.) It also tells you to avoid negative aspects to Mars, Saturn, Uranus, Neptune and Pluto. Look in the Moon Tables under June. You will see that the Moon is in the 1st and 2nd quarters from the 1st through the 13th. The only dates out of that time period when the Moon is in a fixed sign are the 4th and 5th (in Leo) and the 10th, 11th and 12th (in Scorpio). So now you can eliminate all of the other dates. Now look at the Lunar Aspectarian for June for the aspects. The 4th has no aspects (there are no letters listed in any of the boxes under the planets). The 5th has a sextile to the Sun (Sx), a sextile to Mercury (Sx), a sextile to Venus, a trine to Mars (T), an opposition to Saturn (O) and a square to Pluto (Sq). Looking back at aspects to avoid, you will see that there should be no negative aspects to Mars, Saturn, Uranus, Neptune or Pluto. June 5th has an opposition (negative aspect) to Saturn and a square (neg. aspect) to Pluto. Even with the positive aspect (sextile) to the Sun, this day should be avoided.

Looking at the 10th, you will find an opposition to Mars. Rule out this date. On the 11th, the only aspect is a sextile to Jupiter. This date is fine even though there is no positive aspect to the Sun. On June 12th there is a square to Saturn and a conjunction (C) to Pluto (considered negative in most cases). So rule out this date as well. The only two dates that would be good for getting your car repaired in June are the 4th (no aspects) and the 11th (no negative aspects). You will notice that neither date has a positive aspect to the Sun, but they are the proper signs, phases and do not have negative aspects.

After you have looked under all of the planets listed for the activity and eliminated those dates that have negative aspects under those planets, you are ready to make your appointment. Use the Favorable and Unfavorable table for your Sun Sign in choosing between dates.

You have just gone through the entire process of choosing the best dates for a special event. With practice, you will be able to scan the information in the tables and do it very quickly. You will also begin to get a feel for what works best for you. Everyone has his or her own high and low cycle.

Gardening activities are dependent on many outside factors, weather being one of the major ones. Obviously, you can't go out and plant when there is still a foot of snow on the ground or when it is raining cats and dogs. You have to adjust to the conditions at hand. If the weather was bad or you were on vacation during the 1st quarter when it was best to plant, do it during the 2nd quarter while the Moon is in a fruitful sign instead. If the Moon is not in a fruitful sign during the 1st or 2nd quarter, choose a day when it is in a semi-fruitful sign. The best advice is to choose either the sign or the phase that is *most* favorable when the two don't coincide.

So, to summarize, in order to make the most of your plans and activities, check with the *Moon Sign Book*. First, look up the activity in the corresponding section under the proper heading. Then, look for the information given there in the proper tables (the Moon Table, Lunar Aspectarian or Favorable and Unfavorable Dates, or all three). Choose the best date according to the number of positive factors in effect. If most of the dates are favorable, then there is no problem choosing the one that will best fit your schedule. However, if there just don't seem to be any really good dates, pick the ones with the least number of negative influences. We guarantee that you will be very pleased with the results if you use nature's influences to your advantage.

For a quick reference, look at the Astro-Almanac. This is a *general guide* and does not take aspects into account.

HOW TO USE THE MOON TABLES AND ASPECTARIAN

First, read the preceding section on how to use your *Moon Sign Book*. You will be using the tables on the following pages in conjunction with the information given in the individual sections: Home & Family, Business & Finances, Health & Beauty, Leisure & Recreation and Farm & Garden.

The Moon Tables pages include the date, day, sign the Moon is in, the element of that sign, the nature of the sign, the Moon's phase and the times that it changes sign or phase. FM signifies *Full Moon* and NM signifies *New Moon*. The times listed directly after the day are the times when the Moon changes sign. The time listed after the phase indicate the times when the Moon changes phase. All times are listed in Central Standard Time. You need to change them to your own time zone. See the time conversion tables.

On the page next to the Moon Tables you will find the Lunar Aspectarian and the Favorable and Unfavorable Dates. To use the Lunar Aspectarian, find the planet that the activity lists and run down the column to the date desired. If you want to find a favorable aspect to Mercury, run your finger down the column under Mercury until you find an Sx or T. Positive or good aspects are signified by an Sx or T. Negative or adverse aspects are signified by an Sq or O. The conjunciton, or C, is sometimes good, sometimes bad, depending on the activity or planets involved. The Lunar Aspectarian gives the *aspects of the Moon to the other planets.*

The Favorable and Unfavorable Days table lists all of the Sun Signs. To find out if a day is positive for you, find your sign and then look down the column. If it is marked F, it is very favorable. If it is marked f, it is slightly favorable. A U means very unfavorable and a small u means slightly unfavorable.

SYMBOL KEY

Sx: Sextile/positive   T: trine/positive
Sq: square/negative   O: opposition/negative
C: conjunction/positive/negative/neutral

F: very favorable
f: slightly favorable
U: very unfavorable
u: slightly unfavorable

To find out the exact times of the daily aspects, see *Llewellyn's 1992 Daily Planetary Guide.* This will help you refine your timing even more!

TABLE OF TERMS REFERRING TO LUNAR QUARTERS (PHASES)

Sun-Moon Angle	Moon Sign Book Term	Common Terms	Division by:		
		2	4	8	
0-90° after Conjunction	First Quarter	Increasing Waxing Light New	New Moon	New Moon	
				Crescent	
90-180°	Second Quarter		First Quarter	First Quarter	
				Gibbous	
180-270°	Third Quarter	Decreasing Waning Dark Old	Full Moon	Full Moon	
				Disseminating	
270-360°	Fourth Quarter		Last Quarter	Last Quarter	
				Balsamic	

COMMON ALMANACS
ARE WORTHLESS FOR
PLANTING PURPOSES

For **astronomical** calculations the Moon's place in almanacs is given as being in the **constellation**.

For **astrological** purposes the Moon's place is figured in the **zodiacal sign**, which is its true place in the zodiac, and nearly one sign (30 degrees) different from the astronomical constellation.

To illustrate: If the common almanac gives the Moon's place in Taurus (constellation) on a certain date, its true place in the zodiac is in Gemini (zodiacal sign). Thus, it is readily seen that those who use the common almanac may be planting seeds, or engaging in other endeavors, when they think the Moon is in a **fruitful sign**, while in reality it would be in one of the most **barren signs** in the zodiac.

Common almanacs are worthless to follow for planting. Some almanacs even make a bad matter worse by inserting at the head of their columns "Moon's Sign" when they mean "Moon's *Constellation*," and this has brought much unmerited discredit on the value of planting by the Moon. The constellations form a belt outside the zodiac, but do not conform with the signs in position or time.

The constellations are correct in astronomical but not in astrological calculations. This fact not being generally known, a great deal of criticism and skepticism has developed regarding the Moon's influence in planting. To obtain desired results, planting must be done according to the Moon's place in the signs of the zodiac.

Therefore using *Llewellyn's Moon Sign Book* for all of your planting and planning purposes is the best thing to do!

LUNAR ACTIVITY GUIDE

ACTIVITY	SIGN	PHASE
Buy animals	—	New Moon, 1st
Baking	Aries, Cancer, Libra, Capricorn	1st or 2nd
Hair care:		
Permanent waves, Hair straightening, Coloring	Aquarius	1st quarter
Cut hair to stimulate growth	Cancer, Scorpio, Pisces	1st or 2nd
Cut hair for thickness	Any sign except Virgo	Full Moon
Cut hair to decrease growth	Gemini, Leo, Virgo	3rd or 4th
Start a diet to lose weight	Aries, Leo, Virgo, Sag., Aquarius	3rd or 4th
Start a diet to gain weight	Cancer, Scorpio, Pisces	1st or 2nd
Buy clothes	Taurus, Libra	1st or 2nd
Buy antiques	Cancer, Scorpio, Capricorn	—
Borrow money	Leo, Sagittarius, Aquarius, Pisces	3rd or 4th
Start a savings account	Taurus, Scorpio, Capricorn	1st or 2nd
Join a club	Gemini, Libra, Aquarius	—
Give a party	Gemini, Leo, Libra, Aquarius	—
Travel for pleasure	Gemini, Leo, Sagittarius, Aquarius	1st or 2nd
Begin a course of study	Gemini, Virgo, Sagittarius	1st or 2nd

ACTIVITY	SIGN	PHASE
Enter a new job	Taurus, Virgo, Capricorn	1st or 2nd
Can fruits and vegetables	Cancer, Scorpio, Pisces	3rd or 4th
Preserves, jellies	Taurus, Scorpio, Aquarius	3rd or 4th
Dry fruits and vegetables	Aries, Leo, Sag.	3rd
Remove teeth	Gemini, Virgo, Sagittarius, Capricorn, Pisces	1st or 2nd
Fill teeth	Taurus, Leo, Scorpio, Aquarius	3rd or 4th
Dressmaking, mending	—	1st or 2nd
Buy health foods	Virgo	—
Buy medicine	Scorpio	—
Buy permanent home	Taurus, Leo, Scorpio, Aquarius	—
Buy property for speculation	Aries, Cancer, Libra, Capricorn	—
Send mail	Gemini, Virgo, Sagittarius, Pisces	—
Wood cutting	Any sign but Cancer, Scorpio	3rd or 4th
Beauty treatments	Taurus, Cancer, Leo, Libra, Scorpio, Aquarius	1st or 2nd
Brewing	Cancer, Scorpio, Pisces	3rd or 4th
Start building	Taurus, Leo, Aquarius	3rd or 4th
Bulbs for seed	Cancer, Scorpio, Pisces	2nd or 3rd
Canning	Cancer, Scorpio, Pisces	3rd or 4th
Pour cement	Taurus, Leo, Aquarius	Full Moon
Plant cereals	Cancer, Scorpio, Pisces	1st or 2nd

ACTIVITY	SIGN	PHASE
Cultivation	Aries, Gemini, Leo, Virgo, Sag., Aquarius	4th
Breaking habits	Gemini, Leo, Virgo	3rd or 4th
Fix your car	Taurus, Virgo	1st or 2nd
Weddings	Taurus, Cancer, Leo, Libra, Pisces	2nd
Move	Taurus, Leo, Scorpio, Aquar.	—
Painting	Taurus, Leo, Scorpio, Aquarius	3rd or 4th
Train a pet	Taurus	3rd or 4th
Buy a car	Taurus, Leo, Scorpio, Aquarius	3rd or 4th
Collect debts	Aries, Cancer, Libra, Capricorn	3rd or 4th

THE SIGNS OF THE ZODIAC

Aries. The ram. Ruled by Mars. Masculine, fire, cardinal, barren, hot, dry. Rules the head and face. Colors: red and scarlet. Sun in Aries: 22 March to 20 April. Energetic, original, impulsive.

Taurus. The bull. Ruled by Venus. Feminine, earth, fixed, semi-fruitful, cold, moist. Rules the throat and neck. Colors: pink and turquoise. Sun in Taurus: 21 April to 21 May. Peaceful, practical, stubborn.

Gemini. The twins. Ruled by Mercury. Masculine, air, mutable, barren, moist. Rules the hands, arms, lungs, and nerves. Color: silver. Sun in Gemini: 22 May to 22 June. Versatile, imaginative, superficial.

Cancer. The crab. Ruled by the Moon. Feminine, water, cardinal, fruitful, cold, moist. Rules the breasts and stomach. Colors: grey, silver and brown. Sun in Cancer: 23 June to 23 July. Mothering, affectionate, possessive.

Leo. The lion. Ruled by the Sun. Masculine, fire, fixed, barren, hot, dry. Rules the heart and back. Colors: gold and scarlet. Sun in Leo: 24 July to 23 August. Confident, vital, domineering.

Virgo. The virgin. Ruled by Mercury. Feminine, earth, mutable, barren, cold, dry. Rules the bowels. Colors: navy and grey. Sun in Virgo: 24 August to 23 September. Efficient, analytical, critical.

Libra. The scales. Ruled by Venus. Masculine, air, cardinal, semi-fruitful, hot, moist. Rules the kidneys and ovaries. Color: blue-green. Sun in Libra: 24 September to 23 October. Friendly, diplomatic, weak-willed.

Scorpio. The scorpion. Ruled by Pluto. Feminine, water, fixed, fruitful, cold. Rules the sex organs. Color: blood red. Sun in Scorpio: 24 October to 22 November. Intense, forceful, proud.

Sagittarius. The archer. Ruled by Jupiter. Masculine, fire, mutable, barren, hot, dry. Rules the hips and thighs. Colors: purple and green. Sun in Sagittarius: 23 November to 22 December. Independent, sporting, undisciplined.

Capricorn. The goat. Ruled by Saturn. Feminine, earth, cardinal, semi-fruitful, cold, dry. Rules the knees, bones and skin. Colors: black and dark brown. Sun in Capricorn: 23 December to 19 January. Patient, responsible, ambitious.

Aquarius. The water bearer. Ruled by Uranus. Masculine, air, fixed, barren, moist. Rules the calves and ankles. Colors: checks and stripes. Sun in Aquarius: 20 January to 19 February. Intellectual, humanitarian, impersonal.

Pisces. The fish. Ruled by Neptune. Feminine, water, mutable, fruitful, cold, moist. Rules the feet. Colors: lavender and sea-green. Sun in Pisces: 20 February to 21 March. Sensitive, emotional, submissive.

TIME ZONE

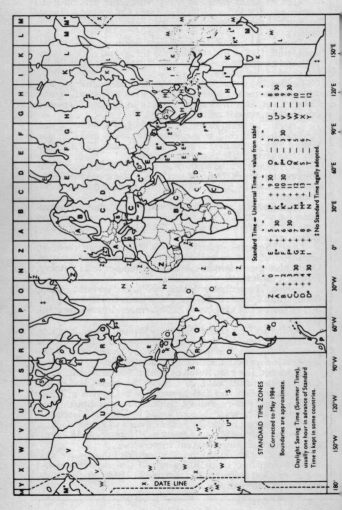

STANDARD TIME ZONES

Corrected to May 1984

Boundaries are approximate.

Daylight Saving Time (Summer Time),
usually one hour in advance of Standard
Time is kept in some countries.

X — DATE LINE

CONVERSIONS

WORLD TIME ZONES
Compared to Central Standard Time

( ) From Map
(S) CST - Used
(R) EST - Add 1 hour
(Q) Add 2 hours
(P) Add 3 hours
(O) Add 4 hours
(N) Add 5 hours
(Z) Add 6 hours
(T) MST - Subtract 1 hour
(U) PST - Subtract 2 hours
(V) Subtract 3 hours
(W) Subtract 4 hours
(X) Subtract 5 hours

(Y) Subtract 6 hours
(A) Add 7 hours
(B) Add 8 hours
(C) Add 9 hours
(D) Add 10 hours
(E) Add 11 hours
(F) Add 12 hours
(G) Add 13 hours
(H) Add 14 hours
(I) Add 15 hours
(K) Add 16 hours
(L) Add 17 hours
(M) Add 18 hours

Standard Time = Universal Time
+ value from table

	h	m			h	m			h	m
Z	0	00	H	+	8	00	Q	−	4	00
A	+ 1	00	I	+	9	00	R	−	5	00
B	+ 2	00	I*	+	9	30	S	−	6	00
C	+ 3	00	K	+	10	00	T	−	7	00
C*	+ 3	30	K*	+	10	30	U	−	8	00
D	+ 4	00	L	+	11	00	U*	−	8	30
D*	+ 4	30	M	+	12	00	V	−	9	00
E	+ 5	00	M*	+	13	00	V*	−	9	30
E*	+ 5	30	N	−	1	00	W	−	10	00
F	+ 6	00	O	−	2	00	W*	−	10	30
F*	+ 6	30	P	−	3	00	X	−	11	00
G	+ 7	00	P*	−	3	30	y	−	12	00

JANUARY

Date	Moon's Sign	Element	Nature	Moon's Phase
1 Wed. 1:31 am	Sagit.	Fire	Barren	4th
2 Thurs.	Sagit.	Fire	Barren	4th
3 Fri. 1:10 pm	Capri.	Earth	Semi-fruit	4th
4 Sat.	Capri.	Earth	Semi-fruit	NM 5:10 pm
5 Sun.	Capri.	Earth	Semi-fruit	1st
6 Mon. 2:00 am	Aquar.	Air	Barren	1st
7 Tues.	Aquar.	Air	Barren	1st
8 Wed. 2:53 pm	Pisces	Water	Fruitful	1st
9 Thurs.	Pisces	Water	Fruitful	1st
10 Fri.	Pisces	Water	Fruitful	1st
11 Sat. 2:23 am	Aries	Fire	Barren	1st
12 Sun.	Aries	Fire	Barren	2nd 8:33 pm
13 Mon. 11:01 am	Taurus	Earth	Semi-fruit	2nd
14 Tues.	Taurus	Earth	Semi-fruit	2nd
15 Wed. 3:56 pm	Gemini	Air	Barren	2nd
16 Thurs.	Gemini	Air	Barren	2nd
17 Fri. 5:27 pm	Cancer	Water	Fruitful	2nd
18 Sat.	Cancer	Water	Fruitful	2nd
19 Sun. 4:58 pm	Leo	Fire	Barren	FM 3:30 pm
20 Mon.	Leo	Fire	Barren	3rd

The SUN enters Aquarius at 1:34 pm

Date	Moon's Sign	Element	Nature	Moon's Phase
21 Tues. 4:23 pm	Virgo	Earth	Barren	3rd
22 Wed.	Virgo	Earth	Barren	3rd
23 Thurs. 5:43 pm	Libra	Air	Semi-fruit	3rd
24 Fri.	Libra	Air	Semi-fruit	3rd
25 Sat. 10:33 pm	Scorpio	Water	Fruitful	3rd
26 Sun.	Scorpio	Water	Fruitful	4th 9:28 am
27 Mon.	Scorpio	Water	Fruitful	4th
28 Tues. 7:21 am	Sagit.	Fire	Barren	4th
29 Wed.	Sagit.	Fire	Barren	4th
30 Thurs. 7:08 pm	Capri.	Earth	Semi-fruit	4th
31 Fri.	Capri.	Earth	Semi-fruit	4th

Set in Central Standard Time

JANUARY 1992
Lunar Aspectarian / Favorable & Unfavorable Days

SUN	MERCURY	VENUS	MARS	JUPITER	SATURN	URANUS	NEPTUNE	PLUTO	ARIES	TAURUS	GEMINI	CANCER	LEO	VIRGO	LIBRA	SCORPIO	SAGITTARIUS	CAPRICORN	AQUARIUS	PISCES
		C			Sx				f		U		f	u	f		F		f	u
	C		Sq						f		U		f	u	f		F		f	u
		C							f		U		f	u	f		F		f	u
C				T			C	C	u	f		U		f	u	f		F		f
								Sx	u	f		U		f	u	f		F		f
		Sx			C				f	u	f		U		f	u	f		F	
		Sq		O		Sx			f	u	f		U		f	u	f		F	
Sx							Sx	T	f	u	f		U		f	u	f		F	
	Sq		Sq		Sx					f	u	f		U		f	u	f		F
Sq		T		T						f	u	f		U		f	u	f		F
			T	T	Sq	T	T			f	u	f		U		f	u	f		F
T								O	F		f	u	f		U		f	u	f	
				Sq	T				F		f	u	f		U		f	u	f	
		O								F		f	u	f		U		f	u	f
	O		O	Sx		O	O			F		f	u	f		U		f	u	f
O								T	f		F		f	u	f		U		f	u
		T						Sq	f		F		f	u	f		U		f	u
			T	C		T	T		u	f		F		f	u	f		U		f
T	T	Sq						Sx	u	f		F		f	u	f		U		f
			Sq	T	Sq		Sq		u	f		F		f	u	f		U		f
Sq	Sx	Sx	Sx	Sx	Sq				f	u	f		F		f	u	f		U	
						Sx	Sx	C	f	u	f		F		f	u	f		U	
	Sx								f	u	f		F		f	u	f		U	
Sx			Sq		Sx					f	u	f		F		f	u	f		U
		C		T						f	u	f		F		f	u	f		U

FEBRUARY

Date	Moon's Sign	Element	Nature	Moon's Phase
1 Sat.	Capri.	Earth	Semi-fruit	4th
2 Sun. 8:09 am	Aquar.	Air	Barren	4th
3 Mon.	Aquar.	Air	Barren	NM 1:00 pm
4 Tues. 8:51 pm	Pisces	Water	Fruitful	1st
5 Wed.	Pisces	Water	Fruitful	1st
6 Thurs.	Pisces	Water	Fruitful	1st
7 Fri. 8:16 am	Aries	Fire	Barren	1st
8 Sat.	Aries	Fire	Barren	1st
9 Sun. 5:37 pm	Taurus	Earth	Semi-fruit	1st
10 Mon.	Taurus	Earth	Semi-fruit	1st
11 Tues.	Taurus	Earth	Semi-fruit	2nd 10:16 am
12 Wed. 0:09 am	Gemini	Air	Barren	2nd
13 Thurs.	Gemini	Air	Barren	2nd
14 Fri. 3:32 am	Cancer	Water	Fruitful	2nd
15 Sat.	Cancer	Water	Fruitful	2nd
16 Sun. 4:16 am	Leo	Fire	Barren	2nd
17 Mon.	Leo	Fire	Barren	2nd
18 Tues. 3:48 am	Virgo	Earth	Barren	FM 2:05 am
19 Wed.	Virgo	Earth	Barren	3rd
The SUN enters Pisces at 3:45 am				
20 Thurs. 4:05 am	Libra	Air	Semi-fruit	3rd
21 Fri.	Libra	Air	Semi-fruit	3rd
22 Sat. 7:12 am	Scorpio	Water	Fruitful	3rd
23 Sun.	Scorpio	Water	Fruitful	3rd
24 Mon. 2:27 pm	Sagit.	Fire	Barren	3rd
25 Tues.	Sagit.	Fire	Barren	4th 1:57 am
26 Wed.	Sagit.	Fire	Barren	4th
27 Thurs. 1:34 am	Capri.	Earth	Semi-fruit	4th
28 Fri.	Capri.	Earth	Semi-fruit	4th
29 Sat. 2:35 pm	Aquar.	Air	Barren	4th

Set in Central Standard Time

FEBRUARY 1992
Lunar Aspectarian / Favorable & Unfavorable Days

SUN	MERCURY	VENUS	MARS	JUPITER	SATURN	URANUS	NEPTUNE	PLUTO	ARIES	TAURUS	GEMINI	CANCER	LEO	VIRGO	LIBRA	SCORPIO	SAGITTARIUS	CAPRICORN	AQUARIUS	PISCES
			C			C	C	Sx	u	f		U		f	u	f		F		f
	C								f	u	f		U		f	u	f		F	
C					C				f	u	f		U		f	u	f		F	
								Sq	f	u	f		U		f	u	f		F	
				O						f	u	f		U		f	u	f		F
		Sx	Sx			Sx	Sx	T	f	u	f		U		f	u	f			F
									F	f	u	f		U		f	u	f		
Sx	Sx	Sq				Sx	Sq	Sq	F	f	u	f		U		f	u	f		
			Sq						F	f	u	f		U		f	u	f		
				T	Sq	T				F		f	u	f		U		f	u	f
Sq	Sq	T	T				T	O		F		f	u	f		U		f	u	f
			Sq		T				f		F		f	u	f		U		f	u
T	T								f		F		f	u	f		U		f	u
			Sx						u	f		F		f	u	f		U		f
		O				O	O	T	u	f		F		f	u	f		U		f
		O			O				f	u	f		F		f	u	f		U	
								Sq	f	u	f		F		f	u	f		U	
O	O			C						f	u	f		F		f	u	f		U
						T	T	Sx		f	u	f		F		f	u	f		U
		T	T		T				U		f	u	f		F		f	u	f	
				Sq	Sq				U		f	u	f		F		f	u	f	
T		Sq	Sq							U		f	u	f		F		f	u	f
	T			Sx	Sq	Sx	Sx			U		f	u	f		F		f	u	f
								C	f		U		f	u	f		F		f	u
Sq		Sx	Sx	Sq	Sx				f		U		f	u	f		F		f	u
	Sq								u	f		U		f	u	f		F		f
Sx				T					u	f		U		f	u	f		F		f
						C	C		f	u	f		U		f	u	f		F	
		Sx						Sx	f	u	f		U		f	u	f		F	

MARCH

Date	Moon's Sign	Element	Nature	Moon's Phase
1 Sun.	Aquar.	Air	Barren	4th
2 Mon.	Aquar.	Air	Barren	4th
3 Tues. 3:12 am	Pisces	Water	Fruitful	4th
4 Wed.	Pisces	Water	Fruitful	NM 7:23 am
5 Thurs. 2:08 pm	Aries	Fire	Barren	1st
6 Fri.	Aries	Fire	Barren	1st
7 Sat. 11:06 pm	Taurus	Earth	Semi-fruit	1st
8 Sun.	Taurus	Earth	Semi-fruit	1st
9 Mon.	Taurus	Earth	Semi-fruit	1st
10 Tues. 6:04 am	Gemini	Air	Barren	1st
11 Wed.	Gemini	Air	Barren	2nd 8:37 pm
12 Thurs. 10:51 am	Cancer	Water	Fruitful	2nd
13 Fri.	Cancer	Water	Fruitful	2nd
14 Sat. 1:21 pm	Leo	Fire	Barren	2nd
15 Sun.	Leo	Fire	Barren	2nd
16 Mon. 2:14 pm	Virgo	Earth	Barren	2nd
17 Tues.	Virgo	Earth	Barren	2nd
18 Wed. 2:56 pm	Libra	Air	Semi-fruit	FM 12:19 pm
19 Thurs.	Libra	Air	Semi-fruit	3rd
20 Fri. 5:21 pm	Scorpio	Water	Fruitful	3rd
The SUN enters Aries at 2:49 am				
21 Sat.	Scorpio	Water	Fruitful	3rd
22 Sun. 11:14 pm	Sagit.	Fire	Barren	3rd
23 Mon.	Sagit.	Fire	Barren	3rd
24 Tues.	Sagit.	Fire	Barren	3rd
25 Wed. 9:09 am	Capri.	Earth	Semi-fruit	4th 8:31 pm
26 Thurs.	Capri.	Earth	Semi-fruit	4th
27 Fri. 9:45 pm	Aquar.	Air	Barren	4th
28 Sat.	Aquar.	Air	Barren	4th
29 Sun.	Aquar.	Air	Barren	4th
30 Mon. 10:24 am	Pisces	Water	Fruitful	4th
31 Tues.	Pisces	Water	Fruitful	4th

Set in Central Standard Time

ARCH 1992
nar Aspectarian / Favorable & Unfavorable Days

SUN	MERCURY	VENUS	MARS	JUPITER	SATURN	URANUS	NEPTUNE	PLUTO	ARIES	TAURUS	GEMINI	CANCER	LEO	VIRGO	LIBRA	SCORPIO	SAGITTARIUS	CAPRICORN	AQUARIUS	PISCES
		C	C		C				f	u	f		U		f	u	f		F	
								Sq	f	u	f		U		f	u	f		F	
				O						f	u	f		U		f	u	f		F
C						Sx	Sx			f	u	f		U		f	u	f		F
	C							T		f	u	f		U		f	u	f		F
			Sx		Sx	Sq			F		f	u	f		U		f	u	f	
		Sx					Sq		F		f	u	f		U		f	u	f	
				T					F		f	u	f		U		f	u	f	
Sx		Sq	Sq		Sq	T	T	O	F		f	u	f		U		f	u	f	
	Sx		Sq							F		f	u	f		U		f	u	f
Sq			T		T					F		f	u	f		U		f	u	f
		T							f		F		f	u	f		U		f	u
	Sq			Sx		O	O		f		F		f	u	f		U		f	u
T								T	f		F		f	u	f		U		f	u
	T		O		O				u	f		F		f	u	f		U		f
		O						Sq	u	f		F		f	u	f		U		f
				C		T	T		u	f		F		f	u	f		U		f
O								Sx	u	f		F		f	u	f		U		f
	O				T	Sq	Sq		f	u	f		F		f	u	f		U	
			T						f	u	f		F		f	u	f		U	
		T		Sx	Sq				f	u	f		F		f	u	f		U	
			Sq			Sx	Sx	C	f	u	f		F		f	u	f		U	
T	T	Sq		Sq						f	u	f		F		f	u	f		U
					Sx					f	u	f		F		f	u	f		U
Sq	Sq		Sx	T					U		f	u	f		F		f	u	f	
		Sx				C	C		U		f	u	f		F		f	u	f	
								Sx	U		f	u	f		F		f	u	f	
Sx	Sx									U		f	u	f		F		f	u	f
					C			Sq		U		f	u	f		F		f	u	f
		C	O							U		f	u	f		F		f	u	f
						Sx	Sx			U		f	u	f		F		f	u	f

APRIL

Date	Moon's Sign	Element	Nature	Moon's Phase
1 Wed. 9:05 pm	Aries	Fire	Barren	4th
2 Thurs.	Aries	Fire	Barren	NM 11:02 pm
3 Fri.	Aries	Fire	Barren	1st
4 Sat. 5:19 am	Taurus	Earth	Semi-fruit	1st
5 Sun.	Taurus	Earth	Semi-fruit	1st
6 Mon. 11:34 am	Gemini	Air	Barren	1st
7 Tues.	Gemini	Air	Barren	1st
8 Wed. 4:19 pm	Cancer	Water	Fruitful	1st
9 Thurs.	Cancer	Water	Fruitful	1st
10 Fri. 7:47 pm	Leo	Fire	Barren	2nd 4:07 am
11 Sat.	Leo	Fire	Barren	2nd
12 Sun. 10:10 pm	Virgo	Earth	Barren	2nd
13 Mon.	Virgo	Earth	Barren	2nd
14 Tues.	Virgo	Earth	Barren	2nd
15 Wed. 0:11 am	Libra	Air	Semi-fruit	2nd
16 Thurs.	Libra	Air	Semi-fruit	FM 10:43 pm
17 Fri. 3:11 am	Scorpio	Water	Fruitful	3rd
18 Sat.	Scorpio	Water	Fruitful	3rd
19 Sun. 8:41 am	Sagit.	Fire	Barren	3rd

The SUN enters Taurus at 1:58 pm

Date	Moon's Sign	Element	Nature	Moon's Phase
20 Mon.	Sagit.	Fire	Barren	3rd
21 Tues. 5:41 pm	Capri.	Earth	Semi-fruit	3rd
22 Wed.	Capri.	Earth	Semi-fruit	3rd
23 Thurs.	Capri.	Earth	Semi-fruit	3rd
24 Fri. 5:39 am	Aquar.	Air	Barren	4th 3:41 pm
25 Sat.	Aquar.	Air	Barren	4th
26 Sun. 6:21 pm	Pisces	Water	Fruitful	4th
27 Mon.	Pisces	Water	Fruitful	4th
28 Tues.	Pisces	Water	Fruitful	4th
29 Wed. 5:14 am	Aries	Fire	Barren	4th
30 Thurs.	Aries	Fire	Barren	4th

Set in Central Standard Time

SUN	MERCURY	VENUS	MARS	JUPITER	SATURN	URANUS	NEPTUNE	PLUTO	ARIES	TAURUS	GEMINI	CANCER	LEO	VIRGO	LIBRA	SCORPIO	SAGITTARIUS	CAPRICORN	AQUARIUS	PISCES
	C	C						T		f	u	f		U		f	u	f		F
C									F		f	u	f		U		f	u	f	
					Sx	Sq	Sq		F		f	u	f		U		f	u	f	
			Sx	T						F		f	u	f		U		f	u	f
					Sq	T	T	O		F		f	u	f		U		f	u	f
	Sx	Sx		Sq					f		F		f	u	f		U		f	u
Sx			Sq		T				f		F		f	u	f		U		f	u
Sq	Sq								f		F		f	u	f		U		f	u
			T	Sx		O			u	f		F		f	u	f		U		f
Sq	T						O	T	u	f		F		f	u	f		U		f
	T								f	u	f		F		f	u	f		U	
T					O			Sq	f	u	f		F		f	u	f		U	
			O	C					f	u	f		F		f	u	f		U	
						T	T	Sx		f	u	f		F		f	u	f		U
	O	O								f	u	f		F		f	u	f		U
O					T	Sq	Sq			f	u	f		F		f	u	f		U
				Sx					U		f	u	f		F		f	u	f	
			T		Sq	Sx	Sx	C	U		f	u	f		F		f	u	f	
	T			Sq					U		f	u	f		F		f	u	f	
		T	Sq		Sx					U		f	u	f		F		f	u	f
T										U		f	u	f		F		f	u	f
	Sq			T					f		U		f	u	f		F		f	u
		Sq	Sx			C	C	Sx	f		U		f	u	f		F		f	u
Sq	Sx								f		U		f	u	f		F		f	u
					C				u	f		U		f	u	f		F		f
		Sx						Sq	u	f		U		f	u	f		F		f
Sx				O					f	u	f		U		f	u	f		F
			C			Sx	Sx	T		f	u	f		U		f	u	f		F
	T								F		f	u	f		U		f	u	f	
	C				Sx	Sq	Sq		F		f	u	f		U		f	u	f	

MAY

Date	Moon's Sign	Element	Nature	Moon's Phase
1 Fri. 1:10 pm	Taurus	Earth	Semi-fruit	4th
2 Sat.	Taurus	Earth	Semi-fruit	NM 11:45 am
3 Sun. 6:29 pm	Gemini	Air	Barren	1st
4 Mon.	Gemini	Air	Barren	1st
5 Tues. 10:11 pm	Cancer	Water	Fruitful	1st
6 Wed.	Cancer	Water	Fruitful	1st
7 Thurs.	Cancer	Water	Fruitful	1st
8 Fri. 1:08 am	Leo	Fire	Barren	1st
9 Sat.	Leo	Fire	Barren	2nd 9:45 am
10 Sun. 3:57 am	Virgo	Earth	Barren	2nd
11 Mon.	Virgo	Earth	Barren	2nd
12 Tues. 7:06 am	Libra	Air	Semi-fruit	2nd
13 Wed.	Libra	Air	Semi-fruit	2nd
14 Thurs. 11:16 am	Scorpio	Water	Fruitful	2nd
15 Fri.	Scorpio	Water	Fruitful	2nd
16 Sat. 5:23 pm	Sagit.	Fire	Barren	FM 10:04 am
17 Sun.	Sagit.	Fire	Barren	3rd
18 Mon.	Sagit.	Fire	Barren	3rd
19 Tues. 2:13 am	Capri.	Earth	Semi-fruit	3rd
20 Wed.	Capri.	Earth	Semi-fruit	3rd

The SUN enters Gemini at 1:13 pm

Date	Moon's Sign	Element	Nature	Moon's Phase
21 Thurs. 1:44 pm	Aquar.	Air	Barren	3rd
22 Fri.	Aquar.	Air	Barren	3rd
23 Sat.	Aquar.	Air	Barren	3rd
24 Sun. 2:26 am	Pisces	Water	Fruitful	4th 9:54 am
25 Mon.	Pisces	Water	Fruitful	4th
26 Tues. 1:53 pm	Aries	Fire	Barren	4th
27 Wed.	Aries	Fire	Barren	4th
28 Thurs. 10:17 pm	Taurus	Earth	Semi-fruit	4th
29 Fri.	Taurus	Earth	Semi-fruit	4th
30 Sat.	Taurus	Earth	Semi-fruit	4th
31 Sun. 3:20 am	Gemini	Air	Barren	NM 9:58 pm

Set in Central Standard Time

MAY 1992

Lunar Aspectarian / Favorable & Unfavorable Days

SUN	MERCURY	VENUS	MARS	JUPITER	SATURN	URANUS	NEPTUNE	PLUTO	ARIES	TAURUS	GEMINI	CANCER	LEO	VIRGO	LIBRA	SCORPIO	SAGITTARIUS	CAPRICORN	AQUARIUS	PISCES
		C		T					F		f	u	f		U		f	u	f	
C					Sq	T	T			F		f	u	f		U		f	u	f
			Sx					O		F		f	u	f		U		f	u	f
				Sq					f		F		f	u	f		U		f	u
	Sx		Sq		T				f		F		f	u	f		U		f	u
		Sx			Sx				u	f		F		f	u	f		U		f
Sx	Sq					O	O	T	u	f		F		f	u	f		U		f
		Sq	T						f	u	f		F		f	u	f		U	
Sq					O			Sq	f	u	f		F		f	u	f		U	
	T			C						f	u	f		F		f	u	f		U
T		T				T	T	Sx		f	u	f		F		f	u	f		U
			O						U		f	u	f		F		f	u	f	
					T	Sq	Sq		U		f	u	f		F		f	u	f	
	O		Sx							U		f	u	f		F		f	u	f
	O				Sq	Sx	Sx			U		f	u	f		F		f	u	f
O								C	f		U		f	u	f		F		f	u
			T	Sq					f		U		f	u	f		F		f	u
			Sx						u	f		U		f	u	f		F		f
		Sq		T					u	f		U		f	u	f		F		f
	T					C	C	Sx	f	u	f		U		f	u	f		F	
T		T							f	u	f		U		f	u	f		F	
			Sx							f	u	f		U		f	u	f		F
	Sq	Sq			C			Sq		f	u	f		U		f	u	f		F
Sq				O					F		f	u	f		U		f	u	f	
						Sx	Sx	T	F		f	u	f		U		f	u	f	
	Sx	Sx								F		f	u	f		U		f	u	f
Sx			C		Sq					F		f	u	f		U		f	u	f
						Sx	Sq		f		F		f	u	f		U		f	u
				T					f		F		f	u	f		U		f	u
					Sq	T	T	O	u	f		F		f	u	f		U		f
C	C	C		Sq					u	f		F		f	u	f		U		f

JUNE

Date	Moon's Sign	Element	Nature	Moon's Phase
1 Mon.	Gemini	Air	Barren	1st
2 Tues. 5:59 am	Cancer	Water	Fruitful	1st
3 Wed.	Cancer	Water	Fruitful	1st
4 Thurs. 7:36 am	Leo	Fire	Barren	1st
5 Fri.	Leo	Fire	Barren	1st
6 Sat. 9:29 am	Virgo	Earth	Barren	1st
7 Sun.	Virgo	Earth	Barren	2nd 2:48 pm
8 Mon. 12:34 pm	Libra	Air	Semi-fruit	2nd
9 Tues.	Libra	Air	Semi-fruit	2nd
10 Wed. 5:28 pm	Scorpio	Water	Fruitful	2nd
11 Thurs.	Scorpio	Water	Fruitful	2nd
12 Fri.	Scorpio	Water	Fruitful	2nd
13 Sat. 0:30 am	Sagit.	Fire	Barren	2nd
14 Sun.	Sagit.	Fire	Barren	FM 10:51 pm
15 Mon. 9:51 am	Capri.	Earth	Semi-fruit	3rd
16 Tues.	Capri.	Earth	Semi-fruit	3rd
17 Wed. 9:20 pm	Aquar.	Air	Barren	3rd
18 Thurs.	Aquar.	Air	Barren	3rd
19 Fri.	Aquar.	Air	Barren	3rd
20 Sat. 10:01 am	Pisces	Water	Fruitful	3rd

The SUN enters Cancer at 9:15 pm

Date	Moon's Sign	Element	Nature	Moon's Phase
21 Sun.	Pisces	Water	Fruitful	3rd
22 Mon. 10:04 pm	Aries	Fire	Barren	3rd
23 Tues.	Aries	Fire	Barren	4th 2:12 am
24 Wed.	Aries	Fire	Barren	4th
25 Thurs. 7:29 am	Taurus	Earth	Semi-fruit	4th
26 Fri.	Taurus	Earth	Semi-fruit	4th
27 Sat. 1:15 pm	Gemini	Air	Barren	4th
28 Sun.	Gemini	Air	Barren	4th
29 Mon. 3:43 pm	Cancer	Water	Fruitful	4th
30 Tues.	Cancer	Water	Fruitful	NM 6:19 am

Set in Central Standard Time

JUNE 1992

Lunar Aspectarian   **Favorable & Unfavorable Days**

SUN	MERCURY	VENUS	MARS	JUPITER	SATURN	URANUS	NEPTUNE	PLUTO	ARIES	TAURUS	GEMINI	CANCER	LEO	VIRGO	LIBRA	SCORPIO	SAGITTARIUS	CAPRICORN	AQUARIUS	PISCES
			Sx		T				f		F		f	u	f		U		f	u
			Sx						u	f		F		f	u	f		U		f
		Sq				O	O	T	u	f		F		f	u	f		U		f
									f	u	f		F		f	u	f		U	
Sx	Sx	Sx	T		O			Sq	f	u	f		F		f	u	f		U	
				C						f	u	f		F		f	u	f		U
Sq		Sq				T	T	Sx		f	u	f		F		f	u	f		U
Sq	Sq									f	u	f		F		f	u	f		U
T		T			T	Sq	Sq		U		f	u	f		F		f	u	f	
	T		O						U		f	u	f		F		f	u	f	
			Sx							U		f	u	f		F		f	u	f
				Sq		Sx	Sx	C		U		f	u	f		F		f	u	f
				Sq					f		U		f	u	f		F		f	u
O		O		Sx					f		U		f	u	f		F		f	u
			T						u	f		U		f	u	f		F		f
		O		T		C	C		u	f		U		f	u	f		F		f
								Sx	u	f		U		f	u	f		F		f
			Sq						f	u	f		U		f	u	f		F	
				C				Sq	f	u	f		U		f	u	f		F	
T		T	Sx						f	u	f		U		f	u	f		F	
				O		Sx	Sx			f	u	f		U		f	u	f		F
	T							T		f	u	f		U		f	u	f		F
Sq		Sq							F		f	u	f		U		f	u	f	
					Sx	Sq	Sq		F		f	u	f		U		f	u	f	
Sx	Sq	Sx	C						F		f	u	f		U		f	u	f	
			T		Sq	T	T	O		F		f	u	f		U		f	u	f
	Sx									F		f	u	f		U		f	u	f
			Sq	Sq	T				f		F		f	u	f		U		f	u
									f		F		f	u	f		U		f	u
C		C	Sx	Sx		O	O		u	f		F		f	u	f		U		f

JULY

Date	Moon's Sign	Element	Nature	Moon's Phase
1 Wed. 4:16 pm	Leo	Fire	Barren	1st
2 Thurs.	Leo	Fire	Barren	1st
3 Fri. 4:38 pm	Virgo	Earth	Barren	1st
4 Sat.	Virgo	Earth	Barren	1st
5 Sun. 6:28 pm	Libra	Air	Semi-fruit	1st
6 Mon.	Libra	Air	Semi-fruit	2nd 8:44 pm
7 Tues. 10:54 pm	Scorpio	Water	Fruitful	2nd
8 Wed.	Scorpio	Water	Fruitful	2nd
9 Thurs.	Scorpio	Water	Fruitful	2nd
10 Fri. 6:18 am	Sagit.	Fire	Barren	2nd
11 Sat.	Sagit.	Fire	Barren	2nd
12 Sun. 4:16 pm	Capri.	Earth	Semi-fruit	2nd
13 Mon.	Capri.	Earth	Semi-fruit	2nd
14 Tues.	Capri.	Earth	Semi-fruit	FM 1:07 pm
15 Wed. 4:04 am	Aquar.	Air	Barren	3rd
16 Thurs.	Aquar.	Air	Barren	3rd
17 Fri. 4:45 pm	Pisces	Water	Fruitful	3rd
18 Sat.	Pisces	Water	Fruitful	3rd
19 Sun.	Pisces	Water	Fruitful	3rd
20 Mon. 5:08 am	Aries	Fire	Barren	3rd
21 Tues.	Aries	Fire	Barren	3rd
22 Wed. 3:37 pm	Taurus	Earth	Semi-fruit	4th 4:13 pm

The SUN enters Leo at 8:10 am

Date	Moon's Sign	Element	Nature	Moon's Phase
23 Thurs.	Taurus	Earth	Semi-fruit	4th
24 Fri. 10:45 pm	Gemini	Air	Barren	4th
25 Sat.	Gemini	Air	Barren	4th
26 Sun.	Gemini	Air	Barren	4th
27 Mon. 2:09 am	Cancer	Water	Fruitful	4th
28 Tues.	Cancer	Water	Fruitful	4th
29 Wed. 2:40 am	Leo	Fire	Barren	NM 1:36 pm
30 Thurs.	Leo	Fire	Barren	1st
31 Fri. 2:02 am	Virgo	Earth	Barren	1st

Set in Central Standard Time

ar Aspectarian / Favorable & Unfavorable Days

SUN	MERCURY	VENUS	MARS	JUPITER	SATURN	URANUS	NEPTUNE	PLUTO	ARIES	TAURUS	GEMINI	CANCER	LEO	VIRGO	LIBRA	SCORPIO	SAGITTARIUS	CAPRICORN	AQUARIUS	PISCES
								T	u	f		F		f	u	f		U		f
	C		Sq		O				f	u	f		F		f	u	f		U	
								Sq	f	u	f		F		f	u	f		U	
Sx		T		C		T	T			f	u	f		F		f	u	f		U
		Sx						Sx		f	u	f		F		f	u	f		U
Sq	Sx					Sq			U		f	u	f		F		f	u	f	
	Sq				T		Sq		U		f	u	f		F		f	u	f	
	Sq		Sx							U		f	u	f		F		f	u	f
		T	O		Sq	Sx	Sx	C	f		U		f	u	f		F		f	u
									f		U		f	u	f		F		f	u
•	T		Sq		Sx				u	f		U		f	u	f		F		f
									u	f		U		f	u	f		F		f
			T		C				f	u	f		U		f	u	f		F	
•			T				C	Sx		f	u	f		U		f	u	f		F
		O							F		f	u	f		U		f	u	f	
	O				C			Sq	F		f	u	f		U		f	u	f	
			Sq							F		f	u	f		U		f	u	f
•				O						F		f	u	f		U		f	u	f
		Sx				Sx	Sx	T	f		F		f	u	f		U		f	u
•		T							u	f		F		f	u	f		U		f
		T			Sx	Sq	Sq		u	f		F		f	u	f		U		f
									f	u	f		F		f	u	f		U	
Sq	Sq	Sq		T	Sq	T	T		f	u	f		F		f	u	f		U	
		C						O		f	u	f		F		f	u	f		U
Sx			Sq							f	u	f		F		f	u	f		U
Sx	Sx	Sx			T				U		f	u	f		F		f	u	f	
			Sx			O	O	T	U		f	u	f		F		f	u	f	
C	C		Sx							U		f	u	f		F		f	u	f
		C			O			Sq		U		f	u	f		F		f	u	f
			Sq						f		U		f	u	f		F		f	u

AUGUST

Date	Moon's Sign	Element	Nature	Moon's Phase
1 Sat.	Virgo	Earth	Barren	1st
2 Sun. 2:18 am	Libra	Air	Semi-fruit	1st
3 Mon.	Libra	Air	Semi-fruit	1st
4 Tues. 5:17 am	Scorpio	Water	Fruitful	1st
5 Wed.	Scorpio	Water	Fruitful	2nd 5:00 am
6 Thurs. 11:58 am	Sagit.	Fire	Barren	2nd
7 Fri.	Sagit.	Fire	Barren	2nd
8 Sat. 10:01 pm	Capri.	Earth	Semi-fruit	2nd
9 Sun.	Capri.	Earth	Semi-fruit	2nd
10 Mon.	Capri.	Earth	Semi-fruit	2nd
11 Tues. 10:07 am	Aquar.	Air	Barren	2nd
12 Wed.	Aquar.	Air	Barren	2nd
13 Thurs. 10:52 pm	Pisces	Water	Fruitful	FM 4:28 am
14 Fri.	Pisces	Water	Fruitful	3rd
15 Sat.	Pisces	Water	Fruitful	3rd
16 Sun. 11:12 am	Aries	Fire	Barren	3rd
17 Mon.	Aries	Fire	Barren	3rd
18 Tues. 10:11 pm	Taurus	Earth	Semi-fruit	3rd
19 Wed.	Taurus	Earth	Semi-fruit	3rd
20 Thurs.	Taurus	Earth	Semi-fruit	3rd
21 Fri. 6:37 am	Gemini	Air	Barren	4th 4:02 am
22 Sat.	Gemini	Air	Barren	4th

The SUN enters Virgo at 3:11 pm

Date	Moon's Sign	Element	Nature	Moon's Phase
23 Sun. 11:37 am	Cancer	Water	Fruitful	4th
24 Mon.	Cancer	Water	Fruitful	4th
25 Tues. 1:16 pm	Leo	Fire	Barren	4th
26 Wed.	Leo	Fire	Barren	4th
27 Thurs. 12:47 pm	Virgo	Earth	Barren	NM 8:43 pm
28 Fri.	Virgo	Earth	Barren	1st
29 Sat. 12:12 pm	Libra	Air	Semi-fruit	1st
30 Sun.	Libra	Air	Semi-fruit	1st
31 Mon. 1:39 pm	Scorpio	Water	Fruitful	1st

Set in Central Standard Time

UGUST 1992

ar Aspectarian / Favorable & Unfavorable Days

SUN	MERCURY	VENUS	MARS	JUPITER	SATURN	URANUS	NEPTUNE	PLUTO	ARIES	TAURUS	GEMINI	CANCER	LEO	VIRGO	LIBRA	SCORPIO	SAGITTARIUS	CAPRICORN	AQUARIUS	PISCES
				C		T	T	Sx		f	u	f		F		f	u	f		U
x	Sx		T						U		f	u	f		F		f	u	f	
		Sx			T	Sq	Sq		U		f	u	f		F		f	u	f	
	Sq									U		f	u	f		F		f	u	f
q				Sx	Sq	Sx	Sx	C		U		f	u	f		F		f	u	f
		Sq							f		U		f	u	f		F		f	u
T	T		O	Sq	Sx				f		U		f	u	f		F		f	u
									f		U		f	u	f		F		f	u
		T							u	f		U		f	u	f		F		f
				T		C	C	Sx	u	f		U		f	u	f		F		f
	O								f	u	f		U		f	u	f		F	
			T		C				f	u	f		U		f	u	f		F	
O								Sq	f	u	f		U		f	u	f		F	
		O								f	u	f		U		f	u	f		F
			Sq	O		Sx	Sx	T		f	u	f		U		f	u	f		F
									F		f	u	f		U		f	u	f	
	T		Sx		Sx	Sq	Sq		F		f	u	f		U		f	u	f	
T									F		f	u	f		U		f	u	f	
	Sq									F		f	u	f		U		f	u	f
		T		T	Sq	T	T	O		F		f	u	f		U		f	u	f
q									f		F		f	u	f		U		f	u
	Sx	Sq	C	Sq	T				f		F		f	u	f		U		f	u
x									u	f		F		f	u	f		U		f
				Sx		O	O	T	u	f		F		f	u	f		U		f
		Sx							u	f		F		f	u	f		U		f
	C		Sx		O			Sq	f	u	f		F		f	u	f		U	
C									f	u	f		F		f	u	f		U	
			Sq	C		T	T	Sx		f	u	f		F		f	u	f		U
		C								f	u	f		F		f	u	f		U
					T	Sq	Sq		U		f	u	f		F		f	u	f	
	Sx		T						U		f	u	f		F		f	u	f	

SEPTEMBER

Date	Moon's Sign	Element	Nature	Moon's Phase
1 Tues.	Scorpio	Water	Fruitful	1st
2 Wed. 6:51 pm	Sagit.	Fire	Barren	1st
3 Thurs.	Sagit.	Fire	Barren	2nd 4:40 pm
4 Fri.	Sagit.	Fire	Barren	2nd
5 Sat. 4:07 am	Capri.	Earth	Semi-fruit	2nd
6 Sun.	Capri.	Earth	Semi-fruit	2nd
7 Mon. 4:09 pm	Aquar.	Air	Barren	2nd
8 Tues.	Aquar.	Air	Barren	2nd
9 Wed.	Aquar.	Air	Barren	2nd
10 Thurs. 4:57 am	Pisces	Water	Fruitful	2nd
11 Fri.	Pisces	Water	Fruitful	FM 8:17 pm
12 Sat. 5:03 pm	Aries	Fire	Barren	3rd
13 Sun.	Aries	Fire	Barren	3rd
14 Mon.	Aries	Fire	Barren	3rd
15 Tues. 3:48 am	Taurus	Earth	Semi-fruit	3rd
16 Wed.	Taurus	Earth	Semi-fruit	3rd
17 Thurs. 12:41 pm	Gemini	Air	Barren	3rd
18 Fri.	Gemini	Air	Barren	3rd
19 Sat. 7:00 pm	Cancer	Water	Fruitful	4th 1:54 pm
20 Sun.	Cancer	Water	Fruitful	4th
21 Mon. 10:20 pm	Leo	Fire	Barren	4th
22 Tues.	Leo	Fire	Barren	4th

The SUN enters Libra at 12:44 pm

Date	Moon's Sign	Element	Nature	Moon's Phase
23 Wed. 11:09 pm	Virgo	Earth	Barren	4th
24 Thurs.	Virgo	Earth	Barren	4th
25 Fri. 10:56 pm	Libra	Air	Semi-fruit	4th
26 Sat.	Libra	Air	Semi-fruit	NM 4:41 am
27 Sun. 11:45 pm	Scorpio	Water	Fruitful	1st
28 Mon.	Scorpio	Water	Fruitful	1st
29 Tues.	Scorpio	Water	Fruitful	1st
30 Wed. 3:34 am	Sagit.	Fire	Barren	1st

Set in Central Standard Time

SUN	MERCURY	VENUS	MARS	JUPITER	SATURN	URANUS	NEPTUNE	PLUTO	ARIES	TAURUS	GEMINI	CANCER	LEO	VIRGO	LIBRA	SCORPIO	SAGITTARIUS	CAPRICORN	AQUARIUS	PISCES
					Sq	Sx	Sx			U		f	u	f		F		f	u	f
	Sq				Sx			C		U		f	u	f		F		f	u	f
Sq		Sx			Sx				f		U		f	u	f		F		f	u
			O	Sq					f		U		f	u	f		F		f	u
	T	Sq							u	f		U		f	u	f		F		f
T						C	C	Sx	u	f		U		f	u	f		F		f
		T		C					f	u	f		U		f	u	f		F	
				T					f	u	f		U		f	u	f		F	
			T							f	u	f		U		f	u	f		F
O	O					Sx	Sx	T		f	u	f		U		f	u	f		F
			Sq	O						f	u	f		U		f	u	f		F
		Sx			Sq				F		f	u	f		U		f	u	f	
O							Sq		F		f	u	f		U		f	u	f	
		Sx							F		f	u	f		U		f	u	f	
				Sq		T	T	O		F		f	u	f		U		f	u	f
T				T						F		f	u	f		U		f	u	f
Sq		T		Sq					f		F		f	u	f		U		f	u
			C			O	O		f		F		f	u	f		U		f	u
	Sq		Sx					T	u	f		F		f	u	f		U		f
		Sx		O					u	f		F		f	u	f		U		f
		Sx						Sq	f	u	f		F		f	u	f		U	
		Sx				T			f	u	f		F		f	u	f		U	
			C			T	Sx			f	u	f		F		f	u	f		U
C	C		Sq		T	Sq				f	u	f		F		f	u	f		U
	Sq						Sq		U		f	u	f		F		f	u	f	
C		T			Sq	Sx			U		f	u	f		F		f	u	f	
		Sx				Sx	C			U		f	u	f		F		f	u	f
Sx										U		f	u	f		F		f	u	f
									f		U		f	u	f		F		f	u
									f		U		f	u	f		F		f	u

OCTOBER

Date	Moon's Sign	Element	Nature	Moon's Phase
1 Thurs.	Sagit.	Fire	Barren	1st
2 Fri. 11:30 am	Capri.	Earth	Semi-fruit	1st
3 Sat.	Capri.	Earth	Semi-fruit	2nd 8:13 am
4 Sun. 10:54 pm	Aquar.	Air	Barren	2nd
5 Mon.	Aquar.	Air	Barren	2nd
6 Tues.	Aquar.	Air	Barren	2nd
7 Wed. 11:38 am	Pisces	Water	Fruitful	2nd
8 Thurs.	Pisces	Water	Fruitful	2nd
9 Fri. 11:37 pm	Aries	Fire	Barren	2nd
10 Sat.	Aries	Fire	Barren	2nd
11 Sun.	Aries	Fire	Barren	FM 12:04 am
12 Mon. 9:49 am	Taurus	Earth	Semi-fruit	3rd
13 Tues.	Taurus	Earth	Semi-fruit	3rd
14 Wed. 6:09 pm	Gemini	Air	Barren	3rd
15 Thurs.	Gemini	Air	Barren	3rd
16 Fri.	Gemini	Air	Barren	3rd
17 Sat. 0:37 am	Cancer	Water	Fruitful	3rd
18 Sun.	Cancer	Water	Fruitful	4th 10:13 pm
19 Mon. 5:02 am	Leo	Fire	Barren	4th
20 Tues.	Leo	Fire	Barren	4th
21 Wed. 7:29 am	Virgo	Earth	Barren	4th
22 Thurs.	Virgo	Earth	Barren	4th

The SUN enters Scorpio at 9:58 pm

Date	Moon's Sign	Element	Nature	Moon's Phase
23 Fri. 8:40 am	Libra	Air	Semi-fruit	4th
24 Sat.	Libra	Air	Semi-fruit	4th
25 Sun. 10:05 am	Scorpio	Water	Fruitful	NM 2:35 pm
26 Mon.	Scorpio	Water	Fruitful	1st
27 Tues. 1:30 pm	Sagit.	Fire	Barren	1st
28 Wed.	Sagit.	Fire	Barren	1st
29 Thurs. 8:19 pm	Capri.	Earth	Semi-fruit	1st
30 Fri.	Capri.	Earth	Semi-fruit	1st
31 Sat.	Capri.	Earth	Semi-fruit	1st

Set in Central Standard Time

OCTOBER 1992
Lunar Aspectarian / Favorable & Unfavorable Days

Day	SUN	MERCURY	VENUS	MARS	JUPITER	SATURN	URANUS	NEPTUNE	PLUTO	ARIES	TAURUS	GEMINI	CANCER	LEO	VIRGO	LIBRA	SCORPIO	SAGITTARIUS	CAPRICORN	AQUARIUS	PISCES
1		Sx				Sx				f		U		f	u	f		F		f	u
2				Sq						u	f		U		f	u	f		F		f
3	Sq		Sx	O			C	C		u	f		U		f	u	f		F		f
4		Sq				T			Sx	u	f		U		f	u	f		F		f
5						C				f	u	f		U		f	u	f		F	
6	T		Sq						Sq	f	u	f		U		f	u	f		F	
7		T									f	u	f		U		f	u	f		F
8			T	T			Sx	Sx			f	u	f		U		f	u	f		F
9				O					T		f	u	f		U		f	u	f		F
10						Sx				F		f	u	f		U		f	u	f	
11	O			Sq			Sq	Sq		F		f	u	f		U		f	u	f	
12											F		f	u	f		U		f	u	f
13		O		Sx		Sq	T	T			F		f	u	f		U		f	u	f
14			O			T			O		F		f	u	f		U		f	u	f
15						T				f		F		f	u	f		U		f	u
16	T									f		F		f	u	f		U		f	u
17				Sq						u	f		F		f	u	f		U		f
18	Sq	T		C			O	O	T	u	f		F		f	u	f		U		f
19			T		Sx					f	u	f		F		f	u	f		U	
20		Sq				O			Sq	f	u	f		F		f	u	f		U	
21	Sx		Sq								f	u	f		F		f	u	f		U
22		Sx		Sx			T	T	Sx		f	u	f		F		f	u	f		U
23			Sx		C					U		f	u	f		F		f	u	f	
24				Sq		T	Sq	Sq		U		f	u	f		F		f	u	f	
25	C										U		f	u	f		F		f	u	f
26			T			Sq	Sx	Sx	C		U		f	u	f		F		f	u	f
27		C			Sx						U		f	u	f		F		f	u	f
28			C			Sx				f		U		f	u	f		F		f	u
29										f		U		f	u	f		F		f	u
30	Sx					Sq				u	f		U		f	u	f		F		f
31				O			C	C	Sx	u	f		U		f	u	f		F		f

NOVEMBER

Date	Moon's Sign	Element	Nature	Moon's Phase
1 Sun. 6:44 am	Aquar.	Air	Barren	1st
2 Mon.	Aquar.	Air	Barren	2nd 3:12 am
3 Tues. 7:13 pm	Pisces	Water	Fruitful	2nd
4 Wed.	Pisces	Water	Fruitful	2nd
5 Thurs.	Pisces	Water	Fruitful	2nd
6 Fri. 7:20 am	Aries	Fire	Barren	2nd
7 Sat.	Aries	Fire	Barren	2nd
8 Sun. 5:20 pm	Taurus	Earth	Semi-fruit	2nd
9 Mon.	Taurus	Earth	Semi-fruit	2nd
10 Tues.	Taurus	Earth	Semi-fruit	FM 3:21 am
11 Wed. 0:50 am	Gemini	Air	Barren	3rd
12 Thurs.	Gemini	Air	Barren	3rd
13 Fri. 6:20 am	Cancer	Water	Fruitful	3rd
14 Sat.	Cancer	Water	Fruitful	3rd
15 Sun. 10:24 am	Leo	Fire	Barren	3rd
16 Mon.	Leo	Fire	Barren	3rd
17 Tues. 1:29 pm	Virgo	Earth	Barren	4th 5:40 am
18 Wed.	Virgo	Earth	Barren	4th
19 Thurs. 4:04 pm	Libra	Air	Semi-fruit	4th
20 Fri.	Libra	Air	Semi-fruit	4th
21 Sat. 6:53 pm	Scorpio	Water	Fruitful	4th

The SUN enters Sagittarius at 7:27 pm

Date	Moon's Sign	Element	Nature	Moon's Phase
22 Sun.	Scorpio	Water	Fruitful	4th
23 Mon. 11:02 pm	Sagit.	Fire	Barren	4th
24 Tues.	Sagit.	Fire	Barren	NM 3:12 am
25 Wed.	Sagit.	Fire	Barren	1st
26 Thurs. 5:39 am	Capri.	Earth	Semi-fruit	1st
27 Fri.	Capri.	Earth	Semi-fruit	1st
28 Sat. 3:20 pm	Aquar.	Air	Barren	1st
29 Sun.	Aquar.	Air	Barren	1st
30 Mon.	Aquar.	Air	Barren	1st

Set in Central Standard Time

SUN	MERCURY	VENUS	MARS	JUPITER	SATURN	URANUS	NEPTUNE	PLUTO	ARIES	TAURUS	GEMINI	CANCER	LEO	VIRGO	LIBRA	SCORPIO	SAGITTARIUS	CAPRICORN	AQUARIUS	PISCES
	Sx			T					f	u	f		U		f	u	f		F	
Sq		Sx			C				f	u	f		U		f	u	f		F	
								Sq	f	u	f		U		f	u	f		F	
T	Sq									f	u	f		U		f	u	f		F
		Sq	T			Sx	Sx	T		f	u	f		U		f	u	f		F
	T			O					F		f	u	f		U		f	u	f	
						Sx	Sq	Sq	F		f	u	f		U		f	u	f	
		T	Sq							F		f	u	f		U		f	u	f
O			Sx				T	O		F		f	u	f		U		f	u	f
	O			T	T				f		F		f	u	f		U		f	u
									f		F		f	u	f		U		f	u
		O		Sq					u	f		F		f	u	f		U		f
T						O	O	T	u	f		F		f	u	f		U		f
	T		C	Sx					f	u	f		F		f	u	f		U	
					O				f	u	f		F		f	u	f		U	
Sq	Sq	T						Sq	f	u	f		F		f	u	f		U	
						T	T			f	u	f		F		f	u	f		U
Sx	Sx		Sx					Sx		f	u	f		F		f	u	f		U
		Sq		C	T	Sq	Sq		U		f	u	f		F		f	u	f	
		Sq							U		f	u	f		F		f	u	f	
		Sx			Sq	Sx				U		f	u	f		F		f	u	f
	C		T				Sx	C		U		f	u	f		F		f	u	f
C				Sx	Sx				f		U		f	u	f		F		f	u
									f		U		f	u	f		F		f	u
				Sq					u	f		U		f	u	f		F		f
		C				C	C		u	f		U		f	u	f		F		f
	Sx		O					Sx	u	f		U		f	u	f		F		f
Sx				T	C				f	u	f		U		f	u	f		F	
	Sq							Sq	f	u	f		U		f	u	f		F	

DECEMBER

Date	Moon's Sign	Element	Nature	Moon's Phase
1 Tues. 3:24 am	Pisces	Water	Fruitful	1st
2 Wed.	Pisces	Water	Fruitful	2nd 0:18 am
3 Thurs. 3:50 pm	Aries	Fire	Barren	2nd
4 Fri.	Aries	Fire	Barren	2nd
5 Sat.	Aries	Fire	Barren	2nd
6 Sun. 2:17 am	Taurus	Earth	Semi-fruit	2nd
7 Mon.	Taurus	Earth	Semi-fruit	2nd
8 Tues. 9:38 am	Gemini	Air	Barren	2nd
9 Wed.	Gemini	Air	Barren	FM 5:42 pm
10 Thurs. 2:06 pm	Cancer	Water	Fruitful	3rd
11 Fri.	Cancer	Water	Fruitful	3rd
12 Sat. 4:48 pm	Leo	Fire	Barren	3rd
13 Sun.	Leo	Fire	Barren	3rd
14 Mon. 6:57 pm	Virgo	Earth	Barren	3rd
15 Tues.	Virgo	Earth	Barren	3rd
16 Wed. 9:34 pm	Libra	Air	Semi-fruit	4th 1:14 pm
17 Thurs.	Libra	Air	Semi-fruit	4th
18 Fri.	Libra	Air	Semi-fruit	4th
19 Sat. 1:21 am	Scorpio	Water	Fruitful	4th
20 Sun.	Scorpio	Water	Fruitful	4th
21 Mon. 6:43 am	Sagit.	Fire	Barren	4th

The SUN enters Capricorn at 8:45 am

22 Tues.	Sagit.	Fire	Barren	4th
23 Wed. 2:05 pm	Capri.	Earth	Semi-fruit	NM 6:44 pm
24 Thurs.	Capri.	Earth	Semi-fruit	1st
25 Fri. 11:44 pm	Aquar.	Air	Barren	1st
26 Sat.	Aquar.	Air	Barren	1st
27 Sun.	Aquar.	Air	Barren	1st
28 Mon. 11:29 am	Pisces	Water	Fruitful	1st
29 Tues.	Pisces	Water	Fruitful	1st
30 Wed.	Pisces	Water	Fruitful	1st
31 Thurs. 0:08 am	Aries	Fire	Barren	2nd 9:39 pm

Set in Central Standard Time

DECEMBER 1992
Lunar Aspectarian / Favorable & Unfavorable Days

	SUN	MERCURY	VENUS	MARS	JUPITER	SATURN	URANUS	NEPTUNE	PLUTO	ARIES	TAURUS	GEMINI	CANCER	LEO	VIRGO	LIBRA	SCORPIO	SAGITTARIUS	CAPRICORN	AQUARIUS	PISCES
1											f	u	f		U		f	u	f		F
2	Sq						Sx	Sx			f	u	f		U		f	u	f		F
3		T	Sx	T					T		f	u	f		U		f	u	f		F
4	T				O	Sx	Sq			F		f	u	f		U		f	u	f	
5			Sq	Sq				Sq		F		f	u	f		U		f	u	f	
6											F		f	u	f		U		f	u	f
7						Sq	T	T	O		F		f	u	f		U		f	u	f
8		O	T	Sx						f		F		f	u	f		U		f	u
9	O					T	T			f		F		f	u	f		U		f	u
10										f		F		f	u	f		U		f	u
11					Sq		O	O		u	f		F		f	u	f		U		f
12		T		C					T	u	f		F		f	u	f		U		f
13			O		Sx	O				f	u	f		F		f	u	f		U	
14	T								Sq	f	u	f		F		f	u	f		U	
15		Sq				T					f	u	f		F		f	u	f		U
16	Sq			Sx				T	Sx		f	u	f		F		f	u	f		U
17		Sx	T		C	T				U		f	u	f		F		f	u	f	
18	Sx			Sq		Sq	Sq			U		f	u	f		F		f	u	f	
19											U		f	u	f		F		f	u	f
20			Sq	T		Sq	Sx	Sx	C		U		f	u	f		F		f	u	f
21										f		U		f	u	f		F		f	u
22		C	Sx		Sx	Sx				f		U		f	u	f		F		f	u
23	C									f		U		f	u	f		F		f	u
24				Sq		C				u	f		U		f	u	f		F		f
25			O					C	Sx	u	f		U		f	u	f		F		f
26										f	u	f		U		f	u	f		F	
27		Sx	C		T	C				f	u	f		U		f	u	f		F	
28									Sq		f	u	f		U		f	u	f		F
29	Sx						Sx				f	u	f		U		f	u	f		F
30		Sq		T				Sx	T		f	u	f		U		f	u	f		F
31	Sq									F		f	u	f		U		f	u	f	

ASTRO-ALMANAC

How to Use the ASTRO-ALMANAC

Llewellyn's unique Astro-Almanac is provided for quick reference. Because the dates indicated may not be the best for you personally, be sure to read the instructions on page 15 and then go to the proper section of the book and read the detailed description provided for each activity.

Most of the time, the dates given in the Astro-Almanac will correspond to the ones you can determine for yourself from the detailed instructions. But just as often, the dates given may not be favorable for your Sun Sign or for your particular interests. *That's why it's important for you to learn how to use the entire process to come up with the most beneficial dates for you.*

The following pages are provided for easy reference for those of you who do not want detailed descriptions. The dates provided are determined from the sign and phase of the Moon and the aspects to the Moon. These are approximate dates only and do not take into account retrogrades or Moon voids. For more information, please see *Llewellyn's Astrological Calendar*.

Please read the instructions on how to come up with the dates yourself, though. This is very important in some instances (such as planning surgery or making big purchases). You will find other lists of dates in the proper sections of *The Moon Sign Book*. We list Fishing and Hunting Dates, Gardening Dates, Dates for Destroying Plant and Animal Pests, and other types of activities. See the Table of Contents for a complete listing.

What to Do When in JANUARY

Entertain: 6-8, 16-17, 20-21, 24-25
Sports activities: 20-21
Marriage for happiness: None
End a romance or file for divorce: 20-21
Cut hair to increase growth: 10, 18
Cut hair to retard growth: 20-21
Cut hair for added thickness: 19
Permanents and hair coloring: 6-7
Start a weight loss program: 1-3, 20-23, 28-30
Stop a bad habit: 20-23
See dentist for fillings: 21, 27
See dentist for extractions: 4-5, 10, 17
Consult physician: 4-5, 11-12, 18-19, 24-25, 31
Purchase major appliances: None
Buy a car or have repairs done: 7, 15, 21, 27
Purchase electronic equipment: 8
Buy antiques or jewelry: 4-5, 15
Buy real estate for speculation: 4-5, 11-12, 18-19, 24-25, 31
Buy permanent home: 6-8, 13-15, 20-21, 26-27
Selling home, property, or possessions: 2-4, 8, 13, 22-23, 28, 31
Sign important papers: 8, 13
Building: None
Ask for credit or loan: 26
Start new ventures or advertise: 7-8, 13, 15
Apply for job: 4, 13
Ask for raise or promotion: 2, 23, 28
Collect money: 4, 12, 31
Move into new home: 6, 21
Do roofing: 20-21, 26-27
Pour concrete: 6-8, 13-15, 20-21
Painting: 20-21, 26-27
Cut timber: 1-3, 28-31
Travel for business: 1-2, 4-5, 7-10, 12-13, 15-17, 19, 21-23, 25, 27-31
Travel for pleasure: 4, 10, 12, 15, 21, 23, 29, 31
Air travel: 16-17, 25
Buy animals: 5, 7
Neutering or spaying an animal: 5-7, 31
Dock or dehorn animals: 1-8, 26-31
Make sauerkraut: 19
Brewing: 19, 26-27
Canning: 19, 26-27
Mow lawn to retard growth: 1-3, 19-31

What to Do When in FEBRUARY

Entertain: 2-4, 12-13, 16-17, 20-21
Sports activities: 17
Marriage for happiness: 14
End a romance or file for divorce: None
Cut hair to increase growth: 5-6, 14
Cut hair to retard growth: None
Cut hair for added thickness: None
Permanents and hair coloring: 3-4
Start a weight loss program: 2, 18-19, 25-26
Stop a bad habit: 18-19
See dentist for fillings: 2, 24
See dentist for extractions: 6, 13
Consult physician: 1, 7-9, 14-15, 20-21, 27-29
Purchase major appliances: 2
Buy a car or have repairs done: 2, 4, 17, 24
Purchase electronic equipment: 13
Buy antiques or jewelry: 14-15
Buy real estate for speculation: 1, 7-9, 14-15, 20-21,
    27-29
Buy permanent home: 2-4, 10-11, 16-17, 22-24
Selling home, property, or possessions: 1-2, 6, 8, 11, 13-
    14, 18, 20, 25, 27, 29
Sign important papers: 2, 23
Building: None
Ask for credit or loan: None
Start new ventures or advertise: 4, 11, 14-15
Apply for job: None
Ask for raise or promotion: 2, 13, 29
Collect money: 14, 20, 27
Move into new home: 11
Do roofing: 2, 22-24
Pour concrete: 2-4, 10-11, 16-17
Painting: 2, 22-24
Cut timber: 1-2, 25-29
Travel for business: 2, 4-8, 11-15, 17-21, 24-29
Travel for pleasure: 6, 8, 11, 13-14, 20, 25, 27
Air travel: 12-13, 20
Buy animals: 4-5, 7, 9
Neutering or spaying an animal: 1-2, 4-6
Dock or dehorn animals: 1-4, 25-29
Make sauerkraut: 22-24
Brewing: None
Canning: 22-24
Mow lawn to retard growth: 1-2, 18-29

What to Do When in MARCH

Entertain: 1-2, 10-11, 15-16, 19-20, 28-29
Sports activities: 16
Marriage for happiness: 8, 12
End a romance or file for divorce: None
Cut hair to increase growth: 4-5, 12-14
Cut hair to retard growth: None
Cut hair for added thickness: None
Permanents and hair coloring: None
Start a weight loss program: 1-2, 18, 23-24, 28-29
Stop a bad habit: 18
See dentist for fillings: 1-2, 28-29
See dentist for extractions: 4-5, 11, 17
Consult physician: 6-7, 12-14, 19-20, 25-27
Purchase major appliances: 1-2
Buy a car or have repairs done: 2, 8
Purchase electronic equipment: 10
Buy antiques or jewelry: 8, 12-14
Buy real estate for speculation: 6-7, 12-14, 19-20, 25-27
Buy permanent home: 1-2, 8-9, 15
Selling home, property, or possessions: 1, 5-6, 8, 10-11, 13, 17, 20, 23, 25, 28, 30
Sign important papers: 15
Building: None
Ask for credit or loan: None
Start new ventures or advertise: 8, 12-14
Apply for job: 8
Ask for raise or promotion: 5, 10, 23, 28
Collect money: 7, 12-13, 25-26
Move into new home: None
Do roofing: 1-2, 21-22, 28-29
Pour concrete: 1-2, 8-9, 15-16, 28-29
Painting: 1-2, 21-22, 28-29
Cut timber: 1-2, 25-29
Travel for business: 2-8, 10-14
Travel for pleasure: 7-8, 12-14
Air travel: 10-11
Buy animals: 8
Neutering or spaying an animal: 1-3, 5-7, 30-31
Dock or dehorn animals: 1-2, 10, 25-29
Make sauerkraut: 21-22
Brewing: 3, 30-31
Canning: 3, 21-22, 30-31
Mow lawn to retard growth: 1-3, 18-31

What to Do When in APRIL

Entertain: 6-8, 11-12, 15-16, 24-26
Sports activities: 11-12
Marriage for happiness: 11
End a romance or file for divorce: None
Cut hair to increase growth: 9-10
Cut hair to retard growth: None
Cut hair for added thickness: 16
Permanents and hair coloring: None
Start a weight loss program: 19-21, 24-26, 29-30
Stop a bad habit: None
See dentist for fillings: 17, 24-26
See dentist for extractions: 8, 14
Consult physician: 2-3, 9-10, 15-16, 22-23, 29-30
Purchase major appliances: 24-26
Buy a car or have repairs done: 11, 17, 24, 26
Purchase electronic equipment: 24
Buy antiques or jewelry: 10, 15
Buy real estate for speculation: 2-3, 9-10, 15-16, 22-23, 29-30
Buy permanent home: 11-12, 17-18, 24-26
Selling home, property, or possessions: 1, 4, 6, 9-10, 17, 19, 22-24, 28, 30
Sign important papers: 24
Building: None
Ask for credit or loan: 26
Start new ventures or advertise: 9-10
Apply for job: None
Ask for raise or promotion: 1, 6, 10, 19, 24
Collect money: 9, 22
Move into new home: 11, 26
Do roofing: 17-18, 24-26
Pour concrete: 4-5, 11-12, 24-26
Painting: 17-18, 24-26
Cut timber: 24-26, 29-30
Travel for business: 9-11, 14-17, 19, 21-24, 26-27, 29-30
Travel for pleasure: 9, 11, 17, 21-22, 26-27
Air travel: 15
Buy animals: 4, 9
Neutering or spaying an animal: 1, 3-5, 29-30
Dock or dehorn animals: 6-9, 24-26
Make sauerkraut: 17-18
Brewing: 1, 27-28
Canning: 1, 17-18, 27-28
Mow lawn to retard growth: 1, 16-30

What to Do When in MAY

Entertain: 4-5, 8-9, 12-13, 22-23, 31
Sports activities: 8-9
Marriage for happiness: 6
End a romance or file for divorce: None
Cut hair to increase growth: 6-7, 14
Cut hair to retard growth: None
Cut hair for added thickness: 16
Permanents and hair coloring: None
Start a weight loss program: 1, 17-18, 22-23, 27-28
Stop a bad habit: None
See dentist for fillings: 16, 22-23, 29
See dentist for extractions: 10-11
Consult physician: 1, 6-7, 12-13, 19-21, 27-28
Purchase major appliances: 22-23
Buy a car or have repairs done: 14, 16, 29
Purchase electronic equipment: 5
Buy antiques or jewelry: 6-7
Buy real estate for speculation: 1, 6-7, 12-13, 19-21,
   27-28
Buy permanent home: 2-3, 8-9, 14-16, 22-23, 29-30
Selling home, property, or possessions: 1, 3, 6, 8, 10, 14,
   17, 20, 22, 26-27, 29, 31
Sign important papers: None
Building: 16
Ask for credit or loan: 26
Start new ventures or advertise: 3, 6-7
Apply for job: 3, 10
Ask for raise or promotion: 10, 20, 26, 31
Collect money: 1, 6, 21
Move into new home: None
Do roofing: 16, 22-23, 29-30
Pour concrete: 2-3, 8-9, 22-23, 29-30
Painting: 16, 22-23, 29-30
Cut timber: 1, 27-30
Travel for business: 1, 3-4, 6-8, 10-11, 13-14, 16-18,
   20-22, 24-26, 28-29, 31
Travel for pleasure: 1, 6-7, 11, 14, 21, 26, 29
Air travel: 4, 31
Buy animals: 3-4
Neutering or spaying an animal: 1, 3-5, 28-30
Dock or dehorn animals: 4-8, 31
Make sauerkraut: 16
Brewing: 16, 24-26
Canning: 16, 24-26
Mow lawn to retard growth: 1, 16-30

What to Do When in JUNE

Entertain: 1, 4-5, 9-10, 18-19, 28-29
Sports activities: 4-5
Marriage for happiness: 2
End a romance or file for divorce: None
Cut hair to increase growth: 2-3, 11-12, 30
Cut hair to retard growth: 28-29
Cut hair for added thickness: None
Permanents and hair coloring: None
Start a weight loss program: 14, 18-19, 23-24
Stop a bad habit: 28-29
See dentist for fillings: 19, 25, 27
See dentist for extractions: 1, 6-8
Consult physician: 2-3, 9-10, 15-17, 23-24, 30
Purchase major appliances: 19
Buy a car or have repairs done: 4, 11, 27
Purchase electronic equipment: 10
Buy antiques or jewelry: 2
Buy real estate for speculation: 2-3, 9-10, 15-17, 23-24, 30
Buy permanent home: 4-5, 11-12, 18-19, 25-27
Selling home, property, or possessions: 1-2, 6, 11, 15-16, 20, 22, 25, 27, 30
Sign important papers: 5, 27
Building: None
Ask for credit or loan: None
Start new ventures or advertise: 2, 13, 30
Apply for job: None
Ask for raise or promotion: 22, 27
Collect money: 2, 9, 16, 30
Move into new home: 25
Do roofing: 18-19, 25-27
Pour concrete: 4-5, 18-19, 25-27
Painting: 18-19, 25-27
Cut timber: 23-29
Travel for business: 1-2, 4, 6-9, 11, 13-17, 20-24, 27-30
Travel for pleasure: 2, 9, 11, 16, 20, 30
Air travel: 1, 28-29
Buy animals: 2-4, 6
Neutering or spaying an animal: 1-3, 27-29
Dock or dehorn animals: 1-6, 28-30
Make sauerkraut: 20-22
Brewing: None
Canning: 20-22
Mow lawn to retard growth: 14-29

What to Do When in JULY

Entertain: 2-3, 6-7, 15-17, 25-26, 29-30
Sports activities: 3, 29-30
Marriage for happiness: None
End a romance or file for divorce: None
Cut hair to increase growth: 1, 8-9
Cut hair to retard growth: 25-26
Cut hair for added thickness: 14
Permanents and hair coloring: None
Start a weight loss program: 15-17, 20-22
Stop a bad habit: 25-26
See dentist for fillings: 15-16, 24
See dentist for extractions: 4-5, 13
Consult physician: 1, 6-7, 13-14, 20-22, 27-28
Purchase major appliances: 15-16
Buy a car or have repairs done: 3, 8, 15
Purchase electronic equipment: None
Buy antiques or jewelry: 1, 6, 13
Buy real estate for speculation: 1, 6-7, 13-14, 20-22, 27-28
Buy permanent home: 2-3, 8-9, 15-17
Selling home, property, or possessions: 4, 6, 8, 11, 13-14, 19, 21, 24, 26, 28-29
Sign important papers: 2
Building: None
Ask for credit or loan: None
Start new ventures or advertise: 1, 10-12
Apply for job: 4, 13
Ask for raise or promotion: 6
Collect money: 13, 20, 28
Move into new home: None
Do roofing: 15-17, 23-24
Pour concrete: 2-3, 15-17, 23-24, 29-30
Painting: 15-17, 23-24
Cut timber: 22-26
Travel for business: 1, 3-8, 10-15, 18
Travel for pleasure: 4-5, 8, 13
Air travel: 7
Buy animals: 1, 3, 31
Neutering or spaying an animal: 1-3, 26-28, 30
Dock or dehorn animals: 1-5, 25-31
Make sauerkraut: 18-19
Brewing: 27-28
Canning: 18-19, 27-28
Mow lawn to retard growth: 14-28

What to Do When in AUGUST

Entertain: 2-3, 11-13, 21-22, 26-27, 30-31
Sports activities: 26-27
Marriage for happiness: None
End a romance or file for divorce: 26
Cut hair to increase growth: 4-5
Cut hair to retard growth: 21, 26
Cut hair for added thickness: 13
Permanents and hair coloring: None
Start a weight loss program: 13, 16-18, 26
Stop a bad habit: 21-22, 26
See dentist for fillings: 13, 19
See dentist for extractions: 1, 9-10, 29
Consult physician: 2-3, 9-10, 16-18, 23-25, 30-31
Purchase major appliances: 13
Buy a car or have repairs done: 13, 19, 27
Purchase electronic equipment: 22, 31
Buy antiques or jewelry: 9-10
Buy real estate for speculation: 2-3, 9-10, 16-18, 23-25, 30-31
Buy permanent home: 12-13, 19-20, 26-27
Selling home, property, or possessions: 1-2, 10, 12, 17, 22, 24, 31
Sign important papers: 26
Building: 13
Ask for credit or loan: None
Start new ventures or advertise: None
Apply for job: None
Ask for raise or promotion: None
Collect money: 3, 9-10, 24-25
Move into new home: None
Do roofing: 13, 19-20, 26
Pour concrete: 11-13, 19-20, 26-27
Painting: 13, 19-20, 26
Cut timber: 21-22, 26
Travel for business: 13-14, 16-19, 21, 23-25, 27, 29-31
Travel for pleasure: 18, 23-25
Air travel: 21-22, 31
Buy animals: 1, 28
Neutering or spaying an animal: 24-26
Dock or dehorn animals: 1-4, 21-31
Make sauerkraut: 14-15
Brewing: 23-25
Canning: 14-15, 23-25
Mow lawn to retard growth: 13-26

What to Do When in SEPTEMBER

Entertain: 8-9, 18-19, 22-23, 26-27
Sports activities: 22-23
Marriage for happiness: None
End a romance or file for divorce: 22-23
Cut hair to increase growth: 1-2, 10, 28-29
Cut hair to retard growth: 18-19, 22-23
Cut hair for added thickness: 11
Permanents and hair coloring: None
Start a weight loss program: 13-14, 22-25
Stop a bad habit: 18-19, 22-25
See dentist for fillings: 15, 17, 23
See dentist for extractions: 5-7, 10
Consult physician: 5-7, 13-14, 20-21, 26-27
Purchase major appliances: None
Buy a car or have repairs done: 2, 9, 17, 23, 29
Purchase electronic equipment: None
Buy antiques or jewelry: 5-7, 27
Buy real estate for speculation: 5-7, 13-14, 20-21, 26-27
Buy permanent home: 1-2, 8-9, 15-17, 22-23, 28-29
Selling home, property, or possessions: 2, 5, 7, 10, 15, 17, 20-21, 24-25, 29
Sign important papers: 17, 22
Building: None
Ask for credit or loan: 23
Start new ventures or advertise: 3, 9, 30
Apply for job: 5, 7
Ask for raise or promotion: 5, 17
Collect money: 7
Move into new home: 8, 23
Do roofing: 15-17, 22-23
Pour concrete: 8-9, 15-17, 22-23
Painting: 15-17, 22-23
Cut timber: 19, 22-25
Travel for business: 2-3, 5-7, 9-11, 13-15, 17-19, 21, 23-25, 27, 29-30
Travel for pleasure: 2-3, 6-7, 17, 19, 21, 23, 29-30
Air travel: 18-19, 27
Buy animals: 27, 29
Neutering or spaying an animal: 23
Dock or dehorn animals: 1-2, 19-30
Make sauerkraut: 11-12
Brewing: 11, 20-21
Canning: 11-12, 20-21
Mow lawn to retard growth: 11-25

What to Do When in OCTOBER

Entertain: 5-6, 15-16, 19-20, 23-24
Sports activities: 19-20
Marriage for happiness: None
End a romance or file for divorce: 19-20
Cut hair to increase growth: 7-9, 25-27
Cut hair to retard growth: 15-16, 19-20
Cut hair for added thickness: 11
Permanents and hair coloring: None
Start a weight loss program: 11, 19-22
Stop a bad habit: 15-16, 19-22
See dentist for fillings: 12, 14, 19
See dentist for extractions: 4, 7-8
Consult physician: 2-4, 10-11, 17-18, 23-24, 30-31
Purchase major appliances: None
Buy a car or have repairs done: 6, 12, 14, 19, 25, 27
Purchase electronic equipment: None
Buy antiques or jewelry: 2, 4, 30
Buy real estate for speculation: 2-4, 10-11, 17-18, 23-24, 30-31
Buy permanent home: 5-6, 12-14, 19-20, 25-27
Selling home, property, or possessions: 1, 4, 7-8, 14, 18-19, 22-23, 27
Sign important papers: 27
Building: None
Ask for credit or loan: 19
Start new ventures or advertise: 1, 6, 28-29
Apply for job: None
Ask for raise or promotion: 7, 27
Collect money: 4, 23
Move into new home: 19
Do roofing: 12-14, 19-20
Pour concrete: 5-6, 12-14, 19-20
Painting: 12-14, 19-20
Cut timber: 19-24
Travel for business: 1-2, 4, 6-10, 12, 14-17, 19, 21-23, 25, 27-30
Travel for pleasure: 4, 6, 8, 14, 16, 19, 21, 23, 27, 30
Air travel: 15-16, 23
Buy animals: 2, 29, 31
Neutering or spaying an animal: None
Dock or dehorn animals: 1-2, 18-31
Make sauerkraut: 17
Brewing: 18
Canning: 17-18
Mow lawn to retard growth: 11-24

What to Do When in NOVEMBER

Entertain: 1-3, 11-12, 15-17, 20-21, 29-30
Sports activities: 15-17
Marriage for happiness: None
End a romance or file for divorce: 15-17
Cut hair to increase growth: 4
Cut hair to retard growth: 11-12, 15-17
Cut hair for added thickness: 10
Permanents and hair coloring: 1, 29-30
Start a weight loss program: 15-19
Stop a bad habit: 11-12, 15-19
See dentist for fillings: 10, 15, 17, 23
See dentist for extractions: 4-5, 27
Consult physician: 6-8, 13-14, 20-21, 26-28
Purchase major appliances: None
Buy a car or have repairs done: 1, 3
Purchase electronic equipment: 1
Buy antiques or jewelry: 26-27
Buy real estate for speculation: 6-8, 13-14, 20-21, 26-28
Buy permanent home: 1-3, 9-10
Selling home, property, or possessions: 1, 5-6, 10-11, 15, 19-20, 23-24, 29
Sign important papers: 1
Building: None
Ask for credit or loan: None
Start new ventures or advertise: 1, 3
Apply for job: None
Ask for raise or promotion: 1, 6
Collect money: None
Move into new home: 2, 17
Do roofing: 10, 15-17, 22-23
Pour concrete: 1-3, 9-10, 15-17, 29-30
Painting: 10, 15-17, 22-23
Cut timber: 17-21
Travel for business: 1, 3-7, 10
Travel for pleasure: 1, 4
Air travel: None
Buy animals: 25-26
Neutering or spaying an animal: 26-27
Dock or dehorn animals: 1, 17-30
Make sauerkraut: 13-14
Brewing: 22-23
Canning: 13-14, 22-23
Mow lawn to retard growth: 10-23

What to Do When in DECEMBER

Entertain: 8-10, 13-14, 17-18, 26-27
Sports activities: 13-14
Marriage for happiness: None
End a romance or file for divorce: 13-14
Cut hair to increase growth: 1-3, 28-30
Cut hair to retard growth: 9-10, 14
Cut hair for added thickness: 9
Permanents and hair coloring: 26-27
Start a weight loss program: 13-16, 21-22
Stop a bad habit: 9-10, 13-16
See dentist for fillings: 14, 19
See dentist for extractions: 1-3, 8, 28-30
Consult physician: 4-5, 11-12, 17-18, 24-25, 31
Purchase major appliances: None
Buy a car or have repairs done: 6, 14, 19, 26
Purchase electronic equipment: 17, 27
Buy antiques or jewelry: 6, 24
Buy real estate for speculation: 4-5, 11-12, 17-18, 24-25, 31
Buy permanent home: 6-7, 13-14, 19-20, 26-27
Selling home, property, or possessions: 3, 8-9, 12, 16-17, 22, 27, 30
Sign important papers: 27
Building: None
Ask for credit or loan: 22
Start new ventures or advertise: 6, 23, 26
Apply for job: None
Ask for raise or promotion: None
Collect money: 17
Move into new home: None
Do roofing: 13-14, 19-20
Pour concrete: 6-7, 13-14, 26-27
Painting: 13-14, 19-20
Cut timber: 16-18, 21-22
Travel for business: 1-4, 6, 8-11, 14-17, 19, 21-24, 26, 28-31
Travel for pleasure: 3-4, 8-9, 14, 17, 22, 29
Air travel: 8-10, 17
Buy animals: 1, 24-26, 28
Neutering or spaying an animal: 24-26
Dock or dehorn animals: 16-27
Make sauerkraut: 11-12
Brewing: 19-20
Canning: 11-12, 19-20
Mow lawn to retard growth: 9-22

RETROGRADES

When the planets cross the sky, they occasionally appear to move backwards as seen from Earth. When a planet turns "backwards" it is said to be "retrograde." When it turns forward again it is said to go "direct." The point at which the movement changes from one direction to another is called a "station."

When a planet is retrograde its expression is delayed or out of kilter with the normal progression of events. Generally, it can be said that whatever is planned during this period will be delayed, but usually it will come to fruition when the retrograde is over. Of course, this only applies to activities ruled by the planet which is retrograde.

Although retrogrades of all the planets are of significance, those involving Mercury and Venus are particularly easy to follow and of a personal use.

Mercury Retrograde Mercury rules informal communications—reading and writing, speaking and short errands. Whenever Mercury goes retrograde, personal communications get fouled up or misunderstood more often. Letters get lost, friends misunderstand each other, more misspellings occur and so on. So the rule astrologers have developed is, *when Mercury is retrograde, avoid means of communication of an informal nature*.

Venus Retrograde This is the planet of love and affection, friendship and marriage, so the retrograde is an unreliable time for these activities. Misunderstandings and alienations of an affectional nature are more common.

Planetary Stations for 1992
(Central Standard Time)

Planet	Begin		End	
JUPITER	12/30/91	1:29 p.m.	04/30/92	12:10 p.m.
PLUTO	02/24/92	10:37 a.m.	07/30/92	12:02 p.m.
MERCURY	03/16/92	9:59 p.m.	04/09/92	12:27 a.m.
NEPTUNE	04/20/92	2:10 a.m.	09/27/92	6:16 a.m.
URANUS	04/21/92	2:58 p.m.	09/22/92	1:34 p.m.
SATURN	05/28/92	7:01 a.m.	10/15/92	7:46 p.m.
MERCURY	07/19/92	6:44 p.m.	08/12/92	8:47 p.m.
MERCURY	11/11/92	3:09 a.m.	12/01/92	1:39 a.m.
MARS	11/28/92	6:20 p.m.	02/15/93	12:18 a.m.

BEST DAYS FOR YOUR SPECIAL PURPOSES

When you wish to choose a favorable day for something other than matters governed by your own ruling planet, read the following list and note the planet which rules the matter in question. Turn to the list of *Favorable and Unfavorable Days* in the **Moon Tables** section of the *Moon Sign Book*. Choose a date for the activity listed below that is both marked "favorable" (F or f) for your Sun sign and one that is marked with an "Sx" or "T" in the *Lunar Aspectarian* under the planet described. Never choose a date for any of these activities which is marked with an "O" or "Sq" under Saturn, Mars or Uranus, as these are negative aspects. They tend to counteract the good results promised.

The more good aspects in operation on the date you choose, the better the outlook for your affairs. "The better the day the better the deed." To recapitulate: Choose a date from the proper lists of dates marked "Sx" or "T" under the planet ruling the activity and also marked "F" or "f" to your own sign, but never a date marked "O" or "Sq" in the *Lunar Aspectarian* to Mars, Saturn or Uranus.

Moon

For doing housecleaning or a big baking, putting up preserves, washing, using liquids or chemicals, for matters connected with babies or small children, and to deal with the public in general, choose the good aspects of the Moon.

Sun

To gain favors of persons of high rank, title or prominent social standing, or those in responsible government office, to make a change or try for promotion, choose the good dates of Sun.

Mercury

For writing or signing an important document, seeking news or information, shopping, study, dealing with literary matters, choose the good dates of Mercury.

Venus

To give a successful party, ball or entertainment, to marry, for matters of courtship, art, beauty, adornnent; to cultivate the friendship of a woman, choose the good dates of Venus.

Mars

For dealing with surgeons, dentists, hair stylists, assayers, contractors, mechanics, lumbermen, police, personnel of army or navy, choose the good dates of Mars.

Jupiter

To deal with physicians, educators, sportspeople, bankers, brokers, philanthropists; to collect money or make important changes, choose the good dates of Jupiter.

Saturn

For dealing with plumbers, excavators or miners, for starting a new building, letting or leasing a house or dealing in land, choose the good dates of Saturn.

Uranus

For successful work on an invention, for dealing with inventors, metaphysicians, astrologers or new thought people, for new methods, or starting a journey, choose the good dates of Uranus.

Neptune

For all affairs connected with the deep sea or liquids in general, for practicing psychometry or developing mediumship, photography, tobacco and drugs, choose the good dates of Neptune.

Pluto

For uncovering errors, overcoming habits, healing, fumigation, pasteurizing, pest control, choose the good dates of Pluto. Also for matters related to the affairs of the dead, taxes, inheritance, etc.

THE TWELVE HOUSES
OF THE ZODIAC

You may run across mention of the houses of the zodiac while reading certain articles in the *Moon Sign Book*. These houses are the 12 divisions of the horoscope wheel. Each house has a specific meaning assigned to it. Below are the descriptions normally attributed to each house.

First House. Self-interest, physical appearance, basic character.

Second House. Personal values, monies earned and spent, movable possessions, self-worth and esteem, resources for fulfilling security needs.

Third House. Neighborhood, communications, siblings, schooling, buying and selling, busy activities, short trips.

Fourth House. Home, family, real estate, parent(s), one's private sector of life, childhood years, old age.

Fifth House. Creative endeavors, hobbies, pleasures, entertainments, children, speculative ventures, loved ones.

Sixth House. Health, working environment, co-workers, small pets, service to others, food, armed forces.

Seventh House. One-on-one encounters, business and personal partners, significant others, legal matters.

Eighth House. Values of others, joint finances, other people's money, death and rebirth, surgery, psychotherapy.

Ninth House. Higher education, religion, long trips, spirituality, languages, higher education, publishing.

Tenth House. Social status, reputation, career, public honors, parents, the limelight.

Eleventh House. Friends, social work, community work, causes, surprises, luck, rewards from career, circumstances beyond your control.

Twelfth House. Hidden weaknesses and strengths, behind-the-scenes activities, institutions, confinement, psychic attunement, government.

Home, Family & Pets

- Building
- Buying
- Home
- Cooking
- Romance
- Pets
- Brewing
- Moving

HOME, FAMILY & PETS

Automobiles

Choose a favorable date for your Sun sign, when the Moon is in a fixed sign (Taurus, Leo, Scorpio, Aquarius), well-aspected by the Sun (Sx or T) and not aspected by Mars and Saturn (the planets of accidents).

Several years ago a reader wrote to say that she bought her car according to the directions in the Special Activities section, that it now had over 100,000 miles on it, and had *never* had any major repairs.

Automobile Repair

Repair work is more successful when begun with the Moon in a fixed sign (Taurus, Leo, Scorpio or Aquarius), and well-aspected to the Sun. First and second quarters are the best Moon phases. Avoid unfavorable aspects (Sq or O) with Mars, Saturn, Uranus, Neptune or Pluto.

Baking

Baking should be done when the Moon is in the cardinal signs, Aries, Cancer, Libra or Capricorn. Bakers who have experimented with these rules say that dough rises higher and bread is lighter during the increase of the Moon (1st or 2nd quarter).

Brewing

It is best to brew during the Full Moon and the fourth quarter. Plan to have the Moon in a water sign (Cancer, Scorpio, Pisces).

Building

Turning the first sod for the foundation of a home or laying the cornerstone for a public building marks the beginning of the building. Excavate, lay foundations, and pour cement when the Moon is full and in a fixed sign, Taurus, Leo, or Aquarius. Saturn should be aspected but not Mars, for Mars aspects may indicate accidents.

Canning

Can fruits and vegetables when the Moon is in either the third or fourth quarters, and when it is in one of the water signs, Cancer, Scorpio or Pisces. For preserves and jellies, use the same quarters but see that the Moon is in one of the fixed signs: Taurus, Scorpio or Aquarius.

Cement and Concrete

Pour cement for foundations and concrete for walks and pavements during the Full Moon. It is best too for the Moon to be in one of the fixed signs, Taurus, Leo or Aquarius.

Dressmaking

Design, cut, repair or make clothes during the first and second quarters on a day marked favorable for your Sun sign. Venus, Jupiter and Mercury should be aspected, but avoid Mars or Saturn aspects.

Williams Lily wrote in 1676, "make no new clothes, or first put them on when the Moon is in Scorpio or afflicted by Mars, for they will be apt to be torn and quickly worn out." (Also see *Buying Clothing* in the Business Section.)

Fence Posts and Poles

Set the posts or poles when the Moon is in the third or fourth quarters. The fixed signs Taurus, Leo and Aquarius are best for this.

House

If you desire a permanent home, buy when the Moon is in one of the fixed signs, Taurus, Leo, Scorpio or Aquarius. If you're buying for speculation and a quick turnover, be certain that the Moon is not in a fixed sign, but in one of the cardinal signs, Aries, Cancer, Libra, or Capricorn.

House Furnishings

Follow the same rules for buying clothing, avoiding days when Mars is aspected. Days when Saturn is aspected make things wear longer and tend to a more conservative purchase. Saturn days are good for buying, and Jupiter days are good for selling.

Lost Articles

Search for lost articles during the first quarter and when your Sun sign is marked favorable. Also check to see that the planet ruling the lost item is trine, sextile, or conjunct the Moon. The Moon governs household utensils, Mercury letters and books, and Venus clothing, jewelry and money.

Marriage

As a general rule, the best time for marriage to take place is during the increase of the Moon, just past the first quarter. Such marriages will tend more towards optimism. Good signs for the Moon to be in are Taurus, Cancer, Leo, Libra and Pisces. Moon in Taurus produces the most steadfast marriages, but if the partners later want to separate they may have a very difficult time. Avoid Aries, Gemini, Virgo, Scorpio and Aquarius. Make sure that the Moon is well-aspected (Sx or T), especially to Venus or Jupiter. Avoid aspects to Mars, Uranus or Pluto.

Moving into a House or Office

Make sure that Mars is not aspected to the Moon. Try to move on a day which is favorable to your Sun sign, or when the Moon is conjunct, sextile or trine the Sun.

Mowing the Lawn

Mow the lawn in the first or second quarters to increase growth. If you wish to retard growth, mow in the third or fourth quarters.

Painting

The best time to paint buildings is during the decrease of the Moon (third and fourth quarters).

If the weather is hot do the painting while the Moon is in Taurus; if the weather is cold, paint while the Moon is in Leo. By painting in the fourth quarter, the wood is dryer and the paint will penetrate, while painting around the New Moon the wood is damp and the paint is subject to scalding when hot weather hits it. It is not advisable to paint while the Moon is in a water sign if the temperature is below 70 degrees, as it is apt to creep, check, or run.

Pets

Take home new pets when the date is favorable to your Sun sign, or the Moon is well-aspected by the Sun, Venus, Jupiter, Uranus or Neptune. Avoid days when the Moon is afflicted by the Sun, Mars, Saturn, Uranus, Neptune or Pluto. Train pets starting when the Moon is in Taurus. Neuter them in any sign but Virgo, Libra, Scorpio or Sagittarius. Avoid the week before and after the Full Moon.

Declaw cats in the Dark of the Moon. Avoid the week before and after the Full Moon and the sign of Pisces.

When selecting a new pet it is good to have the Moon well-aspected by the planet which rules the animal. Cats are ruled by the Sun, dogs by Mercury, birds by Venus, horses by Jupiter, and fish by Neptune.

Predetermining Sex

Count from the last day of menstruation to the day next beginning, and divide the interval between the two dates into halves.

Pregnancy occurring in the first half produces females, but copulation should take place when the Moon is in a feminine sign.

Pregnancy occurring in the later half, up to within three days of beginning of menstruation, produces males, but copulation should take place when the Moon is in a masculine sign. From this 3-day period, to the end of the first half of the next period, again produces females.

Romance

The same principles hold true for starting a relationship as for marriage. However, since there is less control over when a romance starts it is sometimes necessary to study it after the fact. Romances begun under an increasing Moon are more likely to be permanent, or at least satisfying. Those started on the waning Moon will more readily transform the participants. The general tone of the relationship can be guessed from the sign the Moon is in. For instance, those begun when the Moon is in Capricorn will take greater effort to bring to a desirable conclusion, but may be very rewarding. Those begun when the Moon is in Aries may be impulsive and quick to burn out. Good aspects between the Moon and Venus are excellent influences. Avoid those of Mars, Uranus and Pluto. Ending relationships is facilitated by a decreasing Moon, particularly in the fourth quarter. This causes the least pain and attachment.

Sauerkraut

The best tasting sauerkraut is made just after the Full Moon in a fruitiul sign (Cancer, Scorpio, Pisces).

Shingling

Shingling should be done in the decrease of the Moon (3rd or 4th quarters) when it is in a fixed sign (Taurus, Leo, Scorpio, Aquarius). If shingles are laid during the New Moon, they have a tendency to curl at the edges.

Weaning Children

This should be done when the Moon is in Sagittarius, Capricorn, Aquarius or Pisces. The mother should nurse the child in a fruitiul sign the last time. Venus should then be trine, sextile or conjunct the Moon.

Wine and Other Drinks Besides Beer (See Brewing)

For wine and spirits it is best to start when the Moon is in Pisces or Taurus. Good aspects (Sx or T) with Venus are favorable. Avoid aspects with Mars or Saturn.

THE MAGIC OF MEDICINAL PLANTS
by Louise Riotte

Recently I have become intensely aware of the importance of preserving our forests as so many vital medicinal plants grow there.

Consider that native of the Andes, cinchona (*Cinchona lancifolia*), sometimes called Jesuit's bark or Peruvian bark, now also found in the East Indies, India and tropical America. It is valued for its bitter bark from which quinine and other drugs are obtained. It was named for the Countess of Chinchon, wife of a Spanish viceroy of Peru, who introduced the bark in Europe. The Incas are believed to have used several of the species in the treatment of fevers long before they came to the attention of the Western world.

And what of the chaulmoogra the East Indian tree whose seeds yield an acrid oil which was used for centuries to treat leprosy and is still used in treating skin diseases.

Leaving the rain forest, we go to Australia and Tasmania to look with wonder at the eucalyptus trees which grow rapidly and may attain a height of 300 feet. In Australia this is the most important timber tree but these trees also have antiseptic value according to Joseph Kadans (*Encyclopedia of Medicinal Herbs*). He states that the aromatic eucalyptus may be inhaled freely for sore throat and other bacterial infections of the bronchial tubes or lungs. It has also been found to relieve asthma. Ulcers may be healed by preparing an application of one ounce of the powdered leaves to a pint of lukewarm water, applied directly to the parts needing treatment. A third use of the fragrant oil is in cases of fevers and in conditions of muscular spasms. A unique feature of eucalyptus is that it causes offensive odors to cease almost immediately.

After admiring the impressive eucalyptus we come closer to the ground to take a look at a gentle little herb called eyebright (*Euphrasia officinalis. Scrophulariaceae*).

Juliette de Bairacli Levy, in her book *Herbal Handbook for Everyone*, describes this as being found in meadows and by waysides. "Leaves are tiny, in keeping with the whole miniature quality of this plant. Flowers also tiny, white tinged with purple and having a yellow eye. The name of the plant comes from its remarkable power over the eyes; it has restored sight to the blind where blindness resulted from neglected inflammation. The plant is also an astringent and a nerve medicine."

Who would have thought that ferns were medicinal? But, as Levy tells us, one variety, male fern (*Aspidium filix mas.*), found in shady woodlands and on bank-sides, contains a green oil, also, gum, resin, pectin, tannic acid and albumen, a very impressive rhizome for such a tiny plant. It is used as a general tonic and a vermifuge, especially against tapeworms of all kinds.

And it may come as a surprise to many that the rose, dripping with fragrant blossoms, is also a medicinal plant, particularly *R. rugosa*, generally regarded, according to Nelson Coon (*Using Plants for Healing*), as being richer in vitamin C than oranges. The hips are considered to be valuable in the maintenance of health. Rose oil is also useful, as well as being deliciously fragrant, in medicine and rose petals may be used as an astringent.

Many of us have been amused by the story of the old-time cowboy who entered the local saloon, put his foot on the rail, and called for a "sarsaparilla." According to Kadans, this herb has been widely reported as an alterative, tending to restore an abnormal system to normalcy. Many also believe it has aphrodisiac qualities. It is also in high repute as a purifier of the blood and has had considerable use in coping with syphilis infections. In the early days of the west it was popular as a sort of "soft drink."

The rose family has many cousins, including wild black cherry, or rum cherry, the apple, blackberry and raspberry. Levy tells us the raspberry is particularly helpful in a difficult labor, or afterwards to bring down retained afterbirth—strong drinks of raspberry tea made of the leaves, with a teaspoon of crushed ivy leaves to every two teaspoons of raspberry leaves, every two or three hours.

Goldenseal, the very name has a beautiful ring to it. This small perennial plant has a thick, fleshy yellow rhizome the substance of which has the effect of constricting or tightening the blood vessels—known medically as a vasoconstrictor.

Influenza seems to visit us every year, sometimes in a more virulent form than others. I was very interested to read about it in the *Encyclopedia of Medical Astrology* by H.L. Cornell, M.D. Dr. Cornell states:

"Influenza—La Grippe—contagious and epidemic. First called influenza in Italy in the seventeenth century because attributed to the 'Influenze of the Stars,' and this name has passed into medical use. This disease occurs in countries at the time of an eclipse, and where the eclipse is visible, and especially in parts under the Central Line of the Shadow. It also occurs when three or four superior planets are in conjunction or opposition. Said to be caused by electrical conditions in the atmosphere, due to planetary influence."

One of the treasures of my library is *Materia Medica and Therapeutics*, the 1890 edition, formerly owned by an Indian territory doctor. This book asserts that, "Influenza first becomes apparent each year in the East and then travels westward, reaching the U.S. about January." Apparently it still follows this pattern though some years it gets here sooner.

Like the *Materia Medica*, my copy of *Pharmacopeia of the United States* lists a number of remedies for influenza which were used at that time. Among these are arsenic, asaprol, benzol, camphor, carbolic acid, creosote, eucalyptus, oil of sandalwood, quinine, salicin, and sodium salicylate. I found this very interesting in view of the number of trees mentioned.

It has been said that primitive humans learned of the valuable properties of plants by observing the animals nibbling on them—even today the observant may note dogs and cats partaking of various grasses to promote cleansing vomiting when they have eaten something that disagrees with them. Cats also rid themselves of hairballs in this manner.

Those mysterious people, the Gypsies, are also credited with knowing the values of many herbs long before anyone else. Jeanne Rose, in her book *Herbs & Things*, relates that foxglove was used for hundreds of years by the

Gypsies for all manner of heart conditions before it was "discovered" by modern doctors. She tells us that this biennial herb should not be picked until its second year when it is flowering and the alkaloids are most concentrated. Its leaves yield the drug digitalis—a powerful cardiac stimulant.

Levy tells us that the great doctor Paracelsus von Hohenheim forsook the medical universities of the world and lived with the Gypsy and peasant herbalists in many parts of Europe in order to learn the *true* medicine.

Geoffrey Marks and William K. Beatty, authors of *The Medical Garden*, give an interesting insight into the history of colchicine, "an alkaloid obtained from the seeds and bulbous root of the *Colchicum autumnale* or meadow saffron. Colchicum rivals opium for the honor of being the oldest plant remedy still in use. Both are mentioned in the *Ebers papyrus*, the Egyptian record dating back to the sixteenth century B.C. Colchicum's major claim to medical fame has been as a remedy for gouty arthritis, a painful affliction of a single joint, frequently the great toe."

Today aspirin is a household word, credited with even more valuable properties than bringing down a fever. The use of salicylic acid in the treatment of pain and fever is far from new. Ancient records show the Romans obtained it from willow-bark and used it as early as 400 B.C. And our own pioneers, moving westward, found that the North American Indians had long used willow bark as a remedy.

As is often the case, these early users of what would someday be aspirin knew what the natural product did but not why it did it. Indeed, even today nobody knows why colchicine or digitalis, or many other drugs work—they only know that they do "work."

Myrten.   Roßen.   Kräuß baßilien.   Violen.   Gilgen.   Cuonen.   Alraun öpffel.

HERBS AND HEALTH

In a modern society with countless synthetic drugs, the question may be asked: Why use herbs? After witnessing the side effects of medicines artificially prepared, people today are turning again to the valuable remedial properties of herbs and fruit and vegetable juices. Nature's cures are the herbs and their seeds that have grown naturally for centuries all over the earth. For every disease that afflicts humankind there is a natural remedy—an herb.

Herbs are food for the human body and mind. They contain the vitamins and minerals necessary to the balance of the body's systems, as do the other natural foods we eat (vegetables, fruits, grains, etc.).

The purpose of a remedy is to help the body cure itself. When certain organic minerals and vitamins necessary for balance are lacking in our diet, disease results. Therefore, the body must be supplied with the essential elements it needs to rebuild the areas weakened or damaged by disease.

Natural herbs have an advantage over modern drugs. As they are grown, herbs contain an organic combination of substances in the proportions needed by the human body. In their natural form the body can easily convert them into healing remedies. Further, because of these elements, herbs can be used effectively as an aid to the body in preventing as well as healing disease.

How to Prepare Herbal Remedies

Infusions are made as is regular tea, by pouring 1 pint boiling water over 1/2 ounce of herb flowers or leaves and steeping for a few minutes. Honey is sometimes added for sweetening.

Decoctions are made of the hard parts of the herb—the stems, roots, bark, seeds—and they have to boil for some time to extract their full value.

To make a **fomentation**, dip a cloth or heavy towel into

a decoction or an infusion. Wring out the extra moisture and apply externally to the affected area.

For **salves**, take 8 parts vaseline or lard to 2 parts herbal, stir, and mix well while hot. Use when cool.

To make a **poultice**, put the herbs loosely in a flannel bag large enough to cover the area. Pour boiling water over the bag and then wring out the extra moisture inside a towel. Use the poultice as hot as possible. It is good for nerve pains, painful joints and muscles, and promotes restful sleep when applied to the abdomen.

Backache

Exercise is important: lie on floor on back with legs up—cycle! Teas of nettle, rosinweed.

Bites, insect

Apply eucalyptus oil, thyme oil or distilled witch hazel extract.

Boils and Blisters

Poultice of lobelia and slippery elm; hops; skunk cabbage; Solomon's seal; for blisters use onion juice plus salt.

Burns

Poultice of comfrey; mustard; yarrow (excellent). Particularly good salves are made from elderberry blossom, golden seal, or red clover. You may also use wheat germ oil.

Colds

Teas of balsam; catnip (plus hot foot bath); elderberry and peppermint; golden seal; mullein; rosemary; sarsaparilla. A hot foot bath for 20 minutes plus epsom salts. For quick recovery take 2t. honey and 2t. cider vinegar in a glass of water; or eat raw or cooked onions.

Constipation

Teas of blue flag and cascara sagrada are the best known remedies; also red clover.

Corns

Tie lemon slices over the corn overnight. Apply this fluid extract morning and night; or tie a cloth soaked in turpentine around them overnight.

Dandruff

After your hair is rinsed massage well into the scalp: oils of rosemary and eucalyptus; a tea made of willow leaves and bark. A very successful remedy is a tea made of 1 oz. rosemary steeped in a pint of boiling water. (Be sure to let the water cool before you use it!)

Diarrhea

Raw apples and bananas (children also); teas of crowfoot (best); peppermint; red raspberry; slippery elm (most useful).

Eczema

Make an ointment of apple cider vinegar or boric acid instead of soap and water. Internally, you can take lecithin daily, or spikenard, valerian, plantain.

Eyes, black or sore

Use arnica in water if the skin isn't broken, or witch hazel in water if it is broken. A poultice made of scraped raw potato is also effective.

Fevers

Teas of chamomile (most effective); sweet cicely; yarrow (said to relieve fever in 24 hours if taken every 30 minutes); catnip; elderberry; peppermint and honey. Also sponge patient with common baking soda water. Spearmint tea for children.

Frostbite

Paint the area with Friar's Balsam and rub olive oil gently onto same place after a few minutes.

Gums, tender

Try a mixture of orris root, myrrh, and borax.

Headache

Most important is to lie down and rest where there is quiet and fresh air. Also: hot teas of peppermint (most popular); catnip; spearmint; chamomile; a very hot foot bath for 5-10 minutes with 1T. mustard; hot water with lemon juice; onion plus honey.

Hiccoughs

Most popular and effective are: the juice of half an orange; swallowing very hot or very cold water; sipping peppermint tea; pineapple juice; a very hot foot bath; a mouthful of cold water taken, held in mouth, the middle fingers of each hand placed in both ears, the water swallowed, and the fingers removed after a moment.

Insomnia

Teas of chamomile; catnip; hops (or pillow stuffed with under head); lady's slipper (highly recommended); eating raw onions; a very hot foot bath before bed; rose leaves with mint heated as compress.

Irritations, skin

Take citrus fruits; teas of balsam root; yarrow or red clover blossoms and chickweed internally.

Pains, Menstrual

Teas of pennyroyal (best); black cohosh (depressed feelings); chamomile; catnip; sweet cicely.

Sores, Cuts, Wounds

Poultice of grated raw carrot; comfrey, dandelion; juniper; red clover; sweet cicely; skunk cabbage; yarrow and yerba mansa (best); cod-liver oil (stops infection); elderberry blossom salve; and grindelia decoction.

Stomachache

A glass of milk taken 2 hours after each meal; for gas—caraway and sweet cicely teas; teas of sage (most useful); golden seal; chamomile; marigold leaves (highly recommended); mint; peppermint; slippery elm; valerian; yarrow; and dandelion.

Sunburn

Make an ointment of glycerine, witch hazel, and sunflower seed oil.

Sunstroke

Put your feet in a hot mustard foot bath and apply hot or cold cloths to the forehead and back of neck.

Swellings, Sprains

Poultices of chamomile and hops; caraway and hyssop (black and blue marks); juniper; mullein plus pennyroyal; sweet cicely; skunk cabbage; Solomon's seal; yarrow; yerba mansa. You may also use a comfrey fomentation.

Toothache

The most liked remedy is the poultice; juniper; willow; and hops plus coarse salt. Herbs directly put into a cavity are: yarrow; raw cow parsnip; grindelia; sweet cicely (pain reducer). Chewed herbs are: tobacco (best); yarrow; yerba mansa; blue flag. Hops tea is given for baby teething.

Travel Sickness

Sips of a cup of hot water every ten or fifteen minutes help; take only a light meal before starting a trip; ingest lemon juice plus salt every few minutes at the first signs of illness.

Varicose veins

Lie on your back and elevate your legs to relieve the pressure. Try bathing your legs with white oak bark. Sea salt baths are also effective. Overnight, apply cloths soaked in distilled witch hazel extract and cover with a dry towel until morning. Stroke your legs upward toward your hips whenever possible. Teas made of golden seal, myrrh, tansy or bran, taken internally, help strengthen the veins.

Care of the Hair
Baldness

Try massaging oils of clove and eucalyptus into your scalp; or, after washing, rinse your hair with marsh mallow tea. You might also drink sarsaparilla tea and eat more wheat germ, carrots, apples, bananas, tomatoes, strawberries, lettuce, cantaloupe and dried peas.

Grey Hair

To darken, use a rinse made from a handful of stinging nettle boiled in a quart of water; or use an ounce of chamomile or sage boiled in a quart of water for twenty minutes.

Growth

To encourage growth ingest wheat germ, cod-liver oil or lecithin daily.

Texture

To brighten and improve the texture of your hair, use rinses of plantain and shepherd's purse; any mixture of peppergrass; marsh mallow; mullein; nettle; sage or burdock. Chamomile rinses are good for blondes.

Beauty Treatments for Skin

Aging

Apply leaves and roots of comfrey.

Dry

The oldest known moisturizers are glycerine and honey; next to these is lecithin. Lanolin, natural menthol, and oils of quince, avocado, apricot kernel, almond, sesame and wheat germ.

To soften your complexion, smooth mashed papaya on your face and rest with your feet up, then rinse.

Bath oils: Hang a bag of meadow sweet, or a bag of rosemary, lavender, or comfrey in the bath. Or combine a pint of vegetable oil, a small amount of liquid shampoo and a few drops of perfume and add 2T. to your bath.

Dry hands

You can make a good hand lotion of glycerine and benzoin; or 1/2 oz. each of glycerine and rosewater and 1/4 oz. of witch hazel, mixed and shaken well. If your hands are chapped after having been in water, rub dampened table salt on them and rinse.

Oily

Make an astringent of honey and glycerine, cucumber slices on the face daily; or witch hazel on a cloth over the eyes and rest for 15 minutes.

Texture
The skin is one of the ways the body breathes, so try a cold friction bath in the morning to open the pores and improve skin texture. Wet your hands and body and slap yourself for a few moments. Dry yourself well and massage your skin tenderly with almond oil until it's all absorbed.

Wrinkles
Make a lotion of benzoin, glycerine and honey plus a few drops of cologne. Or try warm olive oil massaged into the forehead. Barley water plus a few drops of balm of gilead also works.

Other Beauty Aids
Breath
Improve your breath by chewing anise seed, orris root, angelica root, cardamon seed or nutmeg; or by drinking chamomile tea.

Eyes
For dark circles and faded eyes, try eating more blueberries, tomatoes, avocados, eggplant, and sunflower seeds.

Teeth
To whiten teeth, an old English recipe suggests a mixture of honey and vegetable charcoal.

ANNIVERSARY GEM LIST

1st	Gold Jewelry
2nd	Garnet (All Colors)
3rd	Pearls
4th	Blue Topaz
5th	Sapphire (All Colors)
6th	Amethyst
7th	Onyx
8th	Tourmaline (All Colors)
9th	Lapis Lazuli
10th	Diamond Jewelry
11th	Turquoise
12th	Jade
13th	Citrine
14th	Opal
15th	Ruby
16th	Peridot
17th	Watches
18th	Cat's Eye Chrysoberyl
19th	Aquamarine
20th	Emerald
21st	Iolite
22nd	Spinel (All Colors)
23rd	Imperial Topaz
24th	Tanzanite
25th	Silver Jubilee
30th	Pearl Jubilee
35th	Emerald
40th	Ruby
45th	Sapphire
50th	Golden Jubilee
55th	Alexandrite
60th	Diamond Jubilee

Leisure &
Recreation

LEISURE & RECREATION

Fishing

During the summer months the best time of the day for fishing is from sunrise to three hours after, and from about two hours before sunset until one hour after. In the cooler months, the fish are not actively biting until the air is warmed. At this time the best hours are from noon to 3:00p.m. Warm and cloudy days are good. The most favorable winds are from the south and southwest. Easterly winds are unfavorable. The best days of the month for fishing are those on which the Moon changes quarters, and especially if the change occurs on a day when the Moon is in a watery sign, Cancer, Scorpio, or Pisces. The best period in any month is the day after the Full Moon.

Friends

The need for friendship is greater when Uranus aspects the Moon, or the Moon is in Aquarius. Friendship prospers when Venus or Uranus is trine, sextile, or conjunct the Moon. The chance meeting of informed acquaintances and friends is facilitated by the Moon in Gemini.

Parties, Giving or Going To

The best time for parties is when the Moon is in Gemini, Leo, Libra, or Sagittarius with good aspects to Venus and Jupiter. There should be no aspects to Mars or Saturn.

Sports

The Sun rules physical vitality, Mars rules coordination and competition, and Saturn rules strategy but hinders coordination. Plan activities to coincide with good aspects from the appropriate planets. Specific sports are ruled by specific planets, from which they benefit. Horse racing is ruled by Jupiter. Mars rules baseball, football, boxing, and wrestling. The Sun rules exercising. Swimming is ruled by

Neptune and the Moon. Accidents are associated with squares or oppositions to Mars, Saturn, or Uranus.

Travel

Short journeys are ruled by Mercury, long ones by Jupiter. The Sun rules the actual journey itself. Long trips which threaten to exhaust the traveller are best begun when the Sun is well-aspected to the Moon and the date is favorable for the traveller. If travelling with other people, good aspects from Venus are desirable. For enjoyment, aspects to Jupiter are profitable. For visiting, aspects to Mercury. To avoid accidents, avoid squares or oppositions to Mars, Saturn, Uranus or Pluto.

When to Fly

Choose a day when the Moon is in Gemini or Libra, and well-aspected by Mercury and/or Jupiter. Avoid adverse aspects of Mars, Saturn or Uranus.

Writing

Write for pleasure or publication when the Moon is in Gemini. Mercury should be direct. Favorable aspects to Mercury, Uranus and Neptune promote ingenuity.

RECREATION ACTIVITIES

Everyone is affected by the lunar cycle. Your lunar high occurs when the Moon is in your Sun sign, and your lunar low occurs when the Moon is in the sign opposite your Sun sign. The handy *Favorable and Unfavorable Dates* tables in the Moon Tables section give the lunar highs and lows for each Sun sign every day of the year. This lunar cycle influences all your activities: your physical strength, mental alertness, and manual dexterity are all affected.

Astrological Rulership

By combining the *Favorable and Unfavorable Dates* tables and the *Lunar Aspectarian* tables with the information given below in the list of astrological rulerships, you can choose the best time for a variety of activities.

The best time to perform an activity is when its ruling planet is in favorable aspect to the Moon or when the Moon is in its ruling sign—that is, when its ruling planet is trine, sextile, or conjunct the Moon, marked with a T, Sx, or C, in the *Lunar Aspectarian* or when its ruling sign is marked F in the *Favorable and Unfavorable Dates* tables.

For example, go bicycling when Uranus or Mercury are marked with a T, Sx, or C, or when Gemini is marked with an F. Ice skating is enjoyed more when Neptune is trine, sextile, or conjunct the Moon, and films are more rewarding when Neptune or Uranus is marked T, Sx, or C or when Leo or Aquarius is marked F.

ARTS
Acting, actors Neptune, Pisces, Sun, Leo
Art in general Venus, Libra
Ballet Neptune, Venus
Ceramics Saturn
Crafts Mercury, Venus
Dancing Venus, Taurus, Neptune, Pisces
Drama Venus, Neptune
Embroidery Venus
Etchings Mars
Films, filmmaking Neptune, Leo, Uranus, Aquarius
Literature Mercury, Gemini
Music Venus, Libra, Taurus, Neptune
Painting Venus, Libra
Photography Neptune, Pisces, Uranus, Aquarius
Printing Mercury, Gemini
Theaters Sun, Leo, Venus

HUNTING AND PETS
Animals in general Mercury, Jupiter, Virgo, Pisces
　　　Game animals Sagittarius
　　　Animal training Mercury, Virgo
Cats Leo, Sun, Virgo, Venus
Dogs Mercury, Virgo
Fish Neptune, Pisces, Moon, Cancer
Pet birds Mercury, Venus
Horses, trainers, riders Jupiter, Sagittarius
Hunters Jupiter, Sagittarius

SPORTS
Acrobatics Mars, Aries
Archery Jupiter, Sagittarius

Ball games in general Venus
      Baseball Mars
      Football Mars
Bicycling Uranus, Mercury, Gemini
Calisthenics Mars, Neptune
Deep-sea diving Neptune, Pisces
Horseracing Jupiter, Sagittarius
Jogging Mercury, Gemini
Polo Uranus, Jupiter, Venus, Saturn
Racing (other than horse) Sun, Uranus
Ice skating Neptune
Roller skating Mercury
Sports in general Sun, Leo
      Competive sports in general Mars
      Sporting equipment Jupiter, Sagittarius
Swimming Neptune, Pisces, Moon, Cancer
Tennis Mercury, Venus, Uranus, Mars

TRAVEL
Air travel Mercury, Sagittarius, Uranus
Automobile travel Mercury, Gemini
Boating Moon, Cancer, Neptune
Camping Leo
Helicopters Uranus
Hotels Cancer, Venus
Motorcycle travel Uranus, Aquarius
Parks Sun, Leo
Picnics Venus, Leo
Restaurants Moon, Cancer, Virgo, Jupiter
Rail travel Uranus, Mercury, Gemini
Long journeys Jupiter, Sagittarius
Short journeys Mercury, Gemini
Vacations, holidays Venus, Neptune

OTHER ENTERTAINMENTS
Barbeques Moon, Mars
Casinos Venus, Sun, Jupiter
Chess Mercury, Mars
Collections Moon, Cancer
Festivals Venus
Parades Jupiter, Venus
Parties Venus, Leo

FISHING AND HUNTING BY THE MOON

by Louise Riotte

Hundreds of books have been written about the art of fishing since Izaak Walton penned the first edition of the *Compleat Angler* in 1653. The serious fisherperson has probably read a number of these books, and most of us have studied something of the creature that we pursue. We know that fish are creatures of instinct and habit. The problem is that anglers, too, are creatures of habit. We also develop patterns of behavior, and most of us are painfully aware of how seldom our patterns coincide with the fish's pattern.

Owning the best equipment and reading the best books will not improve anyone's fishing unless that person knows how to use that equipment and knowledge. It becomes evident to the student of astrology that most anglers need to *forget* some of their unproductive fishing habits and learn a variety of new approaches. In the final analysis, being a successful fisherperson means being versatile. What is written here is for everyone who pursues fish not only for the pure joy of relaxing in the outdoors but also in the hopes that someday he or she will catch the lunker of a lifetime.

As creatures captive to their environment, fish are closely attuned to changes in weather and water conditions, and they respond to these changes by moving around in lakes and rivers. Season, time of day, and many other factors have a bearing on whether or not you will catch fish at a particular time.

From sunset to one hour after during the summer months, fishing should be great. In the cooler months, fishing is best from noon to three in the afternoon. The best day to fish is a warm, close and cloudy day that follows a bright moonlit night. This is because fish have no eyelids. On a cloudy day, there is no bright light to distress them, so they feed near the surface.

Wind, too, has a bearing on these matters with the most favorable winds from the south, southwest, and west. East winds are unfavorable.

> When the wind is in the north
> The skilful fisher goes not forth,
> When the wind is in the south
> It blows the bait in the fish's mouth,
> When the wind is in the east
> 'Tis neither good for man nor beast,
> When the wind is in the west
> Then fishing's at its very best.

The concept of fish movement is really very simple. Most game fish spawn in the spring of the year, migrating into shallow waters. This migration is triggered by water temperature with each species responding to a different temperature. Each species also prefers a certain set of bottom conditions over which to spawn. Walleyes, for instance, like hard gravel bottoms while northern pike prefer shallow, weedy sloughs. After spawning, fish begin movement into a summer location pattern, often choosing another area of the lake. Again, this movement is triggered by water temperature and is in response to locating prey that the game fish will feed on all summer long. Once this pattern is established, fish location will be fairly predictable throughout the summer.

With the arrival of the first cold nights that come in the fall, lakes and rivers cool off rather quickly, and once more the fish move to a new location. In the North where lakes and rivers ice over, ice fishermen usually find a gradual movement of game fish from shallow to deeper waters as the winter progresses. In Southern waters fish also move deeper and become less active, but daily weather conditions can make dramatic changes if a warm spell sends the water temperature soaring.

There are many who believe that fish can sense weather changes and are particularly active three days before a storm. But on the day of the actual weather change, the fish will not bite. This may be because the winds often stir up the water, inducing the smaller fish to come out. And small fish are followed by big fish which consider them

their lawful prey. The big fish, in turn, are followed by anglers who have the same idea.

A wise old fisherman once told me to watch out for a storm if insects were flying low and fish were jumping out of the water to catch them. Insects fly lower to avoid the thin atmosphere above due to the lowering air pressure. He also said to take note of the variety of insect that was flying and to set flies for bait accordingly.

After heavy rains fish may not bite since plenty of food has been washed into the lake. They are also hard to catch when fresh snow water is in a stream. Generally speaking, June is usually the best fishing month and July the worst.

It is generally conceded that the best days of the month for fishing are those on which the Moon changes quarters (plus the day before and day after), especially if the change occurs on a day when the Moon is in a water sign (Cancer, Scorpio or Pisces). The best period in any month is the day after the Full Moon. Three days before and after the Full Moon are also favorable.

My friend and expert fisherlady Lucy Hagen, who works by day and often fishes at night, says she has her best luck when she fishes "down the moonbeam."

And which sign of the three water signs is the best? An experienced fisherman took a day off from his job, and it happened to fall under the sign of Scorpio. He caught the fish he had been after for so long but was so delighted to win the fight of wills that he put it back and gave it its freedom. His theory was that fish are more hungry in the sign of Scorpio and less cautious and more likely to be caught.

He also told me that he had his best luck when using an active lure. "With live bait," he said, "attach the hook so the bait will have natural movements. With artificial lures, jig or pop the bait and vary the pace of the retrieve. Present the lure to the water in a manner that will be interesting to fish both in location and in action. Fish the shady sides of logs and rocks, the down-current sides of boulders and large stumps, and the windless side of ledges and cliffs. Let "the bait sink and keep it moving all the time."

You must polish your techniques to fit the fish. Their pattern is not likely to change, so your pattern must if you are to be successful.

Although they don't have eyelids, fish possess remarkable sight. Sensitive to light, they adjust their eyesight to the rhythms of the natural night and day cycle. Any sudden light thrown on them will cause them to quit the area rapidly. Because of the placement of their eyes, it is impossible for them to see objects on the level or directly under them. However, they can see all that is occurring above and around them for distances of 50 feet or more.

They also have a keen sense of smell and don't like strong aromas. Certain odors can be attractive, however. Many fisherpersons believe that bait rubbed with oil of anise will draw the fish. Others swear by the juice of smallage or lovage.

According to Clarence Meyer in *The Herbalist Almanac*, the Chinese use the following method for catching fish: "Take *Cocculus indicus*, pulverize and mix with dough, then scatter it broadcast over the water, as you would with seed. The fish will seize it with great avidity, and they will instantly become so intoxicated that they will turn belly up on top of the water by dozens, hundreds or even thousands, as the case may be. All that you have to do, is to have a boat, gather them up and put them in a tub of clean water, and presently they will be as lively and healthy as ever." Some American Indian tribes also used herbs, such as blue-curls, camphorweed, vinegarweed, wild cucumber and marsh in a similar fashion.

Remember that fish have very good hearing as evidenced by their sensitivity to vibrations. Be as quiet in your movements as possible—talking does not seem to bother them as much as walking about or dropping something heavy.

As previously indicated, fish are usually on three levels of most lakes, ponds and streams. Some, according to season, time of day, etc., are near the surface, some mid-water, and some on the bottom. Work the various levels to find the area of biting fish.

Troll whenever possible. This enables you to cover large or otherwise inaccessible areas to locate fish. Furthermore, you learn more about the water you are working.

Position yourself with your back to the wind, and don't let your shadow fall on the water. If fishing in moving water, cast upstream and let your bait drift down with the flow.

Fish are greedy by nature. They also have a built-in sense as to the size of an object they can swallow and will go for larger baits up to their maximum swallowing capacity.

Fishing for an abundant catch will be most rewarding in the sign of Cancer. Big ones may be caught in the sign of Scorpio, but they do tend to slack off a little bit when the Moon is in Pisces, although this is still a good fishing sign. Other possibilities are the moist signs of Taurus, Virgo, Libra and Capricorn.

A fishing guide states: "The best time to catch fish is when the Moon is directly overhead and the two hours before and after. The next best time is the hour before and after the Moon is straight down on the other side of the earth." The author insists these periods work every time.

Fish are creatures of habit and usually feed on a regular time schedule. If they feed in the early morning, they will be likely to feed again in the late afternoon and again early the next morning. Night feeders are just as regular.

Often fish will feed on only one insect or food for quite lengthy periods. When this happens, it is almost impossible to lure them with any other bait.

Before and after spawning season, fish will eagerly take a variety of baits. Brook trout and many other species will absolutely refuse food during spawning.

The larger the fish, the faster its swimming ability. It has been calculated that fish can swim about eight miles per hour for each foot of body length. But after striking a bait or making any other sudden move, a fish can accelerate up to about 50 percent over its usual cruising speed.

· During the summer months black bass go in pairs—if you catch one, try for its mate. Don't try to catch black bass when the water is perfectly smooth, it's a waste of time.

There are other water creatures besides fish that deserve honorable mention. When the Moon is full, residents of Chatham on Cape Cod head for the beach where they dig up bushels of giant sea clams, which are about four times as big as the quahogs favored by most New Englanders. Clams are ruled by the Moon. An experienced clam digger says they should be dug at the entrance of the wet Sun sign of Libra—its first week, September 22 to 29, is thought to be the best time. She says she marks special spots that look good for digging and then uses this Libra week for harvesting. She, too, thinks they are best and most plentiful during the Full Moon.

According to Louisiana folk, crabs ruled by the Moon and Cancer are best caught when the Moon is full. They use a chicken neck for bait, and the crabs bite quickly. They claim the meat at this time is full and juicy, but at other times the crabs are mostly shell.

Hunting by Moonlight

In early days when the country was young and Daniel Boone was busy making a name for himself, there were no hunting laws. Deer especially like to feed by moonlight, and the hunter could go out any time and kill a deer. Things aren't so easy now, and hunting deer by moonlight is against the law.

Even so, the Moon can be your guide, legally, to better sport. Just as in other activities, you should check for favorable and unfavorable days. Hunting is best when the Moon is in the hunters' sign of Libra.

Most game animals like to feed when the Moon is overhead, and during the Full Moon this is at night, but *during the New Moon this is by day.* My husband, whom I often accompanied on hunting trips to Utah and Colorado, always averred that hunting deer was best at daylight, just before dark. At those times the bucks (the does are protected by law in many places) are starting to move and are much easier to spot. The New Moon rises at dawn, a second quarter

Moon rises at noon, a Full Moon rises at dusk and a fourth quarter Moon rises at midnight. Many hunters like to pursue their sport when the Moon is in the last quarter; the day of and the day after the phase change are also considered favorable.

An Oklahoma hunter who usually "gets his deer" also uses the Moon, following the moonlight more than the sign. He says that when deer are not disturbed they will feed almost as much in the daytime when the Moon is up as they do at night. If the Moon shines all night, they will feed at night and rest during the day. If the Moon is up all day, they will feed during those hours and lie quietly at night. During the Moon's last quarter when it has been down and out of sight all day, the deer become very hungry and will range out and feed all night. For still hunting in the daytime, he tries to go when the Moon is up or is rising, whether it is the morning or afternoon.

So far as I can ascertain, it is still permitted to hunt raccoons at night, and many Southerners think this is great sport, training "coon hounds" to accompany them.

There is a prevailing belief in the mountains that an animal tastes only as good as what it eats. For this reason, animals such as coon and possum are hunted by many only when and if the corn, chestnut, acorn, and grape crops are good. When the mast is good, so is the flesh of the animals that feed on it.

A good place for hunting is around branches and the heads of little springs where coons have been turning over rocks looking for crayfish and spring lizards. Often their tracks or "sign" can be found along sandbars and in soft damp places beside cricks. Raccoons also scratch around oaks and other trees for nuts.

Once a coon is suspected, the hunter brings coon dogs to the spot that night. Then s/he follows the dogs as best s/he can when the coon is "treed," which may actually be any place from a hole in the ground to a rock cliff or even the top of a real tree.

But the tricky coon is no fool, and sometimes when the dogs are at the base of one tree, the hunter might find the coon two or three trees away. If it's actually in a tree, pine knot torches are lit or a brush fire built at the base of the tree. The coon looks at the fire, and the hunter watches for shining eyes and then shoots. If that doesn't work, the hunter usually waits till daylight so the coon can be seen— provided it's still there.

I was told that sometimes when the Moon was shining the coon would look at the Moon and not the fire. Other hunters said that on a moonlit night a coon would always head for a sinkhole, so it was best to hunt them on cloudy nights.

Duck hunting, too, has its advocates. One successful hunter who studied ducks and duck hunting for over 20 years says the best times for shooting are just before daylight and just before dark. He ties a red bandanna on a stick, keeping out of sight while waving it over his head. He contends that ducks have an inquisitive nature and will swim close to investigate unless they are extremely wild. He also favors October and November for his duck hunting on moonlit nights. He works smooth, sheltered water when the wind is up and fully believes a good duck hunter should spend more time looking for the favorite feeding and resting spots than waiting for them to come to you at a blind or by decoys.

Grouse or partridge hunting, another hunter claims, is most successful in the early morning during stormy or cold weather. The best places are around berry bushes or where there is plenty of feed. Learn their roosting places to find them towards night.

Quail are best found at midday during sunny weather in October and November. Look in the middle of fields, around brush and stubble and the edges of woods. A good pointer dog is very valuable.

Woodcock are best hunted late in the evening and at dawn. Best hunting places are moist lowlands, swamps and the north or wet sides of hills.

Wild geese are very regular in going to and from their feeding grounds. Learn their timetable and get your goose.

General Hunting Hints

It is a poor time for hunting when there is a high wind and dry leaves. Most good hunters agree that a period of steady light, after some rain is good hunting weather.

Just about any animal you hunt will be most alert on windy days. Small game grow cautious and burrow up, and big game seek safety in heavy ground cover when it is windy. Wise hunters use this knowledge to creep upward to these hiding places, being careful to be as quiet as possible and remaining out of sight as the game will instinctively bed down where they have the best visibility.

Folks who like to bird hunt and have the area would do well to plant wild rice around ponds and streams in the fall of the year. Ducks and other birds will linger near areas of good feed.

If it has rained over a long period of time and looks like it will never quit, watch for woodchucks. They follow the Sun and will tell you that it will soon clear up sufficiently to bring out game.

HUNTING AND FISHING DATES

Dates	Sign	Phase
Dec 29, 4:04 pm-Jan 1, 1:31 am	Scorpio	4th qtr.
Jan 8, 2:53 pm-Jan 11, 2:23 am	Pisces	1st qtr.
Jan 17, 5:27 pm-Jan 19, 3:30 pm	Cancer	2nd qtr.
Jan 19, 3:30 pm	Cancer	Full Moon
Jan 19, 3:30 pm-Jan 19, 4:58 pm	Cancer	3rd qtr.
Jan 25, 10:33 pm-Jan 28, 7:21 am	Scorpio	3rd/4th
Feb 4, 8:51 pm-Feb 7, 8:16 am	Pisces	1st qtr.
Feb 14, 3:32 am-Feb 16, 4:16 am	Cancer	2nd qtr.
Feb 18, 2:05 am	Leo	Full Moon
Feb 22, 7:12 am-Feb 24, 2:27 pm	Scorpio	3rd qtr.
Mar 3, 3:12 am-Mar 5, 2:08 pm	Pisces	4th/1st
Mar 12, 10:51 am-Mar 14, 1:21 pm	Cancer	2nd qtr.
Mar 18, 12:19 pm	Virgo	Full Moon
Mar 20, 5:21 pm-Mar 22, 11:14 pm	Scorpio	3rd qtr.
Mar 30, 10:24 am-Apr 1, 9:05 pm	Pisces	4th qtr.
Apr 8, 4:19 pm-Apr 10, 7:47 pm	Cancer	1st/2nd
Apr 16, 10:43 pm	Libra	Full Moon
Apr 17, 3:11 am-Apr 19, 8:41 am	Scorpio	3rd qtr.
Apr 26, 6:21 pm-Apr 29, 5:14 am	Pisces	4th qtr.
May 5, 10:11 pm-May 8, 1:08 am	Cancer	1st qtr.
May 14, 11:16 am-May 16, 10:04 am	Scorpio	2nd qtr.
May 16, 10:04 am	Scorpio	Full Moon
May 16, 10:04 am-May 16, 5:23 pm	Scorpio	3rd qtr.
May 24, 2:26 am-May 26, 1:53 pm	Pisces	3rd/4th
Jun 2, 5:59 am-Jun 4, 7:36 am	Cancer	1st qtr.
Jun 10, 5:28 pm-Jun 13, 0:30 am	Scorpio	2nd qtr.
Jun 14, 10:51 pm	Sagit.	Full Moon
Jun 20, 10:01 am-Jun 22, 10:04 pm	Pisces	3rd qtr.
Jun 29, 3:43 pm-Jul 1, 4:16 pm	Cancer	4th/1st
Jul 7, 10:54 pm-Jul 10, 6:18 am	Scorpio	2nd qtr.
Jul 14, 1:07 pm	Capri.	Full Moon
Jul 17, 4:45 pm-Jul 20, 5:08 am	Pisces	3rd qtr.

Jul 27, 2:09 am-Jul 29, 2:40 am	Cancer	4th qtr.
Aug 4, 5:17 am-Aug 6, 11:58 am	Scorpio	1st/2nd
Aug 13, 4:28 am	Aquar.	Full Moon
Aug 13, 10:52 pm-Aug 16, 11:12 am	Pisces	3rd qtr.
Aug 23, 11:37 am-Aug 25, 1:16 pm	Cancer	4th qtr.
Aug 31, 1:39 pm-Sep 2, 6:51 pm	Scorpio	1st qtr.
Sep 10, 4:57 am-Sep 11, 8:17 pm	Pisces	2nd qtr.
Sep 11, 8:17 pm	Pisces	Full Moon
Sep 11, 8:17 pm-Sep 12, 5:03 pm	Pisces	3rd qtr.
Sep 19, 7:00 pm-Sep 21, 10:20 pm	Cancer	4th qtr.
Sep 27, 11:45 pm-Sep 30, 3:34 am	Scorpio	1st qtr.
Oct 7, 11:38 am-Oct 9, 11:37 pm	Pisces	2nd qtr.
Oct 11, 12:04 pm	Aries	Full Moon
Oct 17, 0:37 am-Oct 19, 5:02 am	Cancer	3rd/4th
Oct 25, 10:05 am-Oct 27, 1:30 pm	Scorpio	4th/1st
Nov 3, 7:13 pm-Nov 6, 7:20 am	Pisces	2nd qtr.
Nov 10, 3:21 am	Taurus	Full Moon
Nov 13, 6:20 am-Nov 15, 10:24 am	Cancer	3rd qtr.
Nov 21, 6:53 pm-Nov 23, 11:02 pm	Scorpio	4th qtr.
Dec 1, 3:24 am-Dec 3, 3:50 pm	Pisces	1st/2nd
Dec 9, 5:42 pm	Gemini	Full Moon
Dec 10, 2:06 pm-Dec 12, 4:48 pm	Cancer	3rd qtr.
Dec 19, 1:21 am-Dec 21, 6:43 am	Scorpio	4th qtr.
Dec 28, 11:29 am-Dec 31, 0:08 am	Pisces	1st qtr.

YOUR TIME TO WIN: MOON GUIDE TO GAMBLING
by Ralph Jordan Pestka

Astrology and gambling have one important thing in common. Both are concerned with the probable outcome of events. For example, in the game of poker you can expect to be dealt a full house in the first five cards once in 693 deals. The number of times a person can expect to hold the winning number for a lottery drawing is once in millions of drawings. Astrologers also work with probabilities. Particular types of events are more likely to occur under particular astrological influences. The ancients said, "To every thing there is a season, and a time to every purpose under the heaven." That is pure astrological insight. My own study of astrology and gambling has proven to me there is definitely a time to take a chance and a time to minimize your risk.

I have been interested in probabilities, speculation and gambling for over twenty-five years. I have known all kinds of gamblers, card room operators and bookies. They bet on sports, horses, the dogs, lotteries, dice, casino games and every type of card game. I have spent thousands of hours gambling in Las Vegas, in casinos in Michigan, and in poker clubs in the midwest. I have asked hundreds of people their birth dates, and then watched when they have won or lost. I have also examined the detailed horoscopes of hundreds of gamblers, and come to understand many of the astrological factors that point to winning at gambling. I specialize in poker, as it is a game that combines pure chance with a degree of decision making and skill. But most gamblers gamble on luck, and some gamble on systems. I know gamblers that thought they had discovered *the* system for beating the dice or roulette table—they all went broke. Others say that winning is "all luck." But winning at gambling is more than skill, systems or pure luck. It is, above all these other things, a matter of timing. You can have your skill, your system, and the mathematical laws of probability can be functioning (pure luck), but the one thing you must have in addition to these is the cosmic trigger of timing.

The Sun and the Moon are the great timekeepers of astrology. Together they mark the days, months and years. The Moon is considered the greatest "trigger." Its fast moving aspects to other planets trigger the many events we see around us. The Sun rules the sign of Leo and the Fifth House, which rule speculation, games of chance and gambling in the individual horoscope. The aspects that the transiting Moon makes to your Sun sign reveal when your timing is right for winning at gambling. The transits also show when the timing is not right. A good aspect from the Moon to your Sun can trigger good fortune in games of chance. A difficult aspect can trigger difficulties and losses. The following delineations tell you when to gamble, when to wait, and give you particular hints on your gambling activities for the Moon in each of the signs. Follow the transits of the Moon through the signs. Gamble on your best days, hold off on your less fortunate days, and you will be using the most basic and dependable astrological factor for timing and winning at gambling.

ARIES SUN SIGN
Moon Transiting In:

Aries—Can produce wins, but don't get egotistical and think you have a license to win.

Taurus—Winning is possible, but you may just have the urge to splurge—control your spending.

Gemini—A neutral influence, but can stimulate your mind for numbers, memorization and problem solving.

Cancer—Better hold back and save your money for a more fortunate day.

Leo—You could be fired up to gamble. Others are too. Control your impulses and you can win. Lose control and you can lose big!

Virgo—Good for the professional gambler. The average gambler is better off holding back now.

Libra—Competitive sports or games in which you directly compete can attract your betting dollars. Keep self-control. Avoid impulse or emotional betting and you could come out ahead.

Scorpio—You may borrow to gamble, go into debt, or gamble with the bill money. If you avoid these pitfalls you have a chance to win.

Sagittarius—Impulse and risk abound, so don't take any crazy chances. You could win, but control yourself.

Capricorn—Your wins may be small most of the time, but if you're going to hit the lottery, this could be the time.

Aquarius—Surprises abound. You can win among friends, or a friend can give you a winning tip.

Pisces—You may not be in the mood to gamble. If you are you may be uncertain, indecisive or distracted. Stay conservative if you are in the action.

TAURUS SUN SIGN
Moon Transiting In:

Taurus—If you risk your money now you will probably play the favorites. Look for the long shot that pays big. Your financial intuition is sharp.

Gemini—You can be fascinated by numbers games, and by the numbers that have dollar signs in front of them. Keep your investment small, and you may multiply your resources.

Cancer—Security concerns can dominate your thinking. Winning is possible, but if you start losing don't be stubborn—learn when to quit.

Leo—Others around you may be stimulated to gamble. Your own chances of winning are not that great. Bet small.

Virgo—Your best laid plans and systems can now be put to the test. Stay alert, analyze things and watch the details, and you can come out ahead.

Libra—You spend best by studying, planning and organizing your gambling activities. Wait for a better period to put down your cash.

Scorpio—You may feel the challenge to hit it big. Sports and competitions you bet on or participate in are most likely to win you money.

Sagittarius—You have to spend it to make it, and bet it to win it, but if you borrow it you'll most likely lose it. You can win, but don't let your blind optimism cause you to gamble for more than you can afford.

Capricorn—You could be ready for some serious speculation. Depend on your experience and expertise in financial matters and you can find the winning bets.

Aquarius—Lotteries, sweepstakes and electronic gambling machines may be fortunate now. You may hit a big pay off that makes you famous among your friends.

Pisces—Your intuition is heightened, but make sure it's not just wishful thinking. Winning is possible. Don't loan money to gambling friends.

Aries—You are better off holding back right now. Events may be too fast breaking, or too anxious and distracting for you to use your best judgment.

GEMINI SUN SIGN
Moon Transiting In:

Gemini—You naturally thrive on action, and you can be ready to gamble big. Self-control is essential to end up in the winner's circle.

Cancer—Your better money making instincts dominate now. Winning is possible. Memory serves you well.

Leo—You may get carried away by the gambling fever surrounding you. Lotteries, number games and casinos can hold winning opportunities, but don't risk it all.

Virgo—This transit favors detailed analysis, looking over the forms, refining your systems. Don't bet yet, however; save your cash for a better transit.

Libra—Many opportunities for speculative gains. You can apply what you have learned and test your skills and systems.

Scorpio—Not a fortunate period. You may be better off reviewing your wins and losses, refining your techniques and investigating new strategies.

Sagittarius—Sports and racing competitions can attract your attention. Winning is possible, but remain objective and reserved. Don't let optimism carry you away.

Capricorn—You may have visions of scoring big. There is money to be won, and you may get a piece of it now.

Aquarius—Your friends could be a part of your gambling scene now. You may think you have finally got the perfect system—be cautious. Winning is possible, but don't lose more than you can afford to.

Pisces—Draw on your sixth sense and gain the intuitive insights that lead to winning. Remain sensitive to your inner promptings.

Aries—Your mind may be too fast for your pocket-book. Winning is possible, but you had better set your budget before you begin to gamble.

Taurus—This period is better used for socializing, entertainment or relaxation. Wins may be small, or you may risk more than you should.

CANCER SUN SIGN
Moon Transiting In:

Cancer—Security interests can dominate now. Winning is possible, and this can be fortunate. You will know how to get the best from your gambling dollars.

Virgo—A generally neutral influence with a down tendency. You may be better off saving your money now.

Libra—You are not likely to win big now, although you may win the door prize.

Scorpio—Your instincts and intuition are sharp for risky business. You can turn a small bet into a big pay off. Draw on your memory, and remain sensitive to your psychic promptings.

Sagittarius—If you make a living through speculation this transit could produce a tidy profit. The average gambler may be swept away by visions of riches, and should probably remain conservative.

Capricorn—You are inclined to bet on the favorites, or stay conservative. You'd be smart to keep your bets small as wins can be equally meager.

Aquarius—Your brain may be working overtime, trying to figure out how to win big. Number games can be lucky. Do not lend money to gambling friends.

Pisces—A fortunate time. Stay in touch with your feelings and intuitions. They can lead you to a big winner.

Aries—You may win in competition or sports. Maintain composure and self-control, or you can gamble fast and lose.

Taurus—Sweepstakes and contests may be lucky now. The lotteries may produce a winner. Remain conservative, as this is not your very best time.

Gemini—You would just as well save your money under this transit. Distractions, indecision or anxieties can keep you from using your best judgment.

LEO SUN SIGN
Moon Transiting In:

Leo—Your time to shine! Good fortune will usually come your way, but don't think you can do no wrong, or you can lose everything you've won.

Virgo—You are more pragmatic and perhaps even nervous about taking risks. Be particular about your bets.

Libra—You may gain by mixing social activities with your gambling. A neighbor or relative may prove a fortunate influence.

Scorpio—This is a less fortunate period. It may produce some wins, but you should remain conservative in the amount you risk.

Sagittarius—You may really want to gamble, especially if you like sports or races. You can win big if you are smart, but don't let your enthusiasm cause you to lose too much if you see that it's not your day.

Capricorn—You are probably better off taking care of more serious business. Winning is not that likely, and you will really hate yourself if you lose.

Aquarius—You think you have it all figured out, ready to battle the bookies or the casinos, but it's not a very fortunate time. Keep your eyes on the competition.

Pisces—Winning is possible. Depend on your best financial instincts and intuition to produce the winners.

Aries—Sports, competitions and contests are strongly favored. Your tendency is to gamble too much, so keep self-control.

Taurus—Get the most value from your betting dollar. Stick with your most dependable gambles. A big win from a small bet is possible.

Gemini—Picking numbers may prove surprisingly profitable. Lotteries, bingo and keno games give you a big chance on a small investment.

Cancer—Not very fortunate. You are better off renewing your inner resources in preparation for a new cycle of excitement and risk.

VIRGO SUN SIGN
Moon Transiting In:

Virgo—Luck through wagering in very particular and limited ways. Bet one horse out of ten races, or buy only one lottery ticket.

Libra—Winning is possible, but you may be indecisive or influenced by others' opinions. Keep your risk small if you gamble.

Scorpio—Your skill with numbers and odds can serve you well. This may not produce a big win but it can be profitable.

Sagittarius—You are better off holding back. If you do gamble, keep it small.

Capricorn—Your instincts for finding the best bet will come now. Though your winnings may be modest.

Aquarius—If you are numbers crazy this transit may be lucky. Others are better off studying forms and systems and saving their bets for another day.

Pisces—You are not at your best for picking the winners. Confusion or indecision can cost you.

Aries—Decisive and exacting application of your best gambling instincts may produce a big win on a small investment.

Taurus—This transit could produce winners. Take your time to find the very best odds for your money.

Gemini—You should have at least one lottery ticket, as you can achieve public recognition for numbers games.

Cancer—Don't let feelings cloud your thinking or you may imagine you have the perfect system. Winning is possible, but bet conservatively.

Leo—You could get caught up in an urge to gamble. Keep it at the level of entertainment. Lose control and you can lose big.

LIBRA SUN SIGN
Moon Transiting In:
Libra—Winning is possible if you keep your balance. Don't let the lure of luxury cause you to risk too much.

Scorpio—You may know just how to extract the cash. Your sense of values serves you well.

Sagittarius—Numbers games or racing events may be fortunate. Maintain your self-control. You could lose much if not lucky, and lose your winnings if too self-confident.

Capricorn—Forget this transit for winning. If you do win, it could be small, and a loss will leave you very sour.

Aquarius—You can win in social settings, numbers games and electronic gambling, A most fortunate transit.

Pisces—Not that fortunate. Relax, take care of yourself and save your betting dollars for a better time.

Aries—Competition of every type can attract your bets. You can pick the winners. Stay in touch with your intuitive/psychic impulses.

Taurus—A lottery ticket may be a good idea. If you are destined to win a massive sum, this could be the time.

Gemini—Big numbers attract you. You understand the patterns behind numbers. You can win now, but don't risk more than you can afford to lose.

Cancer–Winning is possible, but security matters may occupy your attention. Remain realistic, as your emotions could get in the way of smart betting.

Leo—Electronic games, lotteries and casinos could prove profitable. A generally favorable transit.

Virgo—Get in touch with facts and real figures. You could be too confused, distracted or undecided to bet right. Proceed cautiously.

SCORPIO SUN SIGN
Moon Transiting In:

Scorpio—Your desire for gain could be great. Draw on your deep insights and intuition.

Sagittarius—Maintain self-control, remain realistic, and this can produce some wins.

Capricorn—Tends toward the down side. You may be better off waiting, learning and planning.

Aquarius—Unusual or surprising events could surround your gambling and end up costing you money. Remain conservative.

Pisces—Your deepest insights and intuition serve you well. Winning could be easy, almost like magic!

Aries—If you dig in and work at it you may come up a winner. Pace yourself and maintain your discipline, or you may end up losing.

Taurus—Don't let feelings cause you to take a poor risk. Winning is possible, but this is not your best time.

Gemini—You have a chance to win if you use your head. You may tend to bet too often or stay in the action long after you have gotten ahead. Learn to quit a winner.

Cancer—Your intuitive knowledge of gambling can make you a winner. Definitely one of your better periods.

Leo—You could strike it rich under this transit! If you are going to achieve fame for winning, this is when it could happen, but don't get carried away.

Virgo—Adept with numbers, you may want to play the lottery, bingo or keno. Not your most fortunate time, but it can produce some wins.

Libra—You could bet emotionally, be undecided or not get the best value for your dollar. You should probably wait for a more fortunate transit.

SAGITTARIUS SUN SIGN
Moon Transiting In:

Sagittarius—You can be off and running, ready for action and willing to gamble big. Maintain perspective and self-control and you can cash in a winner.

Capricorn—You could have one eye on your bank book and one on the racing form. Betting the favorites or remaining conservative would be wise now.

Aquarius—Gambling among friends, neighbors or in social settings may prove favorable. Electronic and numbers games are possible winners.

Pisces—Subconscious desires for grandeur and great wealth may cloud your betting choices. Not your most fortunate transit. Bet small if you bet at all.

Aries—You can put your natural instincts for gambling and risk to good use. Depend on your intuition.

Taurus—If you work at it, this can produce some winners. Try to get a big payoff for a small investment. Not especially fortunate, so be prudent.

Gemini—You may want to "show 'em" and prove you are a winner. Maintain your perspective and composure. Winning in competitive events is possible, but remain conservative.

Cancer—Don't let your feelings or sentiments cause you to bet more than you can afford. Winning is possible, but you should look for small bets that pay big.

Leo—You could be too willing to gamble, lose big money if you lose self-control. Depend on your experience and common sense.

Virgo—Numbers games may be lucky. Watch out for

races, sports and competitions, as these things could go against you.

Libra—Groups and social settings can be favorable. You can be good at picking the winners in competitions.

Scorpio—A time for caution. Your desire to gamble can overcome your best judgment and cause you to lose more than you can afford to. It wouldn't hurt to wait.

CAPRICORN SUN SIGN
Moon Transiting In:

Capricorn—You are inclined to limit your bets. Bet on the favorites. Don't risk much money. Your gambling forte is your conservative and realistic approach.

Aquarius—Gambling among friends, in groups, or on electronic and numbers games can turn a profit.

Pisces—A dream or your intuition may lead you to pick winning numbers. This transit is a neutral influence so you should not risk a lot.

Aries—Emotion and impulse could get the best of you and cause losses.

Taurus—Your heightened sense of values can lead you to get good odds. Definitely one of your better times to risk your resources.

Gemini—Worry, indecision or mental irritations may get in the way of your winning. You should probably save your money for a more fortunate time.

Cancer—Cautions against emotional betting. Keep in touch with your intuition and competitive events could produce winners.

Leo—A strong transit for the urge to win big. Research or inside information could mean big gains. Maintain self-control.

Virgo—Pay attention to details, examine records, tables, charts. Possible wins.

Libra—You can pick between individuals or teams in competitions. You can evaluate the important factors for winning.

Scorpio—You can profit among friends or by pooling a great deal of money. Your mind is sharp for gambling with multiple numbers.

Sagittarius—This is not the time to get carried away by the gambling fever surrounding you. Control yourself and you can win. Blind faith could cost you.

AQUARIUS SUN SIGN
Moon Transiting In:

Aquarius—Gambling among friends, with groups or in social settings is favored now. Stay in tune to ingenious bets—they could surprise you with a winner.

Pisces—Subtle and intuitive insight can lead to winning, but don't risk everything.

Aries—Using your computer brain is a good idea, but guard against impulse betting.

Taurus—Tough to win under this transit. Winnings small and slow to come. Minimize risk.

Gemini—This transit could produce wins. Don't go off on a tangent, betting too much or too often. Control your betting with your mind and you can win.

Cancer—If you work with a gambling system this is a good time to apply what you have learned. Remain sensitive to your intuitive impulses. Not your most fortunate time, but winning is possible.

Leo—You can place your gambling in perspective now. Casino gambling, and gambling among friends or in groups could be productive. Remain reserved.

Virgo—Maintain your mental balance, don't risk more than you can afford to lose. Investigation and detailed digging could reveal winners.

Libra—A fortunate influence in general. Numbers games or competitions could bring in winners. Remain in control, as you are more willing to risk a great deal.

Scorpio—Past research and experience can lead you to winners. Gains come through hard work, but the possibility for success is present.

Sagittarius—You can win big among friends, groups or in social settings. Lotteries and numbers games are also favored. Stay within a budget, as you are more inclined to risk too much.

Capricorn—If you have a hidden advantage you may be able to profit in speculation. Proceed with caution and you may show a small profit.

PISCES SUN SIGN
Moon Transiting In:

Pisces—Intuition is your guide. Remain sensitive to dreams, visions, larger concepts and you can find winners.

Aries—A willingness to risk your resources boldly. You can win, but don't let impulse masquerade as courage. Stay within a budget.

Taurus—A rather neutral influence. You may have intuitive insight into numbers. Modest wagering could be worth it.

Gemini—You may be too distracted, bet emotionally or rely too much on the opinions of others. You might want to skip it during this transit.

Cancer—Your psychic and intuitive insight could pay big dividends in risk and speculation. This is definitely the time to have a bet in.

Leo—A willingness to risk too much could cost you dearly. Others may be eager to gamble but this may not be your time. Keep wages small if you do bet.

Virgo—Good fortune will not fall now. You need to be very alert to come out ahead.

Libra—You may receive a tip or be directed to a winning bet by someone else. This could produce winners, but remember you are responsible for the final decisions.

Scorpio—Your desire to win could overcome your best judgment. Winning is possible, but you will do best by risking little.

Sagittarius—A profitable transit for you. You know how to take advantage of others' willingness to take big risks. Maintain your self-control.

Capricorn—People places and things from the past could produce winners now. Gambles sponsored by governments, institutions or organizations contain special promise.

Aquarius—Lotteries and electronic gambles could produce a winner. Strong intuition directs your winning choices. Protect yourself by remaining on a budget, or you could go into debt.

Health &
Beauty

- Diet
- Herbs
- Surgery
- Skin care
- Hair care
- Dental
- Habits
- Eye care

HEALTH AND BEAUTY

Beauty Care

For beauty treatments, skin care and massage, the Moon should be in Taurus, Cancer, Leo, Libra, Scorpio or Aquarius and sextile, trine, or conjunct Venus and/or Jupiter. Plastic surgery should be done in the increase of the Moon, when the Moon is not in square or opposition to Mars. Nor should the Moon be in the sign ruling the area to be operated on. Avoid days when the Moon is square or opposite Saturn or the Sun.

Fingernails should be cut when the Moon is not in any aspect with Mercury or Jupiter. Saturn and Mars must not be marked Sq or O because this makes the nails grow slowly or thin and weak. The Moon should be in Aries, Taurus, Cancer, or Leo. For toenails, the Moon should not be in Gemini or Pisces. Corns are best cut when the Moon is in the third or fourth quarter.

Dieting: Weight gain occurs more readily when the Moon is in a Water sign, Cancer, Scorpio or Pisces. Experience has shown that weight may be lost though, if a diet is started when the Moon is decreasing in light (third and fourth quarters), and when it is in Aries, Leo, Virgo, Sagittarius or Aquarius. The lunar cycle should be favorable on the day you wish to begin your diet.

Dental Work

For this pick a day that is marked favorable for your Sun sign. Mars should be marked Sx, T, or C and Saturn, Uranus and Jupiter should not be marked Sq or O.

Teeth are best removed during the increase of the Moon in the first or second quarters in Gemini, Virgo, Sagittarius, Capricorn or Pisces. The day should be favorable for your lunar cycle and Mars and Saturn should be marked C, T, or Sx.

Filling should be done when the Moon is in a fixed sign (Taurus, Leo, Scorpio, Aquarius) and decreasing in light.

The same applies for having impressions made for plates.

Dieting
Weight gain occurs more readily when the Moon is in a Water sign; Cancer, Scorpio or Pisces. Experience has shown that weight may be lost though if a diet is started when the Moon is decreasing in light (third and fourth quarters), and when it is in Aries, Leo, Virgo, Sagittarius or Aquarius. The lunar cycle should be favorable on the day you wish to begin your diet.

Eyeglasses
Eyes should be tested and glasses fitted on a day marked favorable for your Sun sign and on a day which falls during your favorable lunar cycle. Mars should not be in aspect with the Moon. The same applies for any treatment of the eyes, which should also be started during the increase of the Moon (1st or 2nd quarter).

Habits
To end any habit, start on a day when the Moon is in the third or fourth quarter and in a barren sign. Gemini, Leo or Virgo are the best times, while Aries and Capricorn are suitable too. Make sure your lunar cycle is favorable. Avoid lunar aspects to Mars or Jupiter. Aspects to Neptune or Saturn are helpful. These rules apply to smoking and will produce a good start. Every time you wish to overcome a habit, watch for these positions of the Moon to help you.

Hair Care
Haircuts are best when the Moon is in a mutable (Gemini, Sagittarius, Pisces) or earthy sign (Taurus, Capricorn), well-placed and aspected, but not in Virgo, which is barren. For faster growth, the Moon should be in a water sign (Cancer, Scorpio, Pisces). To make hair grow thicker, cut it when the Moon is in opposition to the Sun, or when it is a Full Moon, which is marked O in the Lunar Aspectarian. However, if you want your hair to grow more slowly, the Moon should be in Gemini or Leo in the third or fourth quarters with Saturn square or opposite the Moon.

Permanent waves, straightening and hair coloring will take

well if the Moon is in Aquarius and Venus is marked T or
Sx. You should avoid doing your hair if Mars is marked Sq
or O, especially if heat is to be used. For permanents, a
trine to Jupiter is helpful. The Moon also should be in the
first quarter and at the same time check the lunar cycle for
a favorable day in relation to your Sun sign.

Health

Diagnosis is more likely to be successful when the
Moon is in a cardinal sign (Aries, Cancer, Libra, Capricorn)
and less so when in a mutable sign. Begin a program for
recuperation or recovery when the Moon is in a cardinal or
fixed sign and the day is favorable to your sign. Enter hospitals at these times. For surgery, see "Surgical Operations." Buy medicines when the Moon is in Scorpio if they
are made from natural substances.

Surgical Operations

The flow of blood, like the ocean tides, appears to be related by the Moon's phases. *Time* magazine (page 74, June
6, 1960) reports on 1,000 tonsilectomy case histories analyzed by Dr. Edson J. Andrews, only 18% of associated
hemorrhaging occurred in the fourth and first quarters.
This, a new astrological rule: To reduce the hazard of hemorrhage after a surgical operation, plan to have the surgery
within one week before or after the New Moon. Avoid surgery within one week before or after the Full Moon. Select,
too, a date when the Moon is not in the sign governing the
part of the body involved in the operation. The farther removed the Moon sign is from the sign ruling the afflicted
part of the body, the better for healing. There should be no
lunar aspects to Mars, and favorable aspects to Venus and
Jupiter should be present. For more information, read the
article on Medical Astrology.

MEDICAL ASTROLOGY

by Louise Riotte

In his book *Powerful Planets*, Llewellyn George, one of the greatest and most respected astrologers of all time, stated, "Medical astrology in its relation to diagnosis and the prevention and cure of disease, is a valuable adjunct to metaphysicians, doctors, surgeons and dentists." What he said in 1931 is just as true today.

And physicians in the days of old, such as Hippocrates, "the Father of Medicine," used a knowledge of planetary influences to perform their wonders. They well knew the subject of sympathy and antipathy; they knew that the angle of crystallization at sixty degrees, called sextile, was *creative*; they knew that bodies in opposite points of the zodiac were disintegrative in their effects. They knew that sulphur corresponds to the planet Mercury, and, being students of astrology, they knew many other facts that will not be clear to modern scientists until they, too, take up a serious study of planetary influences.

And so it may be seen that the subject of medical astrology takes in much more than the title implies. This fact is readily evidenced by many physicians, surgeons, non-drug-oriented practitioners, and dentists who are now using knowledge of astrology to enhance their skills and to assure more definite and satisfactory results by acting in harmony with the duly timed workings of nature.

By examining a person's natal chart, the physician skilled in medical astrology can see what disorders the patient is predisposed to at birth; by examining the progressed horoscope s/he can see which tendencies are now coming into expression, whether complications are about to set in, or whether the sickness is about to break up. S/he can calculate the time of crisis in advance, for s/he knows that in acute situations the crises come about on the 7th, 14th, 21st, and 28th days from the time the patient was taken sick. The Moon makes a revolution in her orbit in about 28 days, and the 7th, 14th, 21st days, and her return to her place at the time of the New Moon correspond to the quarters, adverse aspects, and crisis times in the illness. Therefore, the first, second, and third quarters of the Moon from the time the illness began are crisis days in diseases.

If the patient lives through these crises, and until the Moon returns to her place, the disease will dissolve itself. The crisis days are the dangerous ones. The most serious crisis day is the 14th, as a rule, when the Moon arrives at the opposite aspect to her place at the beginning of the illness. This crisis day is called the "Criticus Primus," the one of prime importance. More patients usually die on the 14th day of a serious illness than on the other crisis days, and if they survive, their chances for recovery are usually good.

One of the simple but potent rules that is interesting to surgeons is as follows: **"Pierce not with steel that part of the body represented by the sign which the Moon occupies on that day."** Another astrological rule may also be invoked: **"To reduce the hazard of hemorrhage after a surgical operation, plan to have the surgery occur within one week before or after the New Moon; avoid, whenever possible, submitting to surgery within one week before or after the Full Moon."**

These rules are best applied to cases where one can "elect" whether or not to have surgery at a given time; in emergency cases, of course, they cannot be applied as the delay of one or two weeks might prove fatal.

In his book Llewellyn George tells a most interesting story of what occurred at the time when he was located in Portland, Oregon. "I was called upon frequently for some years by two prominent surgeons to make the charts of patients and determine the best date and time for surgical operations. During that period each of the operations was a success—and the patients recovered.

"I recall one extreme case of a lady who had already been operated on five times by other surgeons. Because she was in great distress on account of serious adhesions it was necessary to operate again. As she was very ill and weak, another operation would obviously be precarious.

"As usual, it became my duty to find the proper time for this operation. A task it proved to be. The lady had so many planetary afflictions that it was difficult to find a good place in her chart. I worked all night on it and at last found a spot wherein if the Moon was located it gave promise of success—but that time would be at midnight! Fortunately the patient was willing to have the operation when the Moon was favorable if it promised relief.

"But midnight is a difficult time for securing the use of the operating room. However, the doctors went to the Good Samaritan hospital and frankly told the Sister Superior in charge the reason for wanting the operation at that unusual hour. Somewhat to their surprise she said, 'Certainly you may have the room, for we understand the importance of the Moon.'

"The operation proved satisfactory to all concerned. In fact, the patient was so delighted with the results that she became a student of astrology—and so did the surgeons; now they draw all such horoscopes themselves."

Dr. H.L. Cornell, author of the *Encyclopedia of Medical Astrology*, has stated that statistics show that surgical operations, including operations on the eyes, are apt to be most successful when the Moon is increasing in light, that is, between the New and Full Moons, and that the patients heal more rapidly and have fewer complications than when the Moon is decreasing.

During the decrease of the Moon the vitality is usually less, and the bodily fluids at low ebb; these fluids rise and fill the vessels of the body to a greater fullness when the Moon is increasing.

The Rules for Operations Are As Follows

1. Operate in the increase of the Moon if possible.
2. Do not operate at the exact time of the Full Moon, as the fluids are running high at this time.
3. Never operate when the Moon is in the same sign as at the patient's birth (the Sun sign).
4. Never operate upon that part of the body ruled by the sign through which the Moon is passing at the time, but wait a day or two until the Moon passes into the next sign below—this rule is of great importance in major operations.
5. Let the Moon be in a fixed sign, but not in the sign ruling the part to be operated on, and such sign of the Moon also not on the ascendant.

6. Do not operate when the Moon is applying to (moving
   toward) any aspect of Mars, as such tends to promote
   the danger of inflammation and complications after
   the operation.
7. There should be good aspects to Venus and Jupiter
   (sextile or trine).
8. Avoid, when possible, operations when the Sun is in
   the sign ruling the part upon which the operation is to
   be performed.
9. The Moon should be free from all manner of impedi-
   ment.
10. Fortify the sign ruling the part of the body to be oper-
    ated upon.
11. A Mars hour is not desirable for surgical operations.
12. Do not cut a nerve when Mercury is afflicted (square
    or opposition).
13. When the Moon is under the Sun's beams and op-
    posed by Mars, it is considered a dangerous time for
    amputations.
14. Avoid abdominal operations when the Moon is pass-
    ing through Virgo, Libra or Scorpio. Good times are
    when the Moon is passing through Sagittarius, Capri-
    corn or Aquarius.

Consideration of the Moon's phases is no less important in the practice of dentistry. Teeth should be extracted
in either the first or second quarter—waxing Moon—
which promotes healing.

Best signs for extraction are Gemini, the arms; Virgo,
the bowels; Sagittarius, the thighs; Capricorn, the knees;
and Pisces, the feet. Note that all these signs are some distance from the head. Mars and Saturn should be marked C,
T or Sx.

Avoid extractions when the Moon is passing through
Aries, Cancer, Libra, Taurus, Leo, Scorpio or Aquarius.

Fillings should be done when the Moon is waning in
the third and fourth quarters, in a fixed sign such as Taurus, the neck; Leo, the heart; Scorpio, the genitals; or
Aquarius, the legs.

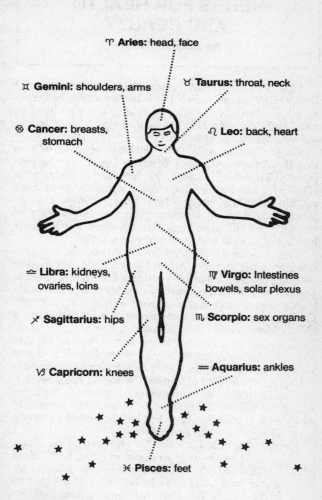

HERBS FOR HEALTH AND BEAUTY

by Louise Riotte

Most of us are primarily interested in maintaining good health but if we can snatch a little beauty along the way—why not? Actually, health and beauty often go hand in hand and clear, firm skin is usually a sign of both, so lets see what herbs can be helpful.

David Conway, writing in *The Magic of Herbs*, tells us that the common burdock (*Arctium lappa*) may be prepared as a standard infusion, or a decoction made from the sliced root. Used externally, either preparation provides a soothing skin and scalp lotion. Burnet (*Sanguisorba officinalis*) used as an infusion promotes the healing of wounds and will cure most skin ailments. Fresh burnet leaves are good to add to all summer salads.

Camomile (*Anthemis nobilis*) was probably the first herb brought to my attention when I was a child. My mother used to prepare a tea of camomile for headaches. She also found it useful as a face-wash, the standard infusion clearing the complexion, and as a rinse for lightening fair hair. Camomile tea, tastier sweetened with a bit of honey, is tonic, digestive and tranquilizing.

Camomile is a familiar weed, with daisy-like flowers and feathery grey-green leaves, often found in many waste places. One of the nicest things about camomile is the odor, reminiscent of apples. Camomile has a reputation as a lawn plant and sometimes it is grown in dry areas where it is difficult to establish lawn grasses—it not only wears well in such locations but has the added attraction of smelling good when walked upon.

Note: A "standard infusion" is prepared by pouring a pint of boiling water over an ounce of dried herb leaves (three handfuls of the fresh) and leaving the mixture for three to four hours. Cut large leaves first and finely chop tough herbs. Strain. Infusions will usually keep fresh for

126

up to four days (refrigerate in extremely hot weather). They may also be poured into bottles and stored in a cool dark place. It is best not to cork but to place a piece of muslin or perforated greaseproof paper over their tops. According to Vicki Zastrow, honey is sometimes added to infusions for sweetness.

Decoctions are made from the hard parts of the herb—the stems, roots, bark and seeds—and must be boiled for some time to extract their full value.

Chickweed (*Stellaria media*), long favored as an iron-rich tonic for cage birds and equally of value for the ordinary variety of chicken, affords similar benefits to us, aiding digestion and useful in the treatment of stomach ulcers and all forms of internal inflammation. We may take chickweed raw or in a standard infusion, drinking a sherry-glassful three times a day. The same infusion refines the texture of the skin when it is applied as a face lotion.

Cleavers (*Calium aparine*) may be made into an infusion and used as a skin lotion, making a good tonic for the scalp (helping to clear dandruff) and for the skin.

In *Household Ecology*, Julia Percivall and Pixie Burger recommend the use of the rind of the avocado for skin-beautifying purposes. They also say that citrus rind is useful against roughened elbows, lemon halves being the best but squeezed out orange or grapefruit halves can also be used, having both a softening and lightening effect that smooths and clears the elbows if they are discolored or chapped.

For a cleansing facial try mixing a cup of oatmeal, a quarter cup of water, and two tablespoons of honey; the proportions need not be exact. Blend the ingredients together to make a nice squishy paste and apply to your face, covering all areas except, of course, your eyes. Let the pack dry and then remove it with warm water.

Different kinds of ordinary fruit, obtainable at the nearest grocery, can hold different benefits as facials—you don't need to use hothouse exotica. Just mash the pulp and apply directly to your skin. Oranges are restful and soothing; lemons are astringent and drying; strawberries, toning and brightening; melon, refreshing and soothing; peaches, soothing and cooling; tomatoes, cleansing and renewing; cucumber, cooling and astringent; bananas, softening and soothing.

All such packs should remain on the skin about 15 to thirty minutes, dependng on individual reaction and personal preference, before being washed off with tepid water. And, by the way, the skin of banana rubbed on warts several times a day is said to remove them.

Garlic, which seems to be good for just about everything, will also rid the skin of parasites. Taken internally it is said to promote skin beauty. Garlic is easy to grow but non-gardeners can readily purchase it at the supermarket.

Heartsease (*Viola tricolor*), also known as pansy, love-in-idleness and butterfly flower, used as a lotion heals sores and other skin ailments. Make the standard infusion from the plant leaves and take a tablespoonful three times daily either as a cure or a preventive measure.

Comfrey (*Symphytum officinale*) was once known as a wound herb, being unrivaled in repairing broken bones and battered bodies. It is often combined with boneset (*Eupatorium perfoliatum*). Eye injuries also respond well to its action. You may use an infusion of the leaves or make a decoction from the bruised root.

Loosestrife (*Lythrum salicaria*) was one of the best herbs recommended for sight, and it is still used, often in the company of eyebright, as an eye lotion. Use half an ounce of herb to half a pint of boiling, slightly salty water. Steep for 30 minutes, strain and use.

Other useful eye herbs are lady's mantle (*Alchemilla vulgaris*), lovage (*Ligustrum scoticum*), summer savory (*Satureja hortensis*) and mugwort (*Artemisia vulgaris*).

Pimpernel (*Amagallis arvensis*) was a favorite of the ancient Greeks, used in the treatment of eye diseases. (It is possible that the pimpernel's habit of folding its petals at dusk may have suggested to them a connection with the eyes.) This plant also has cosmetic properties and may be used as a skin lotion. A standard infusion regulates the pigmentation and helps in the removal of freckles and other minor blemishes. It has a reputation as a hair restorer as well.

A standard infusion of maidenhair fern (*Adiantum capillus-veneris*) may be used as a scalp lotion to improve the hair and stop premature baldness. The leaves of the fern, which may be eaten raw, are also reputed to have a therapeutic effect on the heart and lungs.

Rosemary (*Rosmarinus officinalis*) has a well-deserved reputation as a fine tonic for the scalp and skin, adding luster to the hair, and is a common ingredient of many commercial shampoos.

According to David Conway, rosemary and distilled water were the constituents of Hungary Water, a rejuvenating lotion named after Queen Elizabeth of Hungary, whose use of it kept her free from wrinkles. The good doctors of Myddfai counselled the use of the plant for the same purpose.

"A fine thing it is to boil in water the leaves and flowers and to use the mixture as a face wash. Do not wipe the face afterwards, but let it dry naturally. The truth is that by regularly washing their faces in this way the wise will keep their youth until the day they die."

Sea kale (*Crambe maritima*) is a mineral-rich herb useful in fighting a curious assortment of ills, including dental decay, general debility, rheumatism, constipation and urinary problems. You may eat a few leaves raw in salads but use discretion for it is slightly laxative. Externally, the infusion acts as a mouth wash which strengthens the gums, heals ulcers and fights against oral infection.

At last we come to something really pleasant: strawberry (*Fragaria vesca*). Juliette de Baircli Levy describes the plant thus: "This is a plant of shady banks and woodlands. Also cultivated in gardens. Distinguished by its grey-green, rose-form leaves, rounded, white flowers and soft fleshed, round, red, very juicy berries. The whole plant is very refrigerant. A valuable herb, being rich in minerals and antiseptic." As strawberries are remarkably cooling, eaten with cream on a hot summer's day, they are more than indulgent. They also have cosmetic virtues, the juice being useful in treating more serious skin ailments (eczema, pruritis, etc.). An infusion of the leaves works as well, and is helpful in curing styes. Even teeth which have become discolored or encrusted with tartar may be cleansed with strawberry juice.

CHINESE HERBAL MEDICINE

by Louise Riotte

My mother often told me of her adventures as a young farmgirl in Indiana and of how she roamed the woods searching for ginseng as well as other medicinal herbs which she sold. The virtues and values of ginseng seem to be somewhat controversial—it is both highly praised and considered by others to be of little value. The late Dr. H.S. McMaster wrote: "Ginseng is a mild non-poisonous plant, well adapted to domestic as well as professional uses. The medicinal qualities are known to be a mild tonic, stimulant, nervine, and stomachic. It is especially a remedy incident to old age." And that is as good a summation as any I have found.

In *Secrets of the Chinese Herbalists*, Richard Lucas tells us of its habits: "Asiatic ginseng grows wild in deep shaded mountain forests of the Far East. It shuns direct and heavy sunlight, and its leaves are uniquely arranged to receive only a weak amount of light evenly. While other plants gather their nutrients in the root, leaves, flowers, and buds, the nutrients of ginseng are concentrated mainly in the root. At one time it was believed that ginseng could not be cultivated but today we find that it is successfully grown in many lands."

When we discuss varieties or land of cultivation we again sometimes run into arguments but a former Vice-Consul in Korea once stated: "As to the merits of Korean ginseng, the Chinese at any rate have no doubts. Where vitality is becoming extinct from age or strength, or has been reduced by long illness, ginseng is employed with equal faith and success."

Indeed, according to S.E. Zemlinsky, who has authored a book on the medical botany of Russia (where ginseng is highly regarded): "Ginseng is not only a very popular Chinese medicine for longevity, but is used in all parts of Asia. Its use is to prolong life, youth, virility, and health."

It always seems to me that when something has been

used over centuries, like astrology or a plant remedy, it must be of proven value or it would have been discarded long ago. The Western world should not regard the virtues of ginseng claimed by the East contemptuously, as imagination or based on superstition. A report submitted some decades ago by a U.S. Consul of Korea states, "The evidence is that the mystical value attached itself to ginseng after its virtues had been practically ascertained."

According to Lloyd J. Harris, writing in the *Book of Garlic*, the Chinese along with the Epyptians, Romans, Russians and Indians (of India) have always had a high regard for garlic. Garlic, called "suan," has been used for bowel complaints, colds, coughs, asthma, bronchitis, hypertension, menstrual cramps, nasal congestion, protective power, tonsilitis, tuberculosis, and vaginal infection.

Lu-Ts'-AO (*Humulus lupulus*) is the common wild hop which is native to China, Japan and many other lands. The hop is a twining vine of the mulberry family with 3-lobed or 5-lobed leaves and inconspicuous flowers of which the pistillate ones are seen in glandular cone-shaped catkins. The ripe dried catkins are used in the U.S. and elsewhere to impart a bitter flavor to malt liquors.

Centuries ago Chinese hop pickers began claiming that the strong aroma of the plant imparted a soothing, calming influence on the nerves. Thus it came about that they began stuffing pillows with hops as treatment for insomnia. With the passing years this custom spread to other lands, becoming popular throughout the world. There are records to show that the use of such a pillow was prescribed for George III in 1787 with good results. And an excellent effect is claimed for the Prince of Wales in 1879.

Another Chinese remedy for insomnia is one-half ounce each of catnip, skullcap, valerian, and passiflors (*Passiflora incarnata*). These are mixed and placed in a container, a quart of boiling water poured on, the container covered and the infusion allowed to stand 20 minutes and then strained. It is recommended that a teacupful be taken four times a day, one hour after meals, and about a half hour before bedtime.

Vervain which grows wild in low grounds is odorless and bears small purple flowers, and has a long-standing reputation as an excellent remedy for relieving various types of headaches—nervous-sick, mild congestive or those brought on by fatigue or tension. For this purpose the dried herb is used and made into a tea. It is said to be of great relief in migrane headaches.

According to Richard Lucas, the Chinese have long maintained that the leaves of the ginko contain medicinal properties helpful in quickly curing the common cold and also effective in relieving sinus congestion, stubborn coughs and asthma. Used for any of these purposes the leaves are infused in boiling water and the steamy vapors inhaled. The exact substance in the ginko leaves that produces the therapeutic effect has not, as yet, been explained but Dr. Joachim H. Volkner, a nose, ear and throat specialist in Berlin, verifies that it does work.

Where no emergency exists there are also gentle remedies that give good results in coping with acid indigestion and other forms of stomach distress. One of these is Chieh-Keng (*Platycodon grandiflorum*), otherwise known as Chinese bell flower. This is a very decorative beauty with a red stem, large dark-blue flowers, and smooth strong leaves. The Chinese eat it as a pot herb and consider it very wholesome, also believing it to be an excellent stomach tonic.

Chiang (*Zingiber officinale*), with the English name of ginger, is another favorite. Recently, here in the U.S. this herb has been thought to be of help in cases of high cholesterol. I love the taste of ginger and sprinkle it on my crushed bran and oatmeal cereal.

This top-ranking botanical is given for dyspepsia, nausea, loss of appetite, vomiting and alcoholic gastritis. The digestive juices are stimulated by chewing the root. Used in the form of tea, ginger improves sluggish digestion, often relieves gas bloat and is stimulating to the appetite. Candied ginger is one of my own favorites—try it sometime, it's delicious.

More than a half century ago, two Chinese brothers, Aw Boon Par and Aw Boon Haw, developed the popular Oriental herb ointment called Tiger Balm. The stronger formula, Red Tiger Balm, comes wrapped in reddish-pink paper and the milder product, White Tiger Balm, is wrapped in white paper. Tiger Balm relieves tightness of the chest and is soothing to the pains caused by colds, fatigue, exposure, strain, or rheumatism. It is used externally by rubbing the affected areas with the ointment several times a day and covering with warm flannel.

Who would have ever thought of celery as an herb that might be used to alleviate the discomforts of rheumatism, arthritis, gout, lumbago, neuralgia and nervousness. But the Chinese consider celery not only a food but also a medicine. The remedy, made from the seeds, is a strong tea prepared from two tablespoons of the seeds in two quarts of water. Cover the container and simmer slowly for three hours, strain, and use one cup of tea taken hot, three or four times daily.

Kuei (*Juniperus communis*), the juniper berry, is a Chinese remedy for relieving kidney and bladder complaints and is said to be agreeable to even the weakest stomach and useful also in flatulent indigestion.

Juliette de Baircli Levy describes the evergreen shrub as being of medium size, liking chalky districts and distinguished by its red, woody stems, needle leaves and blue-black berries. She also tells us that the young shoots are very beneficial to animals as well as humans, and are sought by horses, goats, sheep and deer. She states that the whole plant is tonic and stimulant, the bark and berries included. Healing juniper "tar" is made from the interior reddish wood of the trunk and branches. She considers it helpful as well in cases of sciatica and rheumatism, inflamed liver and kidneys, gallstones, jaundice and obesity.

Licorice root, called Kan-Ts'-AO (*Glycyrrhiza glabra*), grows abundantly in Northern China and more is brought in from Mongolia. Considered of great importance by the Chinese, it is thought to be corrective and harmonizing used as an ingredient in many prescriptions.

Richard Lucas writes that it is demulcent, pectoral, alterative, emollient, expectorant and slightly laxative. It may be used to relieve thirst, feverishness, coughs, hoarseness, sore throat and distress in breathing.

Here in the States we also use it for much the same purpose and it is often an ingredient of cough lozenges, syrups and pastilles. It is so pleasant of taste that it is hard to regard it as a medicine. We can enjoy licorice, unlike many bad-tasting medicines, while we are getting "cured"!

ASTROLOGICAL
BIRTH CONTROL

Astrological birth control is as old as the proverbial hills. Although ABC has been brought to public attention only relatively recently, the concept has existed for millennia.

The publication of *Psychic Discoveries Behind the Iron Curtain* by Lynn Schroeder and Sheila Ostrander was responsible for the popularization of astrological birth control. In that book, the authors included a chapter on the work of a Czechoslovakian gynecologist-psychiatrist, Dr. Eugen Jonas, who has been carrying out studies and experiments with ABC for over a decade. During his research period, and before he ran into some political trouble, Jonas tested certain astrological hypotheses on hundreds of women and came up with an astonishing accuracy of 98 percent.

Widespread general interest in the Czechoslovakian techniques prompted Schroeder and Ostrander to co-author a separate volume called *Astrological Birth Control* in 1972. This book laid out the methods in detail and included a history of the research and tables of reference for plotting ABC charts.

The methods of Dr. Jonas were based on two major hypotheses whose sources, interestingly enough, were some ancient Indian texts on astrology. The two principles were as follows: 1) that conception takes place when the Sun and the Moon return every month to the same angular relationship that they held in the mother's birth chart; and 2) that the sex of the offspring depends on the position of the Moon at the time of conception, i.e., whether it is in a positive or negative field of the ecliptic.

To illustrate: if a woman were born three days after a New Moon, then each month the time when the Moon is three days old would be her astrologically fertile period. Or, if she were born at the Full Moon, then it is during this phase of the lunar cycle that she is most fertile.

Also, sex-determination depends on whether the Moon at conception is passing through a positive (traditionally masculine) or a negative (feminine) sign. If the Moon is in one of the six positive fields, the resulting child will be male; if it is in one of the negative signs, the child will be female.

The Jonas method of astrological birth control is to be used in conjunction with the regular menstrual cycle, commonly known as the rhythm method, which postulates that ovulation occurs midway during the feminine monthly cycle. This implies that there may be two fertile periods during the month.

These two periods, are the days to consider fertile—thus, the days to use for birth prevention or promotion.

Business, Finance & Legal

- Buying
- Selling
- Loans
- Travel
- Media
- Career
- Legal
- Writing

BUSINESS, FINANCE & LEGAL

Advertising

Write advertisements when it is a favorable day for your Sun sign and Mercury or Jupiter is conjunct, sextile or trine the Moon. Mars and Saturn should not be aspecting the Moon by square, opposition or conjunction. Advertising campaigns are best begun when the Moon is in Taurus, Cancer, Sagittarius, or Aquarius, and well-aspected. Advertise to give away pets when the Moon is in Sagittarius or Pisces.

Business

As you begin training for any occupation, see that your lunar cycle is favorable that day and that the planet ruling your occupation is marked C, T, or Sx.

In starting a business of your own, see that the Moon is free of afflictions and that the planet ruling the business is marked C, T, or Sx.

When you take up a new job, Jupiter and Venus should be sextile, trine, or conjunct the Moon.

To make contracts, see that the Moon is in a fixed sign and sextile, trine, or conjunct Mercury.

Buying

Buy during the third quarter, when the Moon is in Taurus for quality, in a mutable sign (Gemini, Virgo, Sagittarius, Pisces) for savings. Good aspects from Venus or the Sun (C, Sx, T) are desirable. If you are buying for yourself it is good if the day is favorable to your Sun sign. See also machinery, appliances, tools.

Buying Electronic Equipment

Choose a day when the Moon is in an air sign (Gemini, Libra or Aquarius) and well-aspected by Mercury and/or

Uranus. A favorable Saturn aspect aids with sound equipment.

Clothes Buying

For buying clothes, there are several astrological guidelines. First see that the Moon is sextile or trine to the Sun, and that the Moon is in the first or second quarters. When the Moon is in Taurus, buying clothes will bring pleasure and satisfaction. Do not buy clothing or jewelry or wear them for the first time when the Moon is in Scorpio or Aries. Buying clothes on a favorable day for your Sun sign and when Venus or Mercury are well-aspected (T or Sx) is best; but avoid aspects to Mars and Saturn.

Collections

Try to make collections on days when your Sun is well-aspected. Avoid days in which Mars or Saturn are aspected. If possible, the Moon should be in a cardinal sign: Aries, Cancer, Libra or Capricorn. It is more difficult to collect when the Moon is in Taurus and Scorpio.

Employment, Promotion or Favors

Choose a day when your Sun sign is favorable. Mercury should be marked C, T, or Sx. Avoid days when Mars or Saturn is aspected.

Furniture

Follow the rules for Machinery and Appliances but buy when the Moon is in Libra as well. Buy antique furniture when the Moon is in Cancer, Scorpio, or Capricorn.

Legal Matters

In general, a good aspect between the Moon and Jupiter is the best influence for a favorable decision. If you are starting a lawsuit to gain damages, begin during the increase of the Moon (1st and 2nd quarters). If you are seeking to avoid payment, get a court date when the Moon is decreasing (3rd and 4th quarters). A good Moon-Sun aspect strengthens your chance of success. In divorce cases, a favorable Moon-Venus aspect may produce a more amicable settlement. Moon in Cancer or Leo and well-aspected by the Sun brings the best results in custody cases.

Loans
   Moon in the first and second quarters favors the lender, in the third and fourth it favors the borrower. Good aspects of Jupiter and Venus to the Moon are favorable to both, as is the Moon in Leo, Sagittarius, Aquarius or Pisces.

Machinery, Appliances, Tools
   Tools, machinery and other implements should be bought on days when your lunar cycle is favorable and when Mars and Uranus are trine, sextile, or conjunct the Moon. Any quarter of the Moon is suitable. When buying gas or electiical appliances, the Moon should be in Aquarius. The same applies for electronic equipment.

Mailing
   For best results, send mail on favorable days for your Sun sign. The Moon in Gemini is good, while Virgo, Sagittarius and Pisces are helpful too.

Mining
   Saturn rules drilling and mining. Begin this work on a day when Saturn is marked C, T, or Sx. If mining for gold, pick a day in which the Sun is also marked C, T, or Sx. Mercury rules quicksilver, Venus copper, Jupiter tin, Saturn lead and coal, Uranus radioactive elements, Neptune oil, and the Moon water. Choose a day when the planet ruling whatever is being drilled for is marked C, T or Sx.

New Ventures
   Things usually get off to a better start during the increase of the Moon, the first and second quarter. If there is impatience, anxiety or deadlock, it can often be broken at the Full Moon. Agreements can be reached then.

News
   The handling of news is related to Uranus, Merury, and all of the air signs. When Uranus is aspected, there is always an increase in the spectacular side of the news. Collection of news is related to Saturn.

Photography, Radio, T.V., Film and Video

For all these activities it is best to have Neptune, Venus, and Mercury well-aspected, that is, trine, sextile, or conjunct the Moon. The act of photographing is not dependent on any particular phase of the Moon, but Neptune rules photography while Venus is related to beauty in line, form, and color.

Selling or Canvassing

Contacts for these activities will be better during a day favorable to your Sun sign. Otherwise, make strong efforts to sell on days when Jupiter, Mercury, or Mars is trine, sextile, or conjunct the Moon. Avoid days when Saturn is square or opposite the Moon.

Signing Important Papers

Sign contracts or agreements when the Moon is increasing (first and second quarter) in a fruitful sign, and on a day when Moon-Mercury aspects are operating. Avoid days when Mars, Saturn, or Neptune are square or opposite the Moon (Sq or O). Don't sign anything if it is an unfavorable day for you.

Travel

Short journeys are ruled by Mercury, long ones by Jupiter. The Sun rules the actual journey itself. Long trips which threaten to exhaust the traveller are best begun when the Sun is well-aspected to the Moon and the date is favorable for the traveller. If travelling with other people, good aspects from Venus are desirable. For employment, aspects to Jupiter are profitable. For visiting, aspects to Mercury. To avoid accidents, avoid afflictions from Mars, Saturn, Uranus or Pluto, and again, look for good aspects from the Sun.

When to Fly

Choose a day when the Moon is in Gemini or Libra, and well-aspected by Mercury and/or Jupiter. Avoid adverse aspects of Mars, Saturn or Uranus.

Writing

Writng for pleasure or publication is best done when the Moon is in Gemini. Mercury should be direct. (To find out when Mercury is retrograde and direct, see *Llewellyn's Astrological Calendar*.) Favorable aspects to Mercury, Uranus and Neptune promote ingenuity.

Writing A Will

The Moon should be in a fixed sign (Taurus, Leo, Scorpio, Aquarius) in the first or second quarters. There should be favorable aspects to Saturn, Venus and Mercury and no afflictions (Sq or O) from Pluto.

USING THE MOON FOR BUSINESS AND LEGAL DECISIONS
by Bruce Scofield

When making a decision that pertains to business, legal, financial or real estate matters, attention to the phase of the Moon could prove a real benefit. Decisions made at the right time usually result in a neater, more efficient result than those made at less auspicious times. Fewer complications stemming from a decision means less time wasted—and time means money. Before you sign away your money or your property, read ahead and take the Moon into account.

Since ancient times, the cycle of the Moon from New to Full to New has been observed and correlated with events on Earth. The earliest farmers learned that sowing seeds of aboveground plants before the Full Moon led to a better harvest. Sailors learned to time their travels by the phase of the Moon, which everyone knows controls the tides. In many cultures, specific guidelines for activities on each day of the Moon cycle were given. Today much of this lore is lost to us or is irrelevant to our modern culture, but a few basic principles remain and continue to serve those who use them well.

In general, it is better to initiate a business deal or legal suit or make an offer as the Moon is increasing in light from New Moon to Full Moon. The object is to time your event when the Moon is on the upswing. As the Moon moves from New to Full, it symbolizes the unfolding of a new cycle. Exactly what form it will take may not be known, but there is room to move and time to make adjustments. There are a few details that also should be taken into consideration as well. Do not initiate a process exactly (within 12 hours) at the time of the New Moon or the first quarter. An event started precisely at the New Moon may tend to be premature, while an event started exactly at the first quarter may be conflict-ridden.

It is best to culminate a business deal or a real estate

transaction or sign legal agreements at the Full Moon. The
Full Moon symbolizes the climax of the cycle that began
two weeks earlier at the New Moon. What was sown earlier blooms at the Full Moon. In essence, the Full Moon
sheds light on whatever is occurring, it symbolizes an objectivity that is not found during the previous two weeks.
In practice, it may be best to avoid a business climax or
agreement or other practical matter within 12 hours of the
exact Full Moon. Some astrologers feel that conditions are
best the day after the Full Moon when the second half of
the lunar cycle has actually begun. Here, just past the exact opposition of the Sun and the Moon, the turning point
which led to the agreement is seen in full perspective.

The sign that the New Moon falls in should also be
taken into consideration. If the New Moon occurs in a sign
that is square your Sun sign, then perhaps you should wait
until the next lunar cycle to make your moves. In real estate transactions, which often take months, making the
first move just after a New Moon in a sign that favorably
relates to your Sun sign is recommended. The culmination
of the transaction should be timed for a Full Moon, even
though it most likely won't be the one that occurs two
weeks later. In astrology, the first step is the most important.

If one follows news events carefully, particularly bar-
gaining sessions and political conflicts, the truth of these
general rules will be apparent. Some years ago, President
Carter negotiated with the leaders of Egypt and Israel in
search of a peace treaty. Both the agreement and the signing of the Camp David Accords occurred on a Full Moon.
Frequently, decisions made by world leaders are an-
nounced at the Full Moon. The astute observer will learn
much of value by noting when public decisions are made,
mindful of their ultimate outcomes.

STARTING A NEW BUSINESS OR BUSINESS VENTURE

When starting a new business or any type of new venture, check to make sure that the Moon is in the first or second quarter. This will help it get off to a better start. If there is a deadlock or anxiety, it will often be broken during the Full Moon. Agreements can then be reached.

You should also check the aspects of the Moon to the type of venture with which you are becoming involved. Look for positive aspects to the planet that rules the activity (listed as Sx or T in the *Lunar Aspectarian*).

Activities ruled by the **Sun** are advertising, executive positions, acting, banking, finance, government, jewelry, law and public relations.

Activities ruled by **Mercury** are accounting, brokerage, clerical, disc jockey, doctor, editor, inspector, librarian, linguist, medical technician, scientist, teaching, writing, publishing, communication and mass media.

Activities and occupations ruled by **Venus** are architect, art and artists, beautician, dance, design, fashion and marketing, music, poetry and chiropractors.

Activities ruled by **Mars** are barber, butcher, carpenter, chemist, construction, dentist, metal worker, surgeon and the military.

Activities and occupations that are ruled by **Jupiter** are counseling, horse training, jockey, judge, lawyer, legislator, minister, pharmacist, psychologist, public analyst, social clubs, research and self-improvement.

Activities and occupations ruled by **Saturn** are agronomy, math, mining, plumbing, real estate, repairperson, printers, paper making and dealing with older people.

Activities and occupations ruled by **Uranus** are aeronautics, broadcasting, electricians, inventing, lecturing, radiology, and computers.

Activities and occupations ruled by **Neptune** are photography, investigators, institutions, shipping, pets, movies, wine merchants, health foods, resorts, travel by water and welfare.

Activities and occupations ruled by **Pluto** are acrobatics, athletic managers, atomic energy, research, speculation, sports, stockbrokers, and any purely personal endeavors.

If you follow the guidelines given above and apply them to the occupations or activities for each planet, you should have excellent results in your new business ventures. Even if it is not a new venture, check the aspects to the ruler of the activity before making moves in your business. Avoid any dates marked Sq or O to that planet ruler in the *Lunar Aspectarian*. You are sure to have trouble with the client or deal.

Farm & Garden

- Moon Gardening

- Best Planting Dates

- Breeding Animals & Setting Eggs

Articles:
- Bat Houses
- Organic Pest Control
- Garden Ornaments
- Much More!

GARDENING BY THE MOON

Today, we still find scientists who reject the notion of Moon gardening—but the usual non-believer is not the scientist, but the half-dead city dweller who has never had any real contact with nature, and no conscious experience of natural rhythms.

The true scientist is at least open-minded about the idea, waiting for us to provide more data—and this every Moon planter is usually able to do in the form of both quantity and quality of produce. The scientist, however, needs more than this, and we earnestly hope that many of our readers will undertake some controlled experiments on their own and report them to us.

Moon planting is old, ancient in fact, but so is humankind itself and merely because something is old is certainly no reason to toss it out. Really the opposite is true! First of all, we have to presume that it originated because humans observed that it worked, or seemed to work. Second, we ought to give some credence to the notion that the idea endured because it had merit, even if—as sometimes happens—it might have become exaggerated or even incorrectly applied. Third, our respect for the idea should increase when we learn that the principles of lunar planting have been recognized as fundamentally similar in many cultures that had no contact with each other—in other words, the "discovery" was made independently by many peoples.

Plutarch, two thousand years ago, wrote:

"The Moone showeth her power most evidently in those bodies, which have neither sense nor lively breath; for carpenters reject the timber of trees fallen in the fulmoone, as being soft and tender, subject also to the wormes and putrefaction, and that quickly by means of excessive moisture; husbandmen, likewise, make haste to gather up their wheat and other grain from the threshing-

146

floore, in the wane of the moone, and toward the end of the
month (4th Qtr), that being hardened thus with drinesse,
the heaps, in the garner may keep the better from being
fustie, and continue the longer; whereas corne which is
inned and laide up at the full of the moone, by reason of the
softnesse and over-much moisture, of all other, doth most
crackle and burst. It is commonly said also, that if a leaven
be laid in the ful-moone, the paste will rise and take leaven
better."

Cato, before the time of Jesus, wrote that "fig, apple, olive, and pear trees, as well as vines, should be planted in
the dark of the Moon in the afternoon, when there is no
south wind blowing."

But, ancient as these quotations are, they are not without modern support by the scientific community! Camille
Flammarian, the French astronomer, testifies to Moon
planting as follows:

"Cucumbers increase at full Moon, as well as radishes,
turnips, leeks, lilies, horseradish, saffron; but onions, on
the contrary, are much larger and better nourished during
the decline and old age of the Moon than at its increase;
than during its youth and fullness, which is the reason the
Egyptians abstained from onions, on account of their antipathy to the Moon. Herbs gathered while the Moon increases are of great efficiency. If the vines are trimmed at
night when the Moon is in the Sign of the Lion, Sagittarius,
the Scorpion, or the Bull, it will save them from field-rats,
moles, snails, flies, and other animals."

Even a Nobel prize winner, Dr. Robert Millikan, en-
dorsed the principles involved when answering a question as to the validity of astrology: "I do know that if man is
not affected in some way by the planets, Sun and Moon, he
is *the only thing on Earth that isn't.*"

The Bible (Book of Ecclesiastes) says: "There is a time to
plant and a time to pluck up that which is planted." Dr.
Clark Timmins is one of the few modern scientists to have
actually conducted tests in Moon planting. The following
is a summary of some of his experiments:

1. Beets. When sown with Moon in Scorpio had a germination rate of 71%; when sown in Sagittarius, germination
rate was only 58%.

2. Scotch Marigold. When sown with Moon in Cancer the germination rate was 90%; when sown in Leo, germination rate was 32%.

3. Carrots. When sown with Moon in Scorpio, germination rate was 64%; when sown in Sagittarius, only 47% germinated.

4. Tomatoes. When sown with Moon in Cancer, 90% germinated; in Leo only 58% germinated.

Now let me emphasize two things here: first of all, I am only summarizing the results of the experiments, but the experiments themselves were conducted in a scientific manner to eliminate any variation in soil, temperature, moisture, etc., so that only the Moon's sign used in planting varied. Second, note that these astonishing results were obtained without regard to the phase of the Moon—the other factor we utilize in Moon planting, and which would presumably have increased the differential in germination rates.

Further experiments by Dr. Timmins:

Transplanting: both Cancer-planted and Leo-planted tomato seedlings were transplanted while the Moon was increasing and in Cancer—100% survival. When the transplanting was done with the Moon decreasing and in Sagittarius, all died—0% survival.

The other results of Dr. Timmins' tests, again under scientific controls, show that the Cancer-planted tomatoes had first blossoms twelve days earlier than those planted under Leo; that the Cancer-planted tomatoes had an average height of twenty inches at the same age when the Leo plants were only fifteen inches high; the first ripe tomatoes were gathered from Cancer plantings eleven days ahead of the Leo plantings; and finally, a count of the hanging fruit and comparison of size and weight shows an advantage to the Cancer plants over the Leo plants of 45%.

Students will also be interested to learn that Dr. Timmins also observed that there have been similar tests to the above reported that did not indicate results favorable to the Moon planting theory. As a scientist, he asked why one set of experiments indicated a positive verification of Moon planting, and others did not. He checked these other tests, and found that the experimenters had *not* followed the geocentric system for determining the Moon sign positions, but the heliocentric. When the times used in these other tests were converted to the geocentric system, the dates chosen were found to be often in barren rather than fertile signs. Without going into the technical explanations, it is sufficient to point out that geocentric and heliocentric positions often vary by as smuch as *four* days. This is sufficient to place the Moon in Cancer, for example, in the heliocentric system, and at the same time in Leo by the geocentric system.

Most almanacs and calendars show the Moon's signs heliocentrically—and thus incorrectly for Moon planting—while our *Moon Sign Book* is calculated correctly for planting purposes, using the geocentric system.

In addition, many almanacs only give the Moon's phases, and not the signs. If you plant only according to the phase (quarter), you may be planting during a barren sign. That is why our Gardening Dates in the *Moon Sign Book* are based on both signs and phases.

Some readers are also confused by references to the quarters since the *Moon Sign Book* talks of First, Second, Third and Fourth Quarters, while some almanacs refer to these same divisions as New Moon, First Quarter, Full Moon and Last Quarter. Thus, the almanac says First Quarter when the *Moon Sign Book* says Second Quarter. (Refer to the introductory material in this book for more information.)

The Practice of Moon Gardening

There is nothing complicated about using astrology in agriculture and horticulture in order to increase both pleasure and profit, but there is one very important rule that is often neglected—*use common sense!* Now, of course, that's one rule that should be remembered in every activity we undertake, but in the case of gardening and farming by the Moon we mean that it is not always possible to use the best *dates* for planting or harvesting, and we we must select the next best and just try to do the best we can.

And this brings up the matter of the other factors to consider in your gardening work. The dates we give you as *best* for a certain activity apply to the entire country (with slight time correction), but in your section of the country you may be buried under three feet of snow on a date we say is a good day to plant your flowers. So, we have factors of weather, season, temperature and moisture variations, soil conditions, your own available time and opportunity, and so forth. And don't forget the matter of the "green thumb." Some astrologers like to think it is all a matter of science, but gardening, like anything else, is also an art—and in art you develop an instinctive identification with your work so that you actually influence it with your feelings and *visualization* of what you want to accomplish.

In the *Moon Sign Book* we give you the place of the Moon for every day of the year so that you can more easily select the second best times once you have become familiar with the rules and practices of lunar agriculture. In this article we try to give you the most specific, easy-to-follow directions so that you can get right down to work without any further delay.

We are going to give the best dates for planting, and also for various related activities, including cultivation, fertilizing, harvesting, irrigation, and getting rid of weeds and pests. But we cannot just tell you when it's a good time to plant—we have to tell you also what it's good to plant at the particular time. Many of these rules were learned by observation and experience, but as our body of experience grew we could see various patterns emerging which allow us to make judgments about new things. And then we test the new possible applications, and learn still more. And that's what you should do, too. After you have worked with lunar agriculture for a while and gained a working background of knowledge, you will probably begin to try new things—and we hope you will share your experiments and findings with us. That's how the science grows.

As an example of what we mean: Years ago, Llewellyn George suggested that we try to combine our bits of knowledge about what to expect in planting under each of the Moon signs in order to benefit with several such lunar factors in one plant. From this came our rule for developing "Thoroughbred Seed": To develop thoroughbred seed, save the seed for three successive years from plants grown by the correct Moon sign and phase to breed into the plant the desired characteristics. You can plant in the First Quarter phase and in the sign of Cancer for fruitfulness; the second year plant seeds from the first year plants in Libra for beauty; and in the third year plant the seeds from the second year plants in Taurus to produce hardiness. In a similar manner you can combine the fruitfulness of Cancer, the good root growth of Pisces, and the sturdiness and good vine growth of Scorpio. And don't forget the characteristics of Capricorn, hardy like Taurus, but drier and perhaps more resistant to drought and disease.

Now, unlike common almanacs that are used as planting guides, we consider both the Moon's *phase* and the Moon's *sign* in making our calculations for the proper *timing of our work within nature's rhythm*. It is perhaps a little easier to understand this if we remind you that we are all living in the center of a vast electromagnetic field that is the Earth and its environment in space. Everything that occurs within this electromagnetic field has an effect on everything else within the same field, but since we are living on the Earth we must relate these happenings and effects to our own health and happiness. The Moon and the Sun are the most important and dynamic of the rhythmically changing factors affecting the life of the Earth, and it is their relative positions to the Earth that we project for each day of the coming year.

Many people claim that not only do they achieve larger crops gardening by the Moon, but that their fruits and vegetables are much tastier and more healthful. We now have a growing number of organic gardeners who also have become lunar gardeners, using natural growing methods within the natural rhythm of life forces that we experience through the relative movements of the Sun and Moon. But, as we used to say, *the proof is in the eating*, and that's just what we want you to do.

We want to give you the few basic rules, and then give you, month-by-month and day-by-day the guidance for your farming and gardening work. With these few rules in mind, you will be able to choose the best dates to meet your own needs and opportunities.

Planting by the Moon's Phases
During the *increasing light* (from New Moon to Full Moon), plant annuals that produce their yield above the ground. (An annual is a plant that completes its entire life cycle within one growing season, and has to be seeded

anew each year.)

During the *decreasing light* (from Full Moon to New Moon), plant biennials, perennials, bulb and root plants. (Biennials include crops that are planted one season to winter over and produce crops the next, such as winter wheat. Perennials and bulb and root plants include all plants that grow from the same root year after year.)

A simple, though less accurate rule is to plant crops that produce above the ground during the increase of the Moon, and to plant crops that produce below the ground during the decrease of the Moon. This is the source of the old adage, "plant potatoes during the dark of the Moon."

Llewellyn George went a step further, and divided the lunar month into quarters, and called the first two from New Moon to Full Moon the First and Second Quarters, and the last two from Full Moon to New Moon the Third and Fourth Quarters. Using these finer divisions, we can increase our accuracy in *timing* our efforts to coincide with natural forces still further, and expand our rules to include the following:

First Quarter (increasing). Plant annuals producing their yield above the ground, which are generally of the leafy kind that produce their seed outside the fruit. Also cereals and grain. Examples of such plants are asparagus, broccoli, Brussels sprouts, cabbage, cauliflower, celery, cress, endive, kohlrabi, lettuce, parsley, spinach, etc. As an apparent exception to the rule, we find that cucumber seems to do best in the First Quarter rather than in the Second, even though the seeds are inside the fruit. Also in the First Quarter we plant the cereals and grains.

Second Quarter (increasing). Plant annuals producing their yield above the ground, which are generally of the viney kind that produce their seed inside the fruit. Examples include beans, eggplant, melons, peas, pepper, pumpkin, squash, tomatoes, etc. Also cereals and grains again. These are not hard and fast divisions. If you can't plant during the First Quarter, you will be safe to plant during the Second, and vice versa. And there are many plants that seem to do almost equally well planted in either quarter, such as watermelon, garlic, hay, and—as indicated—the cereals and grains.

Third Quarter (decreasing). Plant biennials, perennials, and bulb and root plants, including crops planted in one season to winter over and produce their crops the next seson. Also trees, shrubs, berries, beets, carrots, onion sets, parsnips, peanuts, potatoes, radishes, rhubarb, rutabagas, strawberries, turnips, winter wheat, grapes, etc.

Fourth Quarter (decreasing). Best for cultivation, pulling weeds and destroying pests of all kinds, turning sod, etc. Especially when the Moon is in the barren signs of Aries, Leo, Virgo, Gemini, Aquarius, and Sagittarius.

Planting by the Moon's Signs

As mentioned before, we also consider the Moon's *signs* in our gardening, and in the dates we will give you for various activities the phases and signs are combined. However, we want to give you some general rules in relation to each of the signs so that you can make various individual decisions as the occasion may require. In each of the twelve zodiacal signs the Moon reflects the special characteristics associated with the sign, and your activities should be coordinated to take benefit of this natural cycle.

Moon in Aries: barren and dry; fiery and masculine. Used for destroying noxious growths, weeds, pests, etc. and for cultivating.

Moon in Taurus: productive and moist; earthy and feminine. Used for planting many crops, more particularly potatoes and root crops, and when hardiness is important. Also used for lettuce, cabbage, and similar leafy vegetables.

Moon in Gemini: barren and dry; airy and masculine. Used for destroying noxious growths, weeds and pests, and for cultivation.

Moon in Cancer: *very fruitful* and moist; watery and feminine. This is the most productive sign and used extensively for planting and irrigation.

Moon in Leo: barren and dry; fiery and masculine. This is the most barren sign, and used only for killing weeds and other noxious growths, cultivation.

Moon in Virgo: barren and moist; earthy and feminine. Considered good for cultivation and destroying weeds and pests.

Moon in Libra: semi-fruitful and moist; airy and masculine. Used for planting of many crops, producing good pulp growth and roots. It is a very good sign for flowers and vines. Also used for seeding hay, corn fodder, etc.

Moon in Scorpio: *very fruitful* and moist; watery and feminine. Very nearly as productive as Cancer and used for the same purposes. Especially good for vine growth, and for sturdiness.

Moon in Sagittarius: considered barren and dry, but often used for onions, seeding for hay, etc. Fiery and masculine, it is also used for cultivation.

Moon in Capricorn: productive and a little more dry than Taurus; earthy and feminine. Used for potatoes, tubers, etc.

Moon in Aquarius: barren and dry; airy and masculine. Used for cultivation, and also for destroying noxious growths, weeds and pests.

Moon in Pisces: *very fruitful* and moist; watery and feminine. Used along with Cancer and Scorpio, but especially good for root growth.

To summarize: We will use Cancer, Scorpio, and Pisces for planting whenever we can unless the nature of the plant itself points to another sign. Taurus and Capricorn are next in the order of preference, especially for root crops; and then Libra, Sagittarius, and Aquarius, in that order. *Don't forget that we are going to combine the Moon signs with the Moon phases in selecting our planting dates.*

PLANETARY RULERSHIPS OF PLANTS

Here are some general guidelines for using the influence of the various planets in timing your gardening activities. These should be used in addition to the lunar information given previously.

Sun-loving plants should be set out while the Sun is in the sky, and shade-loving plants, after it has set. Delicate plants that prefer the Sun should be set out during the period of the waning Sun—in the late afternoon hours when the Sun is yet visible, but not powerful enough to damage them. Sun-loving plants started from seed should be placed in the ground in the early morning hours, during the period of the increasing Sun.

When the *Planetary and Lunar Aspects* tables show a good aspect between Mars and the Moon (the Mars column marked with a T or Sx), it is the best time to plant biennials. A good Jupiter aspect is best for transplanting perennials. For dividing, pruning, and trimming perennials, both Jupiter and Saturn should be in good aspect to the Moon if possible.

Planetary Rulers

It is sometimes necessary to know the planetary ruler of a plant—particularly medicinal herbs and magical plants used in religious ceremonies. It may also be helpful, if you want to invoke a certain feeling in your garden, to cultivate plants ruled by the planet or sign consistent with your purpose. The following information is meant to supplement, not replace, the principles of lunar gardening already given.

Annual plants are ruled by the Sun, for they follow the cycle of the Sun in growth and reproduction. Biennial plants are ruled by Mars, for they follow a two-year cycle in growth, the first year producing a sturdy plant, the second year a full bloom or crop. Perennials are ruled by expansive Jupiter, not following a twelve-year cycle, but requiring much more time for development of the plant than annuals or biennials. Root crops are ruled by Pluto, which rules the underground.

Astrological tradition also assigns specific rulerships to plants, as indicated in the table on the following pages.

EDIBLE PLANTS

Artichoke: Venus
Asparagus: Venus, Jupiter
Barley: Saturn
Beans: Venus
Beets: Saturn
  White Beets: Jupiter
Blackberry: Scorpio, Mars
Cabbage: Moon
Chickory: Sagittarius,
  Jupiter, Sun
Chickpea: Venus
Coffee: Neptune
Corn: Sun
Cress: Mars
  Watercress: Moon
Cucumber: Moon
Endive: Virgo, Mercury,
  Jupiter
Garlic: Aries, Mars

Gooseberry: Venus
Grape: Sun
Horseradish: Scorpio, Mars
Leeks: Scorpio, Mars
Lettuce: Cancer, Moon
Mushrooms: Neptune
Mustard: Aries, Mars, Sun
Onion: Saturn, Mars
Pepper: Aries, Mars
Pineapple: Mars
Pumpkin: Moon
Rhubarb: Mars
Rice: Sun
Rye: Venus, Saturn
Strawberry: Venus
Tomato: Jupiter
Wheat: Venus

HERBS

Agrimony: Sagittarius,
  Jupiter
Aniseed: Jupiter
Basil: Mars
Belladonna: Saturn
Borage: Jupiter
Caraway: Gemini, Mercury
Catmint: Libra, Venus,
  Mars
Chamomile: Sun
Chervil: Jupiter
Cinnamon: Jupiter
Coltsfoot: Taurus, Venus

Medicinal herbs in general:
  Virgo
Mistletoe: Leo, Sun
Motherwort: Venus
Mullein: Virgo, Gemini,
  Mercury, Saturn
Nettles: Aries, Mars
Parsley: Gemini, Mercury,
  Venus
Pennyroyal: Libra, Venus
Plantain: Taurus, Venus,
  Mars, Saturn
Rosemary: Sun

Comfrey: Cancer, Moon, Capricorn, Saturn

Dandelion: Sagittarius, Jupiter

Deadly Nightshade: Taurus, Venus

Fennel: Virgo, Mercury, Aquarius, Saturn

Ginseng: Jupiter

Goldenrod: Taurus, Venus

Hemlock: Capricorn, Saturn

Hemp: Saturn

Hops: Aries, Mars

Horehound: Scorpio, Mars

Licorice: Virgo, Mercury

Sage: Aries, Mars, Taurus, Venus, Jupiter

Sarsaparilla: Scorpio, Mars

Slippery Elm: Capricorn, Saturn

Tansy: Taurus, Venus

Thistle: Aries, Scorpio, Mars, Saturn

Thyme: Taurus, Libra, Venus, Capricorn, Saturn

Valerian: Aquarius, Saturn, Mars

Vervain: Libra, Taurus, Venus

Witchhazel: Mars

Wormwood: Scorpio, Mars

Yarrow: Venus

ORNAMENTAL PLANTS

Buttercup: Aquarius, Uranus, Saturn

Columbine: Venus, Mars

Daisy: Venus
English Daisy: Mars

Ferns: Gemini, Mercury
Maidenhair Fern: Libra, Taurus, Venus

Geranium: Mars, Moon

Gladiola: Gemini, Mercury

Honeysuckle: Aries, Mars, Cancer, Moon

Iris: Jupiter, Moon

Irish Moss: Pisces

Ivy: Saturn

Juniper: Sun, Mars

Lily of the Valley: Gemini, Mercury

Marigold: Leo, Sun

Myrtle: Mars

Orchid: Venus

Pansy: Saturn

Peony: Moon

Pinks: Jupiter

Poppy: Venus, Saturn, Moon

Opium Poppy: Neptune

Roses—
Damask Rose: Venus
Red Rose: Jupiter
White Rose: Libra, Taurus, Venus, Moon

Sunflower: Sun

Violets: Libra, Venus, Cancer, Moon

Waterlily: Cancer, Moon

TREES

Alder: Venus

Almond: Sun

Apple: Venus

Laurel: Sun

Lemon: Sun

Lime: Jupiter

Apricot: Jupiter
Ash: Sun
Aspen: Saturn
Bay: Aries, Mars, Sun
Beech: Saturn
Birch: Venus
Boxwood: Mars
Cherry: Venus
Chestnut: Venus, Jupiter
Citrus fruit in general: Sun
Fig: Jupiter
Hawthorne: Mars
Holly: Saturn

Maple: Jupiter
Oak: Sagittarius, Jupiter
  English Oak: Saturn
Olive: Sun
Orange: Sun
Peach: Venus
Pear: Venus
Pine: Mars
Plum: Venus
Poplar: Saturn
Quince: Capricorn, Saturn
Walnut: Leo, Sun
Willow: Moon

1992
GARDENING DATES

Dec 29, 4:04 pm– Jan 1, 1:31 am Scorpio, 4th qtr.	Plant biennials, perennials, bulbs and roots. Irrigate. Fertilize (organic). Prune.
Jan 1, 1:31 am– Jan 3, 1:10 pm Sagittarius, 4th qtr.	Cultivate. Destroy weeds and pests. Harvest fruits and root crops. Trim to retard growth.
Jan 3, 1:10 pm– Jan 4, 5:10 pm Capricorn, 4th qtr.	Plant potatoes and tubers. Prune.
Jan 4, 5:10 pm– Jan 6, 2:00 am Capricorn, 1st qtr.	Graft or bud plants. Trim to increase growth.
Jan 8, 2:53 pm– Jan 11, 2:23 am Pisces, 1st qtr.	Plant annuals, grains. Irrigate. Fertilize (chemical). Trim to increase growth. Graft or bud plants.
Jan 13, 11:01 am– Jan 15, 3:56 pm Taurus, 2nd qtr.	Plant annuals for hardiness. Trim to increase growth.
Jan 17, 5:27 pm– Jan 19, 3:30 pm Cancer, 2nd qtr.	Plant annuals, grains. Irrigate. Fertilize (chemical). Trim to increase growth. Graft or bud plants.

Jan 19, 3:30 pm Full Moon, Cancer	Gather mushrooms. Harvest root crops for seed.
Jan 19, 3:30 pm– Jan 19, 4:58 pm Cancer, 3rd qtr.	Plant biennials, perennials, bulbs and roots. Irrigate. Fertilize (organic). Prune.
Jan 19, 4:58 pm– Jan 21, 4:23 pm Leo, 3rd qtr.	Cultivate. Destroy weeds and pests. Harvest fruits and root crops. Trim to retard growth.
Jan 21, 4:23 pm– Jan 23, 5:43 pm Virgo, 3rd qtr.	Cultivate, especially medicinal plants. Destroy weeds and pests. Trim to retard growth.
Jan 25, 10:33 pm– Jan 28, 7:21 am Scorpio, 3-4th qtr.	Plant biennials, perennials, bulbs and roots. Irrigate. Fertilize (organic). Prune.
Jan 28, 7:21 am– Jan 30, 7:08 pm Sagittarius, 4th qtr.	Cultivate. Destroy weeds and pests. Harvest fruits and root crops. Trim to retard growth.
Jan 30, 7:08 pm– Feb 2, 8:09 am Capricorn, 4th qtr.	Plant potatoes and tubers. Prune.
Feb 2, 8:09 am– Feb 3, 1:00 pm Aquarius, 4th qtr.	Cultivate. Destroy weeds and pests. Harvest fruits and root crops. Trim to retard growth.
Feb 4, 8:51 pm– Feb 7, 8:16 am Pisces, 1st qtr.	Plant annuals, grains. Irrigate. Fertilize (chemical). Trim to increase growth. Graft or bud plants.
Feb 9, 5:37 pm– Feb 12, 0:09 am Taurus, 1-2nd qtr.	Plant annuals for hardiness. Trim to increase growth.
Feb 14, 3:32 am– Feb 16, 4:16 am Cancer, 2nd qtr.	Plant annuals, grains. Irrigate. Fertilize (chemical). Trim to increase growth. Graft or bud plants.

| Feb 18, 2:05 am
Full Moon, Leo | Gather mushrooms. Harvest root crops for seed. |
| Feb 18, 2:05 am-
Feb 18, 3:48 am
Leo, 3rd qtr. | Cultivate. Destroy weeds and pests. Harvest fruits and root crops. Trim to retard growth. |

Feb 18, 3:48 am- Feb 20, 4:05 am Virgo, 3rd qtr.	Cultivate, especially medicinal plants. Destroy weeds and pests. Trim to retard growth.
Feb 22, 7:12 am- Feb 24, 2:27 pm Scorpio, 3rd qtr.	Plant biennials, perennials, bulbs and roots. Irrigate. Fertilize (organic). Prune.
Feb 24, 2:27 pm- Feb 27, 1:34 am Sagittarius, 3-4th qtr.	Cultivate. Destroy weeds and pests. Harvest fruits and root crops. Trim to retard growth.
Feb 27, 1:34 am- Feb 29, 2:35 pm Capricorn, 4th qtr.	Plant potatoes and tubers. Prune.
Feb 29, 2:35 pm- Mar 3, 3:12 am Aquarius, 4th qtr.	Cultivate. Destroy weeds and pests. Harvest fruits and root crops. Trim to retard growth.
Mar 3, 3:12 am- Mar 4, 7:23 am Pisces, 4th qtr.	Plant biennials, perennials, bulbs and roots. Irrigate. Fertilize (organic). Prune.

Mar 4, 7:23 am- Mar 5, 2:08 pm Pisces, 1st qtr.	Plant annuals, grains. Irrigate. Fertilize (chemical). Trim to increase growth. Graft or bud plants.
Mar 7, 11:06 pm- Mar 10, 6:04 am Taurus, 1st qtr.	Plant annuals for hardiness. Trim to increase growth.
Mar 12, 10:51 am- Mar 14, 1:21 pm Cancer, 2nd qtr.	Plant annuals, grains. Irrigate. Fertilize (chemical). Trim to increase growth. Graft or bud plants.
Mar 18, 12:19 pm Full Moon, Virgo	Gather mushrooms. Harvest root crops for seed.
Mar 18, 12:19 pm- Mar 18, 2:56 pm Virgo, 3rd qtr.	Cultivate, especially medicinal plants. Destroy weeds and pests. Trim to retard growth.
Mar 20, 5:21 pm- Mar 22, 11:14 pm Scorpio, 3rd qtr.	Plant biennials, perennials, bulbs and roots. Irrigate. Fertilize (organic). Prune.
Mar 22, 11:14 pm- Mar 25, 9:09 am Sagittarius, 3rd qtr.	Cultivate. Destroy weeds and pests. Harvest fruits and root crops. Trim to retard growth.
Mar 25, 9:09 am- Mar 27, 9:45 pm Capricorn, 3-4th qtr.	Plant potatoes and tubers. Prune.
Mar 27, 9:45 pm- Mar 30, 10:24 am Aquarius, 4th qtr.	Cultivate. Destroy weeds and pests. Harvest fruits and root crops. Trim to retard growth.
Mar 30, 10:24 am- Apr 1, 9:05 pm Pisces, 4th qtr.	Plant biennials, perennials, bulbs and roots. Irrigate. Fertilize (organic). Prune.
Apr 1, 9:05 pm- Apr 2, 11:02 pm Aries, 4th qtr.	Cultivate. Destroy weeds and pests. Harvest fruits and root crops. Trim to retard growth.

Apr 4, 5:19 am- Apr 6, 11:34 am Taurus, 1st qtr.	Plant annuals for hardiness. Trim to increase growth.
Apr 8, 4:19 pm- Apr 10, 7:47 pm Cancer, 1-2nd qtr.	Plant annuals, grains. Irrigate. Fertilize (chemical). Trim to increase growth. Graft or bud plants.
Apr 15, 0:11 am- Apr 16, 10:43 pm Libra, 2nd qtr.	Plant annuals for fragrance and beauty. Trim to increase growth.
Apr 16, 10:43 pm Full Moon, Libra	Gather mushrooms. Harvest root crops for seed.
Apr 17, 3:11 am- Apr 19, 8:41 am Scorpio, 3rd qtr.	Plant biennials, perennials, bulbs and roots. Irrigate. Fertilize (organic). Prune.

Apr 19, 8:41 am- Apr 21, 5:41 pm Sagittarius, 3rd qtr.	Cultivate. Destroy weeds and pests. Harvest fruits and root crops. Trim to retard growth.
Apr 21, 5:41 pm- Apr 24, 5:39 am Capricorn, 3rd qtr.	Plant potatoes and tubers. Prune.
Apr 24, 5:39 am- Apr 26, 6:21 pm Aquarius, 3-4th qtr.	Cultivate. Destroy weeds and pests. Harvest fruits and root crops. Trim to retard growth.
Apr 26, 6:21 pm- Apr 29, 5:14 am Pisces, 4th qtr.	Plant biennials, perennials, bulbs and roots. Irrigate. Fertilize (organic). Prune.

Apr 29, 5:14 am- May 1, 1:10 pm Aries, 4th qtr.	Cultivate. Destroy weeds and pests. Harvest fruits and root crops. Trim to retard growth.
May 1, 1:10 pm- May 2, 11:45 am Taurus, 4th qtr.	Plant potatoes and tubers. Prune.
May 2, 11:45 am- May 3, 6:29 pm Taurus, 1st qtr.	Plant annuals for hardiness. Trim to increase growth.
May 5, 10:11 pm- May 8, 1:08 am Cancer, 1st qtr.	Plant annuals, grains. Irrigate. Fertilize (chemical). Trim to increase growth. Graft or bud plants.
May 12, 7:06 am- May 14, 11:16 am Libra, 2nd qtr.	Plant annuals for fragrance and beauty. Trim to increase growth.
May 14, 11:16 am- May 16, 10:04 am Scorpio, 2nd qtr.	Plant annuals, grains. Irrigate. Fertilize (chemical). Trim to increase growth. Graft or bud plants.
May 16, 10:04 am Full Moon, Scorpio	Gather mushrooms. Harvest root crops for seed.
May 16, 10:04 am- May 16, 5:23 pm Scorpio, 3rd qtr.	Plant biennials, perennials, bulbs and roots. Irrigate. Fertilize (organic). Prune.
May 16, 5:23 pm- May 19, 2:13 am Sagittarius, 3rd qtr.	Cultivate. Destroy weeds and pests. Harvest fruits and root crops. Trim to retard growth.
May 19, 2:13 am- May 21, 1:44 pm Capricorn, 3rd qtr.	Plant potatoes and tubers. Prune.
May 21, 1:44 pm- May 24, 2:26 am Aquarius, 3rd qtr.	Cultivate. Destroy weeds and pests. Harvest fruits and root crops. Trim to retard growth.

May 24, 2:26 am– May 26, 1:53 pm Pisces, 3-4th qtr.	Plant biennials, perennials, bulbs and roots. Irrigate. Fertilize (organic). Prune.
May 26, 1:53 pm– May 28, 10:17 pm Aries, 4th qtr.	Cultivate. Destroy weeds and pests. Harvest fruits and root crops. Trim to retard growth.
May 28, 10:17 pm– May 31, 3:20 am Taurus, 4th qtr.	Plant potatoes and tubers. Prune.
May 31, 3:20 am– May 31, 9:58 pm Gemini, 4th qtr.	Cultivate. Destroy weeds and pests. Harvest fruits and root crops. Trim to retard growth.
Jun 2, 5:59 am– Jun 4, 7:36 am Cancer, 1st qtr.	Plant annuals, grains. Irrigate. Fertilize (chemical). Trim to increase growth. Graft or bud plants.
Jun 8, 12:34 pm– Jun 10, 5:28 pm Libra, 2nd qtr.	Plant annuals for fragrance and beauty. Trim to increase growth.
Jun 10, 5:28 pm– Jun 13, 0:30 am Scorpio, 2nd qtr.	Plant annuals, grains. Irrigate. Fertilize (chemical). Trim to increase growth. Graft or bud plants.
Jun 14, 10:51 pm Full Moon, Sagittarius	Gather mushrooms. Harvest root crops for seed.
Jun 14, 10:51 pm– Jun 15, 9:51 am Sagittarius, 3rd qtr.	Cultivate. Destroy weeds and pests. Harvest fruits and root crops. Trim to retard growth.
Jun 15, 9:51 am– Jun 17, 9:20 pm Capricorn, 3rd qtr.	Plant potatoes and tubers. Prune.
Jun 17, 9:20 pm– Jun 20, 10:01 am Aquarius, 3rd qtr.	Cultivate. Destroy weeds and pests. Harvest fruits and root crops. Trim to retard growth.

Jun 20, 10:01 am-   Plant biennials, perennials, bulbs
Jun 22, 10:04 pm   and roots. Irrigate. Fertilize (or-
Pisces, 3rd qtr.   ganic). Prune.

Jun 22, 10:04 pm-   Cultivate. Destroy weeds and
Jun 25, 7:29 am   pests. Harvest fruits and root
Aries, 3-4th qtr.   crops. Trim to retard growth.

Jun 25, 7:29 am-   Plant potatoes and tubers. Prune.
Jun 27, 1:15 pm
Taurus, 4th qtr.

Jun 27, 1:15 pm-   Cultivate. Destroy weeds and
Jun 29, 3:43 pm   pests. Harvest fruits and root
Gemini, 4th qtr.   crops. Trim to retard growth.

Jun 29, 3:43 pm-   Plant biennials, perennials, bulbs
Jun 30, 6:19 am   and roots. Irrigate. Fertilize (or-
Cancer, 4th qtr.   ganic). Prune.

Jun 30, 6:19 am-   Plant annuals, grains. Irrigate. Fer-
Jul 1, 4:16 pm   tilize (chemical). Trim to increase
Cancer, 1st qtr.   growth. Graft or bud plants.

Jul 5, 6:28 pm-   Plant annuals for fragrance and
Jul 7, 10:54 pm   beauty. Trim to increase growth.
Libra, 1-2nd qtr.

Jul 7, 10:54 pm-   Plant annuals, grains. Irrigate. Fer-
Jul 10, 6:18 am   tilize (chemical). Trim to increase
Scorpio, 2nd qtr.   growth. Graft or bud plants.

Jul 12, 4:16 pm-   Graft or bud plants. Trim to in-
Jul 14, 1:07 pm   crease growth.
Capricorn, 2nd qtr.

Jul 14, 1:07 pm   Gather mushrooms. Harvest root
Full Moon, Capricorn   crops for seed.

Jul 14, 1:07 pm-   Plant potatoes and tubers. Prune.
Jul 15, 4:04 am
Capricorn, 3rd qtr.

Jul 15, 4:04 am- Jul 17, 4:45 pm Aquarius, 3rd qtr.	Cultivate. Destroy weeds and pests. Harvest fruits and root crops. Trim to retard growth.
Jul 17, 4:45 pm- Jul 20, 5:08 am Pisces, 3rd qtr.	Plant biennials, perennials, bulbs and roots. Irrigate. Fertilize (organic). Prune.
Jul 20, 5:08 am- Jul 22, 3:37 pm Aries, 3rd qtr.	Cultivate. Destroy weeds and pests. Harvest fruits and root crops. Trim to retard growth.
Jul 22, 3:37 pm- Jul 24, 10:45 pm Taurus, 3-4th qtr.	Plant potatoes and tubers. Prune.
Jul 24, 10:45 pm- Jul 27, 2:09 am Gemini, 4th qtr.	Cultivate. Destroy weeds and pests. Harvest fruits and root crops. Trim to retard growth.
Jul 27, 2:09 am- Jul 29, 2:40 am Cancer, 4th qtr.	Plant biennials, perennials, bulbs and roots. Irrigate. Fertilize (organic). Prune.
Jul 29, 2:40 am- Jul 29, 1:36 pm Leo, 4th qtr.	Cultivate. Destroy weeds and pests. Harvest fruits and root crops. Trim to retard growth.

Aug 2, 2:18 am- Aug 4, 5:17 am Libra, 1st qtr.	Plant annuals for fragrance and beauty. Trim to increase growth.
Aug 4, 5:17 am- Aug 6, 11:58 am Scorpio, 1-2nd qtr.	Plant annuals, grains. Irrigate. Fertilize (chemical). Trim to increase growth. Graft or bud plants.
Aug 8, 10:01 pm- Aug 11, 10:07 am Capricorn, 2nd qtr.	Graft or bud plants. Trim to increase growth.
Aug 13, 4:28 am Full Moon, Aquarius	Gather mushrooms. Harvest root crops for seed.
Aug 13, 4:28 am- Aug 13, 10:52 pm Aquarius, 3rd qtr.	Cultivate. Destroy weeds and pests. Harvest fruits and root crops. Trim to retard growth.
Aug 13, 10:52 pm- Aug 16, 11:12 am Pisces, 3rd qtr.	Plant biennials, perennials, bulbs and roots. Irrigate. Fertilize (organic). Prune.
Aug 16, 11:12 am- Aug 18, 10:11 pm Aries, 3rd qtr.	Cultivate. Destroy weeds and pests. Harvest fruits and root crops. Trim to retard growth.
Aug 18, 10:11 pm- Aug 21, 6:37 am Taurus, 3-4th qtr.	Plant potatoes and tubers. Prune.
Aug 21, 6:37 am- Aug 23, 11:37 am Gemini, 4th qtr.	Cultivate. Destroy weeds and pests. Harvest fruits and root crops. Trim to retard growth.
Aug 23, 11:37 am- Aug 25, 1:16 pm Cancer, 4th qtr.	Plant biennials, perennials, bulbs and roots. Irrigate. Fertilize (organic). Prune.
Aug 25, 1:16 pm- Aug 27, 12:47 pm Leo, 4th qtr.	Cultivate. Destroy weeds and pests. Harvest fruits and root crops. Trim to retard growth.

Aug 27, 12:47 pm- Aug 27, 8:43 pm Virgo, 4th qtr.	Cultivate, especially medicinal plants. Destroy weeds and pests. Trim to retard growth.
Aug 29, 12:12 pm- Aug 31, 1:39 pm Libra, 1st qtr.	Plant annuals for fragrance and beauty. Trim to increase growth.
Aug 31, 1:39 pm- Sep 2, 6:51 pm Scorpio, 1st qtr.	Plant annuals, grains. Irrigate. Fertilize (chemical). Trim to increase growth. Graft or bud plants.

Sep 5, 4:07 am- Sep 7, 4:09 pm Capricorn, 2nd qtr.	Graft or bud plants. Trim to increase growth.
Sep 10, 4:57 am- Sep 11, 8:17 pm Pisces, 2nd qtr.	Plant annuals, grains. Irrigate. Fertilize (chemical). Trim to increase growth. Graft or bud plants.
Sep 11, 8:17 pm Full Moon, Pisces	Gather mushrooms. Harvest root crops for seed.
Sep 11, 8:17 pm- Sep 12, 5:03 pm Pisces, 3rd qtr.	Plant biennials, perennials, bulbs and roots. Irrigate. Fertilize (organic). Prune.
Sep 12, 5:03 pm- Sep 15, 3:48 am Aries, 3rd qtr.	Cultivate. Destroy weeds and pests. Harvest fruits and root crops. Trim to retard growth.

Sep 15, 3:48 am- Sep 17, 12:41 pm Taurus, 3rd qtr.	Plant potatoes and tubers. Prune.
Sep 17, 12:41 pm- Sep 19, 7:00 pm Gemini, 3-4th qtr.	Cultivate. Destroy weeds and pests. Harvest fruits and root crops. Trim to retard growth.
Sep 19, 7:00 pm- Sep 21, 10:20 pm Cancer, 4th qtr.	Plant biennials, perennials, bulbs and roots. Irrigate. Fertilize (organic). Prune.
Sep 21, 10:20 pm- Sep 23, 11:09 pm Leo, 4th qtr.	Cultivate. Destroy weeds and pests. Harvest fruits and root crops. Trim to retard growth.
Sep 23, 11:09 pm- Sep 25, 10:56 pm Virgo, 4th qtr.	Cultivate, especially medicinal plants. Destroy weeds and pests. Trim to retard growth.
Sep 26, 4:41 am- Sep 27, 11:45 pm Libra, 1st qtr.	Plant annuals for fragrance and beauty. Trim to increase growth.
Sep 27, 11:45 pm- Sep 30, 3:34 am Scorpio, 1st qtr.	Plant annuals, grains. Irrigate. Fertilize (chemical). Trim to increase growth. Graft or bud plants.
Oct 2, 11:30 am- Oct 4, 10:54 pm Capricorn, 1-2nd qtr.	Graft or bud plants. Trim to increase growth.
Oct 7, 11:38 am- Oct 9, 11:37 pm Pisces, 2nd qtr.	Plant annuals, grains. Irrigate. Fertilize (chemical). Trim to increase growth. Graft or bud plants.
Oct 11, 12:04 pm Full Moon, Aries	Gather mushrooms. Harvest root crops for seed.
Oct 11, 12:04 pm- Oct 12, 9:49 am Aries, 3rd qtr.	Cultivate. Destroy weeds and pests. Harvest fruits and root crops. Trim to retard growth.

Oct 12, 9:49 am–
Oct 14, 6:09 pm
Taurus, 3rd qtr.

Plant potatoes and tubers. Prune.

Oct 14, 6:09 pm–
Oct 17, 0:37 am
Gemini, 3rd qtr.

Cultivate. Destroy weeds and pests. Harvest fruits and root crops. Trim to retard growth.

Oct 17, 0:37 am–
Oct 19, 5:02 am
Cancer, 3–4th qtr.

Plant biennials, perennials, bulbs and roots. Irrigate. Fertilize (organic). Prune.

Oct 19, 5:02 am–
Oct 21, 7:29 am
Leo, 4th qtr.

Cultivate. Destroy weeds and pests. Harvest fruits and root crops. Trim to retard growth.

Oct 21, 7:29 am–
Oct 23, 8:40 am
Virgo, 4th qtr.

Cultivate, especially medicinal plants. Destroy weeds and pests. Trim to retard growth.

Oct 25, 10:05 am–
Oct 25, 2:35 pm
Scorpio, 4th qtr.

Plant biennials, perennials, bulbs and roots. Irrigate. Fertilize (organic). Prune.

Oct 25, 2:35 pm–
Oct 27, 1:30 pm
Scorpio, 1st qtr.

Plant annuals, grains. Irrigate. Fertilize (chemical). Trim to increase growth. Graft or bud plants.

Oct 29, 8:19 pm- Nov 1, 6:44 am Capricorn, 1st qtr.	Graft or bud plants. Trim to increase growth.
Nov 3, 7:13 pm- Nov 6, 7:20 am Pisces, 2nd qtr.	Plant annuals, grains. Irrigate. Fertilize (chemical). Trim to increase growth. Graft or bud plants.
Nov 8, 5:20 pm- Nov 10, 3:21 am Taurus, 2nd qtr.	Plant annuals for hardiness. Trim to increase growth.
Nov 10, 3:21 am Full Moon, Taurus	Gather mushrooms. Harvest root crops for seed.
Nov 10, 3:21 am- Nov 11, 0:50 am Taurus, 3rd qtr.	Plant potatoes and tubers. Prune.
Nov 11, 0:50 am- Nov 13, 6:20 am Gemini, 3rd qtr.	Cultivate. Destroy weeds and pests. Harvest fruits and root crops. Trim to retard growth.
Nov 13, 6:20 am- Nov 15, 10:24 am Cancer, 3rd qtr.	Plant biennials, perennials, bulbs and roots. Irrigate. Fertilize (organic). Prune.
Nov 15, 10:24 am- Nov 17, 1:29 pm Leo, 3-4th qtr.	Cultivate. Destroy weeds and pests. Harvest fruits and root crops. Trim to retard growth.
Nov 17, 1:29 pm- Nov 19, 4:04 pm Virgo, 4th qtr.	Cultivate, especially medicinal plants. Destroy weeds and pests. Trim to retard growth.
Nov 21, 6:53 pm- Nov 23, 11:02 pm Scorpio, 4th qtr.	Plant biennials, perennials, bulbs and roots. Irrigate. Fertilize (organic). Prune.
Nov 23, 11:02 pm- Nov 24, 3:12 am Sagittarius, 4th qtr.	Cultivate. Destroy weeds and pests. Harvest fruits and root crops. Trim to retard growth.

Nov 26, 5:39 am- Nov 28, 3:20 pm Capricorn, 1st qtr.	Graft or bud plants. Trim to increase growth.
Dec 1, 3:24 am- Dec 3, 3:50 pm Pisces, 1-2nd qtr.	Plant annuals, grains. Irrigate. Fertilize (chemical). Trim to increase growth. Graft or bud plants.
Dec 6, 2:17 am- Dec 8, 9:38 am Taurus, 2nd qtr.	Plant annuals for hardiness. Trim to increase growth.
Dec 9, 5:42 pm Full Moon, Gemini	Gather mushrooms. Harvest root crops for seed.
Dec 9, 5:42 pm- Dec 10, 2:06 pm Gemini, 3rd qtr.	Cultivate. Destroy weeds and pests. Harvest fruits and root crops. Trim to retard growth.
Dec 10, 2:06 pm- Dec 12, 4:48 pm Cancer, 3rd qtr.	Plant biennials, perennials, bulbs and roots. Irrigate. Fertilize (organic). Prune.
Dec 12, 4:48 pm- Dec 14, 6:57 pm Leo, 3rd qtr.	Cultivate. Destroy weeds and pests. Harvest fruits and root crops. Trim to retard growth.

Dec 14, 6:57 pm- Dec 16, 9:34 pm Virgo, 3-4th qtr.	Cultivate, especially medicinal plants. Destroy weeds and pests. Trim to retard growth.
Dec 19, 1:21 am- Dec 21, 6:43 am Scorpio, 4th qtr.	Plant biennials, perennials, bulbs and roots. Irrigate. Fertilize (organic). Prune.
Dec 21, 6:43 am- Dec 23, 2:05 pm Sagittarius, 4th qtr.	Cultivate. Destroy weeds and pests. Harvest fruits and root crops. Trim to retard growth.
Dec 23, 2:05 pm- Dec 23, 6:44 pm Capricorn, 4th qtr.	Plant potatoes and tubers. Prune.
Dec 23, 6:44 pm- Dec 25, 11:44 pm Capricorn, 1st qtr.	Graft or bud plants. Trim to increase growth.
Dec 28, 11:29 am- Dec 31, 0:08 am Pisces, 1st qtr.	Plant annuals, grains. Irrigate. Fertilize (chemical). Trim to increase growth. Graft or bud plants.

DATES TO DESTROY WEEDS AND PESTS

There are certain dates, according to the Moon's sign and phase, when it is better to remove or kill weeds, pests, insects, plow, use weed killer on your lawn, spray for pests and diseases, etc. Following is a list of dates for 1992 when these activities will be most effective.

Dates	Sign	Phase
Jan 1, 1:31 am-Jan 3, 1:10 pm	Sagit.	4th qtr.
Jan 19, 4:58 pm-Jan 21, 4:23 pm	Leo	3rd qtr.
Jan 21, 4:23 pm-Jan 23, 5:43 pm	Virgo	3rd qtr.
Jan 28, 7:21 am-Jan 30, 7:08 pm	Sagit.	4th qtr.
Feb 2, 8:09 am-Feb 3, 1:00 pm	Aquar.	4th qtr.
Feb 18, 2:05 am-Feb 18, 3:48 am	Leo	3rd qtr.
Feb 18, 3:48 am-Feb 20, 4:05 am	Virgo	3rd qtr.
Feb 24, 2:27 pm-Feb 27, 1:34 am	Sagit.	3rd/4th
Feb 29, 2:35 pm-Mar 3, 3:12 am	Aquar.	4th qtr.
Mar 18, 12:19 pm-Mar 18, 2:56 pm	Virgo	3rd qtr.
Mar 22, 11:14 pm-Mar 25, 9:09 am	Sagit.	3rd qtr.
Mar 27, 9:45 pm-Mar 30, 10:24 am	Aquar.	4th qtr.
Apr 1, 9:05 pm-Apr 2, 11:02 pm	Aries	4th qtr.
Apr 19, 8:41 am-Apr 21, 5:41 pm	Sagit.	3rd qtr.
Apr 24, 5:39 am-Apr 26, 6:21 pm	Aquar.	3rd/4th
Apr 29, 5:14 am-May 1, 1:10 pm	Aries	4th qtr.
May 16, 5:23 pm-May 19, 2:13 am	Sagit.	3rd qtr.
May 21, 1:44 pm-May 24, 2:26 am	Aquar.	3rd qtr.
May 26, 1:53 pm-May 28, 10:17 pm	Aries	4th qtr.
May 31, 3:20 am-May 31, 9:58 pm	Gemini	4th qtr.
Jun 14, 10:51 pm-Jun 15, 9:51 am	Sagit.	3rd qtr.
Jun 17, 9:20 pm-Jun 20, 10:01 am	Aquar.	3rd qtr.
Jun 22, 10:04 pm-Jun 25, 7:29 am	Aries	3rd/4th
Jun 27, 1:15 pm-Jun 29, 3:43 pm	Gemini	4th qtr.
Jul 15, 4:04 am-Jul 17, 4:45 pm	Aquar.	3rd qtr.

Jul 20, 5:08 am-Jul 22, 3:37 pm	Aries	3rd qtr.
Jul 24, 10:45 pm-Jul 27, 2:09 am	Gemini	4th qtr.
Jul 29, 2:40 am-Jul 29, 1:36 pm	Leo	4th qtr.
Aug 13, 4:28 am-Aug 13, 10:52 pm	Aquar.	3rd qtr.
Aug 16, 11:12 am-Aug 18, 10:11 pm	Aries	3rd qtr.
Aug 21, 6:37 am-Aug 23, 11:37 am	Gemini	4th qtr.
Aug 25, 1:16 pm-Aug 27, 12:47 pm	Leo	4th qtr.
Aug 27, 12:47 pm-Aug 27, 8:43 pm	Virgo	4th qtr.
Sep 12, 5:03 pm-Sep 15, 3:48 am	Aries	3rd qtr.
Sep 17, 12:41 pm-Sep 19, 7:00 pm	Gemini	3rd/4th
Sep 21, 10:20 pm-Sep 23, 11:09 pm	Leo	4th qtr.
Sep 23, 11:09 pm-Sep 25, 10:56 pm	Virgo	4th qtr.
Oct 11, 12:04 pm-Oct 12, 9:49 am	Aries	3rd qtr.
Oct 14, 6:09 pm-Oct 17, 0:37 am	Gemini	3rd qtr.
Oct 19, 5:02 am-Oct 21, 7:29 am	Leo	4th qtr.
Oct 21, 7:29 am-Oct 23, 8:40 am	Virgo	4th qtr.
Nov 11, 0:50 am-Nov 13, 6:20 am	Gemini	3rd qtr.
Nov 15, 10:24 am-Nov 17, 1:29 pm	Leo	3rd/4th
Nov 17, 1:29 pm-Nov 19, 4:04 pm	Virgo	4th qtr.
Nov 23, 11:02 pm-Nov 24, 3:12 am	Sagit.	4th qtr.
Dec 9, 5:42 pm-Dec 10, 2:06 pm	Gemini	3rd qtr.
Dec 12, 4:48 pm-Dec 14, 6:57 pm	Leo	3rd qtr.
Dec 14, 6:57 pm-Dec 16, 9:34 pm	Virgo	3rd/4th
Dec 21, 6:43 am-Dec 23, 2:05 pm	Sagit.	4th qtr.

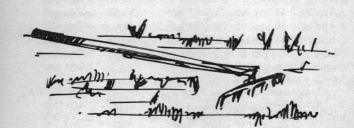

OTHER GARDENING ACTIVITIES

Animals: Easiest to handle when the Moon is in Taurus, Cancer, Libra or Pisces. Avoid the Full Moon. Buy animals during the first quarter. Castrate in any sign except Leo, Scorpio or Sagittarius. Avoid the Full Moon.

Compost: Start compost when Moon is in fourth quarter in a water sign, especially Scorpio.

Cultivating: Best when Moon is in a barren sign and waning. Fourth quarter in Aries, Gemini, Leo, Virgo or Aquarius are best.

Cut Timber: Cut during the third and fourth quarters while the Moon is not in a water sign. This will diminish the rotting.

Dry Crops: Best in the third quarter when the Moon is in a fire sign.

Fertilizer: Do this when the Moon is in a fruitful sign (Cancer, Scorpio or Pisces). Organic fertilizers are best used when the Moon is in the third and fourth quarter; chemical fertilizers: first and second quarter.

Grafting: Do this during Capricorn, Cancer or Scorpio while the Moon is in the first or second quarters.

Harvesting: Harvest root crops when the Moon is in a dry sign (Aries, Leo, Sagittarius, Gemini or Aquarius) and in the third or fourth quarters. Harvest root crops intended for seed when the Moon is Full. Harvest grain which will be stored just after the Full Moon, avoiding the water signs (Cancer, Scorpio and Pisces). Fire signs are best for cutting down on water content. Harvest fruits in the third and fourth quarters in the dry signs.

Irrigation: Irrigate when the Moon is in a water sign.

Lawn Mowing: Mow in the first and second quarters to increase growth and lushness, in the third and fourth quarters to decrease growth.

Pick Mushrooms: Gather at the Full Moon.

Prune: Prune during the third and fourth quarters in

Scorpio to retard growth and to promote better fruit, and in Capricorn to promote better healing.

Slaughter for Food: Do this in the first three days after the Full Moon in any sign except Leo.

Spraying: Destroy pests and weeds during the fourth quarter when the Moon is in a barren sign.

Transplanting: This should be done when the Moon is increasing and preferably in Cancer, Scorpio or Pisces.

Sol actif

Sol inerte

Sous - sol

PLANTING GUIDE

Plant	Phase	Sign
Annuals	1st or 2nd	—
Apple tres	3rd or 4th	Sagittarius
Artichokes	1st	Cancer, Pisces, Virgo
Asparagus	1st	Cancer, Scorpio, Pisces
Asters	1st or 2nd	Virgo
Barley	1st or 2nd	Cancer, Scorpio, Pisces, Libra, Capricorn
Beans (bush & pole)	2nd	Cancer, Scorpio, Pisces, Libra, Taurus
Beans (kidney, white, navy)	3rd or 4th	Leo
Beech trees	3rd	Capricorn
Beets	3rd	Cancer, Scorpio, Pisces, Libra, Capricorn
Biennials	3rd or 4th	—
Broccoli	1st	Cancer, Scorpio, Pisces, Libra
Brussels Sprouts	1st	Cancer, Scorpio, Pisces, Libra
Buckwheat	1st or 2nd	Capricorn
Bulbs	3rd	Cancer, Scorpio, Pisces
Bulbs for seed	2nd or 3rd	—
Cabbage	1st	Cancer, Scorpio, Pisces, Libra, Taurus
Cactus	—	Taurus, Capricorn
Canes (Raspberries, Blackberries, Gooseberries)	2nd	Cancer, Scorpio, Pisces, Sagittarius
Cantaloupes	1st or 2nd	Cancer, Scorpio, Pisces, Libra
Carrots	3rd	Taurus
Cauliflower	1st	Cancer, Scorpio, Pisces, Libra
Celeriac	3rd	Cancer, Scorpio, Pisces

Plant	Phase	Sign
Celery	1st or 2nd	Cancer, Scorpio, Pisces
Cereals	1st or 2nd	Cancer, Scorpio, Pisces, Libra
Chard	1st or 2nd	Cancer, Scorpio, Pisces
Chicory	3rd	Cancer, Scorpio, Pisces, Sagittarius
Chrysanthe-mums	1st or 2nd	Virgo
Clover	1st or 2nd	Cancer, Scorpio, Pisces
Corn	1st	Cancer, Scorpio, Pisces
Corn for fodder	1st or 2nd	Libra
Coryopsis	2nd or 3rd	Libra
Cosmos	2nd or 3rd	Libra
Cress	1st	Cancer, Scorpio, Pisces
Crocus	1st or 2nd	Virgo
Cucumbers	1st	Cancer, Scorpio, Pisces
Daffodils	1st or 2nd	Libra, Virgo
Dahlias	1st or 2nd	Libra, Virgo
Deciduous trees	3rd	Cancer, Scorpio, Pisces
Eggplant	2nd	Cancer, Scorpio, Pisces, Libra
Endive	1st	Cancer, Scorpio, Pisces, Libra
Flowers for beauty	1st	Libra
abundance	1st	Cancer, Pisces, Virgo
sturdiness	1st	Scorpio
hardiness	1st	Taurus
Garlic	3rd or 4th	Scorpio, Sagittarius
Gladiolas	1st or 2nd	Libra, Virgo
Gourds	1st or 2nd	Cancer, Scorpio, Pisces, Libra
Grapes	2nd or 3rd	Cancer, Scorpio, Pisces, Sagittarius
Hay	1st or 2nd	Cancer, Scorpio, Pisces, Libra, Taurus, Sagittarius
Herbs	1st or 2nd	Cancer, Scorpio, Pisces
Honeysuckle	1st or 2nd	Scorpio, Virgo
Hops	1st or 2nd	Scorpio, Libra
Horseradish	1st or 2nd	Cancer, Scorpio, Pisces
House plants	1st	Libra (flowering), Cancer, Scorpio, Pisces, (vines: Scorpio)

Plant	Phase	Sign
Hyacinths	3rd	Cancer, Scorpio, Pisces
Iris	1st or 2nd	Cancer, Virgo
Kohlrabi	1st or 2nd	Cancer, Scorpio, Pisces, Libra
Leeks	2nd	Sagittarius
Lettuce	1st	Cancer, Scorpio, Pisces, Libra, Taurus (late sowings)
Lilies	1st or 2nd	Cancer, Scorpio, Pisces
Maple trees	3rd	Sagittarius
Melons	1st or 2nd	Cancer, Scorpio, Pisces
Moon Vine	1st or 2nd	Virgo
Morning glory	1st or 2nd	Cancer, Scorpio, Pisces, Virgo
Oak trees	3rd	Sagittarius
Oats	1st or 2nd	Cancer, Scorpio, Pisces, Libra
Okra	1st	Cancer, Scorpio, Pisces, Libra
Onion seeds	2nd	Scorpio, Sagittarius, Cancer
Onion sets	3rd or 4th	Libra, Taurus, Pisces
Pansies	1st or 2nd	Cancer, Scorpio, Pisces
Parsley	1st	Cancer, Scorpio, Pisces, Libra
Parsnips	3rd	Taurus, Capricorn, Cancer, Scorpio
Peach trees	3rd	Taurus, Libra
Peanuts	3rd	Cancer, Scorpio, Pisces
Pear trees	3rd	Taurus, Libra
Peas	2nd or 3rd	Cancer, Scorpio, Pisces, Libra
Peonies	1st or 2nd	Virgo
Peppers	2nd	Scorpio, Sagittarius
Perennials	3rd	—
Petunias	1st or 2nd	Libra, Virgo
Plum trees	3rd	Taurus, Libra
Poppies	1st or 2nd	Virgo
Portulaca	1st or 2nd	Virgo
Potatoes	3rd	Cancer, Scorpio, Taurus, Libra, Capricorn, Sagittarius (for seed)
Privet	1st or 2nd	Taurus, Libra
Pumpkins	2nd	Cancer, Scorpio, Pisces, Libra
Quinces	1st or 2nd	Capricorn
Radishes	3rd	Libra, Taurus, Pisces, Sagittarius, Capricorn
Rhubarb	3rd	Aries

Plant	Phase	Sign
Rice	1st or 2nd	Scorpio
Roses	1st or 2nd	Cancer
Rutabagas	3rd	Cancer, Scorpio, Pisces, Taurus
Saffron	1st or 2nd	Cancer, Scorpio, Pisces
Sage	3rd	Cancer, Scorpio, Pisces
Salsify	1st or 2nd	Cancer, Scorpio, Pisces
Shallots	2nd	Scorpio
Spinach	1st	Cancer, Scorpio, Pisces
Squash	2nd	Cancer, Scorpio, Pisces, Libra
Strawberries	3rd	Cancer, Scorpio, Pisces
String beans	1st or 2nd	Taurus
Sunflowers	3rd or 4th	Libra
Sweet peas	1st or 2nd	Cancer, Scorpio, Pisces
Tomatoes	2nd, transplant in 3rd	Cancer, Scorpio, Pisces, Capricorn, if hot and dry
Trees		
Shade	3rd	Taurus, Capricorn
Ornamental	2nd	Libra, Taurus
Erosion Control	3rd	Cancer, Scorpio, Pisces, Taurus, Capricorn
Trumpet vines	1st or 2nd	Cancer, Scorpio, Pisces
Tubers for seed	3rd	Cancer, Scorpio, Pisces, Libra
Tulips	1st or 2nd	Libra, Virgo
Turnips	3rd	Cancer, Scorpio, Pisces, Taurus, Capricorn, Libra
Valerian	1st or 2nd	Virgo, Gemini
Watermelons	1st or 2nd	Cancer, Scorpio, Pisces, Libra
Wheat	1st or 2nd	Cancer, Scorpio, Pisces, Libra

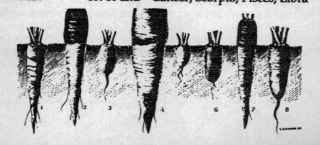

ZODIAC GARDEN

Aries (Mars): aloe, arum, bayberry, cayenne, cowslip, crowfoot, garlic, hemp, holly, hops, juniper, leeks, marjoram, mustard, onions, peppermint, thistle.

Taurus (Venus and Earth): alder, asparagus, beans, coltsfoot, lovage, mint, poppy, sage, spearmint, tansy, thyme, yarrow.

Gemini (Mercury): anise, bittersweet, cabbage, caraway, celery, fern, lily of the valley, parsley, valerian.

Cancer (Moon): chickweed, cucumbers, flax, geraniums, honeysuckle, hyssop, jasmine, lemon balm, lettuce, melons, mushrooms, pumpkins, turnips, wintergreen.

Leo (Sun): almond, angelica, bay, borage, bugloss, celandine, chamomile, citrus, cowslip, heliotrope, marigold, mistletoe, olive, peony, poppy, rue, saffron, St. Johnswort, sunflower.

Virgo (Mercury): artemisia, cabbage, caraway, carrots, celery, cornflower, fennel, hazlenut, lavender, myrtle.

Libra (Venus): asparagus, beans, cloves, daisies, feverfew, orchids, pennyroyal, thyme, violets.

Scorpio (Pluto): basil, blackberry, heather, horehound, horseradish, witch hazel, wormwood.

Sagittarius (Jupiter): agrimony, balm, borage, carnations, clover, dandelions, dock, pinks, sage, tomatoes, wallflowers.

Capricorn (Saturn): aconite, beets, comfrey, flaxseed, heartsease (Viola Wittrockiana tricolor), horsetail grass, ivy, pansies, plantain, shepherd's purse, spinach, wintergreen.

Aquarius (Saturn/Uranus): coltsfoot, grapes, marigold, marsh mallow, pears, primrose, snakeroot, sorrel, southernwood, valerian.

Pisces (Jupiter/Neptune): chamomile, Irish moss, liverwort, mint, sea mosses and other water plants, verbena, wormwood.

COMPANION PLANTING

VEGETABLE	HELPER	HINDERED BY
Asparagus	tomatoes, parsley, basil	
Beans	carrots, cucumbers, cabbage, beets, corn	onions, glads
Bush Beans	cucumbers, cabbage, strawberries	fennel, onions
Beets	onions, cabbage, lettuce	pale beans
Cabbage family	beets, potatoes, onions, celery	strawberries, tomatoes
Carrots	peas, lettuce, chives, radishes, leeks, onions	dill
Celery	leeks, bush beans	
Chives		beans
Corn	potatoes, beans, peas, melons, squash, pumpkins, cucumbers	
Cucumbers	beans, cabbage, radish, sunflowers, lettuce	potatoes, aromatic herbs
Eggplant	beans	
Lettuce	strawberries, carrots	
Melons	morning glories	
Onions, Leeks	beets, chamomile, carrots, lettuce	peas, beans
Garlic	summer savory	
Peas	radish, carrots, corn, cucumbers, beans, turnips	onions
Potatoes	beans, corn, peas, cabbage, hemp, cucumbers	sunflowers
Radishes	peas, lettuce, nasturtium, cucumber	hyssop
Spinach	strawberries	
Squash, Pumpkins	nasturtium, corn	potatoes
Tomatoes	asparagus, parsley, chives, onions, carrots, marigold, nasturtium	dill, cabbage, fennel
Turnips	peas, beans	

HERB	COMPANIONS AND USES
Anise	Coriander
Basil	Tomatoes, dislikes rue, repels flies & mosq.
Borage	Tomatoes and squash
Buttercups	Clover hinders delphiniums, peonies, monkshood, columbines and others of this family.
Chamomile	In small amounts it helps peppermint, wheat, onions, cabbage; destructive in large amounts. Makes spray for damping off.
Catnip	Repels flea beetle
Chervil	Radishes
Chives	Carrots. Spray against apple scab, powdery mildew.
Coriander	Hinders seed formation in fennel.
Cosmos	Repels corn earworm
Dill	Cabbage. Hinders carrots & tomatoes
Fennel	Disliked by all garden plants
Garlic	Aids vetch, roses, hinders peas and beans
Hemp	Beneficial as a neighbor to most plants.
Horseradish	Repels potato bugs
Horsetail	Makes fungicide spray
Hyssop	Attracts cabbage fly away from cabbages. Harmful to radishes.
Lovage	Improves hardiness and flavor of neighbors
Marigold	Pest repellent. Use against Mexican bean beetles, nematodes. Makes spray.
Mint	Repels ants, flea beetles, cabbage worm butterflies.
Morning Glories	Corn. Helps melon germination.
Nasturtium	Cabbage, cucumbers, squash, melons, Deters aphids, squash bugs, pumpkin beetles.
Nettles	Increases oil content in neighbors.
Parsley	Tomatoes, asparagus.
Purslane	Good ground cover.
Rosemary	Cabbage, beans, carrots. Repels cabbage moth, bean beetles, carrot flies.
Sage	Repels cabbage moth and carrot flies.
Summer savory	Deters bean beetles.
Sunflower	Hinders potatoes. Improves soil.
Tansy	Roses. Deters flying insects; Japanese beetles, striped cucumber beetles, ants, squash bugs.
Thyme	Repels cabbage worm.
Yarrow	Increases essential oils of neighbors.

BREEDING ANIMALS
AND SETTING EGGS

Eggs should be set and animals mated so that the young will be born when the Moon is increasing and in a fruitful sign. The fruitful signs are Cancer, Scorpio and Pisces. Young born during the fruitful signs are generally healthier, mature faster and make better breeding stock. Those born during the semi-fruitful signs, Taurus and Capricorn, will generally still mature fast, but will produce leaner meat. The sign of Libra yields beautiful, graceful animals, for showing and racing.

To determine the best date to mate animals or set eggs, subtract the number of days given for incubation or gestation from the fruitful dates given in the following tables. For example, cats and dogs are mated sixty-three days previous to the desired birth date, as shown; chicken eggs are set twenty-one days previous.

Gestation and Incubation Figures

Animal	No. of Young	Gestation
Horse	1	346 days
Cow	1	283 days
Monkey	1	164 days
Goat	1 to 2	151 days
Sheep	1 to 2	150 days
Pig	10	112 days
Chinchilla	2	110 days
Fox	5 to 8	63 days
Dog	6 to 8	63 days
Cat	4 to 6	63 days
Guinea Pig	2 to 6	62 days
Ferret	6 to 9	40 days
Rabbit	4 to 8	30 days
Rat	10	22 days
Mouse	10	22 days

Domestic Fowl	No. of Eggs	Incubation
Turkey	12 to 15	26 to 30 days
Guinea	15 to 18	25 to 26 days
Pea Hen	10	28 to 30 days
Duck	9 to 12	25 to 32 days
Goose	15 to 18	27 to 33 days
Hen	12 to 15	19 to 24 days
Pigeon	2	16 to 20 days
Canaries	3 to 4	13 to 14 days

SETTING EGGS

Dates to be Born	Moon's Sign & Phase	Set Eggs
Jan 4, 5:10 pm- Jan 6, 2:00 am	Capricorn, 1st qtr.	Dec 14-16
Jan 8, 2:53 pm- Jan 11, 2:23 am	Pisces, 1st qtr.	Dec 18-21
Jan 13, 11:01 am- Jan 15, 3:56 pm	Taurus, 2nd qtr.	Dec 23-25
Jan 17, 5:27 pm- Jan 19, 3:30 pm	Cancer, 2nd qtr.	Dec 27-29
Feb 4, 8:51 pm- Feb 7, 8:16 am	Pisces, 1st qtr.	Jan 14-17

Feb 9, 5:37 pm- Feb 12, 0:09 am	Taurus, 1st/2nd qtrs.	Jan 19-22
Feb 14, 3:32 am- Feb 16, 4:16 am	Cancer, 2nd qtr.	Jan 24-26
Mar 4, 7:23 am- Mar 5, 2:08 pm	Pisces, 1st qtr.	Feb 12-13
Mar 7, 11:06 pm- Mar 10, 6:04 am	Taurus, 1st qtr.	Feb 15-18
Mar 12, 10:51 am- Mar 14, 1:21 pm	Cancer, 2nd qtr.	Feb 20-22
Apr 4, 5:19 am- Apr 6, 11:34 am	Taurus, 1st qtr.	Mar 14-16
Apr 8, 4:19 pm- Apr 10, 7:47 pm	Cancer, 1st/2nd qtrs.	Mar 18-20
Apr 15, 0:11 am- Apr 16, 10:43 pm	Libra, 2nd qtr.	Mar 25-26
May 2, 11:45 am- May 3, 6:29 pm	Taurus, 1st qtr.	Apr 11-12
May 5, 10:11 pm- May 8, 1:08 am	Cancer, 1st qtr.	Apr 14-17
May 12, 7:06 am- May 14, 11:16 am	Libra, 2nd qtr.	Apr 21-23
May 14, 11:16 am- May 16, 10:04 am	Scorpio, 2nd qtr.	Apr 23-25
Jun 2, 5:59 am- Jun 4, 7:36 am	Cancer, 1st qtr.	May 12-14
Jun 8, 12:34 pm- Jun 10, 5:28 pm	Libra, 2nd qtr.	May 18-20
Jun 10, 5:28 pm- Jun 13, 0:30 am	Scorpio, 2nd qtr.	May 20-23
Jun 30, 6:19 am- Jul 1, 4:16 pm	Cancer, 1st qtr.	Jun 9-10
Jul 5, 6:28 pm- Jul 7, 10:54 pm	Libra, 1st/2nd qtrs.	Jun 14-16

Jul 7, 10:54 pm- Jul 10, 6:18 am	Scorpio, 2nd qtr.	Jun 16-19
Jul 12, 4:16 pm- Jul 14, 1:07 pm	Capricorn, 2nd qtr.	Jun 21-23
Aug 2, 2:18 am- Aug 4, 5:17 am	Libra, 1st qtr.	Jul 12-14
Aug 4, 5:17 am- Aug 6, 11:58 am	Scorpio, 1st/2nd qtrs.	Jul 14-16
Aug 8, 10:01 pm- Aug 11, 10:07 am	Capricorn, 2nd qtr.	Jul 18-21
Aug 29, 12:12 pm- Aug 31, 1:39 pm	Libra, 1st qtr.	Aug 8-10
Aug 31, 1:39 pm- Sep 2, 6:51 pm	Scorpio, 1st qtr.	Aug 10-12
Sep 5, 4:07 am- Sep 7, 4:09 pm	Capricorn, 2nd qtr.	Aug 15-17
Sep 10, 4:57 am- Sep 11, 8:17 pm	Pisces, 2nd qtr.	Aug 20-21
Sep 26, 4:41 am- Sep 27, 11:45 pm	Libra, 1st qtr.	Sep 5-6
Sep 27, 11:45 pm- Sep 30, 3:34 am	Scorpio, 1st qtr.	Sep 6-9
Oct 2, 11:30 am- Oct 4, 10:54 pm	Capricorn, 1st/2nd qtrs.	Sep 11-13
Oct 7, 11:38 am- Oct 9, 11:37 pm	Pisces, 2nd qtr.	Sep 16-18
Oct 25, 2:35 pm- Oct 27, 1:30 pm	Scorpio, 1st qtr.	Oct 4-6
Oct 29, 8:19 pm- Nov 1, 6:44 am	Capricorn, 1st qtr.	Oct 8-11
Nov 3, 7:13 pm- Nov 6, 7:20 am	Pisces, 2nd qtr.	Oct 13-16
Nov 8, 5:20 pm- Nov 10, 3:21 am	Taurus, 2nd qtr.	Oct 18-20

Nov 26, 5:39 am– Nov 28, 3:20 pm	Capricorn, 1st qtr.	Nov 5-7
Dec 1, 3:24 am– Dec 3, 3:50 pm	Pisces, 1st/2nd qtrs.	Nov 10-12
Dec 6, 2:17 am– Dec 8, 9:38 am	Taurus, 2nd qtr.	Nov 15-17
Dec 23, 6:44 pm– Dec 25, 11:44 pm	Capricorn, 1st qtr.	Dec 2-4
Dec 28, 11:29 am– Dec 31, 0:08 am	Pisces, 1st qtr.	Dec 7-10

THE GLORIES OF GARLIC

by Louise Riotte

In his book *The Herbalist Almanac,* Clarence Meyer tells us: "With quite astonishing consistency the virtues of that homely herb (garlic) have resounded through the annals of the ages. They were known to the Egyptians 5,500 years ago. They are mentioned in the Hindoo writings of 3,000 years ago; in a Sanscrit treatise of Salerno 800 years ago; in a notable medical work published in London 300 years ago; in the report of a series of scientific experiments carried out by doctors in New York 30 years ago; and in the record of investigations by medical men in France some five years later.

"It takes a pretty hardened skeptic to ignore testimony so faithfully documented as that. There can be no suspicion of collusion between experimentalists distributed over a period of fifty centuries!"

Oddly, though garlic is not a universal remedy and a renewer of health and youth, it seems to come nearer to that dream than anything else known and given by a beneficent nature for human use.

Meyer also tells us that garlic was used in great quantities as an antiseptic in World War I, the raw juice being expressed, diluted with water, and put on swabs of sterilized sphagnum moss, which were applied to the wound. Where this treatment was given, it proved there were no septic results, and the lives of thousands of men were saved by its use.

Medicinally, garlic is used as a diaphoretic, stimulant, diuretic and expectorant. And it is still used in many old-fashioned home recipes. In her book *Herbs and Things,* Jeanne Rose tells us that the Russians use a solution of garlic oil in the nostrils to cure infectious rhinitus and sinus infections. She also recommends it as a cure for toothache: "Put a piece of garlic clove inside the cavity. It kills the pain and seems to slow up the infective process. At night place a peeled garlic between your teeth and your cheek. This is also good to keep a cold from becoming worse."

According to Virginia Scully in her book *A Treasury of American Indian Herbs*, "the Indians had highly developed skills for treating snakebite. And while some of these were fantastic, others were sensible, practical and effective." She goes on to say that mashed garlic was considered most helpful and is still used. They also used garlic for a sore throat, mashing it in water and using the water as a gargle.

Joseph Kadans, N.D., Ph.D. confirms garlic's healing properties in *The Encyclopedia of Medicinal Herbs*, stating: "Garlic is also used to advantage in coughs, colds and asthma by making a garlic syrup, mixing a teaspoon of the garlic juice with some honey or sugar for ease of swallowing."

Juliette de Bairacli Levy, in her book *Herbal Handbook for Everyone*, states "Garlic is one of the few herbs found useful in all disorders of the human body. It is further useful when the body is in normal health, as an antiseptic, general tonic and worm deterrent, and in fevers, disorders of the blood, lungs—including tuberculosis, for which it is a specific. Against whooping cough and asthma; for high blood pressure and obesity, for rheumatism, arthritis, sciatica. For expelling all kinds of worms, including tapeworms. Gives protection against all forms of infectious ailments, including epidemic illnesses, and against parasites causing skin ailments." Indeed I have noted from many sources that garlic is considered a beautifier of the skin.

Lloyd J. Harris, writing in *The Book of Garlic*, declares, "One clove of garlic swallowed whole with a glass of water will quickly lower blood pressure in all cases." As an "Old Age Tonic" (especially for arteriosclerosis), one should "fill a pint bottle three-fourths full of finely shredded garlic, adding alcohol to fill and take one tablespoon each hour of the day. Mixture should be warm."

Harris also tells us that garlic may be used as an aphrodisiac. "Like other asphrodisiacs, garlic is used in the East as a temporary and immediate arousal agent, but unlike other short-lived stimulants, garlic is said to create a long-lasting effect."

While all the glories of garlic, the "wonder herb," are acknowledged and proclaimed, it must be admitted that it has some drawbacks. For many, the odor is offensive. Harris, in this regard, comes up with another bit of history: "Anti-Garlic Law Lingers. There are many wacky food laws in cities and states across the U.S.A. Many are no doubt left-overs from earlier days. Since garlic was scorned by our Puritan forefathers, it's not surprising that anti-garlic laws would have been passed. In fact, garlic was seen as a punishment in Colonial America. One surviving law is on the books in Gary, Indiana: *It is illegal to take a streetcar or to go to the theater within four hours of consuming garlic.*"

If it should happen that you eat garlic and wish to avoid being a social outcast, you may try eating parsley or an apple afterward. When I worked in the auxiliary of a local hospital I found that swallowing a small clove of garlic whole, as one would a vitamin tablet, gave me a certain amount of protection and at the same time avoided "garlic breath."

the cloves

Serpent Garlic

Serpent garlic, sometimes called Egyptian garlic, is tall, averaging over two feet. The large, greenish-white heads, containing numerous tiny bulbs, each of which will make a plant, are protected by white sheathing. Garlic is a Russian remedy for arteriosclerosis. Historically it was thought to protect against the evil eye and vampires.

ORGANIC PEST CONTROL
by Louise Riotte

Back in 1975 when I wrote *Secrets of Companion Planting*, now re-named *Carrots Love Tomatoes*, I had no idea that it would sell 350,000 copies and be translated into seven foreign languages. This book also has a companion, *Roses Love Garlic*. Both books are basically concerned with controlling garden pests through companion planting of herbs which repel certain insects, by planting at different levels, as carrots and tomatoes, beets and kohlrabi, onions and lettuce, and by using plants near each other which help to promote health and enhance growth.

Herbs and other protective plants may be planted directly in the row with vegetables or flowers, at the ends of rows, or used as alternate rows. Since the corn earworm for instance preys upon both corn and tomatoes they should not be planted adjacent to each other. A row or two of something else, such as beets or potatoes, will deter them from traveling.

Most of us plant our gardens in straight rows with a walkway between but there are other somewhat more unconventional ways of planting and using protective herbs. A reader of *Organic Gardening* magazine, Diane Crooks, uses a novel approach: "Instead of planting my crops in conventional rows, I group companion plants in odd shapes in and out of the shady areas, as their needs require. This leaves a main curving path, outlined with stakes and string, throughout the garden, which winds closely through crops needing a lot of attention (like tomatoes) and away from crops that don't (like potatoes). This way I have one well-trodden path, leaving the rest of the garden soil very loose and the mulch fluffy, instead of many compacted paths between rows as in conventional garden layouts.

"For plant protection, I plant pest control plants in rings around my vegetables. Then, once a week or so I cut

194

back leaves or flowers from these borders and lay them *on* my vegetables, securing them between stalks and leaves."

From my own book *Carrots* comes a suggestion for using a member of the onion family called allium. These are flowering onions belonging to the lily family. Actually "allium" is a Latin word for garlic. Vegetable alliums are chives, garlic, leek, onion and shallot but there are ornamental allium as well which are excellent to plant with roses, protecting them from aphids and many other pests. They thrive on the same care and culture as onions and are very easy to grow. Alliums also repel moles.

Flowering onions like plenty of compost but will do well even on dry soil. Some of the larger varieties, such as jewel of Tibet, grow to a height of five feet and have a blossom head up to eight inches in diameter. Flowering onions come in many colors besides blue and purple—greenish-white, yellow, rose and dark red. The larger varieties should be staked in windy climates. Alliums are winter hardy and may be left in place year after year.

Edible onions, used in the vegetable garden, do well with all members of the cabbage family. They also like beets, strawberries, tomatoes, lettuce, summer savory and camomile, but do *not* like peas and beans.

Since onion maggots travel from plant to plant when set in a row, scatter your onion plants throughout the garden. I often plant an onion or two between my cabbage, broccoli or Brussels sprouts, giving them protection and me more onions for table use.

Toxic substances in the pigments of red and yellow onion skins appear to be associated with disease resistance. Russian biologist T.A. Tovestole found that a water solution of onion skins, used as a spray three times daily at five-day intervals, gave an almost 100 percent kill of hemiptera attacking more than 100 different species of plants.

A classic all-purpose spray useful on many plants as a pest control consists of onions, ground pepper pods and a bulb of garlic. Cover this mash with water, let stand 24 hours and strain. Add enough water to make a gallon of spray. Use several times daily on roses, azaleas, chrysanthemums or beans to hold down serious infestations. Do not throw away the mash, but bury the residue among the plants where insects occur.

Have you been puzzled and frustrated by a sudden invasion of spider mites? These little nasties thrive in stagnant warm air, whether dry or humid. Actually you can often eliminate most of them with a simple blast of cold water every three or four days, hitting the tops and bottoms of leaves. Adding soap (not detergents) to the water may also be helpful.

Encourage ladybugs and lacewings, their natural predators in your garden. If your infestation is so heavy that you must resort to sprays try pyrethrum or the onion-garlic-pepper spray previously suggested. Also bear in mind that mites can overwinter in perennials and weeds. Practicing good garden sanitation can help avoid the mite problem and many other insects as well. Plowing the garden in the fall will bring many grasshopper eggs to the surface, allowing them to freeze or be eaten.

Gardens Alive! states: "If your lawn has brown patches of dying turf, there's a good chance grubs are chewing on the grass roots. You need milky spore. This naturally occurring bacteria, *Bacillus popilliae*, infects grubs of the Japanese beetle, rose chafer, Oriental beetle and some May and June beetles. As grubs burrow through the soil they eat the spores, stop feeding and die, releasing billions of new spores into the soil, helping spread the disease which will kill other grubs. Once established in your lawn you may not have to apply milky spore again for 15 to 20 years. Harmless to humans and other warm-blooded animals. Apply in spring or fall."

In organic pest control we should always remember the importance of astrological timing. **Spray, weed, and otherwise destroy pests and noxious growths during the fourth quarter and when the Moon is in a barren sign.**

Moon in Aries: barren and dry. Use for destroying noxious growths, weeds, pests and for cultivating. You may also use Moon in Gemini, Leo, Virgo and Aquarius for this purpose. Sagittarius is also used for cultivation.

If weeds, briars, and bushes are cut off in the fourth quarter of the Moon in August when it is in Leo, they will be more certainly destroyed than at any other time. This is also a good time for destroying unwanted trees and roots.

Plants that grow quickly are less apt to be subject to insect damage, so fertilize when the Moon is in a fruitful sign (Cancer, Scorpio, Pisces); Taurus or Capricorn if necessary. Organic fertilizer is best applied during the Moon's decrease, third or fourth quarters.

Chrysanthemum cinerariaefolium, the "bug-killing daisy," from which pyrethrum powder is obtained, is one of our most important plants. It is native principally to the Dalmatian Coast, although grown in other countries such as Japan. The plant has bright golden, daisy-like flower heads on solitary stalks and blooms in June.

THE FLOWERS' DANCE
by Carly Wall

The simple dandelion plant (*Taraxacum officinale*) has a curious little nickname; called peasant's clock from way back when. It obtained that name from its habits of always closing at dusk and opening up very early the next morning. The peasants could set a clock by it. Of course, we all know of the dandelion if we have ever had lawns to mow or have ever gone on a picnic. It is an admirably adaptable plant. It is the first one to join us in spring. It will reach two to four feet in its stretch to the sun, but if mowed will hug the ground and gleam up at one as if to say, "You can't beat me." Native to Europe and Asia, it is common to temperate climates all over the world, for as we know, it is a master seed scatterer.

However, never having really thought of it before, and just taking it for granted, the idea of a flower actually doing such a thing comes to be somewhat amazing when you happen upon it, as I did. One evening after having seriously mowed a part of the several acres of my lawn, I saw it happen. As I wiped the sweat from my brow and leaned back on my arms and surveyed the scene before me, I noticed the heads of the dandelions disappearing. I had never given it a second thought before. Were they "sleeping"?

Apparently, some plants have this habit in common; opening or shutting their flowers at the sun's bidding. The marigold does it, opening its petals at daybreak, the dew dripping from its colorful frills. And there are others: succory, creeping mallow, purple sandwort, small bindweed, common nipplewort, smooth sow-thistle, as well as the common lettuce and many others.

There is the endive plant, which opens its petals at 8 a.m. and closes them at 4 p.m. And I'm told all these plants are so amazingly accurate, no matter where they grow, that there are mere minutes space between the leaves closing up for the night in different parts of the country.

Strangely enough, goatsbeard opens at sunrise too, but for some reason, closes at noon. There's an old-time poem about its habits:

> "And goodly now the noon-tide hour
> When from his high meridian tower
> The sun looks down in majesty,
> What time about, the grassy lea.
> The goatsbeard, prompt his rise to hail,
> With broad expanded disk in veil
> Close mantling wraps its yellow head,
> And goes, as peasants say, to bed."
>
> Bishop Mant

But it is not to sleep they go, surely. Perhaps it is only that they are good barometers of weather changes. After all, chickweed expands its leaves fully when it is going to be a bright sunny day, but folds up in bad weather. There's the saying, if chickweed is wrapped tight, wear your greatcoat when you go out. And the same is believed of the pimpernel and clover. Another belief is that if the marigold doesn't open by 7 a.m., rain or thunder is expected for the day. It is a fact that some plants are so sensitive to the environment that they open or close to light or temperature.

In his book *The Power of Movement in Plants*, Charles Darwin theorized that the habit of moving at certain times of day was common to both plants and animals. He concluded that plants must have a sentient ability, responding to electromagnetic wavelengths from humans, the Earth, Moon, Sun, and stars.

In the 1720's, the French writer and astronomer Jean-Jacques Dertous de Mairan was watering a *Mimosa pudica* (commonly called the sensitive plant). He was surprised to notice that the leaves folded at sunset, just as when he touched them with his hand.

To see if it was a "sleep" response or not, he put the plant in a dark closet to wait for sunrise. The plant, he found, "sensed" the sun without "seeing" it, for its leaves unfolded as the sun rose, even in the dark.

When I see flowers now, waving in the wind, their colorful petals reaching to the sun, I can't help but think of them dancing in the light rays. The Sun and Moon have been close, yet mysterious friends to all the inhabitants of planet Earth. Not only do plants feel the mysterious pull, but so do animals and humans, as well as the waters upon the planet. Primitive humans possessed a vast store of myths concerning the Sun and survival depended upon its daily cycle. In Egypt a whole religion centered around the glowing globe; which brought light, warmth, and food.

The Moon was a more mysterious figure and there are literally thousands of beliefs concerning its powers, many connected to the plant world in some way. For example, in early times consumptive patients were often passed three times through a circular wreath made of woodbine, cut during the increase of the March Moon. In France, vervain was gathered under a particular change of Moon while saying secret incantations. This was done to insure remarkable healing powers to it. And Adder's tongue, if picked during the wane of the Moon, was said to cure tumors.

As I gather the lemon-colored heads of the dandelion flowers in preparation for the dandelion wine to be sampled come Christmas, I can understand why they were named one of the plants of the Sun. The name "dandelion" comes from the French "dent-de-lion" or lion's tooth. In nearly every European language, the plant bears a similar name, for the lion is a symbol of the Sun. With all its uses— wine from flowers, roasted roots for coffee, the new green leaves for salad—and its tenacious will to survive and adapt anywhere, it certainly deserves royal treatment. I must remember to think of this as I mow the grass.

SCARECROWS AND OTHER GARDEN-SAVING DEVICES

by Louise Riotte

From *The Barnhart Dictionary of Etymology* comes an interesting bit of information. It seems that the noun "scarecrow" first appeared in 1553 and was used to describe a person employed in scaring birds. Later, in 1592, it was used to describe an effigy used to scare birds.

The New Encyclopedia Britannica (Vol. No. 10, 15th Ed.) further defines a "scarecrow" as a "device posted on cultivated ground to deter birds or other animals from eating or otherwise disturbing seeds, shoots, and fruit; its name derives from its use *against the crow.*

"The scarecrow of popular tradition is a mannequin stuffed with straw, free-hanging. Often reflective parts movable by the wind are commonly attached to increase effectiveness.

"A scarecrow outfitted in clothes previously worn by a hunter who has fired on the flock is regarded by some as especially efficacious. Another common variant is the effigy or figure of a predator such as an owl or a snake.

"The function of the scarecrow is sometimes filled by audio devices, including recordings of the calls or sounds of predators or noisome insects. Recorded sounds of deerflies in flight, for example, are used to deter deer from young tree plantations. Automatically fired carbide cannons and other simulated gunfire are used to keep migrating geese out of cornfields."

More interesting information comes to us from Beatrice Trum Hunter's book *Gardening Without Poisons:* "Effigies have long been used to scare away predaceous birds. Years ago, a scarecrow, dead crow, the decaying body of a bird of some species, or a salt herring hung from a pole were some of the materials used. When fruit was ripening a stuffed hawk was set out in the orchard. A potato, stuck with many feathers and slung high, simulated a hawk. English gardeners used brown-paper effigies of a death's-head moth to repel bullfinches, mounted so as to move

about in the wind. A hawk effigy suspended in air by hy-
drogen-filled balloons, which permit the figure to hang
high and move, is also being tested over orchards.

"A foot-high replica of an owl is available which can be
hung or mounted in a garden, with the figure visible from
any angle. Presumably it has the same effect on birds and
small creatures as a scarecrow.

"Interestingly, although owl effigies were used successfully at the Busch-Reisinger Museum at Harvard University, they offered no relief from New York City pigeons
in the sculpture garden of the Museum of Modern Art."

Even today, though simple effigies are thought to be
limited in their effectivensss, they are still used. Like everything else scarecrows are now "new and improved"
with more elaborate, lifelike creations being used, some
with moving parts thought to improve their effectiveness,
especially when combined with noise, and when moved
about from time to time to new locations in the garden. If
left too long in one place the birds become accustomed to
them are are no longer frightened.

If a scaring device of any type is to be used it is important to remember that the technique will be most effective
if operations are started early in the season, as soon as
birds start showing an interest in crops to be protected. After birds become accustomed to feeding often in a particular field, it is increasingly difficult to get rid of them.

If scaring devices are used constantly, birds become accustomed to them and lose their fear. Approaches of different types, used on alternate days have been more successful than a single method used day after day.

Noisemakers are most effective used at daybreak,
during the first hours when birds ordinarily start feeding,
after their arrival from roosting at night. Keeping them out
of a field is far easier than frightening them away after they
start to feed. Having settled down they are hard to dis-
perse and quite likely will stay in the area for the rest of the
day.

Noisemakers of various types offer further promise.
Birds may be attracted or repelled by call notes, alarm, distress and food-finding sounds. So specific is their language that a certain species can be affected while other
birds in the area pay no attention. The alarm calls of vari-

ous birds have been recorded for broadcasting over a vicinity. Starlings, startled by distress calls, often fly off in great disorder. These calls have been used to drive them out of fields and even airports where they are often a great nuisance. This technique also gives relief from species which are pests at certain seasons, such as some types of blackbirds, house sparrows, robins and gulls. For such devices to be effective it is important to have a knowledege of the bird's habits, and proper timing and proper placing of the recording.

Something else not generally known is that dialects vary for gulls and crows in different parts of the world and it is very important, if the device is to be effecive, for the correct one to be chosen. A home gardener can use a simplified version of a sound-scaring device by just placing a radio in or near the garden and tuning it to voices, music or even just static sounds. You might even try a tape recording and use it to broadcast bird or human sounds, trying different recordings and changing them from time to time. Birds are smart enough to eventually realize that broadcast noises are synthetic and begin to gradually ignore them. Again such noises often have increased effectiveness if used in conjunction with a visual scare device— such a a scarecrow.

Hunter goes on to describe other possibilities such as using small mirrors on the ground to discourage crows. Glass jugs, placed on their sides so that the wind can whistle into the containers, will also repel birds and small creatures. Empty bottles left in mole runs are said to be effective. Sometimes brightly colored pinwheels have been planted around homes to discourage persistent downy woodpeckers from pecking at shingles. Another pinwheel version is the addition of revolving cowbells to prevent bird depredation of cultivated berry bushes.

Birds are very valuable as insects controllers but we must also recognize that during limited periods, especially when crops are ripening, they can be a nuisance. If we act wisely, damage can be held to a minimum. During the times when fruit or grain is ripening we can use nontoxic devices vey effectively—plastic tubular devices can be slipped over grape clusters or ears of corn while such crops are growing. Netting can protect berries or small seedlings.

One crop most subject to bird depredations is corn and old-time farmers learned that a bucketfull of shelled corn, preferably soaked overnight and scattered where corn was just coming up, would attract the attention of the crows and they would leave the growing corn shoots alone.

BAT HOUSES
by Louise Riotte

> Twinkle, twinkle, little bat!
> How I wonder what you're at!
> Up above the world you fly,
> Like a teatray in the sky.
>
> —Lewis Carroll
> (Charles Lutwidge Dodgson)
> 1832-1898

Bats—creatures of mystery and darkness, their fox-like faces, big ears and wings like sheet rubber shrouding, their fur-covered bodies—often strike terror into the hearts of those who encounter them. Shades of Dracula! Let's just forget all the horror tales associated with these harmless creatures and concentrate on the fact that they play an important part in the balance of nature by holding down insect populations, especially insects which become active at twilight and on into the night.

According to James Poling, writing in *Marvels and Mysteries of Our Animal World*, bats are also useful in other ways not often touched upon and relatively unknown except to scientists and researchers. Bats harbor many of nature's mysteries whose solution has become the goal of specialists in many fields from heat and circulatory diseases to gynecology.

The bat is a warm-blooded animal while active but cold-blooded while slumbering. Because of this bats are able to go into hibernation more quickly and easily than other creatures which is why many leading research laboratories keep them in refrigerators, says James Poling.

It is not unusual to see a sign reading "Contents: Sleeping Bats, Do Not Disturb" hanging over the lab refrigerator. The bat simply drops its body temperature and falls asleep. When it has accumulated some fat—as it ordinarily does in early fall—it can live for months in cold storage, unfed and unattended, the "motor idling" while waiting its turn for laboratory scrutiny. And it is an actual fact that most scientists working with the little creatures develop a real fondness for their small charges.

Bats are exceedingly long-lived, which explains why they are of such great interest to geriatricians and heart specialists—the common brown bat, smaller than a mouse, can live 15 years or more.

Perhaps stranger still they live their entire lives on a diet of fatty insects apparently without suffering any ill effects. Preliminary studies suggest that there is no marked difference between the arterial walls of a 20-year-old bat and those of a one-year-old. This fact has the scientists pondering—just how do they manage to age without arterial deterioration?

The brown bat is a nonconformist even in breeding. The female bat is said to be the only mammal that can apparently hold male sperm in storage to be used when it suits her convenience!

Many bats mate in the fall before hibernation, but not until the following spring does the female finally ovulate and allow fertilization to take place. That's another secret known only to the bats that scientists are curious about—and something that may advance techniques in the artificial insemination of livestock. Further it may offer a clue to human fertility problems.

Bats are the only mammals with the true power of flight, bats fly with their fingers—their wings are the anatomical equivalent of the human hand with a membrane stretched between the fingers. Though they cannot match the speed of the fastest birds they are superior to any, even the swifts and hummingbirds, in maneuverability. At full speed they are able to make a right-angle turn to little more than half their own length. And, while flying, they can carry twice their own weight. All of this added together makes them extremely effective in catching night-flying insects. According to *The Handbook of the Insect World* (U.S. Dept. of Agriculture), these include, but are not limited to, mosquitoes, brown-tail moth, gypsy moth and the moth of the corn earworm.

Hunting insects in flight, bats send out up to 200

Plans for a Simple Bat House

Use a four foot long 1" x 8" board. Cut as shown on the cutting diagram, using a tilting circular or jigsaw to cut the bevel between the back board and roof pieces. The smaller angled ends of this triangular sides must be cut off to allow an opening of about one inch at the bottom of the bat house, as shown in the side view. The cutting angle for this will be approximately 62 degrees, but you will need to adjust it to suit the thickness of your wood.

Assemble the box with nails or screws and glue. The glue will provide some weather sealing and help retain heat. If desired, apply caulk to all joints.

The front door pivots at the bottom on two nails. Drill a hole high up on one side and into the side of the door. A loose fitting nail placed into these holes will hold the door in place. Provide additional weatherproofing by attaching narrow strips (1/2" x 1/2") of wood to the inner sides of the house to act as door stops. Attach a small screw to the front of the door to use as a doorknob. The house may also be built with a fixed instead of hinging door, but this will make it more difficult to clean should birds nest in it before it is inhabited by bats. Apply a coat of polyurethane to the outside of the house only.

Place at least 10 feet up on side of building or tree. Use rough sawn lumber or make many small dents in back board for bats to cling to.

Plans for bat house prepared by Ellen Silva, courtesy of Peter T. Bromley, USDA-ES, Dept. of Fisheries & Wildlife.

"beeps" (echoes) per second. How it distinguishes echoes bouncing off insects from those bouncing off tree branches is as yet unknown. The answer could revolutionize man-made electronic guidance and detection devices.

Peter T. Bromley, USDA-ES, Dept. of Fisheries & Wildlife, who has made an intensive study of bats says, "It has always been assumed that bats caught their prey in their mouths, but recent high-speed photographs reveal that some bats scoop up flying insects in the membrane that stretches between their hind legs, cupping it like a pouch. Then they reach in and consume their meal in full flight! Maybe some clever person copied this idea for the TV dinner we get on planes!"

How effective are bats in controlling insects?

Nature has a complex system of checks and balances, and many animals from frogs and shrews to insectivorous birds and bats are all important. While birds, such as purple martins, play a major role in controlling day-flying insects, bats are by far the most important checks against night-flying species, consuming an almost unbelievable number. The amount a given bat eats varies with season and reproductive conditions, sometimes as much as tripling when mothers are nursing their young—which would normally be in the spring and summer seasons when insects are more abundant and active, laying their eggs. The actual number of insects caught varies according to the size of those eaten in a single night, ranging from less than a hundred moths or beetles to thousands of smaller insects, such as mosquitoes. In fact, bat survival likely requires a mix of several kinds of insects in an area, so that bats can switch among them, according to the abundance of their nightly and seasonal hatches.

Laboratory studies have demonstrated that a single little brown bat can catch up to 600 or more mosquitoes in an hour, and this and other species have been documented in the wild to feed heavily on several species of mosquitoes when they are available. This fact alone makes a very strong argument for establishing a bat house on or near your property.

A single endangered gray bat may catch 3,000 insects in a night, and large colonies can consume countless billions.

The Mexican free-tailed bat colony from Bracken Cave, Texas, for example, catches roughly a quarter of a million pounds of insects nightly! It takes 20 million bats to do that, but even 30 little brown bats from one bat house easily could catch more than 30,000 insects in an evening's feeding.

No control is perfect, but when it comes to mosquitoes, no bug zapper or even purple martins are a match for bats. The alternative is to gamble with the pesticide "treadmill" which increasingly threatens nearly every aspect of our lives—as well as our gardens.

I am well aware that building a "bat house" may seem unusual to some readers. So let's examine some of the pros and cons:

What kinds of bats are most likely to use a bat house?

Throughout the northern two-thirds of the United States and Canada, the little brown bat (*Myotis lucifugus*) and the big brown bat (*Eptesicus fuscus*) are most likely to occur. These species also occur in the southeastern United States but are gradually being replaced by the Southeastern bat (*Myotis austroriparius*) and the Mexican free-tailed bat (*Tadarida brasiliensis*) in the Gulf States. In the southwest and western U.S. the Mexican free-tailed bat and a variety of small bat species (often loosely referred to as little brown bats) may occupy bat houses. Pallid bats (*Antrozous pallidus*) may also use bat houses, especially in arid areas. In general, any species that is known to occupy bridges and buildings is a likely candidate for bat house occupancy.

Can bats live in a bat house year-round?

In Canada and the northern two-thirds of the U.S. all bats must migrate south or find safe hibernating sites for winter. Very few species can long survive sub-freezing temperatures. The roosting species travel south like birds, while species that would generally occupy bat houses move to an undisturbed cave or abandoned mine. The big brown bat is so exceptionally hardy that it sometimes overwinters in the outer walls of buildings. Bats might overwinter in bat houses only in southern or coastal areas where winters are mild. Which brings us to another interesting "bat question."

Will attracting bats to bat houses increase the likelihood that they will move into my attic or wall spaces?

If bats liked your attic or wall spaces, and entry was possible, they probably would be living there already. If bat houses make any difference at all, their effect would be more likely to decrease rather than increase use of buildings in the area.

How can I tell if bats live in my area?

You can watch for them at dusk or around street lights at night. You might also check with local nature centers or pest control companies to see if they receive calls about bats entering buildings.

How does one attract bats to a bat house?

Bats find bat houses just as birds find bird houses. If a house is well located, meets bat requirements and is needed, bats will move in on their own. Most North American bats apparently prefer to live within a few hundred meters of water, especially streams, marshes or lakes, though colonies are sometimes found up to a mile or more from such places. In some western areas they may travel several miles, utilizing only a cattle trough or other similarly small source. Wherever bats live, they must find enough insects to eat, largely explaining their preference for aquatic habitat.

Nursery colonies prefer the most stable available temperatures in the 80-100 degree (F) range, though some can tolerate up to 120 degrees. Bachelor groups are smaller and frequently select cooler roosts.

Since appropriate temperatures may determine how or whether or not a bat house is used, you may wish to consider several geographic factors before mounting it. With increasing latitude and altitude, lower temperatures require that bat houses intended for use by nursery colonies be oriented to receive maximum solar radiation, especially in the morning (southeast exposure). They also may benefit from having the roof painted black. In exceptionally hot climates, plain tops and shaded sites may be preferred. Even if your bat house is too cool for a nursery colony, you may still attract bachelors.

Bat houses are also more likely to be occupied if sheltered from strong winds and when there are no branches or other obstructions near the entrance. Bat houses hung on the sides of buildings have been most successful. Although houses as low as seven feet above ground have been used, heights of 10-15 feet are more acceptable to bats.

Up to 30 or more bats have been reported to live in a bat house, though some are occupied by only one or a few.

When should I hang a bat house—and how soon is it likely to be occupied?

Bat houses can be hung anytime, but it is recommended that fall, winter or early spring are best. Although there are a few reports of bats moving into a house within hours, a year to a year and a half is a more frequent waiting period. Reasons for the delay are unknown but may involve dissipation of odors. If this is the case, hanging houses in the fall or winter night increase the probability of occupancy in the first active season. If a house is not occupied by the end of the second year, try moving it to a warmer or cooler location.

How can I protect my bats from predators such as dogs or cats?

Take the same precautions as for nesting birds. The mere presence of dogs or cats in the yard is unlikely to disturb bats roosting in a bat house. Houses hung on the sides of buildings are probably the safest from predators and seem to be preferred by bats.

If I put up several houses can I attract more bats?

Europeans often put up four bat houses at a time around a tree trunk and arrange them to face north, south, east and west. This is done to provide a variety of temperatures that might better meet the bats' seasonal needs. In some cases, people who put up two or more bat houses at once report they are all occupied. In one case, however, one of two houses mounted side by side was used by 30 bats, while the other was ignored over a period of two years. Although it is difficult to anticipate how many bat

houses might be needed in a given area, one might reasonably assume that more would attract bats. However, use of
more than two to four is not recommended until at least
one bat house has been occupied, confirming a local need.

Do bat houses require maintenance or need adjustments?

Bat houses require no maintenance, as droppings fall
through the open bottom to the ground below. The houses
should be left in place year-round. The inner portions are
of varied widths, designed to meet most bat needs and require no adjustment.

Will bat droppings pose a health threat to my family?

No more so than bird droppings would. It is not a good
idea to unnecessarily stir up and breathe dust associated
with any animal feces. Cat droppings are shown by public
health statistics to be far more dangerous than those from
either birds or bats; although this danger is extremely re-
mote.

Where are bat houses most likely to be needed?

Bats are most likely to need bat houses where roosting
places are insufficient to house as many bats as the local insect population would support. Examples of such places
include areas where forestry practices have largely eliminated old hollow trees or neighborhoods where people
have evicted bats from their attics or wall spaces.

It should be remembered that no bats make nests or any
other form of home for themselves. Even when rearing
their young they merely select an existing site or a suitable
roost. Caves, of course, are very commonly occupied by
bat colonies for they offer equable conditions and freedom
from disturbance.

Less demanding species inhabit buildings, hollow
trees, culverts and even the spaces between boulders. Others roost in the open on trees, cliffs or the outside walls of
buildings.

How can I observe bats in a bat house without disturbing them?

The longer a colony has lived in a bat house, the more tolerant they will be of disturbance. Once they have lived in your bat house for several months, they may quite likely be tolerant of having a flashlight shown on them occasionally. However, any attempt to handle them or to touch the house while they are inside, may cause abandonment. If you would like to know if you have a nursery colony, shine a light inside soon after the mothers leave at dusk (in June or early July). Do this only briefly, and do not repeat more than once a week, or you could disturb them into leaving. Young are left behind in the roost for the first three or four weeks after birth.

Bats, creatures of air and darkness, populate all areas of the world and there are some 1300 known bat species. Contrary to public belief none are blind, and not all of them hibernate. They are not evil and they are not unclean (grooming themselves every morning and after each meal), they are simply a part of nature and often of help to humans.

Do bats try to fly into people's hair?

The last thing a bat wants is to get tangled up in somebody's hair. There have been a few instances where this has happened, usually when the desperate, panic-stricken creatures were trying to find a way out of an attic or enclosed space when some equally frightened person was "shooing" them with waving arms and wild cries! It is unfortunate that a few instances have given these innocent creatures a bad name.

THOSE MYSTICAL MAGICAL PLANTS
by Carly Wall

There's a plant that stands out from all the others because of its strange root. People of long ago discovered the strange resemblance the mandrake root has to human form. What could this mean? A plant with the form of a human must be a special kind of plant, surely. And so the Germans began to make little idols of the root which they clothed and crafted. And these idols were soon consulted as oracles. It became so popular and tales of it spread, so that eventually, great profit was made of the export of the root to various countries.

Many fables of the mandrake abound, all very old. The strangest yet was the tale of how the root must be gathered. It seems the root must be dug up in a certain way, or death would come to the digger. A dog should be employed by tying a rope to its tail and to the plant. The dog then pulls up the plant and in doing so, dies in agony at the screams of the plant. The gatherer could then obtain the root, completely unharmed.

But that's just one plant out of thousands. Yes, it is odd that it resembles the figure of humans, but what about the other plants that came to be known as magical, full of power and, sometimes, connected with evil? How did these plants get their reputations? And why would people spend their time worrying over that fact? Perhaps there was something here that I was missing.

Herbs are used as flavoring in cooking, in sachets and potpourris, but before that they had quite an amazing history; varied and filled with ups and downs in popularity. Some herbs became more popular than others while the "bad" herbs came to be regarded as mystical plants to be used for evil purposes.

Several explanations crop up. If a plant had an unusual appearance or strange manner of growth, it made the mystic list. Some plants seem to be mixed up in mythical leg-

214

ends of old, and also with sacred associations. As with legends, after a period of time, stories become embellished and grow out of proportion.

Magic

Of course, the belief in sorcery and witchcraft is closely linked to the use of plants and herbs in obtaining magic powers. It is a widespread belief which probably had its beginnings in the Paleolithic Age. Anthropologists have found that most every culture has had some sort of belief in magic, superstition, casting of spells, making of storms, or conversing with spirits. In these societies, the "witches" or those employing supernatural magic were looked upon with awe. Although their "wisdom" was sought out in times of need, there was still a fear; an uneasiness of the unknown and the unknowable power they possessed.

It was in the 11th and 12th centuries in Europe that, for the first time, witches were condemned as evil, instead of just being feared. Around this time, the people tried to rid themselves of what they considered the representations on earth of the Prince of Evil or the Devil. The Church encouraged this view as it gave them more control or power over the people; this fear as well as the Church's offers of protection from that fear assured allegiance.

Magic belief is intertwined with many religions and is hard to separate, because of its long history and connection with so many different cultures. As a general guide, the Witch of today, who worships nature and nature spirits with possible ties to Pagan religions; the Satanist, who worships the Devil; and Magicians (including Ceremonial Magicians, Sorcerers, and Witch-doctors or Shamans) all vary in their use of magic, whether using it for good (white) or evil (black), but all believe that magic is a powerful tool that can be harnessed according to different ceremonies, prayers, in-born gifts, invocations or materials gathered.

So we can picture this: an atmosphere filled with superstitions and belief in magic. Through the years, some people would experiment with plants for curing sickness, or as a food source. Early herbalists, if you will. A nearby herb garden would be cultivated, and they would search the fields and woods for new specimens and there would be much time spent in mixing up batches (potions) of new medicines, trying to find new cures or uses. Everyone in the village would come to these people when a loved one was sick. But suppose a new plague swept through the village? And suppose one of the mixtures didn't work? The panicked villagers would then turn on this person and call him or her a witch. Maybe they would run this person out of town, or perhaps burn him or her at the stake. And all that knowledge of plants would then be lost. It's a wonder knowledge of plants survived from the past at all.

Herbalism

Witches didn't corner the market on the use of plants to their own good, however. There were plants believed good, and used in religious ceremonies. Because they were "good" it only made sense to the people that they would repel witches, something they needed in the witch scare in Europe during the 16th and 17th centuries, when the sociey was going through a period of change and unrest. This strain and tension escalated and the so-called witches were used as scapegoats for the problems of the day.

One such good herb was St. Johnswort. According to old tradition, any baptized person whose eyes are annointed with the green juice of its inner bark could see witches in any part of the world and thus reveal them to the general public. So it was naturally believed that witches hated this plant.

In fact, it has been found to be an important herb for good, after all. In the Septmber 1989 issue of *Better Nutrition*, it was reported that this herb is believed to help strengthen the immune system, perhaps making it a candidate in the fight against AIDS and in helping cancer patients go through chemotherapy.

The medicinal qualities of plants cannot be denied. Ancient Egyptians were quite proficient in healing with plants, and their ideas and knowledge were shared with others that came into contact with their culture.

Judy Williams, C.H. (Chartered Herbalist), obtained her degree from the Dominion Herbal College in Burnaby, B.C. and has 25 years experience with herbs. She states, "Herbalism has come to be practiced as a preventative to disease, rather than cure, although plants are used that way also. But the main thrust of herbalism today is to balance the body's vital forces.

"You see, plants have always been used by mankind; for food, health, beauty. And we use these plants today as ingredients in medicines, and beauty products. My interest in herbalism has helped me in my spiritual growth. It's made me aware of nature and how we are all connected—the animals, the earth, humankind, we all depend upon each other to survive. And we are the care-takers, so we must protect the environment. Not only for the other creatures, but our sakes as well. I follow a great deal the teaching of the American Indian, and their heritage. They lived close to nature and knew a great deal about plants and how to use them for good."

Dualism

From earliest times, it seems, humankind has worshipped or paid honor to the plant kingdom or found great significance in it. The strange thing is, I discovered that plants with strong magical connotations were also believed to act against witches, sort of like a counter-charm. In the book *Demonology and Devil Lore* by Moncure Daniel Conway (an American clergyman and author of over 70 works) the author states, "we find the missionaries sprinkling holy water from brushes made of it (rue), whence it was called 'herb of grace'." So although rue was often used in witchcraft, it had a double-life as a good plant too.

Adds Ms. Williams, "In biblical times, herbs were used in burials; like rosemary and myrrh. Illness was thought to be caused by outside influences. Magical properties were attributed to herbs because they cured disease and warded off evil influence, or could kill (with evil overcoming good). In reality, herbs contain either poisons or healing properties according to their chemical make-up."

In European folklore, the association of flowers, trees and plants with pagan gods was later transferred to Christian saints. Thus, Christianity inherited a dual attitude toward the plant world. Tree worship, dating from prehistoric times, can be seen as a prevalent practice in the biblical reference, "And they (the Children of Israel) set them up images and groves in every high hill and under every green tree" (2 Kings 17:10); a period around 1250 B.C. Although plants were used in Christian ceremony, the discouragement and condemnation of plant worship eventually led some plants to be thought of as part of the Devil's work. Some plants were "evil" because of the group with which they were associated. It is interesting to note that evidence exists that the word "church" was a softening of the word "kirk" and originally came from "quercus" which means oak, and this tree was much esteemed by pagans as sacred. The fact is, there were certain herbs different groups deemed important and anyone not going along with that was disrespectful (in their view) of their particular religion.

"The most mystical plants were usually the most poisonous of the herbs," Ms. Williams says. "Every herb has magical properties attributed to them and the herbal practitioners of old might have promoted this thought because it would have given them power in society; as witch doctors, priests of mystical knowledge or just sorcerers to be feared. But the fact remains that if the herb had the power to kill, it was feared."

The Deadly Mix

Of all the herbs associated with magic, there are a few that have just such a reputation: belladonna (deadly nightshade), hemlock, henbane, monkshood, rue and vervain. All are powerful herbs as poisons or soporifics.

In Shakespeare's *Macbeth*, one of the witches speaks of "root of hemlock digg'd i' the dark ... " Hemlock was the execution cup of ancient Greece, and Dioscorides once said it was so poisonous "whosoever taketh of it into his body dieth remediless... " The early magicians used hemlock to help call up demons. It was the most fearsome thing to do, so they used the most fearsome herb with which to do it.

As for vervain and rue, both are narcotic and hallucinogenic. The Druids used vervain to alter conciousness in divination through an ointment made with this herb. Rue, as previously mentioned, also called the herb of grace, is used by magicians as protection in magic circles. It has uses in modern medicine, but is a potent herb, not to be taken lightly. Its synonym is listed in herbal books as

"Devil's herb." Many legends of the Devil and his favored plants are to be found and many plants were connected to the Devil's body parts; a certain ground moss is called "Devil's claws," house leek is called "Devil's beard," and so on, but it is belladonna (deadly nightshade), which seems to have been picked as the Devil's most esteemed plant according to old tradition. Mr. Conway wrote that those in Bohemia considered it a favorite plant of the Devil. It seems only reasonable, for only a few grains of this dried herb causes a strange madness, followed by loss of memory. Ingesting any more from any part of this plant is deadly. Long ago, the priests of a Roman religious group which worshipped Bellona, a goddess of war, drank an infusion of this herb prior to worship. It was often used to produce visions, but at what price? You never knew if you would wake up.

Then there's henbane, also called black nightshade. It's another poisonous plant. It was used, surprisingly, as a love enhancer for lonely men. A naked man would gather it while dew still touched it, but he could only stand on one foot while doing so. Then, he placed it in a pouch and carried it with him to bring love. If eaten, henbane can cause insanity and death. It also causes hallucinations.

Monkshood, which resembles monks of old who wore hooded shrouds, was an ingredient in the famous flying witches' ointment. It was also called "wolfsbane" and used to poison wolves—a menace to the people of medieval Britain.

All these herbs are little used in today's plant magic, because of their deadly consequences. But it is this fatal power that started them off on the road of enchantment. Or is it? Perhaps it wasn't the power of death that attracted those interested in magic. Perhaps it was the power to alter their conciousness, in the end; and death was sometimes an unfortunate side-effect.

Consider this, witches believed plants could give them the ability to fly and visions of the future, the Mazatec Indians in Oaxaca, Mexico eat psilocybin mushrooms in a ceremony to get in contact with the spirit world, and there are many more examples. All the herbs mentioned affect the nervous system in a way as to change the perceptions of the world as we know it. This change of reality was a way of tapping into the great unknown, or a higher spiritual realm.

Eliphas Levi, a 19th century seer, stated in the book *Transcendental Magic*, "Magic is the science of the secrets of nature." These plants may hold the key to locked doors we have not even begun to knock on. Magic may truly be a word for a reality we don't yet understand.

RESEARCH

The Folklore of Plants. Thiselton-Dyer. Chatto & Piccadilly, London, 1889.

The Magic Garden. Anthony Mercatante. Harper and Row, 1976.

A Country Herbal. Lesley Gordon. Webb and Bower Pub. Limited, 1980.

An Illustrated Encyclopedia of the Supernatural: Man, Myth & Magic (Vol. 22). Editor: Cavendish, 1970.

Life Forces: A Contemporary Guide to the Cult and Occult. Lewis Stewart. Andrews and McMeel, Inc. 1980.

MEXICAN-AMERICAN PRODUCE
by Louise Riotte

In early days Mexican fruits and vegetables were not widely known outside the Southwest—the areas that bordered on or were part of Mexico enjoyed many of Mexico's fresh fruits and vegetables. These areas are famous for their outdoor markets fillled with lush and plentiful produce such as avocados, tomatoes, chocolate, vanilla and chiles. Chayotes, members of the squash family, are also higly regarded, and I have grown them successfully in my own Oklahoma garden, as well as jicama and cilantro, a delightful seasoning herb. The Spaniards are credited with introducing new and unusual fruits into Mexico, such as peaches, cherries, apples and plums, as well as nuts, figs, dates and pomegranates.

One of our most widely used flavorings, vanilla, apparently originated in Mexico as a wild vine. "Vanilla," according to *The World Book Encyclopedia*, is the name of a group of climbing orchids. The true vanilla, used to flavor chocolate, ice cream, pastry and candy, comes from these plants. The vanilla vine has been cultivated in Mexico for hundreds of years. Once almost exclusively a Mexican plant it has been introduced into other tropical areas. Madagascar, along with the Comoro and Reunion Islands, now produce over three-fourths of the world's supply. The beans are the part of the plant used.

The vanilla vine has little rootlets by which the plant attaches itself to trees. The cultivated plant lives for about 10 years, producing its first crop at the end of three years.

The jicama, described by Gurney's as a "crisp, sweet snack, best peeled, sliced and eaten raw, has a water chestnut flavor. It does best in a warm, sunny spot and stores well if kept warm and dry." Among its other desirable qualities, it will keep for two weeks if refrigerated, and peeled jicama does not turn brown. The first year I grew jicama I got a real surprise—nobody said anything about the beautiful clusters of purple, sweetpea-like flowers. I

could not bring myself to cut them but later found out that
I should have, for the edible root will not produce well if
the energy of the plant goes into the blossoms. So steel
yourself and cut.

I have also had good luck growing chayotes which are
delicious cooked or eaten raw in salads. With this plant,
also, you must have an understanding of its requirements
for chayotes come in male and female plants and you must
have several plants for them to pollinate. Chayotes are
vines and must have something to climb on—I use my garden fence. The fruits are pale green and pear-shaped. They
may be mashed and stuffed or even sweetened and used
as a dessert. They will also keep well for about two weeks
if refrigerated.

Nopales (cactus) are also beginning to show up in the
supermarkets. Flavorful and succulent, they are somewhat similar in taste to green beans. And beans, of course,
are also one of the great standbys of Mexican cookery. Tomatoes are well known and widely used but what about
tomatillos (fresadillas, green tomatoes)? These, according
to Anne Lindsay Greer, author of *Cuisine of the American
Southwest*, are a small, green member of the nightshade
family, known to the Aztecs. They are covered with a
brown paper husk and range in size from a walnut to a
large lemon. The tart lemony flavor makes them good in
sauces. Do not wash before storing, wrap between paper
towels and they will keep well for 3 to 4 weeks. Remove
husks before using.

Just where would "Tex-Mex" cookery be without
chiles which come in such infinite variety space does not
permit a listing of them all and their uses. We have the
California green chile, green bell pepper, New Mexico
green chile, poblano, and red bell pepper. Fresh chiles include guero, jalapeno (my favorite), and serrano. Dried
and canned chiles begin with ancho, arbol, California chile
pods, cascabel, petite chile pequin, chipotle, japones, ne-
gro (the true pasilla) and New Mexico red chile.

According to Greer, desserts in the Southwest are more
than just a finale to a meal, they serve a salutary purpose.
The sweetness present in a dessert has a tempering and
neutralizing effect on the tongue, disarming the aftermath
of hot chiles and spicy foods.

You might not think that the somewhat bland potato would be an item of interest in Mexican cookery but they do show up in salads, along with much used garlic, peppers and tomatoes. A Mexican gardener told me about an unusual way of growing potatoes. When the tops are well up he said to tie them together into a fairly tight bunch. This, he avers, will cause the energy to go to the roots, producing more and larger potatoes.

Pecans, which are native to Mexico, are popular in pralines and desserts and are often added to make a caramel–nut sauce for crepes. Pine nuts, not too well known outside the Southwest, are the seeds of large pine cones from trees native to Arizona and New Mexico. Mexican cookery also makes use of pumpkin seeds and sesame seeds.

All varieties of squash play an important part in Mexican cookery, as well as another American native, pumpkin. Fresh fruits include coconut, guava, limes, lemons, oranges, papayas, pineapple and many types of melons.

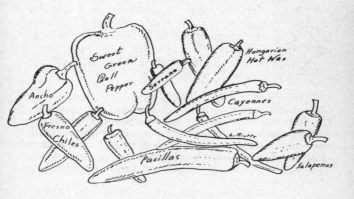

These peppers originated in South America and were brought to Europe by Spanish explorers. From there they spread to Africa and the Far East where they were quickly adapted into the native cuisine. Chiles are the basis for wonderful salsas and they often provide a fiery introduction into "Tex-Mex" cuisine.

THE NEW "OLD" BILLION DOLLAR CROP

Strange as it may seem to us now, the Federal Government once encouraged Americans to grow the hemp plant (sometimes called marijuana). In World War II hemp growers were even exempt from the military draft—so vital was hemp to the war effort. Even that wasn't new: the Massachusetts and Connecticut colonies "ordered" farmers to grow hemp in the 1600s.

Hemp is one of the most efficient plants known to agriculture—as the following commentary reveals. Certainly with modern genetic sciences, plants can be developed without the "drug" content and with greater fiber content for which hemp is superior to other crops.

This commentary was given by Hugh Downs on the ABC Radio Network show "Perspective" on November 5th, 1990. Portions have been edited for length. It is printed here for your information and for its interesting historical value. It is not meant to condone illegal drug use, but to show ways in which a gift of nature could help us in our environmental and economic battle.

... Despite the legal trend against marijuana many Americans continue to buck the trend. Some pro-marijuana organizations, in fact, tell us that marijuana, also known as hemp, could, as a raw material, save the U.S. economy. Would you believe that marijuana could replace most oil and energy needs? That marijuana could revolutionize the textile industry and stop foreign imports? Some people think marijuana, or hemp, may be the epitome of yankee ingenuity.

... The pro-marijuana groups claim that hemp is such a versatile raw material that its products not only compete with petroleum, but with coal, natural gas, nuclear energy, pharmaceutical, timber, and textile companies.

It is estimated that methane and methanol production alone, from hemp grown as biomass, could replace ninety-percent of the world's energy needs. If (that's) right, this is not good news for oil interests and could account for the continuation of marijuana prohibition. The claim is that the threat hemp posed to natural resource companies back in the Thirties accounts for its original ban.

At one time marijuana seemed to have a promising future as a cornerstone of industry. When Rudolph Diesel produced his famous engine in 1896, he assumed that the Diesel engine would be powered "by a variety of fuels, especially vegetable and seed oils." Rudolph Diesel, like most engineers then, believed vegetable fuels were superior to petroleum. Hemp is the most efficient vegetable.

In the nineteen-thirties the Ford Motor company also saw a future in biomass fuels. Ford operated a successful biomass conversion plant that included hemp at their Iron Mountain facility in Michigan. Ford engineers extracted methanol, charcoal fuel, tar, pitch, ethyl acetate, and creosote. All fundamental ingredients for modern industry and now supplied by oil-related industries. The difference is that the vegetable source is renewable, cheap, and clean, and the petroleum or coal sources are limited, expensive, and dirty.

By volume, thirty percent of the hemp seed contains oil suitable for high-grade diesel fuel, as well as aircraft engine and precision machine oil. Henry Ford's experiments with methanol promised cheap, readily renewable fuel, and if you think methanol means compromise, you should know that many modern race cars run on methanol.

About the time Ford was making biomass methanol, a mechanical device to strip the outer fibers of the hemp plant appeared on the market. These machines could turn hemp into paper and fabrics, quickly and cheaply. Hemp paper is superior to wood paper. The first two drafts of the U.S. Constitution were written on hemp paper. The final draft is on animal skin. Hemp paper contains no dioxins, or other toxic residue, and a single acre of hemp can produce the same amount of paper as four acres of trees. The trees take twenty years to harvest and hemp takes a single season. In warm climates hemp can be harvested two, even three times a year. It also grows in bad soil and restores the nutrients.

Hemp fiber-stripping machines were bad news to the Hearst Paper Manufacturing Division, and a host of other natural resource firms. Coincidentally, the DuPont chemical company had, in 1937, been granted a patent on a sulfuric-acid process to make paper from wood pulp. At the time, DuPont predicted their sulfuric-acid process would account for eighty-percent of their business for the next fifty years. Hemp, once a mainstay of American agriculture, became a threat to a handful of corporate giants.

To stifle the commercial threat hemp posed to timber interests, William Randolph Hearst began referring to hemp in his newspapers by its Spanish name "marijuana." This did two things: it associated the plant with Mexicans and played on racist fears, and it mislead the public into thinking that marijuana and hemp were different plants.

Nobody was afraid of hemp. It had been cultivated, processed into useable goods, consumed as medicine, and burned in oil lamps for hundreds of years. But after a campaign to discredit hemp in the Hearst newspapers, Americans became afraid of something called "marijuana." By 1937 the Marijuana Tax Act was passed which marked the beginning of the end of the hemp industry. In 1990, the flagship Hearst paper, the *San Francisco Examiner*, came out for complete legalization.

In 1938, *Popular Mechanics* ran an article about marijuana called "New Billion-Dollar Crop." It was the first time the words "Billion-Dollar" were used to describe a U.S. agricultural product.

Popular Mechanics said, "... a machine has been invented which solves a problem more than 6,000 years old ... The machine ... (is designed to remove) the fiber-bearing cortex from the rest of the stalk, making hemp fiber available for use without a prohibitive amount of human labor. Hemp is the standard fiber of the world. It has great tensile strength and durability. It is used to produce more than 5,000 textile products ranging from rope to fine laces, and the woody 'hurds' remaining after the fiber has been removed contain more than seventy-seven percent cellulose, and can be used to produce more than 25,000 products ranging from dynamite to Cellophane."

Since the *Popular Mechanics* article appeared, over half a century ago, many more applications have come to light. But back in 1935, more than fifty-eight thousand *tons* of marijuana seed were used just to make paint and varnish. All non-toxic, by the way. When marijuana was banned, these safe paints and varnishes were replaced by paints made with toxic petro-chemicals. In the nineteen-thirties, no one knew about poisoned rivers, deadly landfills, and children dying from chemicals in house paint.

People did know something about hemp back then because the plant and its products were so common. All ships' (lines) were made from hemp (as well as much of the sail canvas). In fact, the word "canvas" is the Dutch pronunciation of the Greek word for hemp, *kannabis*. All ropes and hawsers aboard ship, all rigging, nets, flags, and pennants were also made from marijuana stalks. So were all charts, logs and Bibles. Today, many of these items are made, in whole or part, with synthetic petro-chemicals and wood. All oil lamps used to burn hemp-seed oil until whale oil edged it out of first place in the mid-nineteenth century. And then, when all the whales were dead, lamp-lights were fueled by petroleum, coal, and recently, radioactive energy.

This may be hard to believe (in the middle of a war on drugs), but the first law regarding marijuana in the Colonies, at Jamestown in 1619, "ordered" farmers to grow Indian hemp. Massachusetts passed a compulsory-grow law in 1631. Connecticut followed in 1632. The Chesapeake Colonies ordered their farmers, by law, to grow marijuana in the mid-eighteenth century. Names like Hempstead or Hemphill dot the American landscape and reflect areas of intense marijuana cultivation.

During World War II domestic hemp production became crucial when the Japanese cut off Asian supplies to the U.S. American farmers, even their sons, who grew marijuana were exempt from military duty during World War II. A 1942 U.S. Department of Agriculture film, called *Hemp for Victory*, extolled the agricultural might of marijuana and called for hundreds of thousands of acres to be planted. Despite a rather vigorous drug crackdown, 4H clubs were asked by the government to grow marijuana for seed supply. Ironically, war plunged the government into a sober reality about marijuana: it's valuable.

Today, there are anywhere from twenty-five to thirty million Americans who smoke marijuana regularly. As an industry, marijuana clears well more than four billion dollars a year. Obviously, as an illegal business, none of that money goes to taxes, but the modern marijuana trade only sells one product, a drug. Hemp could be worth considerably more than four billion dollars a year if it were legally supplying the fifty-thousand safe products proponents claim it can. If hemp (supplied) the energy needs of the United States, its value would be inestimable ...

As was stated at the beginning of this article, we do not encourage the use of illegal drugs. However, there is a large movement afoot to legalize marijuana for medicinal purposes. This view is supported by many doctors and politicians around the country. Perhaps it is time to take a look at this "war against drugs" and see what is working and what is not. There can be numerous medical, environmental and economic advantages to the growing and proper use of hemp in this country. It certainly could be a boon to farmers and could help stop some of the pollution destroying our air and water.

FIRE-RETARDANT PLANTS
by Louise Riotte

At certain seasons of the year we seem to be reading almost constantly about destructive fires occurring in California and other Southern and Southwestern regions. Brush fires can be started in many ways other than carelessness in burning trash or stamping out campfires, such as lightning. In fact it has been said that such fires are nature's way of "starting over," clearing out forestation which has become too heavy. Should this occur, certain plants first cover the burned area, usually followed by small "soft wood" nurse trees which are in turn followed by the hardwoods. The cycle repeating itself from time to time in different areas of the forest.

Those who live in areas where brush fires are likely to start can, to some exent, protect their property and homes by planting fire-retardant plants. Of course no plants are entirely fire-resistant but some plants do resist burning far better than most and thus may slow a fire's progress, giving time to take other helpful measures. It should be remembered, however, that if sparks are carried by high winds from a fire, even protective fire-retardant plants can be breached.

From *The New Western Garden Book* comes these suggestions for trees and shrubs:

Callistemon (bottlebrush). This Australian native has colorful flowers in dense spikes or round clusters, mostly consisting of long, bristle-like stamens. The flowers are followed by woody capsules that hang on for years, sometimes looking like bands of beads pressed into bark. This drought tolerant plant thrives in full sun but grows best in moist, well-drained soils. It is fast-growing and easy to train and will quickly cover informal espaliers. It is often used as a windbreak.

Ceratonia siliqua (carob or St. John's bread). This evergreen tree or large shrub is native to the eastern Mediterranean region. Allowed to grow naturally it may be multi-

228

stemmed, maintaining a bushy form with branches to the ground. It may be used as a hedge, informal or trimmed. Trained as a tree it reaches a moderate height if the lower branches are removed. The dark green, dense foliage has a "sparkle." The red flowers in the spring are followed by dark brown, leathery pods 1 foot.long. These pods, rich in sugar, are milled to a fine powder and sold as a chocolate substitute.

Heteromeles arbutifolia (Photinia arbutifolia—sometimes called Christmas berry or California holly). It may be grown as an evergreen shrub or small tree. It is native to the Sierra Nevada foothills and from southern California to Baja California. In June and July it bears small white flowers in flattened clusters usually followed by bright red berries (yellow in rare instances). Birds love the berries and it also attracts bees. It is drought-tolerant.

Myoporum. These are evergreen shrubs or small trees. The bell-shaped flowers are attractive at close range but not showy and the fruit is small but colorful. Its best feature is its dark green, shiny leaves with translucent dots, fast growth and toughness. It will take full sun and all its varieties, *M. debile, M. insulare, M. laetum* and *M. parvifolium,* are fire-retardant.

Nerium oleander (dwarf kinds). This is one of the basic shrubs for desert and hot interior valleys. It has narrow leaves, dark green, leathery and glossy, attractive at all seasons. Many of its varieties have leaves with golden variegations and attractive, fragrant flowers ranging from white to shades of yellow, pink, salmon and red. Not particular about soil, it withstands drought, poor drainage, soil with relatively high salt content and thrives on heat and strong light.

Prunus lyonii (Catalina cherry). This native to the Channel Islands off southern California is a broad, dense shrub in hedges and screens, both clipped and informal. The leaves are similar to hollyleaf and the creamy-white flowers bloom in clusters 4 to 6 inches long in April and May. Seldom troubled with diseases or pests, it is drought-tolerant and may be planted in full sun.

Rhamnus alaternus. This plant, with bright, shiny green leaves, tiny greenish-yellow flowers and black fruit, may be trained as a multi-stemmed or single-stemmed small

tree. It is easily sheared or shaped and thrives on drought,
heat, and wind, as well as regular watering.

As may be seen from these brief descriptions, each one
of these trees or shrubs has something going for it by way
of being fire-resistant. Other shrubs or trees which might
be considered as plantings are *Rhus* (evergreen types),
*Rosemarinus officinalis "Prostratus," Schinus molie, Schinus
terebinthifolius* and *Teucrium chamaedrys.*

There are also perennials and vines which afford some
protection:

Achillea (yarrow). These carefree perennials bloom gen-
erously in summer and early fall, thriving in full sun,
needing only routine care and moderate watering. And,
once established, they can endure much drought.

Agave (succulents). This strange plant, which may be
gigantic, has big, but not colorful flower clusters. After
flowering, which may take many years, the foliage clump
dies, usually leaving behind suckers which grow into new
plants. Fire-retardant and drought-resistant, they shrivel
from long water shortage but grow plump again when
rain arrives or watering is given.

Aloe. Most of us are already familiar with this succulent
of the lily family, native to South Africa. We know it is
showy, easy to grow and drought-tolerant loving well-
drained soil and reasonably frost-free areas. There are dozens of varieties available, many variegated and having orange, yellow, cream or red flowers.

Artemisia (low-growing types). These drought-resistant shrubs or woody perennials should be planted in full
sun. Several varieties are valuable for interesting leaf patterns and silvery gray or white aromatic foliage. Many
kinds lend interest and are valuable in mixed borders.

Convolvulus cneorum. An attractive evergreen shrub,
both perennial and annual, all of which have funnel-
shaped flowers very like morning-glories. Actually common, vining morning-glories (*Ipomoea*) are often sold as
Convolvulus. Drought-resistant and heat-tolerant, it will
grow in full sun.

Ice plants (*Mesembryanthemum*). Sometimes called fig
marigold, these are a large group of succulent plants; *M.
crystallinum* being one of the best known and most ornamental. Many varieties have leaves tipped with fine white

hairs.

Solanum jasminoides. Sometimes called "potato vine," this plant has fast growth and a twining habit. The long, narrow leaves turn to a purplish green in mild winters. The flowers are white or tinged blue and are of nearly perpetual bloom. It will grow in sun or light shade and may need control as it is of vigorous growth.

These are but a few possibilities and others include some *Atriplex, Campsis, Gazania, Limonium perezii, Portulacaria afra, Santolina virens, Satureja montana, Senecio cineraria,* and yucca (trunkless varieties).

For those who live in or near desert areas many of these plants are the answer for easy-care ornamentals, being both fire-retardant, or fire-resistant and drought-resistant as well.

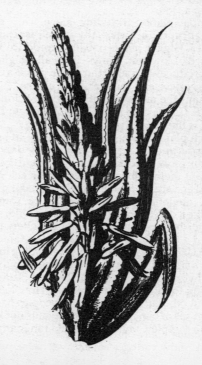

PROPAGATION BY MOON SIGN

by Louise Riotte

Cloning is an important part of gardening operations and should be given a better press—but just what is it?

According to *The World Book Encyclopedia*, a clone is a "group of organisms that are genetically identical. Most clones result from *asexual reproduction*, a process in which a new organism develops from only one parent. Except for rare spontaneous mutations, organisms that are asexually reproduced have exactly the same genetic composition as their parent. Thus, all the off-spring of a single parent make up a clone.

"Simple plants, including algae, club mosses, and fungi, can reproduce asexually as well as sexually and can be clones. Higher plants usually reproduce sexually and form seeds. However, many—if not all—higher plants can also reproduce asexually, through a process called *vegetative propagation*, and they can form clones."

Perhaps the most ancient example of cloning, cited by Joseph F. Goodavage in his book *Astrology: The Space Age Science*, is the banana plant.

"Such plants are not known to exist in nature today. The banana tree has a perennial root. The only way banana trees can grow is to take cuttings from their roots and transplant them. Obviously, Nature herself does not create dead end streets for her species by making them sterile. Equally obviously, the banana tree or something very much like it must once have existed in a wild, self-perpetuating state before man came along and altered it. When we realize the Egyptians raised exactly the same kind of banana 15,000 years ago that we use today, the inference is, of course, that the banana tree was purposefully and intelligently hybridized between 20,000 and 50,000 years ago, according to estimates of botanists. How long the Egyptians and other unknown ancient peoples had been cultivating crops of bananas and other plants not known in the wild, is a complete mystery. It could range anywhere from

35,000 to 2,000,000 years.

"Also obviously, the ancients—whatever they may have called the process without knowing quite how it worked (as we are also aware in other gardening processes)—just knew it worked." It is much the same when we use an almanac to help us with various plant processes of seeding, cultivating and harvesting. And, though few realize it, there is actually a sign—Aquarius—under which cloning is most likely to be successful.

When and how cloning came into being is not known. No doubt primitive humans easily grasped the principle of planting seeds simply by observation. In the fall the plants outside their caves developed seeds and in the spring new plants sprang up. But cloning, the actual process of deriving a new plant from another plant, took a little more thought.

Certain plants do, in nature, lay down their limbs or canes (as raspberries) and the tips take root, form new colonies—so, perhaps this, too, was learned by observation.

Cloning has been practiced for a long time under different names—my mother called it "taking a slip"—or under no name at all. Many plants, such as crepe myrtles, can be easily rooted by cutting a small piece and setting it in the ground under favorable conditions of soil and moisture; this, too, is cloning.

Cloning is very useful to plant breeders who use it to build up their supply of plants with certain desired traits. Farmers and gardeners raise apples, potatoes and roses by means of clones.

According to Rudolf Steiner, the astrological sign **Aquarius** rules the base of the plant stem, the point from which the stem grows up and the root grows down. It also rules clones (defined as an individual grown from a single somatic cell of its parent and genetically identical to it) and asexual reproduction.

Aquarius is a particularly beneficial sign when working with plants in situations involving shock—as in cloning, when a section of a plant is cut and placed rootless in the ground—and in *transplanting* when already rooted plants are moved to a different location. *Wilting will be less of a problem and plants recover more rapidly if they are trans-*

planted under Aquarius.

A great majority of plants can be propagated by vegetative means—cuttings, division and layering. Cuttings are an excellent way of reproducing new plants identical to the parent plants. Parts of plants cut from a parent plant may be inserted in water, sand, soil, peat moss or some other medium where they form roots and become new plants. This method is used for herbaceous perennials, trees and shrubs.

Stem cuttings are obtained from soft-wood (when the stem breaks with a snap) and hardwood (when at the end of the growing season or during the dormant period). The system of leaf cuttings is used with begonias and African violets and these parts can be successfully rooted most easily in a terrarium under ideal conditions of soil, warmth and moisture. Root cuttings are used with such plants as oriental poppies.

Division is a type of cutting, often used with rhubarb, day lilies, peonies and iris. By this method, new plants are not grown from seeds or bulbs, but are separated from the parents.

Suckers developing from such plants as snowberry or red raspberry are individually dug. Black raspberries have a natural habit of bending their canes to the ground and tip rooting.

With strawberries, propagation is by runners, on which new plants form at the nodes along the trailing branches. Runners are simply stems, sometimes several, which grow from the original plant and "run" along the ground. They will root easily in loose soil, forming *daughter* plants. By means of a hairpin or bent wire you can peg them down where you want them to grow. This ability to develop roots at a slight distance from the parent plant is a form of natural layering. Leave the plant until it has formed a good root system. It may then be cut loose and allowed to grow or you may dig it up and plant it elsewhere.

A word of caution about using suckers for propagation. In plants where an improved variety has been grafted on an unimproved root stock, a sucker, arising from the root or stem below the graft, will produce an unimproved variety plant and should be immediately removed.

GARDEN ORNAMENTS
by Louise Riotte

Gazing Globes

At one time gazing globes were very popular garden ornaments. These huge silvery globes were actually a form of the so-called "Witch Ball," once believed to be a protection against the "evil eye." The gazing globe is a glass sphere, silvered on the inside and usually placed on a stand. Not only does it reflect evil but it is also believed to absorb the supposed powers of the Sun, Moon and stars. The entire garden and sky are reflected in its surface.

Just what is the evil eye anyway? Its effects might be felt in two ways: either by physical or nervous illness or by a run of bad luck and unfortunate events. It is worthy to note that through the centuries this has been a very widespread belief in almost every part of the world, even among Native Americans, who also considered the color blue to be efficacious in averting evil effects, particularly among the Navajo who wore turquoise to protect themselves. The Palestinians, the Syrians, as well as Europeans, particularly in Italy, also had a strong belief in the evil eye.

The Sundial

Another beautiful, and even more ancient, garden ornament is the sundial. Its origin is lost in the mists of antiquity but according to Charles Panati, in *Browser's Book of Beginnings*, the earliest device constructed for indicating time is thought to be a vertical stick whose shadow gave a rough estimate of the sun's progression. It was used by the Egyptians about 3500 B.C. and was a crude forerunner of the more accurate sundial.

"The sundial is also believed to have originated in Egypt, somewhere around the start of the 8th century B.C. This was the first known precision time-keeping device. The straight base was inscribed with a scale of six time divisions with a crosspiece at one end. Placed in an east-west position the crosspiece cast shadows at various stages of the day, thus telling the time.

"The hemispherical sundial or hemicycle, devised about 300 B.C. by the Babylonian priest and astronomer Berosus, was an improvement on the Egyptian sundial. A cube was carved with a hemispherical opening, with a pointer or gnomon placed at the space center. The shadow cast by the path of the gnomon swept in a circular arc. Berosus, noting differences in elapsed time during the days of certain seasons, was the first to divide a sundial into twelve equal intervals, or hours. But discrepancies arose throughout the course of the year, because of the differences in a day's length. Berosus' dial was the most accurate instrument of the time and remained in use for years."

The World Book Encyclopedia gives this description of a sundial: "A sundial consists of the *plane* (dial face) and the *gnomon* (style). The dial face is divided into hours and sometimes half and quarter hours. The *gnomon* is a flat piece of metal set in the center of the dial. It points toward the North Pole in the Northern Hemisphere and toward the South Pole in the Southern Hemisphere. The upper edge of the gnomon must slant upward from the dial face at an angle equal to the latitude of the location of the sundial."

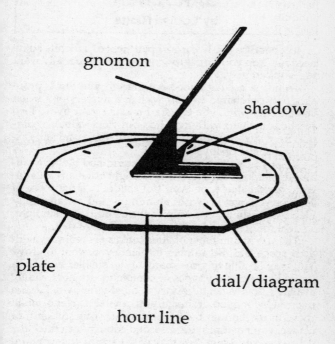

gnomon

shadow

plate

dial/diagram

hour line

A sundial tells time by measuring the angle of a shadow cast by the sun. Many sundials have faces numbered in Roman numerals from 5 a.m. to 8 p.m. A flat piece of metal called a gnomon stands in the center of the dial. When the sun hits the gnomon, it casts a shadow which tells the time. (Illustration from *What's What* by Reginald Bragonier, chapter on Machinery, Tools and Weapons.)

FUN FOR THE WINDOW-BOX GARDENER
by Louise Riotte

Just because you live in an apartment or a mobile home need not stop you from growing herbs, if you really want to—you can play, too!

Your first need is a good potting soil, and this is probably best purchased to start with at a nursery or garden center. Thereafter, you can start making your own. Two plastic containers with tight lids can yield valuable compost from kitchen wastes, layered with some sand and garden soil and occasionally turned.

What you will grow may be determined by the available light. Most herbs thrive on sunlight but many will tolerate partial shade, or even full shade. A large piece of cardboard covered with aluminum foil, strategically placed, can sometimes help capture additional sunlight, try it at different angles and various times of day.

The size and number of your containers will vary with your space and the number of plants you want to grow. You may be able to grow many of the smaller herbs in a limited space. Many types of containers are now widely available, so it is not necessary to build your own. Be sure to provide for good drainage, you can use a layer of small rocks in the bottom before putting in your soil and, of course, you must provide a second container to catch the drip when you water. You may wish to paint your containers an attractive color, deep green or brown, to blend in nicely with their surroundings.

Planting Your Herbs

Here you have the advantage of getting a head start on the growing season. Moisten the soil by placing the container in a pan containing about 2" of water, which will be drawn up through the medium by capillary action, reaching the seeds you have planted without disturbing them. Remove the container when moisture is seen coming to the surface. Place the container in a plastic bag in a warm, well-lighted location or under fluorescent lights, but not in direct sunlight, until the seeds germinate. During this time make sure the growing medium stays moist.

When the seeds have germinated, remove the plastic covering and place the container where it will receive light. When the seedlings develop two true leaves they are ready for transplanting into small pots or wider spacing in flats. The new containers should be filled with a slightly richer mix than for seed sowing.

Seeding is not the only method of propagating herbs, cuttings can be taken any time during the spring and summer from healthy, well-established plants. Perhaps you can trade with a friend. Division is another method of propagating perennial herbs—mint, French tarragon and chives are commonly propagated by division which is usually best done in the spring, under Cancer, Scorpio or Pisces, first or second quarter preferably.

What Will You Grow?

Anise hyssop (Agastache foeniculum). Erect perennial 3'-4' tall. Grown from seed, also self-sows. May be increased by division in spring. Prefers full sun, but will tolerate light shade. Dried leaves make a tea.

Lady mantle (Alchemilla vulgaris). Low mound of foliage about 12 inches tall. Propagate by division in late summer or spring. Full sun or partial shade. Fresh root has been used to stop bleeding and heal wounds. Tea made from the leaves may be used to cure disorders of the female reproductive organs and as a heart tonic. Foliage as well as flowers makes this plant an attractive ornamental.

Coriandrum sativum is an erect annual growing 2' to 3' tall. Seed germinates quickly. Full sun. Ground fruit is used to flavor gingerbread, cookies, pastries, pudding, applesauce, baked apples and pears, salads, ground meat, curry powder bread, sausage and poultry stuffing. Whole fruit used in pickling and confections. Oil derived from fruit used to flavor medicines, liqueurs and confections. Easy to grow but difficult to transplant because of taproot—sow where it is to remain. Plants are relatively short-lived, the fruit ripening in August.

Coriando santo is slow to flower, has upright habit and finely cut leaves of heavy uniform yields for Mexican and

Oriental cooking.

Origanum majorana is a perennial growing 12 to 18" tall. Usually grown from seed each year, but stem cuttings or division is possible. Full sun, light, well-drained, rather dry soil. Leaves used to flavor beef, pork, poultry, fish, sausage, egg dishes, vegetables, poultry stuffing, sauces, soup, and as a garnish for salad. Leaves and flowering top may be used to make a tea to relieve indigestion.

Parsley (Petroselinum crispum) produces 8 to 12" rosettes the first year, flowers the second. Grown from seed. Soaking seed overnight will help germination. Partial shade, moderately rich soil. May be sold as champion moss curled, extra curled dwarf or evergreen. Leaves used as a garnish and to flavor meat, fish, soup, stew, sauces, vegetables, eggs, salad and potatoes. Rich in vitamins C, A and E, and iron as well.

Summer savory (Satureja hortensis) is a compact, bushy annual, growing to 18". Full sun, average garden soil. May need staking. Leaves used to flavor meat, fish, poultry, salad, soup, stews, stuffing, sausage, fried potatoes, egg dishes, beans, and peas. Crushed foliage reputed to relieve the swelling of bee stings.

Lemon thyme (Thymus x citriodorus) grows 6 to 12" tall, and needs full sun. Has lemon scent. Leaves and flowering tops used in sachets and potpourri, to make a tea, and to flavor vegetables, seafood, veal, poultry, tomatoes and fresh fruit dishes. Oil used in perfume and soap. Foliage

variants such as argentus, aureus and silver queen are
very ornamental.

Caraway thyme (Thymus herba-barona) is a prostrate, evergreen perennial, growing just 3 to 5 inches tall. Seed slow
to germinate, best propagated by stem cuttings or division. Needs full sun and light, rather dry soil. Leaves are
used to flavor roast beef.

Mother-of-thyme (Thymus praecox ssp. arcticus). Prostrate
perennial, 2 to 4 inches tall. Full sun, light, dry soil. Grown
from seed which is slow to germinate, or stem cuttings,
layering or division. Leaves and flowering tops used to
flavor meat, fish, poultry, cheese dishes, soup, chowder,
cooked vegetables, stuffing, and sauces. Tea used to treat
colds and as an antiseptic, mouthwash and gargle.

Common thyme (Thymus vulgaris) is a shrubby, evergreen perennial, 8 to 12 inches tall. Grown from seed or
propagted by stem cuttings, division or layering. Full sun,
light, rather dry soil. The most commonly used culinary
thyme. Leaves and flowering tops used to flavor meat,
fish, poultry, game, soup, stew, chowder, stuffing, vegetables, sauces, cheese and egg dishes. Also used in sachets
and potpourri, and to make a tea for coughs. Oil used in
medicine, dentrifices and mouthwash.

Chives (Allium schoenoprasum) is a perennial arising
from clusters of narrow bulbs. Leaves mostly basal, round,
hollow, 10 to 15 inches tall, onion scented. Rose purple
flowers borne in conical umbels about one inch across in
June. Flower stems about as tall as leaves. Seed may be
saved for propagation. Full sun, well-drained, moderately
rich soil. Harvest from the base. Leaves used fresh or dried
to flavor meats, fish, omelets, salad, soup, vegetables,
cheese and egg dishes, sandwiches, potatoes, croquettes,
sauces, cottage cheese, sour cream, butter, vinegar and
salt. Bulbs can be pickled like small onions or used to flavor sausage.

Harvesting
Basil, chives, mint, marjoram, rosemary, parsley, sage
and thyme will provide fresh leaves all season but do not
cut too many at once. Clipping a few sprigs from the ends
of the stems will encourage branching, and produce bushier plants while providing fresh herbs for various culinary

uses. Chives and parsley are always harvested from the base rather than by snipping off the tops.

Home-dried herbs will be of better quality than those purchased at the store provided they are harvested, dried and stored properly. The time to harvest herbs for drying is when they contain the maximum amount of essential oils, usually when the flower buds begin to open. Seeds are harvested when their color changes from green to brown, but before the seeds drop. Herb flowers, such as camomile, just as they reach full flower. Remove seed heads and flowers just below the inflorescence. Cut leafy herbs about halfway down the stem, leaving enough for second growth.

You may dry herbs the picturesque, old-fashioned way by hanging them in bunches to dry—a clothes hanger is handy for drying several bunches. This works best with long-stemmed leafy herbs. Do not dry in the sun as color will be spoiled and the oils dissipated. When thoroughly dry and brittle, strip leaves.

Short-stemmed herbs, leaves and flowers may be spread out on a drying screen such as a window screen propped up off the ground (I use bricks for propping) so there will be good air circulation on all sides.

Once dry, herbs should be stored in air-tight containers in a cool, dry location. Keep glass containers out of the sun. Check occasionally to be sure there is no moisture on the inside of the container.

The Mystic Moon

MOONLORE
by Louise Riotte

Belief in the power of the Moon to influence human and animal behavior is centuries old. It has been approached down through the ages in both scientific and playful ways by practically every culture.

We've all heard about the "Man in the Moon," but what about the "Woman in the Moon"? In Samoan legend "we are told that the Moon came down one evening, and picked up a woman, called Sina, and her child. It was during a time of famine. She was working in the evening twilight, beating out some bark with which to make native cloth. The Moon was just rising, and it reminded her of a great breadfruit. Looking up to it, she said, 'Why cannot you come down and let my child have a bit of you?' The Moon was indignant at the idea of being eaten, came down at once, and took her up, child, board, mallet and all." The popular superstition is not yet forgotten in Samoa of the *woman* in the Moon. "Yonder is Sina," they say, "and her child and her board." The same belief is held in the adjacent Tonga group, or Friendly Islands, as they were named by Captain Cook, on account of the supposed friendliness of the natives.

In Mangaia, the southernmost island of the Hervey cluster, the woman in the Moon is Ina, the pattern wife, who is always busy, and indefatigable in the preparation of resplendent cloth (*i.e.* white clouds). At Atiu it is said that Ina took to her celestial abode a mortal husband, whom, after many happy years, she sent back to the earth on a beautiful rainbow, lest her fair home should be defiled by death.

Hina-papa'i-kua, the Moon Goddess of the ancient Hawaiians, worked in the Moon, beating out tapa (bark). Fishing was very important to the islanders and it was Hina who helped them by tricking the alae birds so they could not warn the fish and prevent a good catch.

The Pennsylvania Dutch, who inherited a lot of their

Moonlore from their European ancestors, have a quaint
legend about the "Posy Lady." This is the name they
fondly give to Virgo, the Virgin, and they consider it a very
good sign for planting flowers if you want profuse blooms.
It is their opinion that the first day she appears is better
than the second or third. It is also considered auspicious to
plant flowers in the increase of the Moon, in Cancer or Libra.

Cato, Vitruvius and Pliny all had their notions of the
advantages of cutting timber at certain stages of the Moon.
As a matter of fact this is still preserved in the royal *or-
donances* of France to the conservators of the forests, who
are directed to fell oaks only "in the wane of the Moon"
and "when the wind is at north." Astrologers affirm that
the Moon rules all plants, trees, and herbs that are juicy
and full of sap.

In minerals and gems the Moon is said to rule pearls,
emeralds, moonstones, opals, selenite, and silver. It rules
white roses, irises, lilies and all water plants such as water
lilies, water violets and waterflag. It rules the colors green
and white, and all opalescent and iridescent hues; all bodies of water, ponds, rivers and lakes, and even bottles of
water!

The Moon was thought to be the source of all moisture.
Everything from the sap of plants to the blood of living
creatures was supposed to be vitalized by the waters of life
which the Moon controlled. In ancient cults, there is a close
connection between Moon, Earth and water worship, all
three representing the female or passive principle in nature. This probably came from the earliest observation of
the relation between the Moon and tides.

In ancient Rome, silver symbolized the Moon and possessed female powers. For this reason young married
women wore silver crescents on their shoes to insure bearing healthy children. This silver ornament in contact with
the foot–symbolic of the masculine generative powers–became a triple passport to protection and to the realization
of their wishes.

As a natural proceeding, we find that the Moon has influence when a child is weaned. Caledonian mothers very
carefully observe the lunar phases on this account. This belief with respect to the fatal influences of a waning Moon

seems to have been general in Scotland. In Angus, it is believed that if a child be put from the breast during the waning of the Moon, it will decline in health all the time that the Moon continues to wane. So in the heart of Europe, "the Lithuanian precept is to wean boys at a waxing, but girls on a waning Moon," no doubt to make the boys sturdy and the girls slim and delicate.

As to marriage, the ancient Greeks considered the day of the Full Moon the most propitious period for such a ceremony.

The rare sight of a star above or in the cusp of the New Moon is considered a sign of good luck even to this day.

It is commonly believed that a "Wet Moon" is a New Moon, with one horn or point lower that the other—somewhat resembling a tilted bowl. But in America, and other countries too, there is disagreement that the up-pointed horns mean that the "bowl" is overflowing and rain will fall. On the other side, it is argued that with the points upward, the Moon is in such a position that it will catch all the rain in the heavens, and so the weather will be clear.

The Moon was the first calendar of early humans, and to some degree, the first timekeeper. The American Indians counted time according to "Moons," hence the phrase "many Moons ago," often quoted at the beginning of a story.

"Once in a Blue Moon"—have you heard that phrase all
your life without really knowing what it meant? Most people believe it to be used it conjunction with a rare or unusual event. Others, like the prophetess Amelia Poroth in
T.E.D. Klein's book *The Ceremonies*, believe a "Blue Moon"
to be a portent of evil or disaster. The author has Amelia
musing, "For just last night, aware that a visitor, an out-
sider, was due among them this May Day, and knowing
with dread that, exactly as prophesied, a month with two
Full Moons lay ahead. ... "

So just what is a Blue Moon, and why is it called "blue"?
A Blue Moon is simply the occurrence of two Full Moons
in one calendar month. The lunar cycle averages 29 1/2
days, and the length of the months vary, so the lunar cycle
"slips" backward in relation to the calendar. It becomes
obvious that two Full Moons (nor any other "double"
Moon phase) can never occur in February, and for the
same reasons (the number of days in the month) would
also be extremely rare in April, June, September and November. With a cycle of 29 1/2 days and one of approximately 365 1/4 days, the time at which the two would
mesh most closely would be around 2 1/2 years, though
this is an approximation, and the actual time from one
Blue Moon to the next can vary as much as three months.

The Egyptians were well acquainted with astronomical
phenomena of all sorts and generally patterned their lives,
in both the physical and spiritual aspects, on their philosophy of the universe. They noticed that the phases of the
Moon occurred thirteen times a year, each of which is
shorter, naturally, than the twelve calendar months.

Undoubtedly the Egyptians were greatly impressed by
the fact that there were thirteen "Moons" in a year, and
gave a name to each, such as Harvest Moon, Fruit Moon,
and others. Once in a great while a "Blue Moon" showed
up as the thirteenth Moon, which was occasion for great
rejoicing when this rare event combined with the lucky
thirteenth month.

A "Blue Moon" is an astral oddity, which, owing to unusual conditions in the upper atmosphere, gives the Moon
the appearance of being blue or green. Blue was the favorite color of the Egyptians, which made them feel even
more strongly that a thirteenth "Blue Moon" was a most

auspicious manifestation. To the Egyptian Moon-gazers of ancient times, the thirteenth Moon was generally called a "Blue Moon" whether or not it was blue, it was simply synonymous with the thirteenth Moon, as a manifestation of the year's complete cycle.

In north temperate latitudes, the Full Moons of September and October are popularly called "Harvest Moons." But to be exact, the Harvest Moon appears at the time of the Autumn Equinox, approximately between the 15th and 20th of September. Some country folk, however, think the October Full Moon is the real Harvest Moon. After the harvesting was over, the next Full Moon was generally called the "Hunter's Moon," because now, in autumn, the work being over, farmers could enjoy their leisure by hunting.

Much Moonlore is scientifically provable, other beliefs would seem to be true, though sometimes difficult to explain, because they have been repeatedly experienced by so many people. Still others may be considered simply in the spirit of fun—interesting to know about as conversation pieces to startle or amuse.

Scientists are beginning to learn, for instance, that the season, even the month of birth, can make a dramatic difference in physique, and mental and emotional attitudes. The lunar phase at birth often makes the difference between introversion and extroversion.

According to your personal lunar cycle, there are times when you cannot succeed at any undertaking, regardless of detailed planning or positive thinking. On the other hand, if you choose the right time to act, you are virtually assured of success. Those who are accustomed to using the Lunar Aspectarian Dates (favorable and unfavorable days) in the *Moon Sign Book*, know just how valuable this knowledge can be in planning your timing and making your decisions.

You can plant a garden, mow your lawn, trim your shrubs or even have your hair cut at the proper phase of the Moon. It results in thicker growth. At the wrong time during the lunar phase, such activities have the opposite effect. Any activity has a greater chance of success when undertaken as the Moon increases in light (from New to Full Moon). With every Full Moon, Nature reaches a crescendo of activity. It's a regular cycle.

Careful observers living by the lunar calendar have noticed certain periodic effects of great importance in daily life. Because we now live exclusively by solar timing, we have been ignoring potentially life-saving information.

It has been demonstrated that at the New and Full Moon our moods will change. If we are tense, our pulse quickens. If we are cut, we bleed more freely. These latter two effects have been seen in ordinary individuals, and with wide statistical bases.

Folk tradition has it that castration of farm animals is dangerous during the Full Moon because of excessive bleeding. In an ancient Jewish tradition, the practice of bleeding patients for medical purposes was limited according to the phases of the Moon. The Talmud states that certain days on the Hebrew lunar calendar that match roughly with the New and Full Moon are too dangerous for bloodletting.

Confronted with the evidence of increased bleeding in surgical patients at times of the New and Full Moon, it must be asked, What is the mechanism responsible? The answer to this difficult question is speculative, and in accord with the theory of biological tides. Blood vessels and cells have semipermeable membranes. Body water passes freely back and forth among the fluid compartments. In a biological high tide situation, bloating and tissue tension make it necessary to establish a new equilibrium among the fluid compartments of the body. It is likely that water under increased pressure will be re-absorbed into the circulatory system, resulting in increased blood volume and higher blood pressure. People with bleeding ulcers or with weak, delicate blood vessels may then tend to have spontaneous hemorrhages because of the sudden rise in volume and pressure. This knowledge is of practical use in timing a date for surgery, because patients may have more of a bleeding tendency at these times.

The Moon is considered by many to have a great influence on health. Richard Mead, a prominent eighteenth-century English physician, made these case observations involving the influence of the Moon on the health of various persons:

"Doctor Pitcairne's case is remarkable ... he was seized,

at nine in the morning, the very hour of the New Moon, with a sudden bleeding at the nose, after an uncommon faintness.

"That the fits of the asthma are frequently periodical, and under the influence of the Moon, and also of the weather ....

"A more uncommon effect of this attractive power is related by the learned Kirchringus. He knew a young gentlewoman, whose beauty depended upon the lunar force, insomuch that at Full Moon she was plump and very handsome; but in the decrease of the planet so wan and illfavored, that she was ashamed to go abroad; till the return of the New Moon gradually gave fullness to her face, and attraction to her charms."

Along with Dr. Mead, such prominent men as Robert Boyle, Francis Bacon, and Henry More believed in the biological influence of the Moon. Dr. Benjamin Rush, the father of American psychiatry, recognized and wrote of the relationship he found between Moon phases and human maladies, especially mental disturbances. Physicians and natural philosophers throughout history—Heraclitus, Aristotle, Paracelsus, Maimonides, and many others— were aware of a relationship between the lunar cycle and physical and emotional health. Anais Nin once wrote: "In watching the Moon she acquired the certainty of the expansion of time by depth of emotion, range and infinite multiplicity of experience."

One aspect of the Earth's environment that is of daily concern is the weather. A connection between the weather and the Moon had long been suspected, but only in the last few decades has it been conclusively demonstrated. In 1962 three meteorologists—D.A. Bradley, M.A. Woodbury, and G.W. Brier—published a paper in *Science* magazine showing a definite lunar periodicity in heavy precipitation. To organize their data, based on weather records from 1900 to 1949, they divided the lunar month according to the synodic decimal scale. They found a "marked tendency for extreme precipitation in North America to be recorded near the middle of the first and third weeks of the synodic month, especially on the third to fifth days after the configurations of both New and Full Moon." Again there is evidence of a lunar periodicity and of precipitation peaks logged just after the New and Full Moon.

So, they finally proved what astrologers and farmers have known all along.

Now science has even come to the support of farmers who for centuries have insisted it was best to plant crops during the increase of the Moon. According to Dr. Geoffrey Keller, assistant director for the National Science Foundation, "Researchers, after poring over weather records going back 91 years, discovered that chances for a heavy rainfall in the week after New Moon and Full Moon were up to three times greater than for the week preceding the New Moon."

Here is a quotation from James Irwin, astronaut and Moon-walker: "You can look at the distortion of the Moon as a result of the Earth pulling on the Moon, because it is kind of pear-shaped, toward the Earth. So you know, if the Earth can do that to the physical Moon, you can imagine what it's doing to the Earth."

It is not generally realized that the gravitational pull of the Earth causes moonquakes, or that the Moon has an effect on earthquakes. Tides of the oceans are accompanied by tidal stresses on the crust of the Earth. When it is a zenith over a particular area of the Earth, the Moon pulls that area's water and land outward in "a tidal bulge." At the same time there is a corresponding bulge on the opposite side of the Earth. This happens because those areas of the planet nearest the Moon are subjected to a stronger gravitational pull. The Moon distorts the Earth as if it were a rubber ball!

The best known and undisputed effect of the Moon is the way in which it creates tides, causing the daily rise and fall of our vast oceans. This is, of course, the result of the Moon's magnetic influence on the earth.

By now probably just about everybody has heard about Dr. Brown's remarkable oysters but the story is so interesting that it bears repeating. Fish, animals, insects and plants also generate magnetic charges and are subject to invisible biological influences from the surrounding universe. Oysters, for example, open and close their shells in perfect synchronization with the rise and fall of the tides.

Dr. Frank Brown of Northwestern University experimented with some oysters taken from the Long Island

Sound. He transported them from New Haven, Connecticut to Evanston, Illinois, where he kept them alive and nourished in a tank of salt water at the same temperature and level under a steady, dim light.

The oysters, completely divorced from changes in temperature, from night and day, and from tidal changes, still continued to open and close their shells in phase with the tides at New Haven!

It seemed to Dr. Brown that the rhythmic opening and closing of the oysters' shells was merely an inherited characteristic—until something totally unforeseen and unexpected happened: after two weeks the oysters closed and remained tightly closed during a period when they should have been open. At the end of this time, the cycle resumed, but with a profound difference; they opened their shells widest at a moment when the Full Moon was directly overhead at Evanston, Illinois, some time *after* high tide in New Haven, Connecticut.

Obviously the oysters were responding to the location of the Moon which triggered some mysterious reaction inside their "biological clocks." And by so doing creating an entirely new mystery for scientists—for no one knows what the connecting link is between stars and planets and the earthly events with which they so often correlate.

Because of their simplicity, the lower life forms that inhabit our planet furnish excellent clues to the effects of cosmic influences. What of the phosphorescent sea worms that rise to the surface and mate on certain nights of the Full Moon? Or of the grunion (a small, silvery fish) which lays its eggs on sandy beaches from late February to early September. This must be done on nights of the highest tide. Many people gather on the beaches at this time of the year and catch the fish. Newspapers in communities along the coast announce "grunion nights" when the fish may be expected to come up on the beaches. The grunion eggs hatch two weeks after they are laid. As the waves wash the eggs out of the sand, the fish break out of them like bursting popcorn!

In the past, farm stock was managed on the lunar analogy. It was thought that if pigs were killed when the Moon was waxing the bacon would be richer and fatter, but if the slaughter took place during the wane the bacon would be shrunken and lean. The sheep's wool grew thick and rich with the waxing Moon, so sheep were sheared at this time. Animals were never gelded during the Moon's wane lest they sickened and died. Farmers said that stock born when the Moon was on the wane would not thrive.

Llewellyn George, in his interesting and delightful little book, *Powerful Planets*, tells us that the poultry dealer, too, can benefit by use of the "signs," as indicated by astrology: "eggs should be set on such date that 21 days later they will be hatched when Moon is *new* and in a 'fruitful' sign.

"Chicks hatched in new of Moon grow faster and are hardier than those hatched in 'old' of Moon. They come out of their shells all on the same day, and are strong and alert.

"Chicks hatched in new of Moon and in a 'fruitful' sign will mature rapidly and be good layers, while those hatched in old of Moon and in a barren sign will not show such good results. They straggle out of their eggs on different days, are weak and sluggish compared to those hatched in New Moon.

"Chicks hatched when Moon is in Gemini will be restless, active, cluckers and fliers, big eaters, but not good layers. Hatched in Leo or Virgo their productiveness will be only of ordinary degree.

"Hatched in new of Moon and in sign Cancer is best of all, for they will mature quickly, be domesticated, maternal, and very productive. Hatched in Scorpio or Pisces (fruitful signs) they will be good layers."

It is said that poultry dealers who have observed these laws of Nature soon had prize-winning stock and sold hatching eggs at very high prices to others who wanted well-bred stock.

What we know about the Moon is tantalizing but insignificant, compared with what we don't know about it! From the question of its origin to the question of how it exerts its power on our daily lives, the Moon remains enigmatic.

ECLIPSES
by Bill Tuma

Eclipses are one of the most important predictive tools that an astrologer can use. An eclipse is an astronomical phenomenon that involves the relative position of the Sun, Moon and Earth. There are two kinds of eclipses, Solar and Lunar. At the time of Solar Eclipse, the Moon is directly between the Earth and Sun, temporarily obscuring the Sun from the Earth's view. Lunar Eclipses occur when the Earth is between the Sun and Moon with the Earth completely blocking the Sun.

Solar Eclipses only take place during the New Moon. Lunar Eclipses always occur during the Full Moon. While a New and Full Moon occur once a month, they are not always eclipses, because the orbit of the Moon does not always lie on the same path as the Earth's. When it does, only then do we have an eclipse.

There are an average of only two Solar and two Lunar Eclipses every year. These usually occur in pairs because of the position of the lunar nodes. The lunar nodes are those imaginary points where the lunar orbit crosses the ecliptic, or solar orbit.

The sign the eclipse occurs in is of extreme importance, because it indicates what kind of intrinsic action will become activated during the eclipse period, and how that action will affect the native. A good way to examine the eclipse is to look at the mode of activity, through the qualities and element of the zodiac.

The quality shows the kind of action the eclipse will present to the native. When an eclipse occurs in a cardinal sign, such as Aries, Cancer, Libra or Capricorn, the action of the eclipse will be swift and decisive. The native must deal with the eclipse in a determined manner, meet the crisis head on, and accept it as an oncoming challenge. The eclipse must be dealt with in a way that allows the individual to rise above the situation. When an eclipse occurs in a fixed sign, Taurus, Leo, Scorpio or Aquarius, the native will want to live with the crisis in order to maintain the status quo. The action initiated by the fixed eclipse will be very slow and deliberate. Usually with the fixed eclipses, one major event or circumstance will be highlighted during the eclipse period. Mutable eclipses occur in the signs of Gemini, Virgo, Sagittarius and Pisces. When presented with a mutable eclipse, the individual may pretend that any problem brought upon him or her does not exist. The native may also try to walk around the crisis at hand and avoid it. The action here will be changeable and fluctuating. More than one crisis can arise with the mutable eclipse.

The element of the eclipse indicates at what level the eclipse will be felt. Eclipses that are fire in element, Aries, Leo or Sagittarius, are usually accepted as a personal challenge, and dealt with in the spirit of the crisis. Great growth can occur under the influence of this particular lunation. Eclipses in an earth sign such as Taurus, Virgo or Capricorn are tangible and real and usually occur on a mundane level. Money or career of the individual are subjects of the crisis. The foundations of these people are usually tested to see if they are on steady ground. Great stability and security can be acquired if the eclipse is handled in a productive manner. Air eclipses that occur in Gemini, Libra or Aquarius can bring about an intellectual development. When an eclipse occurs in a water sign, Cancer, Scorpio or Pisces, a highly emotional crisis can occur in the native's life. Nebulous matters can be the basis of this eclipse. Usually the scope of the crisis is limited to the emotional feelings. Intuitive abilities can be sharpened and used to gain insight into the emotional nature of the native.

During the Solar Eclipse the Sun and Moon are always together in the same sign, occupying the same house. When we experience a Lunar Eclipse, the Moon is always in the opposite sign and house that the Sun is in. A Solar Eclipse's energy will be concentrated in the sign and house that the eclipse occurs. On the other hand, a Lunar Eclipse's energy will fluctuate between the sign and house that holds the Sun, and the sign and house the eclipsed Moon is in. That is why the influence of the Lunar Eclipse will only last for a period of six months, while the Solar Eclipse can be felt for a total year. The energies of a Solar

Eclipse are concentrated with all of the action being focused into one area. With the Lunar Eclipse, both signs and houses are going to be brought into the picture. The Lunar Eclipse is symbolic of the opposition between the two lights of our world.

The Solar Eclipse will almost always be in the sign that is opposite the sign in which the accompanying Lunar Eclipse has occurred. For example, if the Lunar Eclipse falls in the sign of Taurus, then approximately two weeks later the Solar Eclipse will fall in the sign of Scorpio. Six months later the Solar Eclipse will occur in the sign that the Lunar Eclipse was in. Consequently, the Lunar Eclipse will again be in the opposite sign that the Solar Eclipse was in. In this way, the eclipses work off one another. The Lunar Eclipse sets the stage for the upcoming Solar Eclipse because they will occur in the same sign. The Lunar Eclipse awakens us and warns us of the upcoming Solar Eclipse. If we are able to deal with the Lunar Eclipse, then the Solar Eclipse can be worked out in a better way. Lunar Eclipse's signal us to shape up the house that the eclipse occurs in before the Solar Eclipse comes to visit the same house. The successive series of eclipses run backwards through the zodiac. In this way we are tested on how well we are doing in relation to each house in our chart. Occasionally a Solar Eclipse will occur without an accompanying Lunar Eclipse, but the converse is never true. There can never be a Lunar Eclipse without an accompanying Solar Eclipse.

This year we will have a total of five eclipses, three Solar and two Lunar. On January 4th we will have our first Solar Eclipse in 13 Capricorn 51'; the second, June 30th in 8 Cancer 57'; and the third, December 24th in 2 Capricorn 28'. The two Lunar Eclipses will occur on June 15th in 24 Sagittarius 20'; and on December 9th in 18 Gemini 10'. Every person will be affected by these eclipses in accordance to his or her own natal chart. Those who have a heavy Cancer/Capricorn or Gemini/Sagittarius influence will have a very significant year ahead of them.

Cancer is the sign that governs the home and family. Capricorn on the other hand, rules the career and professional matters. 1992 could be a year where many individuals will have to make some important decisions in regards to both areas of their life. Responsibilities at work could prevent many people from spending needed time with family members. Problems at home could limit others as to the amount of time they will be able to put into career matters. Many people will have some problems in trying to strike an appropriate balance between these two areas of their life.

When we begin to delineate the natal chart in order to determine how the eclipse will work, the most important factor to take into consideration is in which house the eclipse falls. In astrology each house in the horoscope represents a different area of the individual's life. Whatever house the eclipse occurs in, those activities and events that the house governs will be highlighted during the eclipse period. An eclipse in the particular house brings the particular need of that house into the life of the native. This need becomes manifest through a crisis related to the activities of that particular house. When we have a Lunar Eclipse, the house that is opposite that of the house the eclipse falls in will additionally be emphasized, because the Sun is directly opposite the eclipse position.

Even though the influence of the eclipse lasts for months, the few weeks that surround the day of the eclipse will be a critical period. This is especially true if any transiting planets are brought into the picture as they aspect the eclipse position, activating the energy of the eclipse.

Obviously, when looking at how an eclipse will effect the natal chart, the chart as a whole must be taken into consideration. For the most part, eclipses are a fascinating territory of astrological study and can be an integral part of chart delineation.

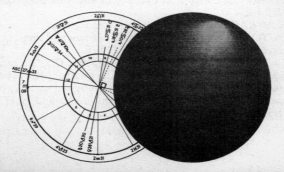

HOW TO FIND YOUR MOON SIGN

Every year we give tables for the position of the Moon during that year, but it is much more complicated to give tables for the Moon position in any year because of the continuous movement of the Moon. But the problem was long ago solved by Grant Lewi, which he published in *Astrology for the Millions*, a do-it-yourself manual which is still available from Llewellyn. Here's Grant Lewi's system:

Directions
1. Find your birth year in the Moon Tables.
2. Run down the left-hand column and see if your date is there.
3. IF YOUR DATE IS IN THE LEFT-HAND COLUMN, run over this line till you come to the column under your birth year. Here you will find a number. This is your BASE NUMBER. Write it down, and go directly to the part of the direction under the heading "What to Do with Your Base Number" on the next page.
4. IF YOUR BIRTH DATE IS NOT IN THE LEFT-HAND COLUMN, get a pencil and paper. Your birth date falls between two numbers in the left-hand column. Look at the date closest *after* your birth date, run over this line to your birth year. Write down the number you find there, and label it TOP NUMBER. Having done this, write directly beneath it on your piece of paper the number printed just above it in the table. Label this BOTTOM NUMBER.
   SUBTRACT the bottom number from the top number. If the TOP NUMBER is smaller, add 360 to it and then subtract. The result is your DIFFERENCE.
5. Go back to the left-hand column and find the date next *before* your birth date. Determine the number of days between this date and your birth date by subtracting or counting on your fingers. Write this down and label it INTERVENING DAYS.

6. In the Table of difference below, note which group your DIFFERENCE (found at 4 above) falls in.

Difference	*Daily Motion*
80-87	12 degrees
88-94	13 degrees
95-101	14 degrees
102-106	15 degrees

Note: If you were born in a leap year *and* use the difference between February 26 and March 5, use the special table following:

Difference	*Daily Motion*
94-99	12 degrees
100-108	13 degrees
109-115	14 degrees
115-122	15 degrees

Write down the DAILY MOTION corresponding to your place in the proper Table of Difference above.

7. Multiply this daily motion by the number labeled IN-TERVENING DAYS (found at 5).

8. Add the result of 7 to your BOTTOM NUMBER (under 4). The result of this is your BASE NUMBER. If it is more than 360, subtract 360 from it and call the result your BASE NUMBER.

What to Do with Your Base Number

Turn to the Table of Base Numbers and locate your Base Number in it. At the top of the column you will find the SIGN your Moon WAS IN. At the left you will find the DE-GREE your Moon occupied at—7 A.M. of your birth date if you were born under Eastern Standard Time.

6 A.M. of your birth date if you were born under Central Standard Time.

5 A.M. of your birth date if you were born under Mountain Standard Time.

4 A.M. of your birth date if you were born under Pacific Standard Time.

If you don't know the hour of your birth, accept this as

your Moon's sign and degree.

IF YOU DO KNOW THE HOUR OF YOUR BIRTH, get the exact degree as follows:

If you were born *after* 7 A.M., Eastern Standard Time (6 A.M. Central Standard Time, etc.), determine the number of hours after this time that you were born. Divide this by two. *Add* this to your BASE NUMBER, and the result in the table will be the exact degree and sign of the Moon on the year, month, date, and hour of your birth.

If you were born *before* 7 A.M. E.S.T. (6 A.M. C.S.T., etc.), determine the number of hours before that time that you were born. Divide this by two. *Subtract* this from your base number, and the result in the table will be the exact degree and sign of the Moon on the year, month, date and hour of your birth.

TABLE OF BASE NUMBERS

	Aries (13)	Taurus (14)	Gemini (15)	Cancer (16)	Leo (17)	Virgo (18)	Libra (19)	Scorpio (20)	Sagittarius (21)	Capricorn (22)	Aquarius (23)	Pisces (24)
0 deg.	0	30	60	90	120	150	180	210	240	270	300	330
1 deg.	1	31	61	91	121	151	181	211	241	271	301	331
2 deg.	2	32	62	92	122	152	182	212	242	272	302	332
3 deg.	3	33	63	93	123	153	183	213	243	273	303	333
4 deg.	4	34	64	94	124	154	184	214	244	274	304	334
5 deg.	5	35	65	95	125	155	185	215	245	275	305	335
6 deg.	6	36	66	96	126	156	186	216	246	276	306	336
7 deg.	7	37	67	97	127	157	187	217	247	277	307	337
8 deg.	8	38	68	98	128	158	188	218	248	278	308	338
9 deg.	9	39	69	99	129	159	189	219	249	279	309	339
10 deg.	10	40	70	100	130	160	190	220	250	280	310	340
11 deg.	11	41	71	101	131	161	191	221	251	281	311	341
12 deg.	12	42	72	102	132	162	192	222	252	282	312	342
13 deg.	13	43	73	103	133	163	193	223	253	283	313	343
14 deg.	14	44	74	104	134	164	194	224	254	284	314	344
15 deg.	15	45	75	105	135	165	195	225	255	285	315	345
16 deg.	16	46	76	106	136	166	196	226	256	286	316	346
17 deg.	17	47	77	107	137	167	197	227	257	287	317	347
18 deg.	18	48	78	108	138	168	198	228	258	288	318	248
19 deg.	19	49	79	109	139	169	199	229	259	289	319	349
20 deg.	20	50	80	110	140	170	200	230	260	290	320	350
21 deg.	21	51	81	111	141	171	201	231	261	291	321	351
22 deg.	22	52	82	112	142	172	202	232	262	292	322	352
23 deg.	23	53	83	113	143	173	203	233	263	293	323	353
24 deg.	24	54	84	114	144	174	204	234	264	294	324	354
25 deg.	25	55	85	115	145	175	205	235	265	295	325	355
26 deg.	26	56	86	116	146	176	206	236	266	296	326	356
27 deg.	27	57	87	117	147	177	207	237	267	297	327	357
28 deg.	28	58	88	118	148	178	208	238	268	298	328	358
29 deg.	29	59	89	119	149	179	209	239	269	299	329	359

		1901	1902	1903	1904	1905	1906	1907	1908	1909	1910
Jan.	1	55	188	308	76	227	358	119	246	39	168
Jan.	8	149	272	37	179	319	82	208	350	129	252
Jan.	15	234	2	141	270	43	174	311	81	213	346
Jan.	22	327	101	234	353	138	273	44	164	309	84
Jan.	29	66	196	317	84	238	6	128	255	50	175
Feb.	5	158	280	46	188	328	90	219	359	138	259
Feb.	12	241	12	149	279	51	184	319	90	221	356
Feb.	19	335	111	242	2	146	283	52	173	317	94
Feb.	26	76	204	326	92	248	13	136	264	60	184
Mar.	5	166	288	57	211	336	98	229	21	147	267
Mar.	12	249	22	157	300	60	194	328	110	230	5
Mar.	19	344	121	250	24	154	293	60	195	325	105
Mar.	26	86	212	334	116	258	22	144	288	69	192
Apr.	2	175	296	68	219	345	106	240	29	155	276
Apr.	9	258	31	167	309	69	202	338	118	240	13
Apr.	16	352	132	258	33	163	304	68	204	334	115
Apr.	23	96	220	342	127	267	31	152	299	77	201
Apr.	30	184	304	78	227	354	114	250	38	164	285
May	7	267	40	177	317	78	210	348	126	249	21
May	14	1	142	266	42	172	313	76	212	344	124
May	21	104	229	350	138	275	40	160	310	85	210
May	28	193	313	87	236	2	123	259	47	172	294
Jun.	4	277	48	187	324	88	219	358	134	258	30
Jun.	11	11	151	275	50	182	322	85	220	355	132
Jun.	18	112	238	359	149	283	48	169	320	93	218
Jun.	25	201	322	96	245	11	133	267	57	180	304
Jul.	2	286	57	197	333	97	228	8	142	267	40
Jul.	9	21	160	283	58	193	330	94	228	6	140
Jul.	16	121	247	7	159	291	57	178	330	102	226
Jul.	23	209	332	105	255	18	143	276	66	188	314
Jul.	30	295	66	206	341	105	239	17	151	275	51
Aug.	6	32	168	292	66	204	338	103	237	17	148
Aug.	13	130	255	17	168	301	65	188	339	111	234
Aug.	20	217	341	113	265	27	152	285	76	197	323
Aug.	27	303	77	215	350	113	250	25	160	283	62
Sep.	3	43	176	301	75	215	346	111	246	27	157
Sep.	10	139	263	27	176	310	73	198	347	121	242
Sep.	17	225	350	123	274	35	161	294	85	205	331
Sep.	24	311	88	223	358	122	261	33	169	292	73
Oct.	1	53	185	309	85	224	355	119	256	35	166
Oct.	8	149	271	36	185	320	81	207	356	130	250
Oct.	15	233	359	133	283	44	169	305	93	214	339
Oct.	22	319	99	231	7	130	271	42	177	301	83
Oct.	29	62	194	317	95	233	5	127	266	44	176
Nov.	5	158	279	45	193	329	89	216	5	139	259
Nov.	12	242	6	144	291	53	177	316	101	223	347
Nov.	19	328	109	239	15	140	280	50	185	311	91
Nov.	26	70	203	325	105	241	14	135	276	52	185
Dec.	3	168	288	54	203	338	98	224	15	148	268
Dec.	10	251	14	155	299	61	185	327	109	231	356
Dec.	17	338	118	248	23	150	289	59	193	322	99
Dec.	24	78	213	333	115	249	23	143	286	61	194
Dec.	31	176	296	61	213	346	107	232	26	155	277

		1911	1912	1913	1914	1915	1916	1917	1918	1919	1920
Jan.	1	289	57	211	337	100	228	23	147	270	39
Jan.	8	20	162	299	61	192	332	110	231	5	143
Jan.	15	122	251	23	158	293	61	193	329	103	231
Jan.	22	214	335	120	256	23	145	290	68	193	316
Jan.	29	298	66	221	345	108	237	32	155	278	49
Feb.	5	31	170	308	69	203	340	118	239	16	150
Feb.	12	130	260	32	167	302	70	203	338	113	239
Feb.	19	222	344	128	266	31	154	298	78	201	325
Feb.	26	306	75	231	353	116	248	41	164	286	60
Mar.	5	42	192	317	77	214	2	127	248	26	172
Mar.	12	140	280	41	176	311	89	212	346	123	259
Mar.	19	230	5	136	276	39	176	308	87	209	346
Mar.	26	314	100	239	2	124	273	49	173	294	85
Apr.	2	52	200	326	86	223	10	135	257	35	181
Apr.	9	150	288	51	184	321	97	222	355	133	267
Apr.	16	238	14	146	286	48	184	318	96	218	355
Apr.	23	322	111	247	11	132	284	57	181	303	96
Apr.	30	61	208	334	96	232	19	143	267	43	190
May.	7	160	296	60	192	331	105	231	4	142	275
May.	14	246	22	156	294	56	192	329	104	227	3
May.	21	331	122	255	20	141	294	66	190	312	105
May.	28	69	218	342	106	240	29	151	277	51	200
Jun.	4	170	304	69	202	341	114	240	14	151	284
Jun.	11	255	30	167	302	65	200	340	112	235	11
Jun.	18	340	132	264	28	151	304	74	198	322	114
Jun.	25	78	228	350	115	249	39	159	286	60	209
Jul.	2	179	312	78	212	349	122	248	25	159	293
Jul.	9	264	39	178	310	74	209	350	120	244	20
Jul.	16	349	141	273	36	161	312	84	206	332	123
Jul.	23	87	237	358	125	258	48	168	295	70	218
Jul.	30	187	321	86	223	357	131	256	36	167	302
Aug.	6	272	48	188	319	82	219	360	129	252	31
Aug.	13	359	150	282	44	171	320	93	214	342	131
Aug.	20	96	246	6	133	268	57	177	303	81	226
Aug.	27	195	330	94	234	5	140	265	46	175	310
Sep.	3	281	57	198	328	90	229	9	138	260	41
Sep.	10	9	158	292	52	180	329	102	222	351	140
Sep.	17	107	255	15	141	279	65	186	312	91	234
Sep.	24	203	339	103	244	13	149	274	56	184	319
Oct.	1	288	68	206	337	98	240	17	148	268	52
Oct.	8	18	167	301	61	189	338	111	231	360	150
Oct.	15	118	263	24	149	290	73	195	320	102	242
Oct.	22	212	347	113	254	22	157	284	65	193	326
Oct.	29	296	78	214	346	106	250	25	157	276	61
Nov.	5	26	177	309	70	197	348	119	240	7	161
Nov.	12	129	271	33	158	300	81	203	329	112	250
Nov.	19	221	355	123	262	31	164	295	73	202	334
Nov.	26	305	88	223	355	115	259	34	165	285	70
Dec.	3	34	187	317	79	205	359	127	249	16	171
Dec.	10	138	279	41	168	310	89	211	340	120	259
Dec.	17	230	3	134	270	40	172	305	81	211	343
Dec.	24	313	97	232	3	124	267	44	173	294	78
Dec.	31	42	198	325	87	214	9	135	257	25	181

		1921	1922	1923	1924	1925	1926	1927	1928	1929	1930
Jan.	1	194	317	80	211	5	127	250	23	176	297
Jan.	8	280	41	177	313	90	211	349	123	260	22
Jan.	15	4	141	275	41	175	312	86	211	346	123
Jan.	22	101	239	3	127	272	51	172	297	83	222
Jan.	29	203	325	88	222	13	135	258	34	184	306
Feb.	5	289	49	188	321	99	220	359	131	269	31
Feb.	12	14	149	284	49	185	320	95	219	356	131
Feb.	19	110	249	11	135	281	60	181	305	93	230
Feb.	26	211	334	96	233	21	144	266	45	191	314
Mar.	5	297	58	197	343	107	230	8	153	276	41
Mar.	12	23	157	294	69	194	328	105	238	6	140
Mar.	19	119	258	19	157	292	68	190	327	104	238
Mar.	26	219	343	104	258	29	153	275	70	200	323
Apr.	2	305	68	205	352	115	240	16	163	284	51
Apr.	9	33	166	304	77	204	337	114	247	14	149
Apr.	16	130	266	28	164	303	76	198	335	115	246
Apr.	23	227	351	114	268	38	161	285	79	208	331
Apr.	30	313	78	214	1	123	250	25	172	292	61
May.	7	42	176	313	85	212	348	123	256	23	160
May.	14	141	274	37	173	314	84	207	344	125	254
May.	21	236	359	123	277	47	169	295	88	217	339
May.	28	321	88	222	11	131	259	34	181	301	70
Jun.	4	50	186	321	94	220	358	131	264	31	171
Jun.	11	152	282	45	182	324	93	215	354	135	263
Jun.	18	245	7	134	285	56	177	305	96	226	347
Jun.	25	330	97	232	20	139	268	44	190	310	78
Jul.	2	58	197	329	103	229	9	139	273	40	181
Jul.	9	162	291	54	192	333	101	223	4	144	272
Jul.	16	254	15	144	294	65	185	315	104	236	355
Jul.	23	338	106	242	28	148	276	54	198	319	87
Jul.	30	67	208	337	112	238	20	147	282	49	191
Aug.	6	171	300	62	202	341	110	231	15	152	281
Aug.	13	264	24	153	302	74	194	324	114	244	4
Aug.	20	347	114	253	36	157	285	65	206	328	95
Aug.	27	76	218	346	120	248	29	156	290	59	200
Sep.	3	179	309	70	213	350	119	239	25	161	290
Sep.	10	273	32	162	312	83	203	332	124	252	13
Sep.	17	356	122	264	44	166	293	75	214	337	105
Sep.	24	86	227	354	128	258	38	165	298	70	208
Oct.	1	187	318	78	223	358	128	248	35	169	298
Oct.	8	281	41	170	322	91	212	340	134	260	23
Oct.	15	5	132	274	52	175	303	85	222	345	115
Oct.	22	97	235	3	136	269	46	174	306	81	216
Oct.	29	196	327	87	232	7	137	257	44	179	307
Nov.	5	289	50	178	332	99	221	349	144	268	31
Nov.	12	13	142	283	61	183	313	93	231	353	126
Nov.	19	107	243	12	144	279	54	183	315	91	225
Nov.	26	206	335	96	241	17	145	266	52	189	314
Dec.	3	297	59	187	343	107	230	359	154	276	39
Dec.	10	21	152	291	70	191	324	101	240	1	137
Dec.	17	117	252	21	153.	289	63	191	324	99	234
Dec.	24	216	343	105	249	28	152	275	60	199	322
Dec.	31	305	67	197	352	115	237	9	162	285	47

		1931	1932	1933	1934	1935	1936	1937	1938	1939	1940
Jan.	1	60	196	346	107	231	8	156	277	41	181
Jan.	8	162	294	70	193	333	104	240	4	144	275
Jan.	15	257	20	158	294	68	190	329	104	239	360
Jan.	22	342	108	255	32	152	278	67	202	323	88
Jan.	29	68	207	353	116	239	19	163	286	49	191
Feb.	5	171	302	78	203	342	113	248	14	153	284
Feb.	12	267	28	168	302	78	198	339	113	248	8
Feb.	19	351	116	266	40	161	286	78	210	332	96
Feb.	26	77	217	1	124	248	29	171	294	59	200
Mar.	5	179	324	86	213	350	135	256	25	161	306
Mar.	12	276	48	176	311	86	218	347	123	256	29
Mar.	19	360	137	277	48	170	308	89	218	340	119
Mar.	26	86	241	10	132	258	52	180	302	69	223
Apr.	2	187	334	94	223	358	144	264	34	169	315
Apr.	9	285	57	185	321	95	227	355	133	264	38
Apr.	16	9	146	287	56	178	317	99	226	349	128
Apr.	23	96	250	18	140	268	61	189	310	80	231
Apr.	30	196	343	102	232	7	153	273	43	179	323
May.	7	293	66	193	332	103	237	4	144	272	47
May.	14	17	155	297	64	187	327	108	235	357	139
May.	21	107	258	28	148	278	69	198	318	90	239
May.	28	205	351	111	241	17	161	282	51	189	331
Jun.	4	301	75	201	343	111	245	13	154	280	55
Jun.	11	25	165	306	73	195	337	117	244	5	150
Jun.	18	117	267	37	157	288	78	207	327	99	248
Jun.	25	215	360	120	249	28	169	291	60	200	339
Jul.	2	309	84	211	353	119	254	23	164	289	64
Jul.	9	33	176	315	82	203	348	125	253	13	160
Jul.	16	126	276	46	165	297	87	216	336	108	258
Jul.	23	226	8	130	258	38	177	300	69	210	347
Jul.	30	317	92	221	2	128	262	33	173	298	72
Aug.	6	41	187	323	91	211	359	133	261	21	170
Aug.	13	135	285	54	175	305	97	224	346	116	268
Aug.	20	237	16	138	267	49	185	308	78	220	355
Aug.	27	326	100	232	10	136	270	44	181	307	80
Sep.	3	49	197	331	100	220	8	142	270	31	179
Sep.	10	143	295	62	184	314	107	232	355	125	278
Sep.	17	247	24	147	277	58	194	317	89	228	4
Sep.	24	335	108	243	18	145	278	55	189	316	88
Oct.	1	58	206	341	108	229	17	152	278	40	188
Oct.	8	151	306	70	193	322	117	240	4	134	288
Oct.	15	256	32	155	287	66	203	324	100	236	13
Oct.	22	344	116	253	27	154	287	64	198	324	98
Oct.	29	68	214	350	116	239	25	162	286	49	196
Nov.	5	161	316	78	201	332	126	248	12	145	297
Nov.	12	264	41	162	298	74	212	333	111	244	22
Nov.	19	353	125	262	36	162	296	73	207	332	108
Nov.	26	77	222	0	124	248	33	172	294	58	205
Dec.	3	171	325	87	209	343	135	257	19	156	305
Dec.	10	272	50	171	309	82	220	341	120	253	30
Dec.	17	1	135	271	45	170	306	81	217	340	118
Dec.	24	86	231	10	132	256	43	181	302	66	214
Dec.	31	182	333	95	217	354	142	265	27	167	313

		1941	1942	1943	1944	1945	1946	1947	1948	1949	1950
Jan.	1	325	88	211	353	135	258	22	165	305	68
Jan.	8	50	176	315	85	219	348	126	256	29	160
Jan.	15	141	276	50	169	312	87	220	340	123	258
Jan.	22	239	12	133	258	52	182	303	69	224	352
Jan.	29	333	96	221	2	143	266	32	174	314	75
Feb.	5	57	186	323	95	227	358	134	265	37	170
Feb.	12	150	285	58	178	320	96	228	349	131	268
Feb.	19	250	20	142	267	62	190	312	78	234	359
Feb.	26	342	104	231	11	152	274	43	182	323	83
Mar.	5	65	196	331	116	236	8	142	286	46	179
Mar.	12	158	295	66	199	328	107	236	10	139	279
Mar.	19	261	28	150	290	72	198	320	102	243	8
Mar.	26	351	112	242	34	161	281	53	204	332	91
Apr.	2	74	205	340	125	244	16	152	294	55	187
Apr.	9	166	306	74	208	337	117	244	19	148	289
Apr.	16	270	36	158	300	81	206	328	112	252	17
Apr.	23	360	120	252	42	170	290	63	212	340	100
Apr.	30	83	214	350	133	254	25	162	302	64	195
May	7	174	316	82	217	346	127	252	27	158	299
May	14	279	45	166	311	90	215	336	123	260	26
May	21	9	128	261	50	179	299	72	221	349	110
May	28	92	222	1	141	263	33	173	310	73	204
Jun.	4	184	326	91	226	356	137	261	36	168	307
Jun.	11	287	54	174	322	98	224	344	134	268	34
Jun.	18	17	137	270	60	187	308	81	231	357	119
Jun.	25	102	231	11	149	272	42	183	318	82	213
Jul.	2	194	335	99	234	7	145	269	44	179	316
Jul.	9	296	63	183	332	106	233	353	144	277	43
Jul.	16	25	147	279	70	195	318	89	241	5	129
Jul.	23	110	240	21	157	280	52	192	327	91	224
Jul.	30	205	343	108	242	18	153	278	52	190	324
Aug.	6	304	71	192	341	115	241	3	153	286	51
Aug.	13	33	156	287	80	203	327	98	251	13	138
Aug.	20	119	250	30	165	289	63	201	336	99	235
Aug.	27	216	351	117	250	28	162	287	61	200	332
Sep.	3	314	80	201	350	125	249	13	161	296	59
Sep.	10	41	165	296	90	211	336	108	260	21	146
Sep.	17	127	261	39	174	297	74	209	345	107	246
Sep.	24	226	359	126	259	38	170	295	70	209	341
Oct.	1	323	88	211	358	135	257	22	170	306	67
Oct.	8	49	174	306	99	220	344	118	269	30	154
Oct.	15	135	272	47	183	305	84	217	353	116	256
Oct.	22	236	8	134	269	47	180	303	80	217	351
Oct.	29	333	95	220	7	144	265	31	179	315	75
Nov.	5	58	181	317	107	229	352	129	277	39	162
Nov.	12	143	283	55	192	314	94	225	1	125	265
Nov.	19	244	18	141	279	55	189	311	90	225	0
Nov.	26	343	104	229	16	153	274	39	189	323	84
Dec.	3	67	189	328	115	237	360	140	284	47	171
Dec.	10	153	292	64	200	324	103	234	9	136	274
Dec.	17	252	28	149	289	63	199	319	100	234	9
Dec.	24	351	112	237	27	161	282	47	199	331	93
Dec.	31	76	198	338	123	246	9	150	293	55	180

		1951	1952	1953	1954	1955	1956	1957	1958	1959	1960
Jan.	1	194	336	115	238	6	147	285	47	178	317
Jan.	8	297	67	199	331	107	237	9	143	278	47
Jan.	15	30	150	294	70	200	320	104	242	9	131
Jan.	22	114	240	35	161	284	51	207	331	94	223
Jan.	29	204	344	124	245	17	155	294	55	189	325
Feb.	5	305	76	207	341	116	246	18	152	287	56
Feb.	12	38	159	302	80	208	330	112	252	17	140
Feb.	19	122	249	45	169	292	61	216	340	102	233
Feb.	26	215	352	133	253	27	163	303	63	199	333
Mar.	5	314	96	216	350	125	266	27	161	297	75
Mar.	12	46	180	310	91	216	351	121	262	25	161
Mar.	19	130	274	54	178	300	86	224	349	110	259
Mar.	26	225	14	142	262	37	185	312	72	208	356
Apr.	2	324	104	226	358	135	274	37	169	307	83
Apr.	9	54	189	319	100	224	360	131	271	34	170
Apr.	16	138	285	62	187	308	97	232	357	118	269
Apr.	23	235	23	150	271	46	194	320	82	217	5
Apr.	30	334	112	235	6	146	282	46	177	317	91
May	7	62	197	330	109	232	8	142	279	42	177
May	14	146	296	70	196	316	107	240	6	127	279
May	21	243	32	158	280	54	204	328	91	225	15
May	28	344	120	244	15	155	290	55	187	326	100
Jun.	4	71	205	341	117	241	16	153	288	51	186
Jun.	11	155	306	79	204	325	117	249	14	137	288
Jun.	18	252	42	166	290	63	214	336	101	234	25
Jun.	25	354	128	253	26	164	298	63	198	335	109
Jul.	2	80	214	351	125	250	24	164	296	60	195
Jul.	9	164	315	88	212	335	126	259	22	147	297
Jul.	16	260	52	174	299	72	223	344	110	243	34
Jul.	23	3	137	261	37	173	307	71	209	343	118
Jul.	30	89	222	2	134	258	33	174	304	68	205
Aug.	6	174	324	97	220	345	134	268	30	156	305
Aug.	13	270	62	182	308	82	232	353	118	254	42
Aug.	20	11	146	269	48	181	316	79	220	351	126
Aug.	27	97	232	11	143	267	43	183	314	76	215
Sep.	3	184	332	107	228	355	143	278	38	166	314
Sep.	10	280	71	191	316	92	241	2	127	265	50
Sep.	17	19	155	278	58	189	325	88	230	359	135
Sep.	24	105	242	20	152	274	54	191	323	84	225
Oct.	1	193	341	116	237	4	152	287	47	174	324
Oct.	8	291	79	200	324	103	249	11	135	276	58
Oct.	15	27	163	287	68	198	333	98	239	8	143
Oct.	22	113	252	28	162	282	64	199	332	92	235
Oct.	29	201	350	125	245	12	162	295	56	182	334
Nov.	5	302	87	209	333	114	256	19	144	286	66
Nov.	12	36	171	297	76	207	341	109	247	17	150
Nov.	19	121	262	37	171	291	73	208	341	101	244
Nov.	26	209	0	133	254	20	173	303	65	190	345
Dec.	3	312	95	217	342	124	265	27	154	295	75
Dec.	10	45	179	307	84	216	348	119	255	27	158
Dec.	17	129	271	46	180	299	82	218	350	110	252
Dec.	24	217	11	141	263	28	184	311	73	199	355
Dec.	31	321	103	225	352	132	273	35	164	303	84

Karen
116

20   14
96   1 ent.

~~88~~   14
~~88~~   90   34
~~88~~   ~~Cancer~~ Taurus

Charlie

161   14
66   6 ent.
        ‾‾‾‾
        84
95   66
~~80~~   150   Virgo

		1961	1962	1963	1964	1965	1966	1967	1968	1969	1970
Jan.	1	96	217	350	128	266	27	163	298	76	197
Jan.	8	179	315	89	217	350	126	260	27	161	297
Jan.	15	275	54	179	302	86	225	349	112	257	36
Jan.	22	18	141	264	35	189	311	74	207	359	122
Jan.	29	105	225	1	136	275	35	173	306	85	206
Feb.	5	188	323	99	225	360	134	270	35	171	305
Feb.	12	284	64	187	310	95	235	357	121	267	45
Feb.	19	26	150	272	46	197	320	81	218	7	130
Feb.	26	113	234	11	144	283	45	182	315	93	216
Mar.	5	198	331	109	245	9	142	280	54	180	313
Mar.	12	293	73	195	332	105	244	5	142	277	54
Mar.	19	34	159	280	71	205	329	90	243	15	139
Mar.	26	122	243	19	167	291	54	190	338	101	226
Apr.	2	208	340	119	253	18	151	290	63	189	323
Apr.	9	303	82	204	340	116	252	14	150	288	62
Apr.	16	42	167	288	81	213	337	99	253	23	147
Apr.	23	130	253	28	176	299	64	198	347	109	235
Apr.	30	216	349	128	261	27	161	298	71	197	333
May	7	314	90	213	348	127	260	23	158	299	70
May	14	51	176	298	91	222	345	109	262	32	155
May	21	137	263	36	186	307	74	207	357	117	245
May	28	225	359	137	270	35	172	307	80	205	344
Jun.	4	325	98	222	357	137	268	31	168	309	78
Jun.	11	60	184	308	99	231	353	119	270	42	163
Jun.	18	146	272	45	195	315	82	217	6	126	253
Jun.	25	233	10	145	279	43	183	315	89	214	355
Jul.	2	336	106	230	6	147	276	40	178	318	87
Jul.	9	70	191	318	108	241	1	129	279	51	171
Jul.	16	154	281	56	204	324	91	227	14	135	261
Jul.	23	241	21	153	288	52	193	323	98	223	5
Jul.	30	345	115	238	16	156	286	47	188	327	97
Aug.	6	79	200	327	116	250	10	138	288	60	180
Aug.	13	163	289	66	212	333	99	238	22	144	270
Aug.	20	250	32	161	296	61	203	331	106	233	14
Aug.	27	353	124	246	27	164	295	55	199	335	106
Sep.	3	88	208	336	126	259	19	147	297	68	189
Sep.	10	172	297	77	220	342	108	249	30	152	279
Sep.	17	260	41	170	304	72	212	340	114	244	23
Sep.	24	1	134	254	37	172	304	64	208	344	115
Oct.	1	97	217	344	136	267	28	155	308	76	198
Oct.	8	180	306	88	228	351	117	259	38	161	289
Oct.	15	270	50	179	312	82	220	350	122	254	31
Oct.	22	10	143	262	47	182	313	73	217	353	123
Oct.	29	105	226	352	146	275	37	163	318	84	207
Nov.	5	189	315	97	237	359	127	268	47	168	299
Nov.	12	281	58	188	320	93	228	359	130	264	39
Nov.	19	19	151	271	55	191	321	82	225	3	131
Nov.	26	113	235	1	157	282	45	172	328	92	215
Dec.	3	197	326	105	245	7	138	276	55	176	310
Dec.	10	291	66	197	328	102	237	7	139	273	48
Dec.	17	30	159	280	63	202	329	91	234	13	139
Dec.	24	121	243	11	167	291	53	183	337	101	223
Dec.	31	204	336	113	254	14	149	284	64	184	320

		1971	1972	1973	1974	1975	1976	1977	1978	1979	1980
Jan.	1	335	109	246	8	147	279	56	179	318	90
Jan.	8	71	197	332	108	243	6	144	278	54	176
Jan.	15	158	283	69	207	328	93	240	18	139	263
Jan.	22	244	20	169	292	54	192	339	102	224	4
Jan.	29	344	117	255	17	156	288	64	188	327	99
Feb.	5	81	204	342	116	253	14	153	287	63	184
Feb.	12	167	291	79	216	337	101	251	26	147	271
Feb.	19	252	31	177	300	62	203	347	110	233	14
Feb.	26	353	126	263	27	164	297	72	199	334	109
Mar.	5	91	224	351	124	262	34	162	296	72	204
Mar.	12	176	312	90	224	346	122	262	34	156	293
Mar.	19	261	55	185	309	72	226	356	118	243	37
Mar.	26	1	149	270	37	172	320	80	208	343	130
Apr.	2	100	233	360	134	270	43	170	307	80	213
Apr.	9	184	320	101	232	355	131	273	42	164	302
Apr.	16	271	64	194	317	82	235	5	126	254	46
Apr.	23	9	158	278	47	181	329	88	217	352	139
Apr.	30	109	242	8	145	278	52	178	318	88	222
May	7	193	329	111	240	3	141	282	50	173	312
May	14	281	73	203	324	92	243	14	134	264	54
May	21	19	167	287	55	191	337	97	226	3	147
May	28	117	251	16	156	286	61	187	328	96	231
Jun.	4	201	339	120	249	11	151	291	59	180	323
Jun.	11	291	81	213	333	102	252	23	143	273	63
Jun.	18	29	176	296	64	201	346	106	234	13	155
Jun.	25	125	260	25	167	295	69	196	338	105	239
Jul.	2	209	349	129	258	19	162	299	68	188	334
Jul.	9	300	90	222	341	111	261	32	152	282	72
Jul.	16	40	184	305	72	212	354	115	243	24	163
Jul.	23	133	268	35	176	303	78	206	347	114	248
Jul.	30	217	0	137	267	27	172	308	77	197	344
Aug.	6	309	99	230	350	120	271	40	161	290	83
Aug.	13	51	192	314	81	223	2	124	252	34	171
Aug.	20	142	276	45	185	312	86	217	356	123	256
Aug.	27	225	10	146	276	36	182	317	86	206	353
Sep.	3	317	109	238	360	128	281	48	170	299	93
Sep.	10	61	200	322	90	232	10	132	262	43	180
Sep.	17	151	284	56	193	321	94	228	4	132	264
Sep.	24	234	20	155	284	45	191	326	94	215	2
Oct.	1	325	120	246	9	136	291	56	179	308	103
Oct.	8	70	208	330	101	241	19	140	273	51	189
Oct.	15	160	292	66	202	330	102	238	12	140	273
Oct.	22	243	28	165	292	54	199	336	102	225	10
Oct.	29	334	130	254	17	146	301	64	187	318	112
Nov.	5	79	217	338	112	249	27	148	284	59	197
Nov.	12	169	300	76	210	339	111	247	21	148	282
Nov.	19	253	36	175	300	63	207	347	110	234	18
Nov.	26	344	139	262	25	156	310	73	195	329	120
Dec.	3	87	226	346	122	257	36	157	294	67	206
Dec.	10	177	310	84	220	347	121	255	31	156	292
Dec.	17	261	45	185	308	72	216	356	118	242	28
Dec.	24	355	148	271	33	167	318	81	203	340	128
Dec.	31	95	235	355	132	265	44	166	303	76	214

		1981	1982	1983	1984	1985	1986	1987	1988	1989	1990
Jan.	1	226	350	129	260	36	162	300	71	205	333
Jan.	8	315	89	225	346	126	260	36	156	297	72
Jan.	15	53	188	309	73	225	358	119	243	37	168
Jan.	22	149	272	35	176	319	82	206	348	129	252
Jan.	29	234	0	137	270	43	172	308	81	213	343
Feb.	5	324	98	234	354	135	270	44	164	306	82
Feb.	12	64	196	317	81	236	6	128	252	48	175
Feb.	19	157	280	45	185	328	90	217	356	138	260
Feb.	26	242	10	145	279	51	182	316	90	222	353
Mar.	5	332	108	242	15	143	280	52	185	313	93
Mar.	12	74	204	326	104	246	14	136	275	57	184
Mar.	19	166	288	55	208	337	97	227	19	147	268
Mar.	26	250	20	154	300	60	191	326	111	230	1
Apr.	2	340	119	250	24	151	291	60	194	322	103
Apr.	9	84	212	334	114	255	22	144	286	66	192
Apr.	16	175	296	66	216	346	106	237	27	156	276
Apr.	23	259	28	164	309	69	199	336	119	240	9
Apr.	30	349	130	258	33	160	302	68	203	331	113
May	7	93	221	342	124	264	31	152	297	75	201
May	14	184	304	75	225	355	114	246	36	165	285
May	21	268	36	175	317	78	207	347	127	249	18
May	28	358	140	266	41	170	311	76	211	341	122
Jun.	4	102	230	350	135	272	40	160	307	83	210
Jun.	11	193	313	84	234	3	123	255	45	173	294
Jun.	18	277	45	185	325	87	216	357	135	258	27
Jun.	25	8	149	275	49	180	320	85	219	352	130
Jul.	2	110	239	359	146	281	49	169	317	92	219
Jul.	9	201	322	93	244	11	133	263	55	181	304
Jul.	16	286	54	196	333	96	225	7	143	266	37
Jul.	23	19	158	284	57	191	328	94	227	3	138
Jul.	30	119	248	7	155	290	57	178	327	101	227
Aug.	6	210	331	101	254	19	142	272	66	189	313
Aug.	13	294	64	205	341	104	236	16	152	274	48
Aug.	20	30	166	293	66	202	337	103	236	13	147
Aug.	27	128	256	17	164	299	65	187	335	111	235
Sep.	3	218	340	110	264	27	151	281	75	197	321
Sep.	10	302	75	214	350	112	247	24	160	282	59
Sep.	17	40	174	302	74	212	345	112	245	23	156
Sep.	24	138	264	26	172	309	73	197	343	121	243
Oct.	1	226	349	119	274	36	159	292	84	206	329
Oct.	8	310	86	222	359	120	258	32	169	291	70
Oct.	15	50	183	310	84	220	354	120	255	31	165
Oct.	22	148	272	35	181	319	81	206	352	130	251
Oct.	29	234	357	130	282	44	167	303	92	214	337
Nov.	5	318	96	230	8	129	268	40	178	300	79
Nov.	12	58	193	318	93	229	4	128	265	39	175
Nov.	19	158	280	44	190	329	90	214	2	139	260
Nov.	26	243	5	141	290	53	175	314	100	223	345
Dec.	3	327	106	238	16	139	277	49	185	310	88
Dec.	10	66	203	326	103	237	14	136	274	48	185
Dec.	17	167	288	52	200	337	98	222	12	147	269
Dec.	24	252	13	152	298	62	184	324	108	232	355
Dec.	31	337	114	248	24	149	285	59	193	320	96

		1991	1992	1993	1994	1995	1996	1997	1998	1999	2000
Jan.	1	111	242	15	145	281	53	185	317	92	223
Jan.	8	206	326	108	244	16	136	279	56	186	307
Jan.	15	289	54	210	337	99	225	21	147	270	37
Jan.	22	18	158	299	61	190	329	110	231	2	140
Jan.	29	119	252	23	155	290	62	193	326	101	232
Feb.	5	214	335	116	254	24	145	287	66	193	315
Feb.	12	298	63	220	345	108	235	31	155	278	47
Feb.	19	29	166	308	69	201	337	119	239	12	148
Feb.	26	128	260	32	164	299	70	202	335	111	240
Mar.	5	222	356	124	265	32	166	295	76	201	337
Mar.	12	306	87	229	354	116	259	39	164	285	72
Mar.	19	39	189	317	77	211	360	128	248	22	170
Mar.	26	138	280	41	172	310	90	212	343	121	260
Apr.	2	230	5	133	275	40	175	305	86	210	345
Apr.	9	314	98	237	3	123	270	47	173	294	83
Apr.	16	49	198	326	86	220	9	136	257	31	180
Apr.	23	148	288	50	180	320	98	221	351	132	268
Apr.	30	238	13	143	284	48	183	315	95	218	353
May	7	322	109	245	12	132	281	55	182	302	93
May	14	57	207	335	95	228	18	144	267	39	190
May	21	158	296	59	189	330	106	230	1	141	276
May	28	247	21	154	292	57	191	326	103	227	1
Jun.	4	330	119	253	21	141	291	64	190	311	102
Jun.	11	66	217	343	105	236	28	152	276	48	199
Jun.	18	168	304	68	199	340	114	238	11	150	285
Jun.	25	256	29	165	300	66	199	337	111	236	10
Jul.	2	339	129	262	29	150	300	73	198	321	111
Jul.	9	74	227	351	114	245	38	160	285	57	209
Jul.	16	177	313	76	210	348	123	246	22	158	293
Jul.	23	265	38	175	309	75	208	347	120	245	19
Jul.	30	349	137	272	37	160	308	83	206	331	119
Aug.	6	83	237	359	123	255	48	169	293	67	218
Aug.	13	186	322	84	221	356	132	254	33	166	302
Aug.	20	273	47	185	318	83	218	356	129	253	29
Aug.	27	358	146	282	45	169	317	93	214	340	128
Sep.	3	93	246	7	131	265	56	177	301	78	226
Sep.	10	194	331	92	231	4	141	263	43	174	311
Sep.	17	281	56	194	327	91	228	5	138	261	39
Sep.	24	8	154	292	53	178	326	102	223	349	137
Oct.	1	104	254	16	139	276	64	186	310	89	234
Oct.	8	202	339	101	241	13	149	273	53	183	319
Oct.	15	289	66	202	337	99	238	13	148	269	49
Oct.	22	16	164	301	61	187	336	111	231	357	148
Oct.	29	115	262	25	148	287	72	195	318	100	242
Nov.	5	211	347	111	250	22	157	283	61	193	326
Nov.	12	297	76	211	346	107	247	22	157	277	58
Nov.	19	24	174	309	70	194	346	119	240	5	159
Nov.	26	126	270	33	156	297	80	203	328	109	251
Dec.	3	220	355	121	258	31	165	293	69	202	334
Dec.	10	305	85	220	355	115	256	31	165	286	67
Dec.	17	32	185	317	79	203	357	127	249	13	169
Dec.	24	135	278	41	166	306	89	211	338	117	260
Dec.	31	230	3	131	266	41	173	303	78	211	343

YOUR PERSONAL MOON SIGN

by Gavin Kent McClung

The Moon is the point of life potential through which we contact the universe at large at the "gut-level" of experience. Here is where we unthinkingly absorb nourishment from outside ourselves, and where we instinctively give sustenance to others. The Moon represents life at the wavelength of feeling and mothering. Both men and women must fulfill this role or operate at this frequency from time to time.

ARIES MOON:

Anyone who knows an Aries Moon also knows the boost of feelings associated with a person of high emotional aspiration. This active, often impetuous force is powered by a keen imagination and a compass-like search for the "true north" of inward, person-to-person situations. This may result in a shy appearing or jumpy person, ready always to be off and away from close confrontations.

Here, the first impulse that occurs is likely to be adopted. There is clearly something chancey, something risky, about this person's approach. Sparks may sometimes fly, if one is not so quick to start up as an Aries Moon. They may *know* they are right, whether they know what they are right about or not. Once the relative steadiness of maturity has arrived, the Aries Moon can be a supportive dynamo for the less adventurous.

Severance from anything that is perpetually binding is likely to tempt them rather sooner than later. The emotional level is transient, yet ever ready to extend the hand of reconciliation. The Aries Moon automatically reassigns him or herself to new tasks and new challenges, and it is wise not to interfere with this constant process of renewal.

TAURUS MOON:

A personal goal for this person is to establish practical results, concrete expression wherever this is appropriate in connection with his or her feelings and emotions, and sometimes where it may *not* be so appropriate. Pie in the sky is not enough to provide satisfaction here. For Taurus Moon, the pie should be on the table, on a plate, and in ample supply. The search for true value in life may be this person's best contribution to society. They can forcibly supply the rest of us with the drive to integrate the idea of "pie in the sky" with the reality of "plate on the table."

Taurus Moon will generally tend to see things in summation, to demand that one's position in life be made manifest in reality. The orientation to material values is primary. The source of all this inward solidity is probably the deep rooted and persistent imagination of this person, which does not allow them to accept substitutes in life, but drives ever onward to obtain "the real thing" ultimately.

GEMINI MOON:

This Moon sign is perpetually drawn toward life itself, living it, feeling it, breathing it in. This in turn results in the effect of breathing life into life itself. Quickness and versatility are exceptional here, though others may sometimes construe these traits as being deceptive. But this perception may simply reflect two persons operating at two different speeds. Gemini adapts very fast, and relatively unjudgmentally, to whatever he or she faces.

There is a mental approach to the feeling level here, but these feelings are the same as everyone else's, and Gemini Moon is quite aware of their presence within. But he or she does not feel bound to dwell on things too long. The result can be a tendency to work things over a little at a time—for a long, long time. It would be a little contradictory for this Moon sign not to be a little contradictory.

With Gemini Moon, a basic assumption is that everything in life is *imminent*, is about to happen. This sense of urgency presses them into a constant search for the true body of experience, and they manage to acquire much knowledge as they go along through life.

CANCER MOON:

Contacting a Cancer Moon will nearly always result in an unusual expansion of what was meant earlier by "gut level" experience in life, for Cancer is itself ruled by the Moon. Everything lunar functions at high pitch in this sign. Moods are enlarged dramatically; sensitivity and changeability may be exaggerated in some way.

This person "lives to feel." The need to nurture others is great. If you need a bowl of chicken soup, the Cancer Moon will usually provide at least a gallon of it. The problem is generally one of keeping things in perspective. For Cancer Moon, it may take some hard work.

There is the sense of "summation" with a Cancer Moon, but powered here by a real feeling for the group need, which they will home in on quite naturally and almost always try to satisfy. They strive to offer every encouragement for development to others in their sphere of activity. Generosity as such is almost an obligation and sometimes he or she will nearly *demand* to help you, as if it were their inborn right. The effects of constructive flux or change for the better that a Cancer Moon produces can benefit all who chance to fall beneath their goodwill beams.

LEO MOON:

This person has a positive feel for leadership and a sense of preeminence in their emotions as well, which they and others must take into account. The air of assurance is always present to some degree, regarding the relative importance of his or her personal position in a given situation, and this fact bulks large for those who must deal with this Moon sign.

Where give and take are involved, there is a notable freedom of giving and the taking is "understood" since Leo feels that what is his or hers is *his*, no questions asked. There is a great air of vitality and fire and also some stubbornness about changing one's way or altering one's position. Yet Leo Moon tends to sense the overall purpose in emotional situations and often takes the lead in resolving them.

Leo Moon communicates a kind of sufficiency to others that is often unmistakeable, as if karma or inevitable forces had put this person into the place she or he occupies.

Sometimes the appearance of overconfidence is a relatively transparent cover for the need of respect from others that may lie deep within the psyche. Leo Moon demands its due in deference from others, and pays for this in kindness and concern for their ultimate welfare.

VIRGO MOON:

Assimilation to the world as it is, the accommodation of reality "the way things are" is a power that activates this person. Virgo Moon will bend and give, in all the right places, to handle whatever comes his or her way, but this is not to suggest that they themselves are able to "feel" adaptively, better than most. In fact, they are often so well organized that small discrepancies are easily detected, and seem more aggravating to them.

Where the mental component allows Gemini to feel intensely present in the moment, the same mental potential is applied by Virgo in terms of mastering technique and routine. Virgo Moon wants to be ready for all eventualities, and may be overly analytical about how to meet them, over planning for the future. This may drive those around them crazy but it certainly is a force for order in general. "Organization" as an actual feeling is paramount.

This Moon sign is exceptionally well equipped to make "gut level" choices, and the craftsmanship with which they pursue life is often a source of amazement for others. For Virgo Moon, prudence is prudent.

LIBRA MOON:

This person has a feeling for an emotional identification with the concept of equality or equivalence, as such. They are forever testing the winds of every situation to see what is needed to bring things into alignment.

They have the acquisitiveness of Taurus, but this force runs more toward aesthetic harmonies than toward materialistic realizations. There is a positive repulsion for things that are out of tune, and the only area where Libra Moon can go overboard is in the rejection of extremism itself. Their sensitive openness to others must not be infringed upon, or they may "turn off" completely.

A sort of dialectic process is forever operative within the breast of the Libra Moon, and thus their alert attendance upon the value of "rightness" in life. They have a special appreciation for poignancy of emotion, and feel a real sense of presence in the life that expresses these in a measured way. The Libra Moon sense of relaxed poise is based on a true fidelity to past experience, which always sees them prepared for newer ventures.

SCORPIO MOON:

These people know the value of true creativity in making active application of some of life's stronger impulses. This comes from a determination and control that is always oriented toward bringing unused or neglected facets of life into fuller expression. Others may be surprised, or even "turned off" by the results, but they will seldom fail to be attracted in one way or another.

Scorpio Moon has the ability to take the initiative in direct and sometimes unsettling ways. There is notable power to focus single mindedly even obsessively on specific goals. It may be difficult for other people to relate to this kind of intensity.

As a product of their drive toward emotional maturity, this Moon sign often appears to be over indulging, when from a certain point of view they are actually "testing the limits," and busily separating the "wheat from the chaff" of experience. Few know sooner than this person when a situation has lost its merit, or has become outmoded. Scorpio Moon can provide the transmutation of experience through a great power to *lift* even if the lifting involves a sudden *drop* of some kind.

SAGITTARIUS MOON:

Sagittarius Moon has a broad spectrum of contact with its surroundings, and prefers not to be held to any specific point for very long. There may be a tendency here to take an overview approach emotionally, or to view present resources as the means to possibly very distant ends.

A level of enthusiasm is present here that carries over into warm and spontaneous feelings. The imagination is open to stimulation, and there is often a sense of great bouyancy. This can sometimes produce a certain fitfulness that must be recognized as being more natural for this person than for most others. One must not expect to pin down a Sagittarius Moon very easily.

The relativity of standpoint is important to a Sagittarius Moon. That is, this person will strive to find out where another person is "coming from" in order to fix or to understand their own position better. There is very little desire, however, to "corral" another person emotionally. The inner liberty of Sagittarius is itself sufficient motivation to allow full freedom for others, and this person expects to receive an equal measure of the leeway he or she gives in return. The secret of the Sagittarius Moon is its fluidity.

CAPRICORN MOON:

An essential function of this placement is discrimination, and not necessarily in the negative sense of putting down a thing. Here also is the power to know imaginatively and instinctively what is discriminating in the sense of being distinctive or "high class." As long as this does not become an obsession, the Capricorn Moon can become the very model of emotional class and style.

There is a high sensitiveness to the correct way of providing structure to life, of getting things in proper order, making them work right. Filling in all the blanks in life is important to a Capricorn Moon, and they may be rather quick to point out where others have failed to do so. As long as they apply the hard rules of life to themselves, then their sense of authority in guiding others is not without constructive foundation.

This Moon sign has a great drive to express *completion* in life, and may suffer a secret fear of the inadequacy of all of us in the face of extremely high or ideals standards in life. Truly adult and responsible guidance of life's course is a major orientation here. If this person consciously or unconsciously calls our own attention to some deficiency in ourselves, perhaps we should heed the implicit advice that is being offered.

AQUARIUS MOON:

The "friendship" potential of this Moon sign will seldom fail to manifest itself. There is a constant opening up and reaching out going on here, which often will provide an inventive twist to his or her relationships. But to maintain a steady course, Aquarius Moon will usually remain somewhat objective.

Sensitiveness to the right of independence in others is usually high in this person's awareness. This is a practice that most of us try to follow, but none with more sincerity than an Aquarius Moon. There may be ingenious or unconventional results, or unusual associations that are often viewed as being ahead of their time somehow. Substantial ability to make feelings have real effects in the world will be seen here.

Aquarius Moon will tend to penetrate to the heart of any emotional dilemma rather quickly, and often this person is a fine reader of character. There is a particular felicity of detachment here, which yet will successfully avoid becoming separated from others. This is because this combination is almost an embodiment of the term "humanitarian," in the best and truest sense of that word.

PISCES MOON:

This combination has exceptionally sympathetic openness to whatever is taking place in one's surroundings. A constant, subtle, "all-surrounding" impulse is at work. Sometimes the Pisces Moon feels so many things at once that there is a muddle in trying to identify them all. There may be a kind of passivity that is based on gentleness or kindliness. But passivity is still passivity.

This Moon sign has an inward leading that requires constant clarification of one's obligations or responsibilities to oneself and to other persons. This means guarding against any unusual lapse into simply letting important things take care of themselves. The beauty of life is highly appreciated, and steps to make oneself part of the action will be taken by the Pisces Moon.

What really drives the Pisces Moon onward is the sense of incompleteness it seems to see in all directions in life. It is a privilege for this individual to sustain others who may themselves have lapsed into vacillation of some kind. The constructive sacrifice that does not infringe upon one's own integrity attracts this person. Simple argument will seldom force them out of their position, partly because this position is seldom very clearly known itself.

YOUR LUNAR CYCLES

The influences of the transiting Moon are evident in our day to day psychological and emotional states. There is a high and a low in every lunar month along with a Lunar Birthday. As the Moon moves through the chart, it transits each natal planet. All of these bring different reactions.

Your Lunar High: This occurs when the Moon is in the same sign as your natal Sun. If you are a Sagittarius, for example, your lunar high will occur when the Moon is in Sagittarius. The result would be a time of inspiration, when new ventures could be successfully implemented. It is a day when you are most emotionally like your Sun sign. It is a day when your thinking is most sound.

Your Lunar Low: Your lunar low occurs when the Moon is in the sign opposite your natal Sun. If you are a Taurus, your lunar low would occur when the Moon is in Scorpio. Since you are least sure of your decisions on this day, try to leave major decisions to another day. While in a lunar low, you will run into opposition in whatever you may start. This is, however, a good day to exchange ideas since you are much more aware of other people. You may feel restless and will want to keep busy. Plan constructive (but not demanding) projects for this day.

Your Lunar Birthday: If you know the sign and degree of the Moon at the time you were born, you can determine your Lunar Birthday. It comes when the transiting Moon is conjunct, that is, in the same sign as your natal Moon. If your natal Moon is in Gemini, your lunar birthday is when the Moon is in Gemini. The lunar birthday is a time when you respond rather than initiate. You might be absorbed in feelings and sensations. You will often want to be in the company of women on this day.

The Moon Transiting Natal Planets: If you know the positions of your natal planets, you can plot the Moon's passage over these points. *Mercury*: A good day for ideas and communications. *Venus*: Go out and have a good time. *Mars*: Do some hard work. You may be irritating or irritated. *Jupiter*: Don't overindulge. You feel optimistic and self-confident. *Saturn*: Look into yourself. You are realistic and feeling serious today. *Uranus*: Surprises and excitement. A good day to explore and experiment. *Neptune*: You are very emotional. You may forget things and feel lost. *Pluto*: You want to be alone.

Moon

+. .47
360
407
3. 322
dif. 85

12 deg
7 int.
48
+322
418
-360
58

Taurus Moon

4 deg Sag. Moon

Dad

+. 6
360
366
3276
90

13 deg
3 int.
39
276
315

2/7
3

Sag.
7 deg
3+4 Boar H
3
2+7 Boar H
60
187

Aquarius

4 millennium chip × 6/0
/4

Mo   difference   15 degree

102
-187
89

360
i 3
42 3
B. 324
_____

99 dif.   5 int.

Ron

                          Kath
                    t. 176
        14 deg.   B. 92
         3   dif. 84
        ____
         70   4 in.
      + 3 24   12 deg.
      _____   4
       3 9 4   ____
                      48
      - 3 60   t 92
      _____   140
        3 4   3
                      ____
      4 dif. Tarus 23 deg. 143
            Moon

                      Leo
                      Moon

World Events

- Weather
- World Predictions
- Date Tables
- Market Forecast
- Earthquakes
- Hurricanes

HOW PREDICTIONS ARE MADE FOR THE NATIONS OF THE WORLD— FOR 1992 AND BEYOND!

by Noel Tyl

Noel Tyl is one of the most celebrated astrologers in modern history. He has authored 15 best-selling astrological textbooks and has lectured throughout the United States and Europe. His most recent work, *Prediction in Astrology*, focuses in major part on predictions about nations, specifically those involved with the Middle East Crisis. Written *before* the war, Tyl's predictions proved accurate in practically every detail. The overview for 1992 that follows here was written in *March 1991*.

Predictions are astrology's claim to fame as well as astrology's Achilles' heel! The technique of making predictions is elusive; it is an art form based upon scientific measurements, but exactness and reliability, while at times astounding, cannot be guaranteed. On the one hand, we can say that not being able to know everything about life keeps all of us human; and on the other hand, we can continue searching for the accuracy and sureness that *do* occur often—indeed, more and more as we learn about applying astrology to revelation of the future.

Some astrologers specialize in mundane astrology, the branch of the art that deals with celestial phenomena and predictions for the nations of the world. It is interesting to note that predictions for nations very often fall into place more reliably than do predictions for individuals! It may be that nations have less volition within the passage of time than individuals do, what with hundreds of millions of people constantly working together within a government structure throughout all of a nation's history to maintain and fulfill a national profile. Where individuals seem to be able to adjust through free will much of what can happen to them in life, nations seem to make fate happen just as it is suggested in the heavens. Nations tend to behave just as they are expected to in terms of national identity developed over centuries.

Mundane astrologers use the same measurements that other astrologers use, with symbolic meanings adjusted to national significances, but they have to deal with the daunting problem of ascertaining the *birthtime of a nation*! Rarely are the date and time of a nation's "birth" known for sure or even generally, especially in history before World War I.

For example, we *do* know that the modern state of Israel was definitely born on May 14, 1948 at precisely 4:00 PM in Tel Aviv! It was at that time that the meeting began to proclaim independence from post-War rule by the British. The reading of the proclamation to clarify the state of independence took thirty-seven minutes, but Ben Gurion regarded 4:00 PM as the critical time of the new nation's birth and recorded it specifically as so in his diary.

Iraq is the oldest land recorded in world history: the site of the Garden of Eden, the birthplace of Abraham, the domain of Nebuchadnezzar and Hammurabi. We do not know when Adam appeared, but we do know definitely that the modern Kingdom of Iraq was founded millennia later on August 23, 1921 at precisely 6:00 AM in Baghdad. This was the moment the British gave formal recognition to Amir Faisal Ebin Husain as he ascended to the throne as King of Iraq. The recognition and declaration were made at a grand public meeting presided over by Sir Percy Cox, personal representative of England's King George.

For the United States, there are many charts suggested for national birth. In many astrologers' opinions, the chart that works best for the birth of our nation is drawn for July 4, 1776 in Philadelphia at the time of 2:13 *in the morning*. It is extremely difficult to explain this time of birth logically in terms of Congressional meeting schedules and diary entries from two centuries ago, yet this horoscope works extremely well under the tests of some 215 years of detailed history.

When astrologers do *not* know the time or date of a nation's birth, they work with techniques that literally bring the heavens down to earth, inscribing the path of eclipses and the paths of planetary phenomena onto the map of the earth and watching for contact points with national capitals. For example, on December 31, 1980 at precisely 10:19 PM Eastern European Time, the awesomely important initial Grand Mutation Conjunction of Jupiter and Saturn— an event that only occurs approximately every 240 years—*was rising precisely on the horizon at Mecca, Saudi Arabia,* the birthplace of Mohammed, the holiest center of devotion for all of Islam, the religious capital for over one-half billion Muslims throughout the world. Finding this position on earth for this planetary phenomenon provided a predictive base for astrology to anticipate the upheavals that have fractured the Arab world since then and *which will continue to do so until about the year 2080.*

Astrologers know that it was no accident or mere coincidence that within four days of Iraq's invasion of Kuwait and within one day of the order for American troops to go to the Gulf there was a mighty Lunar Eclipse (on August 6, 1990) that keyed critically into the horoscopes of all the countries involved in the war to follow. It was no accident or coincidence that the deadline established by the United Nations for Iraqi withdrawal from Kuwait was January 15, 1991, the date of another eclipse, the position of which involved the Iraqi horoscope and the coalition countries involved in the ensuing conflict.

These two eclipses were the major leading measurements along with bold follow-up movements of the planets (transits) that made possible and sure the prediction of the Iraqi invasion, the American attack after the United Nations deadline, and, later, the change of tactics that was ordered on February 11, the involvement of Israel and other nations, and the abrupt cease-fire.

The United States in Trouble!

Although the United States and the Coalition Forces won the war overwhelmingly decisively, the United States will still be harrassed and challenged in its new role as guardian of the so-called New World Order. Despite claims to the contrary, with its national Sun in the sign of Cancer and its Moon in Aquarius, the United States *loves* this role of protector. The United States has always watched out for the so-called less fortunate in the world. The inscription on the Statue of Liberty says just that in the familiar, mighty poem that begins, "Give me your tired, your poor, your huddled masses yearning to breathe free ..."

Caring for the world is always expensive, of course, but now, United States' caring faces historically formidable financial problems with its vigilance now extended over so much of the world and throughout such protracted time spans yet to be seen. The expense will become more costly than any national or international project in world history because the United States is challenged by unrest throughout the entire Arab world (which *will* continue), is eternally tied to the sovereignty of Israel (politically and astrologically), and, at the same time, must watch carefully the almost copy-cat unrest in Russia and other lands. As guardian, the United States faces infinitely complex drains of time, military power, money, diplomacy, and identity positioning at home and abroad.

The Arabs will continue to threaten Israel; the Arabs will continue to fight among themselves for leadership as "the chosen people"; the states of the Soviet Union will continue to tear away from unionist domain to establish independent sovereignty. There will be uprisings in Ethiopia; there will be attempts to overthrow governments throughout many nations.

The reason all of this tension is so centered in the Middle East is because Moscow, Damascus, Beirut, Baghdad, Jerusalem, Amman, Cairo ... Addis Ababa, and, indeed, the countries clustered in South Africa ... all share *the same geographic longitude within a few degrees!* This means that celestial phenomena that key to this region will involve *all* these capital cities and countries at the same time, and, alarmingly, through very special other measurements, extend as well to the United States and certain European capitals. (In 1992, the celestial phenomena continue to stir up the Middle East and the major "players" involved in the conflict.)

Global Warning Signs

Approximately every two years, the planets Mars and
Saturn join each other in the same longitudinal position in
the heavens. While these planets are vast distances apart
in the depth of space, they line up together and appear to
accompany upheaval in nations on earth when their position connects dramatically with planetary positions in a
national horoscope or is located closely overhead or rising
on the horizon at a capital city. Astrologers know that the
conjunction point of these two planets which symbolize
war energies and enforcement becomes very sensitive and
potentially reactant to other planetary transit contact for a
period of one to two years. From 1934 to 1946, for example,
successive Mars-Saturn conjunctions and follow-up transits actually mapped out on earth the build-up and explo-
sion of World War II.

On March 7, 1992, we have a major global warning sign:
Mars and Saturn are in conjunction at 13 Aquarius 29. This
position is extremely close to conjunction with the United
States Midheaven, the very sensitive point directly overhead in the national horoscope. This phenomenon suggests a tremendous strain put on the Bush administration,
continuing a tense vigilance in military preparedness.

Others measurements linked with this Mars-Saturn
conjunction as viewed from the perspective of Washing-
ton D.C. at the moment of its occurrence (12:51 PM, EST)
promise enormous upheaval with other nations; militarism with substantial jeopardy to human lives; and exorbi-
tant financial tension with many countries that owe the
United States money.

This warning sign is reinforced by the Solar Eclipse that
precedes the planetary conjunction, on January 4, 1992 *opposite the United States' national Sun!* The United States sees
a changing international environment, seeks to maintain
power leadership and establish new order. The United
States embarks on a policy of world surveillance that will
bring near financial calamity domestically through the
drain of political attention and financial resources.

This is serious difficulty, which we will see through
major transit activity in the national chart as early as January 26-28, March 6-12, May 4-16, and May 28-29. The
United States will be challenged to throw its weight

around powerfully. Working with the same dates, we can expect major upheaval to continue and be emphasized in Russia and, again, in Iraq and Kuwait. Just because Kuwait was "saved" in the war does not mean that Kuwait will become peaceful (i.e., free from the age-old passions of the Arab people, one over the other and all against Israel).

Throughout the Middle East, we can expect continuance of the Palestinian tensions, Lebanon's return to prominence, along with Syria, especially in June, November, and December 1992.

The Middle East will be a boiling pot of anxiety highlighting Israel in July and October especially, when terrorism and outright enemy interaction can be expected. Jordan will still be caught in the middle; Syria and Egypt will continue to be key forces in determining the outcome of the tensions as long as they can remain rational within the passionate conflicts among all Arab nations.

Overall, we can expect that there will be a tremendous force to overturn governments everywhere. There will be a new regime in Iraq in March 1992. If a new regime will have been installed in Summer/Fall 1991, the odds are high that it then, in turn, will be changed during this March period in 1992. (There will be an attempt to overthrow the government in Iran in May, July, or October, but the regime in power will prevail.)

The United States will be overseeing all of these hostilities and, additionally, be involved in the crisis that will have built up in the Soviet Union. There, the year 1992 will begin with enormous upheaval started in earnest in October 1991. Tremendous upset, especially from the Youth Movement, can be expected in March, perhaps specifically March 10-20. The change in power in the Soviet Union will be resolved between July and November 1992; there will be a decidedly new national image for this largest country on earth. (It is unlikely that Gorbachev's influence will have prevailed past October 1991.)

We can expect rebel uprisings in Ethiopia in response to severe economic crisis. The Mengistu government is likely to be overthrown by Spring 1992.

It is important to realize that elections can "overthrow" governments as thoroughly as rebellion can. In the Middle

East, November 1992 will be the time of elections in Israel, with so very much of all Middle East strategies dependent on the outcome. Israel's horoscope is in grand change of its national perspectives at that time in October and November specifically, with transiting Pluto opposing its Sun, with Saturn opposing its Pluto. The odds are very high that the Shamir party in power will be changed and that a major shift in philosophy will be propelled by severe economic drain of national resources. Something will have to be done to put Israel profitably into the mainstream of international commerce.

The elections in the United States in November 1992 appear to favor re-election of George Bush conclusively, but not without intense activity, discussion, and politicking about financial affairs, the dangerous ill-health of the nation's savings banks, the costs of world supervision and militarism, especially in July and August. The female vote appears extremely important.

The United States suffers a bad Spring within all these affairs, a tremendous exhaustion of funds, and a startling deception by a friendly nation, which is possible in July, all stoking the fires of intense Congressional debate: pressing social issues at home going unchecked in favor of holding up international militaristic vigilance. A fragile, superficial resolution in favor of sticking with the world view will accompany the election.

Another warning sign studied by mundane astrologers involves the changes of seasons, so very important to the symbology of all astrology. Horoscopes for the Spring and Autumnal Equinoxes, the Summer and Winter Solstices (occurring the 21st of March, September, June, and December, respectively) related to capital cities suggest events to come within the following three months, when the next seasonal horoscope takes over. Through these measurements for 1992, we gain strong corroboration of the events we see suggested from the Mars-Saturn conjunction and follow-up transits.

The Spring period shows the civil uprisings in Russia very dramatically; a major power move by Iran, gaining leadership position and extracting promises from other Arab countries, to signal a very important shift in power throughout the region; a great power push by the United

States to take care of the world; and a great upset in the deteriorating political profile in Germany. At the same time, Egypt and Turkey appear positive in their peace-keeping positions.

The Summer introduces Iraq and Kuwait again to the foreground: tremendous upheaval in both these countries, still trying to recover from the war, still fighting for proper government within the scheme of Middle East realignment, always with Iran essential as a growing force, and always with a bow to ancient anti-semitic passions.

The United States will have a heavy Spring and a very hot Summer, as we have seen, and, on the eve of its elections, the United States will have to face the Jordanian question head on. Syria will be very active in this confrontation, which, by all probabilities, will involve a show of force by the United States.

The year 1992 will end with the United States dramatically on top of the world situation—but not without enormous drain of national resources—and beginning to readdress concerns in Europe specifically. Germany's stability will still be threatened by political incredibility domestically, the people's revolt at severe taxation, and an emerging militarism to keep the peace, recalling events of July, August, and September 1991 in that country.

A third warning sign for mundane astrologers involves Solar and Lunar Eclipses. Again, in 1992, we see corroboration by these eclipse measurements of the other measurements and deductions we have already made. Specifically: early in the year, we will see unrest growing in Berlin, with repercussions in Italy, Austria, and Yugoslavia; unrest in Russia, Ethiopia, Jordan, and Kenya. The Spring of the year is again highly dramatized with the United States and Russia very prominent. The "hot" Summer is also traced on the earth by the Solar Eclipse of June 30, involving Israel belligerently, with Syria "standing guard." The Summer is extremely difficult within the whole world view as it is focused on the Middle East and on the United States' role as militaristic peace-keeper.

It is significant to mention that astrological measurements suggest that there will be major economic adjustments in Japan in the late Spring of 1992. Japan may adopt a protectionist philosophy to hoard national assets: they will be regrouping financial forces for concentrated, new image-building work on the home front. Japan may curtail trade ties or diminish trade activity considerably with many of its allies.

Going Further

It appears that the United States has proclaimed the start of a New World Order *prematurely*. The transition time to that new international arrangement will be protracted well into 1993 and beyond. The war with Iraq was just a warm-up, a tune-up, a blowing off of steam. The war turned up the lights for the United States' international reputation; the nation feels proud again though frustrated that the war ended as abruptly and "unfinished" as it did, and will continue the humanitarian role that is its birthright.

Yet, every nation now wants new weapons for new futures, and the United States is in the position of plying weapons for dollars and allegiance, using armaments and treaties to rebuild seriously exhausted revenues, working full-time domestically to relieve social dissatisfaction and continuing recessions. All active nations seem infected by the plague of civil unrest; astrologers recognize this as a global transformation into the Air Family of values, keyed by the Jupiter-Saturn Grand Mutation, which will not be complete for some 80 years.

While the year 1992 is extremely tense and serious, it is a prelude to even more demanding times in 1993. A rare astrological phenomenon occurs that is a particularly frightening global warning signal: the transit conjunction of Uranus and Neptune (February 3, 1993 at 12:51 PM, GMT).

The conjunction of Uranus and Neptune occurs once every 171 years and carries ponderous symbology with it. Throughout history, the conjunction has accompanied enormous change: the Great Plagues that altered populations drastically throughout Europe and Great Britian; religious uprisings in Spain that bloodied history; and Napoleonic conquests, just to mention a few. We can definitely expect the disruption of traditional, perhaps worn-out social institutions, administrations, laws, and constitutions the world over to continue and intensify.

WEATHER PREDICTIONS
by Nancy Soller

Nineteen ninety-two should see continued drought in the Northeast with the possibility of a partial reprieve in the spring and fall. The drought is associated with the Uranus-Neptune conjunction which began forming in 1989 and will be perfect in 1993. The drought should peak then, but there will will be a continuation of dry conditions as the conjunction separates. Normal weather patterns, however, will probably be restored sometime before the planets are fully separated late in 1997.

Also probably associated with the Uranus-Neptune conjunction is the drought in Florida. The Uranus-Pluto conjunction of the Sixties, which coincided drought in the Northeast, also coincided with drought in the Everglades. It appears that conjunctions of Uranus with planets which move more slowly than itself coincide with drought in these two places.

The *winter* of 1991-1992 will probably see generous precipitation and very low temperatures in the Plains and drought in the extreme West. Wide-spread areas in Alaska will be warmer and drier than usual.

The drought in the Northeast may be temporarily broken in the *spring*, but drought is predicted for the Western Plains and cold, dry conditions are predicted for the Rockies. The Alaskan Panhandle will be wet.

Heat and drought are predicted or both the Northeast and the Midwest in the summer. The drought will continue in Florida and a dry *summer* is predicted for the West Coast.

Fall should see a reprieve in the drought in the Northeast, but dry weather is predicted for much of the Plains where temperatures will be above normal. Chilly weather is predicted for the West Coast and much of Alaska will be drier and warmer than usual.

290 Moon Sign Book

Using Your Weather Predictions

The following weather predictions are based on a study of ingress charts, planetary conjunctions and the weather-changing planetary aspects that occur almost daily. The United States extends so far from east to west that *every* weather-changing aspect is prominent at some United States location. Dates in the following weather predictions that indicate precipitation are the dates when the weather-changing aspects are perfect. In actual practice the precipitation could occur on *that day, the day before or the day after*. Dates which indicate wind usually find wind coinciding almost to the very hour the weather-changing aspect is perfect. Wind dates in italics indicate winds ranging from strong to destructive. When planning an important outdoor activity pick a date that does *not* have a precipitation-causing aspect on that day, the day before or the day after.

The Uranus-Neptune Conjunction
and the Turn of the Age

The Earth makes a very slow twenty-five thousand year wobble around its pole. Because of this the point of the Spring Equinox moves backward about one degree every seventy years. For the last two thousand plus years the point of the Spring Equinox has been traveling backwards through the sign of Pisces. Soon it will leave Pisces and begin traveling backwards through the sign of Aquarius.

Many astrologers will not even attempt to indicate a year when we leave the Age of Pisces and enter the Age of Aquarius. It appears that at the turn of an Age the characteristics of both Ages are in evidence.

Each Age brings its own characteristics and accomplishments. Usually these are good: the age of Cancer brought agriculture; the Age of Gemini brought writing. The Age of Aries, however, brought war.

Astrologers call the Age of Pisces the Age of Christianity. It began about the time of the birth of Christ and it was marked at its beginning by a conjunction of Jupiter, Saturn and Mars in the sign of Pisces indicating that the Age would be characterized by a religious movement. Now, nearly two thousand years after the birth of Christ, entire continents have been converted to Christianity. The coming Age, the Age of Aquarius, is supposed to be the Age of Technology.

The Uranus-Neptune conjunction in Capricorn which is altering precipitation patterns and lending strength to earthquakes has a special significance where the change of an Age is concerned. Nicholas de Vore in his *Encyclopedia of Astrology* indicates that conjunctions or oppositions of Uranus and Neptune, always involving the signs of Cancer and/or Capricorn, always coincide roughly with the fading of one Age and the approach of the next. As we enter the period of time when these two planets are conjunct in Capricorn we know that we will soon be seeing whatever comes as the Age changes.

Neptune is the planet that is associated with the sign of Pisces. Uranus is the planet that is associated with the sign of Aquarius. For the first time in over twenty-five thousand years they are conjunct as an Age of Pisces ends and an Age of Aquarius begins.

Uranus will move into the sign of Aquarius before the conjunction fully separates late in 1997. In January of 1998 Neptune will move into the sign of the new Age also. Events occurring during the Uranus-Neptune conjunction in effect now will set the stage for events which will influence the next two thousand years.

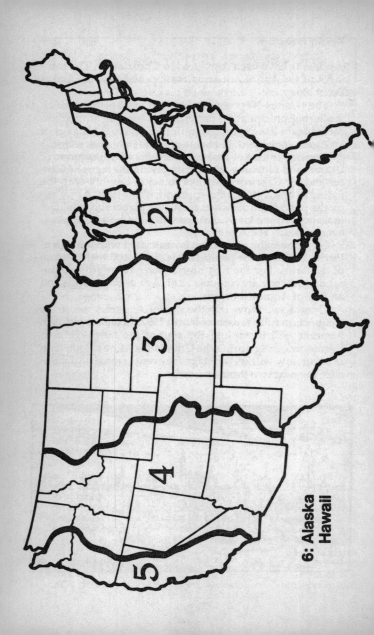

6: Alaska
Hawaii

NOVEMBER 1991 WEATHER

ZONE 1: Wet weather is forecast for the New England area and northern portions of this zone. Temperatures north will be chilly. To the south both temperatures and precipitation should be normal. Thanksgiving will be a memorable day with very heavy snow north and very heavy rain south. Watch for snow on the 3rd, 4th, 7th, 10th, 28th and 30th. New England will see snow on the 25th. This month's weather patterns will continue into December.

ZONE 2: Dry weather is forecast for this zone during the month of November. Temperatures will be colder than normal. Watch for precipitation east on the 3rd and 4th and precipitation west on the 6th and 7th. The 19th and 25th should bring snow to the entire zone. Eastern portions of this zone may see heavy snowfall on Thanksgiving Day. The dry weather should continue into December.

ZONE 3: Dry weather with seasonable to chilly temperatures is the forecast for this zone during the month of November. Precipitation is most likely at the Moon's quarters on the 14th and 28th and following the Full Moon of the 21st. Precipitation on other days should be sparse. Snow is possible on the 19th, but Thanksgiving Day snows will strike farther east. Watch for strong, cold winds November 7th.

ZONE 4: Dry weather is forecast for this zone during the month of November. Temperatures east may be seasonable, but strong, cold winds and below-normal temperatures are forecast for most of this zone. November 14th, 22nd and 28th should bring precipitation, but snow should be sparse north and rainfall minimal south. Strong, cold winds may strike east on the 7th. Dry weather will continue in December.

ZONE 5: Dry weather is predicted for this zone during November. Eastern sections of this zone will be cold and northern and western portions will have above average temperatures. Winds will be prominent. Precipitation will be most likely at the Moon's quarters on the 14th and 28th and the day following the Full Moon of the 21st. Storms forming over the ocean could bring moisture at other times.

ZONE 6: Dry weather and temperatures higher than normal are forecast for Alaska, but some areas in eastern parts of the state north of the Alaskan Panhandle may see generous amounts of precipitation. Hawaii will have a pleasant, normal month with seasonable temperatures. In Alaska, as in the east, Thanksgiving may bring heavy snow. The first and last weeks of the month are the most likely for precipitation.

Dates to Watch:
Watch for rain November 3rd, 5th, 6th, 7th, 10th and 14th.
Watch for snow November 19th, 22nd, 23rd, 25th, 28th and 30th.
Watch for winds November 1st, *3rd,* 5th, 6th, *7th, 8th,* 11th, 12th, *13th, 15th,* 19th, *22nd, 28th* and 30th.

DECEMBER 1991 WEATHER

ZONE 1: Extremely cold with snow is the forecast for this zone north; southern portions of this zone will be cold and wet. Deviations from normal will be most marked in New England. The month will come in with snow and snow is due again on the 7th, 9th, 14th, 17th, 18th, 19th and 21st. A white Christmas Eve promises a white Christmas. Areas south will see generous rainfall on many of the above dates.

ZONE 2: Most locations here will be dry with seasonable temperatures, but some areas east may share in the generous precipitation of *Zone 1*. The month will come in with snow and more precipitation is due on the 3rd. Watch for snow on the 7th, 9th, 14th, 17th, 18th, 19th and 21st. A white Christmas is predicted for this zone with snow and a drop in temperature coming Christmas Eve. Some snow dates above may have merely overcast skies.

ZONE 3: Dry weather with seasonable temperatures is the forecast for this zone in December. The month may come in with snow in the extreme east and there may be snow on the 3rd, but most weather-changing planetary aspects will be prominent *east* of the Mississippi. Snow is predicted for this zone Christmas Eve. A white Christmas is predicted for the plains. Winds will accompany snow then cause drifting.

ZONE 4: Dry conditions and seasonable temperatures are predicted for the Eastern Rockies. To the west it will still be dry, but cold winds will lower temperatures throughout the month. The month will come in with snow and there may be light snow at the Moon's quarters December 14th and 28th. Watch for strong, destructive winds on the 14th and 22nd. The year may end with more strong, cold gusts.

ZONE 5: Dry weather and strong winds are forecast for this zone during December. Temperatures will be above normal on the coast and colder-than-normal east of the mountains. Precipitation is forecast for the 3rd and 18th. Storms originating over the Pacific may reach shore on other dates, but will bring relatively little moisture into the area. Snow is likely to be on the ground north Christmas because snowfall is predicted for the 24th.

ZONE 6: Little precipitation and temperatures above normal are forecast for Alaska, but some areas northeast will receive generous snowfall. Western Alaska will have the most normal weather and Hawaii will have a pleasant, normal month. Temperatures there will be slightly above normal. Dates most likely to result in snowfall in Alaska include the 1st, 7th, 9th, 14th, 17th, 18th, 19th, 21st and 24th.

Dates to Watch:

Watch for snow December 1st, 3rd, 7th, 8th, 9th, 11th, 14th, 17th, 19th, 22nd, 24th and 28th.

Watch for winds December *3rd, 6th, 7th, 8th, 9th, 10th, 11th, 13th, 14th,* 17th, *19th, 22nd, 24th, 25th, 28th* and 31st.

JANUARY 1992 WEATHER

ZONE 1: Little precipitation is forecast for this zone in January with temperatures to the north below normal and temperatures in southern portions of this zone unseasonably high. Snowfall is very likely north on the 12th and is due in wide-spread portions of this zone on the 5th, 13th and 17th. Wind and snow are due the 21st. The 26th and 29th will be wet.

ZONE 2: Areas close to the Mississippi should see much snow this month, but eastern portions of this zone will be dry. Temperatures will be above normal in most of this zone. Watch for snow the 7th and 13th, 15th and 17th. Precipitation is also likely on the 27th and 30th. Strong, cold winds will rake this 8th and these will chill much of *Zone 1* also.

ZONE 3: Areas east of this zone will be relatively dry, but much snow north and generous rainfall south are forecast for this zone. Temperatures will be below normal. The year will begin with wind, snow and cold temperatures. More snow is due the 7th, 14th, 17th, 26th and 27th. An especially heavy snowfall is due the 30th. Strong, cold winds and plunging temperatures are due January 20th.

ZONE 4: The most eastern sections of the Rockies will see a little more snow than usual, but the greatest part of this zone will see far less precipitation than normal. Temperatures will be cold in the extreme east and seasonable elsewhere. The year will begin with wind and snow. More snow is possible the 5th, 7th, 12th, 15th, 26th and 30th. Watch for a dip in temperature January 20th.

ZONE 5: Extremely dry weather is forecast for this zone during the month of January. Temperatures will range from seasonable to a little below normal. The month will begin with wind, rain and cold. Snow is possible the 5th, 12th, 15th and 26th. The 27th should bring snow, wind and a drop in temperature. Areas south may see rain, but precipitation will be sparse the entire month.

ZONE 6: A warm winter with little precipitation is forecast for most of Alaska. Western portions of the state will also be dry, but temperatures here will be extremely cold. Hawaiian temperatures should be a little below normal and precipitation in Hawaii may be less than usual. Likely dates for Alaskan snow include the 5th, 12th, 13th, 17th, 21st, 26th and 29th. Watch for wind in Western Alaska.

Dates to Watch:
Watch for snow January 2nd, 5th, 7th, 12th, 13th, 18th, 21st, 26th, 27th, 28th, 29th and 30th.

Watch for winds January *2nd, 5th, 6th, 8th, 10th,* 12th, 13th, *20th, 21st, 25th,* 27th, *28th* and *29th.*

FEBRUARY 1992 WEATHER

ZONE 1: This zone will see little precipitation in February with below-normal temperatures in New England and warmer-than-normal temperatures in southern portions of this zone. Watch the month open with wind and snow north with more snow due on the 3rd. Dates when precipitation is most likely in this zone include the 6th, 11th, 12th, 15th and 25th. The month, while mostly dry, may end with heavy snow north.

ZONE 2: Dry weather with temperatures above normal is forecast for eastern portions of this zone in February. Areas near the Mississippi will be dealing with temperatures below normal and there is a possibility of generous amounts of precipitation there. The month should begin with wind and snow and precipitation is likely the 4th, 6th, 11th and 15th. The 25th will likely see more precipitation.

ZONE 3: Temperatures below normal are forecast for this zone in February with more snow here than in areas east of the Mississippi. Snow dates here will not be many, but precipitation should be generous when it comes. Watch the end of the month for heavy snowfall; especially the 25th. Two storms originating farther west may reach the plains the 8th and 11th.

ZONE 4: Cold temperatures and little precipitation are forecast for this zone in February. Actual snow dates are few, but snow could be heavy when it comes. February 7th and 11th should bring snowfall in much of this zone; February 19th should bring both snow and wind. Lowest temperatures will be in the east; milder temperatures are forecast for the western portions of this zone.

ZONE 5: Dry weather and normal temperatures are forecast for this zone this month. February 7th could bring both wind and snow north and the 11th may bring rain. Wind and snow are possible the 19th and snow is due north the 25th. A storm originating over the ocean on the 1st could reach land shortly after causing the month to begin with wind and snow. Desert areas of the Southwest will have no precipitation.

ZONE 6: February on the Alaskan Panhandle should be a relatively normal month, but Central Alaska will be dry with above-normal temperatures. Western Alaska will be dry, cold and windy. Hawaii will have temperatures slightly below normal. Most likely dates for precipitation in Alaska include the 1st, 4th, 6th, 11th, 15th and 28th. Winds will accompany some of this precipitation causing drifting when snowfall is generous.

Dates to Watch:
Watch for snow February 1st, 4th, 7th, 8th, 11th, 12th, 15th, 19th, 25th, 26th, 28th and 29th.

Watch for winds February *1st, 3rd, 4th, 7th, 8th, 12th, 15th, 17th, 19th,* 25th, 26th, *27th* and *28th.*

MARCH 1992 WEATHER

ZONE 1: The forecast for most of March calls for cold and dry weather north and dry weather with above-normal temperatures south. Drought should be in evidence this month in the Northeast, but chances for rain will occur on the 8th and 19th with heavy rain possible on the 28th and 29th. Strong winds may accompany the rains of the 19th or precede them by a few hours.

ZONE 2: Eastern portions of this zone should see some very dry weather this month. To the west temperatures will be lower than normal. Also, the greatest chances for precipitation will be found in the western portions of this zone. Rain is possible on the 8th, 19th, 28th and 29th. Heavy winds and/or tornadoes are forecast for the 18th and 19th. Areas north will be drier than areas south.

ZONE 3: Wet at times is the forecast for most of this zone in March. Temperatures west will be a little below normal. Precipitation this month may be relegated to a few dates, but will be ample on those dates. Look for rain on the 19th, 26th and 29th. Tornado activity is likely the 10th, 18th and 29th. Extremely dry conditions are due in April. These will continue through the spring.

ZONE 4: Dry weather is forecast for western portions of this zone in March. Temperatures should be seasonable. To the east there will be a slightly greater chance of rain. The last week of the month should see a temperature dip throughout this zone beginning spring with dry weather and temperatures below normal. This trend will continue through the season. Strong winds are likely this month.

ZONE 5: Dry weather with seasonable temperatures is forecast for this zone in March. The last week of the month may see a temperature dip starting a series of temperature readings slightly below normal which could continue through the spring. Strong winds are possible at the end of the month. Watch for precipitation, a temperature drop and winds on the 6th. Rain is likely the 11th.

ZONE 6: Central Alaska should see clear skies and warmer-than-normal temperatures this month. Western Alaska may be dealing with cold winds. Eastern portions of the state and the panhandle will see normal weather patterns. Hawaii may see temperatures a little below normal. Hawaii may see temperatures a little below normal. Watch for precipitation in Alaska on the 8th, 19th, 28th and 29th. Heavy precipitation in Alaska on the 8th, 19th, 28th and 29th. Heavy precipitation is due east the end of the month.

Dates to Watch:

Watch for snow March 6th, 8th and 12th.

Watch for rain March 19th, 26th, 28th and 29th.

Watch for winds March *6th*, 7th, *8th*, *10th*, 13th, *18th*, *26th*, 28th and *29th*.

APRIL 1992 WEATHER

ZONE 1: April will be wet beginning about three months of relief from dry conditions in the Northeast. Temperatures will be low. To the south precipitation will also be generous and temperatures will be more seasonable. The extreme south is likely to be very dry. Watch for rain on the 1st, 2nd, 8th, 10th, 14th, 17th, 21st and 24th. Cloud seeding over the Everglades in recommended for drought.

ZONE 2: The forecast for this zone in April is for dry weather with seasonable temperatures. Rain dates affecting *Zone 1* are numerous and may also involve rain in *Zone 2*. However, precipitation on these days is likely to be scanty. Best days for rain include April 1st, 2nd, 8th, 10th, 13th, 17th, 21st, 22nd and 24th. Western portions of this zone will be the driest and temperatures highest here.

ZONE 3: Warm and dry is the forecast for most of this zone in April with the driest conditions centering at about 100 degrees west. In the extreme west, close to the Rockies, temperatures will be below normal and winds will be strong. The heaviest rain of the month should come April 13th. Other possible rain dates include the 10th, 17th and 24th. Rain on these days may be scant.

ZONE 4: Cool, dry and windy is the forecast for this zone in April. Watch for rain April 2nd and rain and cold in western portions of this zone April 3rd. Precipitation is also possible on the 8th, 13th and 22nd. Every rain is likely to bring cold, unpleasant conditions because of the low temperatures and wind. The wind and cold will continue through the spring.

ZONE 5: An uneventful month is forecast for this zone in April, but temperatures may be a little below normal and wind is a possibility. The month should come in with a thunderstorm. Rain and cold are predicted for the 3rd and 6th. The last half of the month is likely to be dry unless the numerous storms originating to the west over the Pacific do not die before reaching land.

ZONE 6: The Alaskan Panhandle will be very wet, Central Alaska will be dry and western portions of the state will see some extremely wet weather during the month of April. Rain is likely on the 1st, 2nd, 8th, 10th, 14th, 17th, 21st and 24th of the month. Hawaii will have a wet month with temperatures a little below normal.

Dates to Watch:
Watch for rain April 1st, 2nd, 5th, 6th, 8th, 10th, 18th, 21st, *22nd* and 24th.
Watch for winds April 1st, *2nd, 4th, 6th, 7th, 8th,* 20th, *21st,* 25th and *28th.*

MAY 1992 WEATHER

ZONE 1: May in this zone is likely to see precipitation with cooler-than-normal temperatures north and seasonable temperatures south. Rain is likely on the 3rd, 5th, 9th, 16th, 17th, 21st, 24th and 30th. As in April, the back of the Uranus-Neptune may be temporarily broken, but all rain dates may not bring the promised rain. May 16th and 30th are the best rain dates in New England.

ZONE 2: Pleasant weather with seasonable temperatures and blue skies are forecast for this zone in May. Days most likely to result in rain include the 3rd, 8th, 15th, 16th, 24th, 27th and 30th, but rain coming on these dates may be brief and/or scanty. The beginning of the month may see a tornado, probably on the 3rd, and tornado activity is likely in western portions of this zone May 22nd and 28th.

ZONE 3: A dry month is forecast for this zone in May. Temperatures will run from seasonable to above-normal in most of this zone, but the extreme west will be cold and windy. Dates when rain is likely include the 3rd, 8th, 16th, 27th and 30th. Tornado activity is likely the 22nd and 28th. A trend to dry weather will continue into the summer. Rain, when it comes, should be light.

ZONE 4: Cold, windy weather is predicted for most of the Rockies in May. Western portions of this zone, however, may see more normal temperatures. Precipitation will be sparse, but is most likely on the 3rd, 5th, 9th, 16th and 18th. While wind is predicted, the most destructive winds will strike east of this zone. Western portions of this zone will see the most normal weather.

ZONE 5: Dry weather with temperatures a little below normal is predicted for this zone in May. Wind may increase cold in the northern portions of this zone. May 21st and 26th may see heavy rain in wide-spread areas in this zone, but most other precipitation will originate over the Pacific and will be spent and meager by the time it reaches land. Desert areas will see no rain this month.

ZONE 6: The Alaskan panhandle may be wet, but most of Central Alaska will have little precipitation in May. Both Western Alaska and Hawaii will have both precipitation and temperatures a little below normal. Dry areas will be warmer than normal. Dates when rain is most likely include the 3rd, 5th, 9th, 16th, 17th, 21st, 24th nd 30th. Far Western Alaska should have precipitation on the 8th, 15th and 27th.

Dates to Watch:
Watch for rain May 3rd, 5th, 8th, 9th, 16th, 19th, 21st, 24th, 26th, 27th and 30th.
Watch for winds May *3rd*, 5th, 8th, 9th, *12th*, *13th*, 14th, 16th, *19th*, 20th, *22nd*, *26th*, *27th*, *28th*, *29th*, *30th* and 31st.

JUNE 1992 WEATHER

ZONE 1: June will be a wet month in much of *Zone 1*, with temperatures a little below normal north and seasonable temperatures south. This will be the last month of reprieve in the drought in the Northeast. Watch for rain on the 4th, 7th, 8th, 9th, 13th, 14th and 23rd. In addition, southern portions of this zone will see rain on the 14th, 19th and 26th. Wind will accompany some rains.

ZONE 2: *Zone 2* will see seasonable temperatures and a tendency to dryness. Areas close to the Mississippi will be slightly drier than areas to the east. Watch for rain June 8th and 9th; also on the 13th, 14th, 19th, 20th, 23rd and 26th. Rain, when it occurs, is likely to be light and short-lived. Areas west of the Mississippi will be even drier.

ZONE 3: This zone will see some extremely dry weather this month with high temperatures everywhere but in states bordering the Rockies. There temperatures will be below normal. Watch for rainfall around the 8th and 9th. Rainfall is also possible around the 14th and 19th. The end of the month will be extremely dry with precipitation possible only on the 26th. Winds may accompany low temperatures west.

ZONE 4: Dry weather is predicted for this zone in June. Temperatures will be well below-normal and winds will be prominent. Rainfall will be sparse and precipitation, when it comes, will be short-lived. Best chances for rain come around the 8th of the month, the 26th and at the Moon's quarters June 7th and 23rd. Lack of rain here will lower waters downstream on both sides of the Continental Divide.

ZONE 5: The weather in this zone in June will be the most normal in the nation although the last week of the month may be very dry. Temperatures will be a little below normal except for desert areas where they will range from normal to a little above normal. Rain is likely on the 4th, 8th, 9th, 10th and 26th. After this month precipitation in this zone will be very sparse.

ZONE 6: Precipitation may be generous on the Alaskan Panhandle, but Central Alaska will be dry with temperatures above normal. Both Western Alaska and Hawaii may see precipitation and some temperatures a little below normal. Best chances for rain come on the 4th, 7th, 8th, 9th, 13th, 23rd and 26th. Rain is most likely west on the 14th and 19th. Dry weather will mark the month's end.

Dates to Watch:
Watch for rain June 4th, 7th, 8th, 10th, 11th, 13th, 16th, 19th, 20th, 23rd and 26th.
Watch for winds on the 4th, 7th, *13th, 18th, 19th, 20th, 21st,* 26th and 27th.

JULY 1992 WEATHER

ZONE 1: Blue skies and seasonable temperatures are forecast for most of this zone in July, but this month is likely to see a return of the drought in the Northeast. Dates most likely to result in rain include the 2nd, 5th, 6th, 8th, 22nd, 25th and 26th. July 15th will result in rain south. Some rain dates north will result only in cloudy skies. To the west it will be dry also.

ZONE 2: Dry and hot is the forecast for this zone in July. Rain is possible on the 2nd, 8th, 15th, 22nd and 25th. The 5th and 6th may see rain in the extreme east. Dry weather this month is a harbinger of dry weather the rest of the summer. Rain, when it does come, is likely to be short-lived and scanty. Watch for a tornado July 9th. The rain on the 8th will involve wide-spread areas.

ZONE 3: Hot and dry is the forecast for this zone in July. Eastern portions of this zone will suffer the most. Rain dates include the 2nd in the east, the 5th, the 15th, the 22nd and the 30th. The dry weather evident this month should continue the rest of the summer. Rainfall is likely to be short-lived and scant. Watch for tornado activity July 9th. Temperatures may dip July 2nd.

ZONE 4: Dry weather is forecast for this zone in July. Temperatures should be a little above normal. Rain is predicted for July 6th and in the west on the 8th. A short, heavy downpour is due the 15th. The extreme west may see rain on the 26th and a thunderstorm is due on the 30th. The dry conditions of this month will continue through the summer. Rainfall on the 8th should be wide-spread.

ZONE 5: Dry weather is predicted for this zone during the month of July. Precipitation, when it comes, will be sudden and winds will be strong. A thunderstorm is due July 8th with more rain coming on the 9th and 14th. The month will go out with rain and it is possible that another storm originating out over the ocean will reach land the last week of the month.

ZONE 6: The weather in all of Alaska this month should be normal for the season. Hawaii should have a pleasant July weatherwise. Dates involving precipitation in Alaska include the 2nd, 5th, 6th, 8th, 22nd, 25th and 26th. July 9th should see rain, but only on the Alaskan Panhandle. Precipitation in Hawaii should be normal and may involve some of the same rain dates listed above for Alaska. Good weather this month may continue all summer.

Dates to Watch:
Watch for rain July 2nd, *3rd*, 6th, 7th, 8th, 9th, 15th, 22nd, 23rd, 25th, 26th and 30th.
Watch for winds July *2nd*, 6th, *7th*, *8th*, *9th*, *12th*, 15th, *23rd*, *25th*, *26th*, *30th* and 31st.

AUGUST 1992 WEATHER

ZONE 1: Dry weather with above-normal temperatures north and seasonable temperatures south is predicted for this zone in August. Precipitation is predicted for most of this zone August 5th and 7th and again on the 13th. Rain is also predicted for the 18th and 20th. The 21st, 23rd and 24th are also likely to see precipitation, but most rains in the Northeast will be scant. Some rain dates may just see overcast skies.

ZONE 2: Dry and hot is the prediction for this zone in August. Areas nearest the Mississippi will have the least amount of precipitation. Rain is possible on the 5th and 7th and also on the 13th. More precipitation is due on the 17th, 18th and 20th. The 21st, 23rd and 24th should also see rain. Precipitation, when it comes, will be light and short-lived. Some rain dates may just see overcast skies.

ZONE 3: August in *Zone 3* will be dry. Temperatures will range from seasonable to a little above normal. Areas near the Mississippi will receive the least amount of rainfall. Watch for rain on the 5th and rain east on the 7th. Precipitation is likely on the 9th, 13th, 17th and 18th. August 20th, 21st and 23rd are likely to see rain. Precipitation, when it comes, will be light and short-lived.

ZONE 4: The forecast for this zone is for weather a little drier than normal with temperatures that are seasonable. The first week of the month will be dry, but precipitation is due on the 9th. August 17th and 18th should bring rain as should the 20th. The trend to dry weather will continue the rest of the summer and well into the fall. Precipitation, when it comes, will not be as generous as in other years.

ZONE 5: Very dry weather is predicted for *Zone 5* in August. Temperatures will range from well below normal to seasonable. Winds will be prominent. Dates involving precipitation are few. Watch for rain August 9th, 18th and 20th. August 23rd should result in precipitation also. Some rain originating over the Pacific may reach land on other dates. Dates listed as wet in Alaska would be involved.

ZONE 6: Weather in Central Alaska will be slightly warmer and drier than usual. Weather on the Alaskan Panhandle should be about normal. Western Alaska should see some beautiful, blue skies and Hawaii should have a pleasant, normal month. Rainfall is likely in Alaska on the 5th, 7th, 14th, 18th, 20th, 21st, 23rd and 24th. Much of this precipitation could affect both the Panhandle and the central part of the state.

Dates to Watch:
Watch for rain August 5th, 7th, 9th, 14th, 17th, 19th, 20th, 21st, 23rd and 24th.
Watch for winds August *2nd, 5th,* 7th, *11th, 12th,* 17th, 19th, 20th, 23rd, *24th, 27th, 28th* and 30th.

302

SEPTEMBER 1992 WEATHER

ZONE 1: Blue skies and mild temperatures are forecast for most of this zone this month, but drought conditions will prevail in the Northeast. The last week of the month may bring some relief there. Rain is most likely on both the 26th and 28th north; other dates that could result in rain include the 3rd, 10th and 11th. Next month should bring more normal rainfall patterns north.

ZONE 2: Dry weather is forecast for this zone in September, but the last week of the month may see generous rainfall east. Temperatures should be above normal. Rain is possible September 3rd, 8th and 10th. The 11th may bring both wind and rain. Precipitation is also very likely east on the 26th and 28th. Heavy rain falling in this zone at the end of the month will indicate a wet fall.

ZONE 3: Dry, hot weather is forecast for this zone in September. Records for high temperatures may be broken this month in this zone. Not only do ingress charts suggest dry weather, but there are only a few dates in September when planetary aspects suggest precipitation in this zone. Best dates for rain include September 8th, 11th and possibly 13th. Watch for rain east the 10th. The dry, hot weather will continue all fall.

ZONE 4: Dry weather is forecast for this zone in September. Areas east will be hot and dry; areas in the extreme west dry, cold and windy. The last week of the month should see the beginning of more normal precipitation and temperature patterns. Rain is most likely on the 10th and in the extreme west on the 11th and 19th. Watch for more rain September 26th. Rainfall on the 10th should be wide-spread.

ZONE 5: Dry weather is predicted for this zone in September. Temperatures will be below normal and winds will be prominent. The last week of the month should be extremely cold north beginning a weather pattern that will continue through the fall. Precipitation is likely on the 10th, 11th, and 13th. September 19th is also likely to see rain. The 26th may see a little precipitation north.

ZONE 6: A normal month is predicted for both Alaska and Hawaii although the last week of the month will bring high winds to the Alaskan Panhandle. Temperatures here should be seasonable despite the wind. Watch for precipitation in Alaska on the 3rd, 8th, 10th, 11th, 26th and 28th. The same dates may result in weather changes in parts of Hawaii. The Alaskan Panhandle will see wind the entire fall season.

Dates to Watch:
Watch for rain September 3rd, 8th, 10th, 11th, 12th, *13th*, 19th, 26th and 28th.
Watch for winds September 6th *10th, 11th, 12th, 13th,* 14th, *15th, 16th, 18th, 22nd, 26th, 27th* and *28th.*

OCTOBER 1992 WEATHER

ZONE 1: A reprieve from the drought lasting several months is due to begin this month in the Northeast. The entire *Zone 1* area should see generous rainfall. Temperatures will be seasonable. Rainfall is likely October 4th, 6th, 8th, 9th, 15th, 17th, 18th, 20th and 21st. Conservation of water now and through the rest of the fall could ease water problems when the drought returns. Temperature dips will coincide with rain.

ZONE 2: Eastern portions of this zone should see generous rainfall this month, but areas near the Mississippi will be dry. Temperatures will range from normal east to a little above normal west, but temperature dips will accompany most rains this month. Watch for precipitation on the 4th, 6th, 8th, 15th, 17th, 18th, 20th, 21st, 25th and 29th. Dry areas will see dry conditions for two more months.

ZONE 3: An extremely dry month is predicted for this zone in October. Temperatures will be above normal. Best chances for rain come on the 4th, 8th, 11th, 20th, 25th, 29th and in the far west on the 9th. Rain is likely east on the 15th and 17th. Drops in temperature will accompany most rain. Dry conditions this month should continue through the season and many dates when rain is possible may merely be overcast.

ZONE 4: Eastern portions of this zone will be dry and the extreme west will be cold and windy this month. The central portions of this zone should have seasonable temperatures and normal precipitation. Rain is likely on the 4th, 9th, 11th, 12th, 21st and 29th. Temperature drops will accompany most rain. Areas that are dry this month will continue to be dry the entire fall season.

ZONE 5: Cold, dry and windy weather is predicted for this zone north in October. Areas south will have below-normal temperatures and wind. Watch for rain October 4th, 8th, 9th, 11th, 18th, 21st and 25th. Most rain this month will be accompanied by temperature dips. The cold winds and the tendency to dryness should continue through November and most of December. Some rain dates may merely be overcast.

ZONE 6: A pleasant October is forecast for Hawaii and the central and western portions of Alaska. The Alaskan Panhandle and eastern portions of the state will have the dry, cold winds also predicted for *Zone 5*. Rain is most likely on the 6th, 8th, 15th, 17th, 18th, 20th, 21st and 29th. Blue skies are forecast west on days without rain. Pleasant weather there should continue through the entire fall season.

Dates to Watch:

Watch for rain October 3rd, 4th, 5th, 6th, 8th, 9th, 11th, 12th, 14th, 15th, 17th, 18th, *21st*, 26th and 29th.

Watch for winds October *3rd*, *5th*, 6th, *7th*, *9th*, *12th*, *14th*, *15th*, *17th*, 18th, 20th, 22nd, *26th*, 29th and *30th*.

NOVEMBER 1992 WEATHER

ZONE 1: Wet weather is predicted for this zone in November with the Northeast still getting a reprieve from the drought. Temperatures will be seasonable. Rain is predicted for November 2nd with more rain coming on the 6th, 8th and 11th. The 17th should see precipitation with a drop in temperature. Snow is predicted north for the 19th. Watch for additional precipitation on the 24th and 29th.

ZONE 2: Wet weather is forecast for the eastern portions of this zone, but most of this zone will have dry weather this month. Best chances for rain will come on the 2nd, 6th, 8th, 11th, 17th and 19th. Precipitation is also likely on the 24th, 26th and 29th. Temperatures throughout the month will be seasonable, but watch for temperature dips on the 6th, 17th, 24th and 26th. Snow north is forecast for the 24th and 26th.

ZONE 3: The forecast for this zone is for dry weather during the month of November with temperatures well above normal. Rain is possible on the 4th and likely east on the 6th. Rain south and snow north is predicted for the 17th with precipitation west on the 19th. Watch for snow November 24th. The 27th and 29th could also bring snow in some places. Dry weather this month should continue through most of December.

ZONE 4: This zone will see plenty of sunshine with temperatures ranging from normal to a little above normal. Precipitation, when it comes, will be a little more generous and long-lasting than in *Zone 3*. Precipitation and a temperature drop are due November 4th. Other dates likely to result in rain or snow include the 6th, 13th, 19th, 24th, 27th and 29th. The 6th will be cold and windy.

ZONE 5: Cold, windy weather is forecast for this zone in November. Temperatures should be well below normal and there will be little precipitation. Rain is most likely on the 4th, 17th, 19th and 27th. Some storms originating over the ocean on other dates may reach land, but will not increase the total amount of precipitation appreciably. Weather patterns in effect this month should continue into December.

ZONE 6: The forecast for Alaska is for cold, dry weather on the Alaskan Panhandle with dry weather and seasonable temperatures over most of the rest of the state. Hawaii should have an uneventful month weatherwise. Best dates for snow in Alaska include the 2nd, 6th, 8th, 10th, 17th, 19th, 24th and 29th. Rain could come on many of these dates in Hawaii. Snow will not be generous in Alaska.

Dates to Watch:

Watch for rain November 2nd, 4th, 8th and 11th.

Watch for snow November 17th, 18th, 20th, 24th, 26th, 27th and 30th.

Watch for winds November 3rd, 7th, *15th*, *18th*, 19th, *21st*, 23rd, *24th*, *26th* and *27th*.

DECEMBER 1992 WEATHER

ZONE 1: The break in the drought should continue this month in the Northeast. Southern portions of this zone should have more precipitation than usual. Temperatures will be seasonable. The month will come in with wind and snow. Watch for snow on the 3rd, 6th, 7th, 10th and 16th. Snow is due in New England on the 19th. Snow is also predicted for the 21st and 29th. Winds will be sharp north.

ZONE 2: Most of this zone will see normal precipitation this month, but areas bordering the Mississippi will be dry. The northern part of the Mississippi River Valley will be especially dry and temperatures here will be milder than usual for the season. Precipitation is most likely on the 1st, 3rd, 6th, 10th, 16th, 21st and 29th. Winds will accompany precipitation on most of these dates.

ZONE 3: This zone will be dry in December with temperatures milder than normal. Most days involving precipitation will also have wind. Snow north and rain south will be short-lived and scanty. The first half of the month will see the greatest amount of precipitation. Watch for snow or rain on the 1st, 2nd, 3rd, 6th, 7th, 10th, 11th, 16th, 23rd and 29th. Snow on the 23rd will melt before Christmas.

ZONE 4: Mild temperatures and beautiful blue skies are forecast for this zone in December. The extreme eastern part of the Rockies will see the mildest temperatures, but the extreme west and north will share in the cold, windy weather forecast for *Zone 5*. The entire zone will tend to dry weather. Precipitation is most likely on the 5th, 6th, 9th, 11th, 16th, 23rd, 24th and 29th.

ZONE 5: Cold, windy and dry is the forecast for this zone in December. Temperatures north will be especially chill, but the entire zone could see some record-breaking lows. Precipitation will be sparse. Best dates for snow and rain include the 5th, 6th, 9th, 11th, 16th, 23rd and 29th. There is a possibility of snow north Christmas Eve. Winds will accompany snow the 6th, 23rd and 29th.

ZONE 6: The Alaskan Panhandle may see precipitation, but most other parts of the state will have dry weather with temperatures a little milder than usual. Hawaii will have a pleasant, normal month. Most days this month that do see precipitation will also see wind. Alaskan snow will be scant and short-lived. Best dates for precipitation include the 1st, 3rd, 6th, 7th, 10th, 16th, 19th, 21st and 29th.

Dates to Watch:
Watch for snow December 2nd, 3rd, 5th, 6th, 7th, 10th, *11th*, 16th, 17th, 19th, 21st, 22nd, 23rd, 24th, 26th, 29th and 30th.
Watch for winds December 2nd, 3rd, *5th*, *6th*, 7th, *10th*, 17th, 21st, 22nd, 23rd, *26th*, *28th*, 29th and *30th*.

EARTHQUAKE PREDICTIONS
by Nancy Soller

The most interesting day of the year for earthquake watchers will be January 4th (January 5th in Japan) when an annular solar eclipse, visible at noon over the Pacific, will take place at thirteen degrees of Capricorn. Uranus at thirteen degrees of Capricorn and Neptune at sixteen degrees of Capricorn will conjunct each other and the Sun indicating that an earthquake is likely to coincide with the eclipse and would be likely to occur somewhere in the Pacific area. Uranus is often directly overhead at the time of an earthquake and, since it exactly conjuncts the Sun at the time of the eclipse, it indicates that noon is the time most fraught with danger from a quake.

The ancients believed that when a planet was conjunct the Sun at the time of an eclipse an earthquake occurred in the same part of the world in which the earthquake was visible. Modern observations indicate that earthquakes can occur out of range of the eclipse view and that the time of the quake may not coincide exactly with the eclipse. However, noon anywhere in the Pacific area could result in a quake. Areas in danger include Japan, the Aleutian Islands, the west coast of North America (including California), Australia and the South Pacific.

Venus will be conjunct the Sun during a total solar eclipse June 30, 1992. This eclipse will be visible over much of South America, the South Atlantic and South Africa and could involve land areas bordering the Atlantic in its accompanying quake. Areas north of the equator are probably not exempt.

The solar eclipse of December 24th will not take place with a planet conjunct the Sun and so will not be associated with any earthquakes taking place that day. However, later quakes may involve this eclipse-point as the traveling planets form hard angles to it.

Quakes of the Nineties

Earthquake watching in the Nineties should be an especially rewarding pastime because of the unusually large number of eclipses which take place in the signs of Cancer and Capricorn in 1990, 1991 and 1992. This involves a total of six eclipses and six eclipse-points, most of which will be struck or opposed by the Uranus-Neptune conjunction as it travels through Capricorn.

We are still in the process of finding out how this works, but it has long been known that large earthquakes tend to coincide with planets forming hard earth-centered angles to recent eclipse-points. Conjunctions of the slow-moving outer planets are rare, but show up in the charts of spectacular quakes in the years they do occur.

February, November and December of 1993 will see Uranus and Neptune exactly conjunct each other and opposing the July 11, 1991 eclipse-point of nineteen degrees of Cancer. Watch for at least one spectacular quake during these months.

Nineteen ninety-three will be the last year Uranus and Neptune will be in exact conjunction, but in every year between then and 1999 at least one of them will be opposing or conjuncting a critical eclipse-point in Cancer or Capricorn. The two planets will remain in effective conjunction until the end of 1997. We will probably be seeing more and bigger earthquakes.

Sun-centered hard angles of the Earth to recent eclipse-points also coincide with large earthquakes. Because of the large number of eclipses in Cancer and Capricorn, any month that the Earth is in a cardinal sign (as viewed from the Sun) it forms several such angles and several large quakes are possible. January, April, July and October are the months to watch, but December 31st could also result in a quake in 1992.

EARTHQUAKES AND ECLIPSE-POINTS

by Nancy Soller

Most earthquakes that make headlines occur on days when at least one planet is making an earth-centered hard angle to a recent eclipse-point. The hard angles are the zero, ninety and one hundred eighty degree angles.

Only some days that see a planet forming a hard angle to a recent eclipse-point result in earthquakes. Other factors have to be in effect in order for this to happen. These factors include:

The Moon in critical aspect to its nodes. (This is another way of saying that the Moon is on the equator or at a high point or low point in relation to it.)

Another planet making a hard angle to the recent eclipse-point at the same time.

Two or more other planets forming hard angles to two or more other recent eclipse-points at the same time.

Mars and Neptune in a hard angle to each other.

The Moon at perigee. (The Moon at its near point to the Earth.)

A Full Moon is suspect.

As mentioned before, a planet in conjunction with the sum at the time of an eclipse can trigger an earthquake at about the same time as the eclipse and in the same general part of the world. The eclipses used in this method of earthquake prediction involve solar eclipses. All the hard angles involved in the above are Earth-centered.

When the Earth makes a Sun-centered hard angle to a
very recent eclipse-point an earthquake can occur. It does
not appear that any other factor needs to be in effect, or
possibly that other factors may be necessary, but are not
yet identified.

Large earthquakes do occur that do not appear to involve eclipse-points. However, earthquakes which make
the news media usually do.

High Risk Dates for Earthquakes

January:
Very high risk: 4th, 19th
High risk: 2nd, 5th
Earthquake possible: 1st, 3rd, 7th, 8th, 11th

February:
Very high risk: 17th
High Risk: 27th, 28th
Earthquake possible: 4th, 5th, 8th, 15th, 18th

March:
High risk: 6th, 13th
Earthquake possible: 15th, 16th, 26th, 30th

April:
Earthquake possible: 2nd, 8th, 9th, 13th, 15th, 17th,
    23rd, 28th

May:
High risk: 6th
Earthquake possible: 7th, 19th, 27th

June:
Very high risk: 9th, 30th
High Risk: 14th, 22nd
Earthquake possible: 3rd, 8th, 12th, 14th, 20th, 23rd,
    26-29th

July:
High risk: 13th
Earthquake possible: 3rd, 15th, 18th, 19th

August:
High risk: 23rd, 26th, 27th
Earthquake possible: 8th, 13th, 21st, 24th, 25th, 27th-29th

September:
Very high risk: 12th
High risk: 25th
Earthquake possible: 1st, 9th, 10th, 25th, 30th

October:
High risk: 2nd, 21st
Earthquake possible: 24th

November:
High risk: 19th, 25th
Earthquake possible: 6th, 12th, 13th, 21st, 22nd, 30th

December:
Earthquake possible: 3rd, 5th, 7th, 10th, 11th, 13th, 16th, 30th

January, April, July and October are likely to result in earthquakes not indicated above because the Earth will be forming heliocentric hard angles with recent eclipse-points in Cancer and Capricorn.

Additional high risk dates in *January:* 10th, 16th, 20th
Additional high risk dates in *April:* 3rd, 19th
Additional high risk dates in *July:* 5th, 12th, 15th, 19th
Additional high risk dates in *October:* 6th, 13th, 19th, 23rd
 December 31st

ECONOMIC FORECAST FOR 1992

by Pat Esclavon Hardy

As we enter 1992, we could still be dealing with some of the same issues from 1991, due to the final eclipse in the "7 eclipse series" on January 4, 1992. This Solar Eclipse will be at 13 degrees of Capricorn exactly conjunct Uranus, trine Jupiter and within 3 degrees of conjuncting Neptune. (The last occurrence of a 13 Capricorn Solar Eclipse was in 1935.) This final eclipse really brings home what our unfinished business is all about! There will be a new awareness of factors associated with those important issues of '91. Something we were totally unaware of before, but now must take these new factors into our decision-making processes. And decision-making is what we will be doing this year, more so than ever.

Capricorn eclipse will again focus on laws, how laws are established and the content or true meaning by which we all can use these laws. Government issues such as the all incurring budget deficit, military issues, environmental laws, abortion and naturally the Presidential election will have the greatest impact on our society this year. You will need to do your research and be in touch with what the benefits and/or consequences could be concerning these laws and issues. Big CHANGES are ahead of us as we start to assimilate what we experienced last year and will not tolerate old habit patterns of throw-away America, polluting, chemical waste and politicians who have outworn their stay in Congress, and all the way down the ladder to governor, mayor and commissioners!

This January eclipse will expedite messages pertaining to the exact Neptune/Uranus conjunction which occurs in February 1993. But April 20-21, 1992 Uranus and Neptune will be stationary retrograde within 57 minutes of each other and this is very powerful! Essentially it has the same connotation as the conjunction due to both planets being stationary in the same degree at 18 Capricorn. First of all, the primary message is SPIRITUAL AWARENESS. Now this can come in many ways; it may start out with the awareness and action taken concerning Mother Earth and how we are misusing our planet, concern for the animals and essentially all creatures great and small! We have been hearing about these issues for the last few years, you will see more and more activity associated with them and laws being changed to protect and conserve in many areas.

Mass consciousness can experience tremendous insights into themselves. Psychic awareness will achieve a whole new attitude of acceptance as more and more people are experiencing it. Would you ever think that this could become mainstream? At the close of this second millennium there are unmistakable signs of world-wide multidenominational religious and spiritual revival! Strange new influences will be seen, some even bordering on the bizarre; new kinds of consciousness, some very high, others very low. One of the common denominators is that during this period in our lives, things may get so hectic or moving so fast that we find it hard to keep pace; therefore people will be looking for ways to let their minds escape, since schedules may not provide the time to get away physically. The fad that can become popular will contain the ingredients for people to escape with their minds. Maybe one step further than video and music. In the 60's it was mind altering drugs, hopefully in the 90's it can be through philosophy, belief systems, meditation, psychology and the raising of our consciousness. That's how we make shifts to meet the demands on us that are already in motion in this final decade of the millennium! In turbulent times, in times of great change, people head for two extremes: fundamentalism and personal, spiritual experience.

Baby boomers who rejected organized religion in the 70's are returning to church with their children in tow or joining the New Age movement. They will be the ones who will initiate some of the upcoming changes in religious organizations. When people are buffeted about by change, the need for spiritual belief intensifies. Most seek reassurance in one of two ways: either through inner-directed, "trust the feeling inside" movements or through outer-directed, "this is the way it is," authoritarian religions.

One of the fastest growing professions will be in the area of psychology. This is due to the awareness that people will have on how to train their minds in a completely different and unique way. People want to figure out what makes them tick so they can understand themselves better. Why not program our own minds instead of allowing all those other influences to affect us. More of a take charge and responsibility type attitude for our mental health. Exercising our minds is just as important as our physical health. So we had aerobics in the 80's for physical fitness, there could evolve a trend whereby MENTAL fitness clubs or groups become a new wave for the 90's! We may just have to do it to keep up with the new wave of children growing up with computerized information. . . . What will they be like to talk to?

A quantum leap in the way we think as a human race will be the initial outcome when the Neptune/Uranus conjunction finally moves through mass consciousness by 1994. These attitudes will become mainstream and be seen in advertising, Hollywood, TV, business and everyday activities. Large numbers of people join together in some major effort. Bottom line is "spiritual awareness"!

Uranus/Neptune is also associated with religions and churches. The sign of Capricorn is associated with structures. For example, the Roman Catholic Church in the United States is only lukewarm with its relationship to the Roman Catholic Church in Rome. There have been many disagreements on abortion, gay rights, and divorce with the political church in Rome. These planetary energies can be a catalyst to some significant disruption, rebellion within the structures of the Roman Catholic Church—to the point of a possible split with the Vatican. Other churches may see some of the same underlying problems. As spiritual awareness develops within religious organizations, a pull on the ol' political "chain" occurs to keep members from straying and thinking for themselves. Religious laws and politics are just as powerful as any country's!

Also a new trend could occur in that the post-Communistic countries open their doors to freedom of religion, creating a massive tidal wave of worshipers expressing their spiritual beliefs! The spiritual resurgence would be in full force.

Another issue is that Neptune symbolizes water, oil, gas. In 1990-91 we had the crisis in the Gulf with Iraq. Issues over water, gas, and/or oil rights are of primary focus now. Not just with the oil lords, but with all bodies of water, oil and gas reservoirs. Water pollution and contamination is an issue of which we have all been aware for the past several years. It won't be tolerated any longer! It will be too precious to us—for survival!

Global laws (Capricorn/Saturn) may be made and executed concerning water-rights, and aggressive action taken on or under water. Seaports and piers may see a renovation or new look. Bridges, rivers and streams are spotlighted. The Uranus/Neptune conjunctions of the past show us common denominators as in the 1600's, river protectionism laws were initiated. In the 1800's, seaports were revived and new ones opened. In the 90's bridge/overpass structures could be updated.

This conjunction favors independence, equality, human rights and social progress. There is power with the numbers. Many people pooling their resources together to channel the outcome of a specific issue. You just may see humanitarianism clashing with materialism and elitism. Neptune's limitlessness may get out of control—the most powerful people could get what they want.

JUPITER TRINE URANUS

These four years from 1990 through 1993 will have made us aware of issues and problems that were shouting to be solved. The planet Jupiter symbolizes, among other things, the TRUTH! The decade of the 90's is fast becoming the DECADE OF TRUTH. Being truthful to ourselves about who we are and how we relate with, not only others, but with this planet—our only home! More of a global attitude.

Jupiter trine Uranus is the most significant aspect for the year. This particular cycle started February 18, 1983.

The Jupiter/Uranus cycle is partially responsible for maintaining the economic prosperity that was prevalent through the 1980's under the Sagittarius expansion energy. This year Jupiter will be on it's waning trine (120 degrees) in the Virgo/Capricorn earth energy which brings more contraction, practicality, organization, accountability and effort into making the economy maintain its course. Dates emphasized are November 11, 1991; January 12, 1992; and July 31, 1992.

The general public is very cognizant of the economic problems facing the world right now, and that is why it has temporarily retreated into hibernation until the next course of action becomes apparent. But there are also the map-makers ... aware of the problems, they rise above it all to gather energy and support in creating a new and unique way to bring solutions to these problems. The problem-solvers of the 90's are our most valuable people.

There is a basic need to experience a new kind of freedom and to discover dimensions of living that we have not known before. It will be more traditional in a unique or bizarre kind of way, practical and down to earth. It also signifies a strong desire for us to release the restrictions that have limited us seeing what is real and true. The search for inner truth is on, and the trends of 1992 will be more environmental and earth oriented. Cleaning up our acts will be the main issue on the agenda. Recycling could be put into law forms. With many budgets pulled tight, we are finding unique ways to be effective without the major costs involved. Doing it simpler with better results. These past 24 months have truly been times we have learned to trim the fat from the indulgent 1980's and get down to basic facts and true realism of the 1990's!

An important discovery or invention could be this year's greatest hit! Something totally out of the blue and yet very simple that it could have been overlooked and under our noses for years—just waiting to be seen!

Things of the earth will have our attention. Emphasis also on commodities such as grains, soybeans, oil, gas, gold and silver could have their bullish runs on occasion. We are still trying to acquire our equilibrium from the oil crisis.

This is a Presidential election year. You will see more

mud-slinging than ever. With the computer age delivering data faster than can be assimilated, facts and dates will be easily researched on the candidates to support or tear them apart. You may see large groups (people power) targeting a specific issue(s) and matching it to the person who stands for that issue! It's not just the person! It's how many people can get together to nominate someone who will pass the anti-abortion bill, or gay rights amendments, or whatever the cause. So it will be imperative that you register to vote and vote with your conscience. Research and brush up on the facts. Know for whom and what you are voting!

JANUARY

As we ring in the New Year of 1992, the overtones of this being a Presidential election year will bring more conservatism and possible loosening, but may be too late. The tax law changes and budget changes from 1990 will be filtering into the economy now and the pinch is on. This is the year it will be truly felt.

Wall Street could start the New Year off with a roller coaster month, as the Solar Eclipse on January 4th at 13 Capricorn conjunct Uranus trine Jupiter will complete the seven (7) eclipse year that started last January 1991. Expect the unexpected this month. Should see signs of bullishness early and late in the month and who knows what in between! Truly action oriented!

Best advice is to be flexible and be aware. . . . The technology sector will have the limelight this month! Areas to watch could be space, airlines, utilities, electronics, computers (hardware and software), information systems, and telecommunications. Possible bullishness concerning these areas due to benefic Jupiter.

Since the economy was recession oriented this past year, we could see things improve off and on as we move through the year. Not really coming out of recession, but having a mild recession, after all . . . it is an election year— and whoever acquires the next 4-year term has a challenge keeping the economy from a deeper recession; I think statistics like GNP, unemployment, housing starts, retail sales, etc. are manipulated to reflect a milder recession than what most of us are experiencing.

A major focus we must be aware of this year is the potential for earth disturbances. The Full Moon on January 19th has an above average lunar tidal pull. Earthquakes and/or volcanic activity could be highly prominent between now and the New Moon of February also due to the Mars/Uranus/Neptune conjunction which in itself has a high potential for earth disturbances.

FEBRUARY

New Moon on the 3rd with Mars conjunct Uranus/Neptune brings in an active February also. Oil and gas definitely again in the news. Supported also by Pluto going stationary retrograde on the 24th. Financial markets could be on a roller coaster ride this month, especially with the uncertainties of Uranus! Bearish sentiment is definitely lurking as we get into the middle of the month.

Venus is conjunct Mars at 0 degrees on the Full Moon of the 18th which is also associated with down markets. Soybeans could be due for a correction after a minor run these past few weeks. Commodities such as pork bellies, cattle, grains, metals (gold and silver) and financial instruments such as T-Bonds and currencies could go through a significant down this month. Especially the dollar! Short the metals by the 19th and remain flexible with stops until the 28th.

Venus/Mars contacts are also associated with negotiations and relationships in general. Important business meetings at this time should be well thought out and know where you stand on those weak issues should you have to deliver comments on them. This awareness will help make a strong impact on those business associates you are trying to woo! When the business of the day is over, take advantage of the wonderful Venus/Mars contacts to enjoy your social life and/or the company of one who is special to you.

Pluto will be stationary retrograde from the 24th through July 30, 1992. These two dates are excellent for metals activity. Use technical analysis to help correlate the mentioned dates with the current trend at the time. Significant trend changes should occur.

MARCH

Mars will conjunct Saturn two days after the New Moon of the 4th. This aspect also signifies down market weather. Usually a decline in most stocks and utilities. Interest rates could be focused this month as the contraction belt tightens. My feeling is that correctional measures are going on internally from the Federal Reserve and other government departments to keep the economy from looking too ill ... after all we are in an election year. Also stock portfolio adjustments are taking place as the end of the first quarter nears. Futures/options players be cautious this first week of March, even the last week in February!

IRA deposits will help put some money back into the system, but I don't think it will be given to Wall Street this year! Government secured treasury bonds seem to be the safest bet ... watch those banks! Too much uncertainty in the banking industry to let large amounts of money accumulate there.

Mercury turns stationary retrograde on the 16th just two days before the Full Moon through April 9th and is usually associated with general communications difficulties. Letters, mail, telephone services, office machines, computers, automobiles and coworker communication may run into delays, misunderstandings or break down completely. At the same time this allows us to get caught up on office work that has laid around for some time. It's time to get organized and clean out those drawers, closets and files. Not a favorable time for signing contracts or initiating negotiations or new projects. Re-evaluation is appropriate now. Unions may be in the news, strikes or labor problems emphasized. Basically labor laws are changing due to deregulation and the merger frenzy in the late 80's.

March 20th heralds the Vernal Equinox and this is usually associated with trend changes in the market (hopefully this one is for the better).

APRIL

Tax season is definitely here. New Moon on the 2nd will give renewed energy toward getting those last minute taxes filled out and mailed. Full Moon on the 16th will start to set the pace for the Uranus/Neptune conjunction messages, as Uranus and Neptune turn stationary retrograde within one day of each other and by only 57 minutes at 18 degrees of Capricorn on April 20-21! Uranus will remain retrograde through September 22nd and Neptune, September 27th. Emphasis on "spiritual" renewal. Getting messages concerning our spiritual values and issues. Religious organizations may have the spotlight this month. Also people who are friends of the earth could speak out on some issue.

Mars will trine Pluto on the 25th and financial markets should look better. Political news may indicate some reform being planned or taking place. Great time to set our objectives and long range goals/plans. Keep an eye on political figures now as this is where someone with true substance can be seen.

Jupiter turns stationary direct on the 30th from its retrograde of 12/30/91—keep an eye on those soybeans! A rally should be in the works. Other grains (wheat, corn, meals, etc.) should also be enjoying good market weather.

People born in late August and early September should be enjoying the benefits of Jupiter in Virgo now. Good month for Earth signs Taurus and Virgo (and some Capricorns) to establish their goals and plan ahead. Optimistic time and can be rewarding if the work/effort has been put into something you're wanting. You could get it now!

MAY

Jupiter trine the North Node is a great indication that this is going to be a good month to accomplish or receive what we have been working toward. The economy should show some signs of improvement in this time-frame and therefore the stock market could be on a rally phase. New Moon on the 2nd would be a good time to re-evaluate your financial condition and set up some long range plans concerning your values and resources. If there are areas in which you need to transfer money or valuables, now would be a good time to do this. Be careful of getting stuck in old ways or stubborn over some issue. Do your homework on what you need to accomplish. Recheck your insurance policies, credit card agreements, contracts, etc. and see if you can make the necessary changes that are more in line with your pocketbook. Update as much as possible.

Mars enters 0 degrees of Aries on the 5th which occurs every other year. Mars also changes from south declination to north—when Mars is at 0 degrees Aries it is on the equator and this can bring unstable weather or a mild possibility of earth disturbance. There does not appear to be other supporting factors for this, so it could go without incident. Mars position is usually associated with stock market rallies. Since we should already be in good market weather, this is supportive to an already rising market. If soybeans are bullish, be careful as they could top out here and drop considerably. Previous dates for this planetary phenomenon are May 31, 1990; July 13, 1988; January 8, 1987; February 2, 1985.

You can check your technical charts for the financial markets and get an idea how the specific stock or commodity correlated.

JUNE

We are closing down the second quarter and this month will have TWO NEW MOONS indicating a very busy month. May 31-June 1 is the New Moon and also the 30th, but the second one is attached to a Solar Eclipse in the sign of Cancer. There will also be a Lunar Eclipse in Sagittarius on June 14th. These two eclipses this month will put the finishing touches to any upside momentum to the stock markets. Eclipses are good benchmarks in time to take a look at significant trend changes in the market place.

The Moon and Jupiter are rulers of the two eclipses and therefore can be associated with the public, mass psychology, silver, real estate, soybeans ... budget deficit (overspending), international relations and sports.

The second week of June should get highly volatile with the options and futures since options expiration will be due the following week. Usually market manipulation takes place and you will need to watch premiums on those options carefully!

The Sun will be harmonious with Saturn on the 8th which puts focus on the governmental issues and policies. A little more belt tightening will surface now, but it will be made to appear as stabilizing.

The Summer Solstice occurs on the 20th and it is also as-

sociated with secondary trend changes in most markets.
Usually a correction with the stock market, but also keep
an eye on those metals, they should start to get active, especially as we get closer to mid-July.

Mars trine Jupiter on the 26th and this is usually a more
optimistic time in general. So if the early part of this month
was sluggish for the markets, there could be a short but
quick rally in the making here. Keep your eye on the bond
markets, as there could be a significant trend change.
Mars/Jupiter aspects are usually associated with tops and
bottoms to existing trends. From a general business perspective, you may find yourself busier than usual due to
the unsettling activity of the eclipses. Pace yourself and
you'll do just fine!

JULY

Well the Democratic and Republican National Conven-
tions should be making us more aware of our voting issues. Research those candidates and really know why they
stand for what they do!

We are beginning the third quarter with Venus opposing Uranus on the 2nd and this is usually associated with
an abrupt reversal of trend on the stock market. Research
indicates that this aspect is the single most accurate short-
term (3-10 days) trading mechanism. If a trader or specula-
tor is armed with this kind of knowledge, profits could almost be in the "bank"(a bit of skill is also suggested).

Mars will oppose Pluto on the 12th and since Pluto will
be stationary direct on the 30th, I would suggest a stock
market decline. Other aspects through the month support
this around the 15, 18, 24, 25, 27, 29, 30th. Metals (gold and
silver) should be experiencing some trend changes around
the later part of July. This energy is aggressive and you
may see tempers flare up in the political arenas. It could be
a dog-eat-dog type of energy that must be carefully
watched or it could get nasty. National defense issues
come into the limelight again. From a military standpoint,
a clash in objectives could occur.

Jupiter trines Uranus/Neptune the end of the month
and starts August off in a positive direction. This aspect is
symbolic of sudden expanding energy. Possibly a shot in
the arm for the economy in some way, especially after last

week's issues that would have erupted under the Mars/Pluto aspect. Keep an eye open in the technology sector, as you will find stocks doing well there. Global issues will be of concern now, but from a positive viewpoint. International business could be expanding and that would help in the global economy. Sports, publishing and entertainment associated stocks could find a short term rally in here. As we had mentioned earlier in the general trends, you may find religious issues in the news.

Full Moon on the 14th with Mercury opposing Saturn the following day brings a bit of seriousness to our market weather. New Moon on the 29th near the Pluto station provides an extra boost to this already potent energy that correlates with short-term (10 days to 2 weeks) trend changes.

AUGUST

Jupiter will be 145 degrees from Saturn in the sky which correlates with the 20-year business cycle. Business in general could be "out of focus." The numbers just don't show any real business growth and therefore a slowdown, but a remedy doesn't seem to be in the immediate picture. Also supported by the Sun opposing Saturn on the 7th and the Full Moon within days on the 13th to help stimulate the existing energies. The stock market could be faced with a pull-back! Wall Street is not happy. Government policies could be shifting in here and Wall Street may be a little uptight.

Congress may be challenged by the budget once again. It seems that there may not be a ready solution this time and a freeze in spending is the best cure for the deficit. Congress will just have to give up those expenditures, which could have a real impact. This is a tough one. It just seems no matter what is tried, the results produced are not what you can easily live with. There may be difficult communications with the President over the national budget package. A lot of late night talks going on!

Jupiter trines Neptune exactly (Uranus is within 1 degree of this) on the 9th. ... This aspect will activate your spiritual awareness. Religious, spiritual and mystical issues could be newsworthy. There is a humanitarian side of life, compassion and awareness of others' difficulties are in focus now ... the homeless, drug addiction, old age, vic-

tims of many issues ... I could go on and on, but you will
see these causes get bigger than life for the purpose of public awareness! With these social issues being in the forefront of the campaign, it could lean more toward the
Democrats due to their social programs being emphasized. We also need a good business mind to keep us out of
a deeper recession. At the same time this aspect can shed
light on social issues, it can also create nebulous or miscon-
ceived versions of what really is happening. There is a desire to speculate or gamble on what "they" think could be
accomplished. There may be a display of overconfidence
and the desire to take unnecessary risks that could get us
in a losing situation. Planning and foresight are necessary
to keep focus with these nebulous energies.

New Moon on the 27th along with Jupiter sextile Pluto
will give us an opportunity to research and reevaluate
what is being presented by our politicians. Use this time to
do exactly that ... research and evaluate!

SEPTEMBER

Sun trine Uranus/Neptune from the 6th through the
8th allowing a minor rally on Wall Street. Oil, gas, technology, pharmaceutical, and television/broadcasting stocks
may be the ones on the most active lists. This is also a good
time to submit that unusual proposal or offer that you've
been putting aside. It has the potential to fly now. Make
appointments with people you don't ordinarily connect
with, as you can see a different side to them now. Follow
up any other meetings around the Sun conjunct Jupiter on
the 17th to allow for a more positive approach to your deal
or to finalize it!

Full Moon on 11th with Venus square Uranus—markets and soybeans bumping up against some trend
changes now ... one last acceleration for the beans before
they go south. Keep an eye on those technical charts to ver-
ify trend changes with these dates. Financial markets (i.e.
bonds, currencies, dollar) should be erratic to say the least.
Technical indicators should be watched as you go through
this period, especially if you are in the markets or hedging
in some way.

Congress should be more active than usual in here with
name-calling and aggressive behavior over the budget.

The Autumnal Equinox on the 22nd with Uranus station-ary direct helps to blow issues out of the water so the real-ness can be seen. Either planetary phenomenon is associ-ated with trend changes in the markets across the board. With an active past two weeks, this one should put the ic-ing on the cake for the stock and commodity sectors ... those of you who would hedge futures on your grains, be aware, here is a great opportunity. A quick play and be done with it! Right into the New Moon on the 26th! Nep-tune stationary direct on the 27th along with this New Moon energy provides a bubble-bursting effect. Portfolio stock and commodity managers are closing down the third quarter. Weeding out those non-performers.

OCTOBER

We will start this fourth quarter with Sun square Ura-nus/Neptune and Mars will oppose it between the 6th and 9th. Congress is in session trying to vote on the budget for 1993. This should be a difficult session as there are so many issues to take into consideration. There is also a good bit of mud-slinging with the politicians as this energy could get things a little out of control, stepping over ethical bounda-ries. Congress could have its own private earthquake. This should send the markets into a tailspin for a few days if it hasn't already. These are difficult aspects for the markets to digest. Commodities, like the precious metals, could fair better right now. Full Moon on the 11th should help to bring some decisions. Saturn will be stationary direct on the 15th emphasizing governmental issues coming to the forefront. Not a beneficial time to address people in authority positions for favors or to present your side of the story.

New Moon on the 25th should help to calm everything down and get us braced for a whole new set of challenges for the elections next week!

NOVEMBER

Sun squares Saturn on November 4th (Presidential election). Be sure to vote! Do it for yourself, do it for your children, do it for your future. A serious type of day with Saturn.

Full Moon on the 10th with Mercury going stationary

retrograde on the 11th which remains retrograde through December 1st. Grains and especially wheat and oats could have an active week. Sun will conjunct Pluto over the weekend of the 14th providing us with a slight change in market weather. Keep an eye on those metals as we will start a rally before the end of the year.

New Moon on the 24th with Mercury trine Mars. A great time to use the retrograde period is by cleaning out desk drawers, file cabinets, closets, any place that has storage which has not been organized or checked for some time. Sometimes on a New Moon such as this, you can find articles or things lost from some time ago, or get in touch with someone from your past. Use communications to your advantage these few days around the New Moon with Mercury retrograde. You may have to put forth a little more effort to accomplish your goal, but the results could be worth your while.

Mars will turn stationary retrograde on the 28th and remain through February 15, 1993. The last time this occurred was in the autumn of 1990. This Mars retrograde period could hold the markets in a stagnant pattern of a hundred points trading range for 3 months! Seems as if any momentum that gets started quickly wanes and gets lost in the shuffle.

DECEMBER

HAPPY HOLIDAYS
The Lunar Eclipse on the 9th in the sign of Gemini could produce a stock market correction. Commodities such as wheat, oats, soybeans, corn, and meals should be in for a correction with this eclipse. But keep your eyes on the short rallies of metals, crude oil, copper, and orange juice.

Currencies and foreign markets could be in for a choppy week. OEX, S&P, New York Composite and XMI could have a correction—lots of weeding out before the end of the year and the next administration. The smart people have been weeding out stocks and commodities so they can be flexible with the upcoming changes so close at hand.

A Solar Eclipse on the 23rd. Try to travel to where you

need to be for the Christmas holidays before the 23rd, as Solar Eclipses are associated with unexpected hassles. Try to be flexible in your travel plans as you could get into unexpected delays, routing, changes and time problems. This does not have to be part of your reality, so program a smooth trip. Being aware of potential difficulties can make you plan better ahead of time for all to go well.

The 1990's represent a different decade than what we have experienced the past 50 years. As we enter 1993, I wish you financial prosperity, success and a great new year!

PLANET	HOUSE(S) RULED	CORRESPONDENCES
Sun	5th	Money, investments, gold, government, brokers, stock exchanges.
Moon	4th	The public, mass psychology, silver, aluminum, soybeans, fluctuations, homes and property.
Mercury	3rd & 6th	Business in general, contracts and agreements, communication, travel, wheat and oats.
Venus	2nd & 7th	Partnerships, investments and valuable possessions, copper, national treasures, securities, accumulation, wheat.
Mars	1st & 8th	Activity and energy (used wisely or unwisely), national defense, steel and metals in general, manufacturing.
Jupiter	9th & 12th	Optimism, over-spending, national budget, international relations, judicial system, stocks, tin, financial gain.
Saturn	10th & 11th	Conservatism, agriculture, cattle, barley, rye, grains in general, lead, financial losses or limitations, recession.
Uranus	11th	Inventions, technology, sudden change, uranium, earthquakes, civic and humanitarian organizations, public media (radio, TV, broadcasters & reporters).
Neptune	12th	Inflation, chemicals and pharmaceuticals, medicine, oil industry, unseen influences, idealism.
Pluto	8th	Underground resources, institutions, transformations, rebuilding, space exploration & oceanographic research, insurance, plutonium, atomic energy.

MAKE EXTRA MONEY THE EASY WAY—BECOME A MOON SIGN BOOK SALES AGENT!

Would you like to make a little extra money in your spare time? Why not become a Llewellyn Sales Agent?

It's all very easy. Just order the *Moon Sign Book* in quantities of a dozen and you will receive substantial discounts. Then you can turn around sell the books to your friends and family, at the local farmer's market, at craft fairs, wherever! You will be helping others, spreading the word about lunar planning and making money all at the same time.

The retail cost of 12 copies of the *Moon Sign Book* is $59.40. But, if you buy them as an agent you pay only $35.64 and we pay the postage and handling! *You save $23.76 per dozen*!

Even if you don't intend to resell the *Moon Sign Book*, think of what a great present it would make. Surely there are 11 people out there who would really appreciate a copy of this valuable almanac. (The remaining copy would be yours, of course!) The *Moon Sign Book* is delivered before the holidays, so order your dozen early.

Other Calendars and Almanacs Available:

The rest of our bestselling calendars and almanacs are also available as agent products. Below are the retail and discount prices for each. Think of all the ways you could make money using this special offer!

Llewellyn's 1992 Astrological Calendar: Retail per dozen $119.40. *Quantity discount price $71.64. You save $47.76!*

Llewellyn's 1992 Sun Sign Book: Retail per dozen $59.40. *Quantity discount price $35.64. You save $23.76!*

Llewellyn's Daily Planetary Guide: Retail per dozen $83.40. *Quantity discount price $50.04. You save $33.36!*

To place your order, use the order form on the last page or call toll free 1-800-THE-MOON today!

Horoscopes
by Anne Lyddane

- **Rising Signs**
- **Monthly Horoscopes**
- **Monthly Highlights**
- **All 12 Signs**

Your ascendant is the following if your time of birth was:

If your Sun sign is:	6 to 8 am	8 to 10 am	10 am to Noon	Noon to 2 pm	2 to 4 pm	4 to 6 pm
Aries	Taurus	Gemini	Cancer	Leo	Virgo	Libra
Taurus	Gemini	Cancer	Leo	Virgo	Libra	Scorpio
Gemini	Cancer	Leo	Virgo	Libra	Scorpio	Sagittarius
Cancer	Leo	Virgo	Libra	Scorpio	Sagittarius	Capricorn
Leo	Virgo	Libra	Scorpio	Sagittarius	Capricorn	Aquarius
Virgo	Libra	Scorpio	Sagittarius	Capricorn	Aquarius	Pisces
Libra	Scorpio	Sagittarius	Capricorn	Aquarius	Pisces	Aries
Scorpio	Sagittarius	Capricorn	Aquarius	Pisces	Aries	Taurus
Sagittarius	Capricorn	Aquarius	Pisces	Aries	Taurus	Gemini
Capricorn	Aquarius	Pisces	Aries	Taurus	Gemini	Cancer
Aquarius	Pisces	Aries	Taurus	Gemini	Cancer	Leo
Pisces	Aries	Taurus	Gemini	Cancer	Leo	Virgo

If your Sun sign is:	6 to 8 pm	8 to 10 pm	10 pm to Midnight	Midnight to 2 am	2 to 4 am	4 to 6 am
Aries	Scorpio	Sagittarius	Capricorn	Aquarius	Pisces	Aries
Taurus	Sagittarius	Capricorn	Aquarius	Pisces	Aries	Taurus
Gemini	Capricorn	Aquarius	Pisces	Aries	Taurus	Gemini
Cancer	Aquarius	Pisces	Aries	Taurus	Gemini	Cancer
Leo	Pisces	Aries	Taurus	Gemini	Cancer	Leo
Virgo	Aries	Taurus	Gemini	Cancer	Leo	Virgo
Libra	Taurus	Gemini	Cancer	Leo	Virgo	Libra
Scorpio	Gemini	Cancer	Leo	Virgo	Libra	Scorpio
Sagittarius	Cancer	Leo	Virgo	Libra	Scorpio	Sagittarius
Capricorn	Leo	Virgo	Libra	Scorpio	Sagittarius	Capricorn
Aquarius	Virgo	Libra	Scorpio	Sagittarius	Capricorn	Aquarius
Pisces	Libra	Scorpio	Sagittarius	Capricorn	Aquarius	Pisces

1. Find your Sun sign (left column);
2. Determine correct approximate time of birth column;
3. Line up your Sun sign with birth time to find ascendant.

Sign	Glyph	Dates	Ruler	Element	Quality	Nature
Aries	♈	Mar 21–Apr 20	Mars	Fire	Cardinal	Barren
Taurus	♉	Apr 20–May 21	Venus	Earth	Fixed	Semi-Fruitful
Gemini	♊	May 21–June 21	Mercury	Air	Mutable	Barren
Cancer	♋	June 21–July 23	Moon	Water	Cardinal	Fruitful
Leo	♌	July 23–Aug 23	Sun	Fire	Fixed	Barren
Virgo	♍	Aug 23–Sept 22	Mercury	Earth	Mutable	Barren
Libra	♎	Sept 22–Oct 23	Venus	Air	Cardinal	Semi-Fruitful
Scorpio	♏	Oct 23–Nov 22	Pluto	Water	Fixed	Fruitful
Sagittarius	♐	Nov 22–Dec 22	Jupiter	Fire	Mutable	Barren
Capricorn	♑	Dec 22–Jan 20	Saturn	Earth	Cardinal	Semi-Fruitful
Aquarius	♒	Jan 20–Feb 18	Uranus	Air	Fixed	Barren
Pisces	♓	Feb 18–Mar 21	Neptune	Water	Mutable	Fruitful

ARIES
March 21 to April 20

Aries is the first sign of the zodiac. It represents the indomitable spirit of life, forever renewing itself and moving forward with exuberant, fiery growth.

Always on the alert for action, adventure, and new worlds to conquer, the Aries individual is a natural pioneer and motivator. Your passionate and assertive spirit hates to have limits placed upon it, and you deal quite bluntly with any obstacle to your will. This tendency toward direct aggression may make you the odd one out when it comes to moving people and projects to action using the subtle tools of diplomacy and tact. Still, your zest for life and egocentric worldview shield you from taking the criticisms of more cautious folk too much to heart.

Conquest and the thrill of the chase are prime motivations for you in love. Yet, in some ways, you are also an old-style romantic. You crave the grand gestures of courtship—flowers, constant praise, and declarations of undying love. And woe betide your lover if they ever cast a wandering eye toward another! You truly believe that you should be the one-and-only for your partner; after all, they mean everything to you. You may be a bit selfish, but you are fair.

You will need to cultivate patience and persistence. You get fired up, start a project, and then drop it just as quickly as you began. Though this approach may suit you, think how you will feel when you realize that your life is a string of unfinished projects and unfulfilled potential. Learn to temper your passions with a little staying power, and your wonderful potential for success in life will manifest in a way that is magnificent to behold.

HIGHLIGHTS OF 1992—ARIES

As 1992 begins your region of career and public image is accented. Your talents for organization and leadership suggest potential balance with patience, discipline and factual data to succeed. Uranus and Neptune both in Capricorn indicate materializing and grounding of goals in practical ways now. You may feel at times "on a short leash," with duties and responsibilities highlighted. Hang in there and use your sense of humor and take the long-range outlook. Capricorn, the Tortoise, always wins the race! From the last week in April until the end of September, these two planets will be retrograde. It would be wise for you to "cool it," to avoid appearing arrogant or domineering in career situations. Steady, purposeful work attitudes are important now. Cause and effect can work satisfactorily for you. Slow down but keep a steady pace.

At the end of May Saturn in Aquarius goes retrograde until mid-October affecting your region of friends and groups. This suggests a period of adjustment to keep a balance between avant garde concepts and practical implementation of innovative ideas. When Saturn is again direct, if you have done your homework, your originality and individuality may be rewarded.

Jupiter moves into Libra in mid-October, affecting your chart sector of marriage, love unions and/or bus;iness relationships. Jupiter suggests expansion and enthusiasm. Libra indicates companionship on many levels, for balance, peace and mutual benefits. A sudden union with someone fun and pleasure-loving is a potential here.

Pluto in Scorpio turns retrograde at the end of February until July 31st affecting mutual assets, legacies and regeneration. Pluto is associated with the subconscious and the meaning of dreams. What you have buried, hidden or ignored in these areas now surface for recognition and decisions. These are excellent times for introspection and working with your inner self.

JANUARY

With a New Year opening, practical matters and persistent, disciplined action brings success in your career affairs. New and down-to-earth methods and concepts can be grounded and projected successfully on the 4th, finding total fulfillment on the 19th. Travel for business reasons can also be productive. Home matters appear satisfying and secure. Romance may be exotic. A good month for publishing, communications and specialized educational opportunities. Don't rock employment boats and investigate work ideas before making decisions. Progressive people offer excitment and New Age experiences with groups and organizations. Manipulations and secrecy surround a possible inheritance now. Keep all cards on the table when dealing with mutual funds. Behind-the-scenes data can be important when facing choices concerning changes in energies. Dream symbols helpful, introspection rewarding. After the 21st, openings occur for a position of leadership regarding groups dedicated to large and even planetary interests. There are important balances to be achieved between time and energies spent with career and home matters currently. Support and emotional stability successfully combine with organized goals and ambitions.

FEBRUARY

On the 3rd, your region of friends, groups and organizations receives a strong thrust of energy. What is unexplored, original and progressive appeals to you. People with expansive beliefs offer you exciting opportunities. Avoid, however, those who are charming but irresponsible. After the 18th, research and investigation help you reach intelligent choices. After mid-February, work done in solitude, the past, family traditions, restrictions and institutions are highlighted. Your intuitive qualities are strong now. Romance may have a secretive, hidden quality, even a "karmic" touch. On the 18th, action moves away from the heavy-duty career sector toward working with groups having mutual aims which are original and innovative. Avoid impulsive decisions, impatience or rebellious behavior. Pluto goes retrograde on the 25th, so slow down and go within for important data available at deep levels. Your public image and career situations continue in importance, with routine and practicality basic necessities. Duties and responsibilities tend to bring a sense of boredom, but you are seeking to balance out your Aries fire and Capricorn earth. Build and organize before taking definite career actions. Stability and security are your goals at this time.

MARCH

The past appears emotionally important to you. Spending time alone can prove creative, and occult-psychic studies teach you much about your inner self. Other selves or lives may catch your attention, and healing, teaching, writing and the arts appear as paths for your talents. On the 18th, your work-service-employment sector indicates material rewards for past efforts. A raise, promotion or more profitable position is a potential. Your past discipline now produces successful results. Real estate, hospitals, laboratories and areas connected with the needs of the public indicate fulfilling results. After the 15th when Mercury goes retrograde, you would be wise to "cool it" and use caution before making new beginnings or changes. Travel and communications need to be slowed down and thought out. Signing important papers should be avoided until Mercury is again direct. Journeys will be more productive if postponed now. Romance continues to be tender with strong ties to the past. Psychic and intuitive matters also add emotional fire to relationships. Your creativity receives much potential thrust. History, dance, acting, photography, motion pictures and TV and all types of healing are accented.

APRIL

Your birthday month takes off with much action. On the 3rd, new chapters and opportunities may have successful outcomes. A positive period for changing your image and putting the limelight upon your talents and skills. On the 17th, a legacy could appear from an unusual sector, but watch out for manipulative strings. Transforming your past outlooks and beliefs can be productive. In the use of mutual assets, keep all cards on the table and avoid power plays. Neptune goes retrograde on the 20th and Uranus on the 22nd, both in Capricorn. These planets are accenting your career region. Slow down, be cautious, use patience and self-discipline until these elements turn direct again. You may feel restricted or repressed, but try to keep a light touch. You are building for a stable and secure future, so keep your eyes on the long-range outcomes. Love can be hot and heavy now, with someone independent and exciting. Mercury turns direct on the 19th and suggests new methods and original ideas which may be productive. Travel and communications can be successful, and those papers you have been avoiding signing can be documented. Ask directly for what you desire and project that new charming image.

MAY

Your assets, investments and value system come in for highlighting this month. Starting a new business or making practical, cautious and well-researched investments can be ultimately productive. Taking it slow and easy, working with basic facts and realities can be rewarding. Real estate, farms, animals, gardens and construction are all accented. The theatrical and entertainment fields can also be profitable. Make sure that all contracts and agreements are set forth in clear-cut terms understood by all parties. Travel for pleasure and business can be satisfying. On the 2nd you may start investing and working with your value system successfully. Full results can be felt by the 16th. Romance may be encountered in connnection with money and financial business. Food, cruises, entertainment, sex, elegant surroundings and all those "good things in life" can add color and exhilaration to your life. Jupiter goes direct on the 5th, signifying that your employment sector now has that lid lifted and goodies can appear here. Rewards are returnable in coin similar to those causes you have projected in the past. On the 28th, Saturn becomes retrograde affecting your area of friends and groups. It would be wise to retreat from impulsive actions and to research the realities here.

JUNE

On the 1st your sector of relatives, communications and environment receives vibrations from the air element of Gemini, suggesting travel, changes and new potentials. This is a fine period for writing, lecturing, teaching, communications of all kinds—the media, publishing, and acting. You may be able to get your ideas and needs across with charm and wit. A fun romance is a potential now, right in your own back yard. A companion who needs lots of freedom can offer you excitement. On the 15th travel to faraway places may call and/or you may wish to expand your educational training. Unexplored paths call to you now. You could take a long trip which offers new data to combine with your creative skills. Opening up vistas and large horizons is also available at this time. After the 21st home base offers stable and secure emotional rewards. A new member of the family is also a possibility. Keep on "keeping on" when it comes to your career. Persistence and practicality are important foundations. Don't feel overwhelmed by feeling too serious or restricted here. Avoid appearing critical or impatient. Create a necessary balance so duties and responsibilities do not seem burdensome.

JULY

A summer wedding around the 7th is a potential. If already wed, a more companionable, pleasurable relationship with mutual benefits can result. Business partnerships also may be projected successfully now. Mercury moves into retrogradation on the 20th affecting your sector of love affairs and children's interests. Passion, impulsive power plays and action are all highlighted here. Romance appears fiery, direct, but there may be power struggles. This may also be true of relationships with children, as they appear bright and ambitious but equally strong in arrogance and domination. You may need all of your sense of humor and patience to deal with these people. However, it won't be dull! Make sure you say what you mean and that you think before you speak. Avoid travel now if possible. Money continues to need a practical, persistent approach, with building opportunities highlighted. Pluto becomes direct on the 31st so that mutual funds, legacies and regeneration of time and energies become more free and open. What you have accomplished through introspection can now be transferred to conscious actions with success. On the 14th, career ambitions receive fulfilling results.

AUGUST

The 5th brings potential for new action/beginnings in dealing with a partner's assets. An inheritance may also occur. On the 13th, help and understanding from friends and organizations offer you outlets for talents in new ways. What you have envisioned in the past now appears ripe for achievement. The 23rd suggests further definite and practical rewards around your work site. Discrimination, discretion and patience can bring you raises, promotions and recognition. Mercury goes direct on the 13th, lightening up the lovers and children's region. Some of the power plays cool down, and generosity and affection surface. Creativity can be strong. Communications, travel and changes also indicate recognition of your talents, so fun and pleasure can be enjoyed. Vacations and emotional satisfactions indicated. Romance may be discovered at the work place. The entertainment field can fulfill ambitions. Work with the public is also accented for success. Avoid confrontations with relatives or neighbors. You may speak too quickly or inaccurately, creating divisions. Be charming, and cautious with your signature. Any type of communication and subconscious data can be helpful in making decisions.

SEPTEMBER

Work-service-employment takes the limelight this month. Disciplined causes implemented with patience and perseverance prevail. Your critical and investigative talents help you achieve your goals. On the 3rd a prolonged legacy may surface satisfactorily. Behind-the-scenes manipulations can be understood now. Make sure you obtain facts before making decisions regarding mutual funds. On the 12th, work done in solitude, the past, family traditions and "other selves or lives" (karma) are highlighted. Psychic or occult research may be presented with successful results. On the 12th your home base affairs become active, and you may feel like entertaining. You could enlarge or refurbish your home as well. Uranus goes direct on the 24th and Neptune on the 28th, releasing much of the previous restrictive pressures encountered. Your career sector continues to be accented by these two planets, but it is as though you feel released and much freer here. New ideas, progressive, original skills and abilities can be implimented at this time. Intuition and creativity based on practical foundations can also bring you success. After mid-month an Autumn romance, or wedding is a potential. Someone with mutual interests and a love of peace and quiet is accented.

OCTOBER

If you have not married or made a love union last month, perhaps October will see this consummation. If already in a relationship, a new opportunity for balance and mutual benefit is now available. On the 11th action, ambition and new opportunities appear. Your leadership and executive talents may find new outlets. Romance can be passionate, possessive and intense. Jealousy and attempts for domination need to be avoided. Respect on mutual terms is important here. This is an excellent period for investigation of occult interests. Your ability for critical analysis may extend to music, literature and art. Your subconscious has interesting messages for you. Saturn goes direct on the 16th, lifting some restrictions regarding friends and groups. Home base continues to have an important emotional affect, indicating need for security and stability. You could now work at home, deepening relationships there and creating a strong sense of foundation for family understanding. A new offspring is also a possibility. Avoid procrastination and indecision in this part of your current lifestyle. Your work with organizations could blend harmoniously now with your career opportunities. Friends may introduce you to important people.

NOVEMBER

On the 2nd assistance from groups and friends continues its progressive and helpful vibrations. Inventive and unexplored opportunities are offered to you now. These may be successfully financed by the 10th. Matters connected with real estate, healing, entertainment fields and needs of the public are accented. You could head up a group of avant garde types and make a fine profit for all concerned. On the 11th Mercury goes retrograde, accenting your sector of travel to foreign countries, publishing, specialized education, occult research and dealings with people from other backgrounds or cultures. It would be wise to slow down and think it all through before coming to decisions. Travel, taking risks and making impulsive changes should be avoided until Mercury is again direct. Romance is indicated in this same region; someone colorful and "different" can be appealing. Stimulation can be important to you at this time, but you do need be cautious and discreet. Mars goes retrograde on the 29th affecting your home sector. Watch out for feelings of rebellion, anger, holding grudges and pushing your feelings down into your subconscious. Emotional imbalances also need attention. You may be feeling re-

stricted or repressed, pulled away from career ambitions by duties and family responsibilities.

DECEMBER

As 1992 ends many changes and opportunities appear. On the
2nd, once more the past is highlighted. Much creativity is available through working at your deepest inner level. What is still of
value to you may currently be projected in new ways. On the 9th,
relatives and neighbors may be more communicative and fun-
oriented than in the past. Communication lines are open and
pleasurable. This is a positive period for writing, lecturing, teaching and publishing. Romance is idealistic, discovered among
friends and groups. Mutual goals are important with much need
for mutual freedom and liberty. Caution and compassion continue to be important at home base. Emotional commitments suggest permitting each his/her space without anger. Look at the
good and value it. On the 22nd your public image and career sector loses some of its excitement and becomes more practical. Try
to make peace between your work goals and the necessary time
and energy important for an emotionally stable and enjoyable
home base, having fun with loved ones as the year closes.

TAURUS
April 20 to May 21

Taurus is the preserver of the zodiac, the calm organizer of people and things into pleasing, efficient systems. You take the raw, untamed fire of Aries and mold that energy into something more real and enduring. You instinctively realize how best to bring ideas down to earth. And while you're bringing these heady concepts into being, you usually manage to have a good time!

You possess an intuitive appreciation for the true value in a person or a thing. Your artistic flair will most likely be expressed through things of utility and beauty, and the words "glitz" or "flash" are simply not in your vocabulary.

With all this strength and stability in your character, you must be on your guard against a tendency to overwork. Consider the feelings of your family as well as their creature comforts. In providing a comfortable, stable environment for your loved ones, you may lose sight of the purpose for all your hard work: to show them that you care. Take time to relax and express how you feel, not by working harder at the office, but with a big, earthy hug!

Although you can be possessive in a relationship, this only manifests if you feel unappreciated or insecure with your lover. Remember that the earth, which symbolizes your sign, is firm as well as warm and giving. Discuss your feelings as they surface, and keep the way clear for love.

Your appetite for the pleasures of life and loving are prodigious. It is as if you're forever attuned to the sensual, and the simple pleasures of a touch, a glance, a whisper. When you combine these strengths with your warm, enduring nature, it is little wonder that Taurus has the reputation of being one of the most accomplished lovers in the zodiac.

HIGHLIGHTS OF 1992—TAURUS

1992 appears to be your year for foreign travel. Special training and educational opportunities are also accented, publishing, occult research and connections with people from other cultures. On April 20 Neptune turns retrograde and Uranus on the 22nd, both in Capricorn, indicating caution and slowing down in all of the above affairs. This restrictive influence continues until September 24 for Uranus and Neptune, the 28th when they become direct once more. Pluto goes retrograde on February 25th affecting love unions and/or business partnerships. Pluto suggests a depth of introspection, of listening to your subconscious. If not already committed, it would be wise to wait until Pluto becomes direct on July 31st before taking action. Only you can analyze this part of your relationship region. Be honest with yourself and take time to discover your value system.

Jupiter becomes direct on May 5th affecting your sector of lovers and children. Virgo suggests patience, practicality and persistence. Jupiter is totally opposite, impulsive, expansive and exploratory. Balance is a keyword with these two opposite influences. You need to ground and materialize those big visions and desires in workable order.

Saturn will go retrograde on May 28th accenting career and public image. The suggestion is to play it cool with caution. Saturn is a builder and conserver. Your desire for new, progressive and original methods needs curbing. Organize, plan and wait until October 16th when Saturn is direct before implementing career aims. Jupiter enters Libra on October 11th. You may have some opportunities for new and satisfying work, with raises, promotions or better recognition of your abilities.

JANUARY

You may learn much to add to your current skills through travel to foreign lands and connections with people of different backgrounds. On the 4th, potential "business" is accented for visiting faraway places. On the 19th, you may receive support from relatives and neighbors. Communications are open and fluid. Romance is sudden and exciting. You may receive an unexpected and generous inheritance and/or work successfully with mutual funds. Lovers and children may come in for analytical attention now, with Jupiter retrograde. Balance is important here, rather than a seesawing between generosity and permissiveness and duties and responsibilities. You may tend to be overly-critical at times, and overly-optimistic and enthusiastic at others. Your career situation suggests further balance between not rocking boats and keeping your originality and progressive attitudes alive and healthy. This is not a positive time for demanding changes, but through routine and discipline, your message gets across. Your marriage, love union and/or business partnership region indicates the need for some introspection. Only you know what you desire in these kinds of commitments. A true value system needs to be employed for mutual benefit.

FEBRUARY

Pluto turns retrograde on the 25th, further accenting last month's need for going within to make decisions regarding partnership commitments and desires. Pluto connects with your subconscious and the meaning of dream symbols. Now is the time to recognize all of these areas and to make important decisions. If you are considering marriage or an enduring relationship, it would be wise to wait until July 31st when Pluto turns direct. Your public image and career region on the 3rd suggests new plans, originality and innovations. On the 18th, many of these may be successful. Your individuality will be recognized and applauded. After mid-month friends, groups and organizations offer you opportunities in healing and working with the disadvantaged. Romance may be met in this sector with someone with mutual responses. Accent upon foreign travel continues, with romance also evident here. You add to your basic creativity with meetings and associations with people of different backgrounds. A friend may become a lover, with karmic undertones between you. On the 18th, keep your eye on the career ball.

MARCH

On the 4th the work you have accomplished with groups and among friends receives acclaim. Your sense of being needed is consummated now. The 18th suggests further rewards through recognition of your service-orientation accomplishments by lovers and children. Mercury goes retrograde on the 17th and accents the past, family traditions, restrictions, institutions and creative work done in solitude. It would be wise to use caution in communications and to avoid travel until Mercury turns direct on April 9th. Avoid signing agreements or documents during the retrogradation. Make sure communications are concise. Romance is sweet and tender, found among groups, friends and organizations which are dedicated to helping and healing. You are attracted to someone who is intuitive, sensitive and compassionate. Your career desires can be directed toward progressive expansion this month, after investigation and dealing with realities. Pluto continues its retrogression in your region of love unions and business relationships. Making an honest appraisal of facts, desires and needs can be constructive. After the 20th, your creativity is vigorous, preferably when working alone.

APRIL

On the 3rd, results from creativity consummated in solitude reach new potential. Being individualistic and exploring the unknown can be profitable. Trust yourself and your abilities. Mercury becomes direct on the 9th, adding communicative skills and the capacity to act. Travel and the media as well as dealing with the public can be successful. Love is stimulating and passionate, although hidden perhaps. Uranus turns retrograde on the 22nd and Neptune on the 20th, both accenting your region of foreign travel, publishing, connections with other cultures and occult research. All of these areas need further slowing down and caution. Don't get caught up in the new and unusual. Stay clear of people and situations which may have great charisma but are basically irresponsible and impractical. Avoid self-indulgences, drugs, alcohol or overeating. Drifting and dreaming, procrastination and indecision can also be depleting. You could feel restricted, but keep the long-range viewpoint in sight. Building for endurance can be slow but stable. After the 20th, new beginnings and a new image can be projected satisfactorily. Entertainment, elegant shops, luxury items, cruises, resort hotels, and all those fun things are available to you. Healing and helping are facets of this vibration. A new path is open to you.

MAY

Beginnings and image take the limelight during your birthday month. On the 2nd you may project with success a different path, a new image and concepts. Although slow, this vibration is of enduring value and steady purpose. It is a building influence, meant to last with satisfaction and reward. On the 16th, a partner either personal or professional can be helpful in attaining mutual goals. Jupiter turns direct on the 5th, releasing tensions around your sector of children and love affairs. You take a lighter reaction, with less demands here for "perfection." Saturn turns retrograde on the 28th, affecting career and public image. Slow down and work only with realities. Test, use patience and practical outlooks. Use what has been successful in the past, but keep your progressive and inventive skills sharp for when Saturn turns direct again on October 16th. Romance is newly-minted now, sensual, pleasurable with an exciting flavor. On the 22nd, finances, values and assets take the stage. You may have more than one opportunity available. Avoid indecision and scattering of attention and energies.

JUNE

Finances continue their importance this month, with dualistic influences. Transportation, communications, travel, public relations, the media, change and alternatives are accented. You could feel pulled two ways here. Test and research and work only with facts. On the 15th, expansive opportunities arise through a potential legacy and/or the use of a partner's assets for mutually beneficial goals. Real estate along with transportation and the public's desires are highlighted. Romance is allied with finances, so the dualities remain with emotions as well as money. You may feel flirtatious, able to handle more than one love relationship currently. On the 21st there is emphasis upon relatives, environment and communications. Stability and security are important with commitments and tradition accented. Your intuition and empathy help your communicative skills to be accepted. Memories of the past hold tenderness and you receive nurturing through those around you. You tend to feel active and vigorous, strongly creative in work done alone. Originality, the unknown and freedom to explore blend with your natural talents so your productions hold your signature. Acting, writing, producing, directing, healing, counseling and all the arts appeal to you.

JULY

Your work-service-employment sector takes center stage on the 7th. Cooperation and pleasant circumstances are evident here.

You have the ability to use charisma to your advantage. On the 14th, people from other lands or backgrounds may offer you assistance in materializing your dreams. Practical organizational skills can supplement your talents, so that your output can be used overseas or with special training-educational projects. Pluto goes direct on the 31st, softening and opening up communications with a marriage partner, love union and/or business relationship. If you have done your work here in the past months, you should be well aware now of your basic desires. Deep-seated desires should be successfully projected now. Mercury turns retrograde on the 20th affecting your chart sector of home base. There may be power plays, attempts to dominate with little success. Travel should be delayed until Mercury is direct again on August 13th. From mid-July on, romance may be found on your doorstep. Impulsive, sudden and colorful love opportunities can be exciting. That new beginning continues to build successfully, with applied practical methods.

AUGUST

A summer wedding is a potential perhaps around the 5th. A well-planned commitment and excitement surround this situation. Ambition and social position may also be part of this relationship or that of a business relationship. On the 13th your career matters take on a strong progressive thrust. What is unusual and unexplored may be projected successfully. Inventive concepts and methods reach a position of expansion. Home base is accented, with Mercury turning direct on the 13th. There is a more gregarious, fun-loving and active vibration apparent. Communications, travel and changes are also highlighted. This could be a positive time for a vacation, for expanding a second home, trailer, or boat. Entertainment and at-home activities may help you achieve some of your ambitions. A desire for that "perfect mate" is highlighted, as well as demanding similar perfection from children. Finances and values continue to be important. You may feel indecisive. Making a list of priorities could be helpful. Try not to attempt too many goals at one time. Avoid impulsive actions and impractical monetary decisions.

SEPTEMBER

Lovers and children continue to share the limelight this month. You are always watching their actions. You test and analyze. After the 19th, situations become more cooperative and pleasant. Some of the rigidities and rules drop by the wayside, and a more easygoing response arises. On the 3rd, if you have not wed as of last month, the question may arise again. On the 12th, friends and organizations allied with healing, psychic studies, hospitals, hospices, prisons, orphanages, animal shelters and those in trouble are highlighted. You may find practical ways to achieve goals with groups of similar interests. Romance is available at the work site, with someone able to share your reactions harmoniously. On the 12th attention shifts to relatives, communications and environment. Emotional rewards can be delightful, and feelings of being "at home" are evident. Travel by water especially can offer soothing benefits. Uranus turns direct on the 24th and Neptune on the 28th. Both accent your area of foreign travel, special education, publishing and psychic research. Your intuition and inner voice can be used creatively.

OCTOBER

Your work area continues to be pleasant, satisfying and full of cooperative efforts, as of the 3rd. On the 11th, work done in solitude offers new paths. Your originality and ambition receive rewards and recognition. A Fall wedding or love union has the limelight this month. Romance, communications, your mentality and outer personality all are focussed upon this area of your life now. If already committed, intensity, ambition, and passion arise in these relationships. What has been hidden in the subconscious now surfaces. You will find it important to direct much of this energy toward the deep inner self's desires. Questions will erupt, demanding attention and decisions. Jupiter enters your work area on the 11th, indicating potential raises, promotions and/or recognition of your abilities with financial renumeration. A new and more progressive work position is also evidenced. Saturn turns direct on the 16th indicating career thrust toward unexplored areas. Your individuality and innovative ideas may be consummated successfully now. All of the past restraints are released and your career opportunities suggest the capacity to feel more free to show your talents.

NOVEMBER

The 2nd continues the rise in career opportunities from last month. Keep on showing your originality and progressive methods. On the 10th, a new image can be projected successfully. Much of your past envisioning of career matters and the potential "new you" can be expressed productively. Legacies, mutual funds and regeneration of energies are strongly accented. Mercury turns retrograde here on the 11th, suggesting avoidance of travel, clarity in communications and intellect. Impatience with time restrictions is important at this time. Slow down and take the ultimate outcome viewpoint. Wait for travel and communicative outlets until

Mercury turns direct. Romance is stimulating, fun, exciting and connected with a free-soul type individual. Someone with original romantic ideas can expand your horizons bringing you larger concepts of commitment. This can be a fine month for turning around some of your past habits. Transforming the old into the new—the regeneration of energies—can be successful. You are feeling optimistic, active and enthusiastic. Keep your feet on the ground, and then go for it! Mars turns retrograde on the 29th affecting your region of relatives, environment and communications.

DECEMBER

1992 is winding down and the holidays suggest potential opportunities for change, growth and expansion. The region of regeneration continues its importance from last month. After the 22nd your actions become blended with practicality and persistence. On the 2nd friends, groups and organizations indicate recognition of your nurturing/healing skills. Emotional rewards are fulfilling. On the 9th, finances indicate dualities which need practical focus. More than one monetary alternative can be confusing. Keep on with your list of priorities and don't get too caught up in holiday buying. Romance takes on an idealistic tinge, concentrated within your career sector. Someone unusual may add to your career success. You may feel irresponsible with love choices. Mars turns retrograde this month suggesting a continuation from November of situations involving relatives, environment and communications. Stay with clarity and openess in this part of your life. As the new year approaches, exciting opportunities are waiting in the wings.

GEMINI
May 21 to June 22

You have a friendly, open approach to life. You are a master of the "light" touch. You thrive on the excitement of all that is novel and different, and refuse to allow anyone to place limits on your ideas or your spirit.

To experience life in all its diversity and display is not a whim with you—it is a psychological necessity. You become depressed and despondent if you feel intellectually hemmed in, with no new horizons to explore. Fortunately, the sure-fire cure for the Gemini blues is easy. Simply immerse yourself in a new interest or avocation, and your childlike zest for life will be rekindled anew.

As witty, intelligent company, you are without peer. You are perhaps the single most entertaining sign in the zodiac. You love games of skill, for your restless mind needs constant exercise. You are an impartial debater, and have almost total recall of an astounding variety of information.

You are a mental lover, and need a partner who is compatible with you intellectually. You can lose interest quite rapidly, however. Your mate will have to keep you guessing to retain your interest in the relationship. In love, you require a delicate balance of consistency and variety to keep your heart from roaming.

One drawback to all your mental brilliance is a definite risk of your becoming a superficial thinker, a "jack of all trades" and master of none. Work at disciplining your fine mind and sticking with your undertakings. Treat it as a game if you must, for you have a great many talents that may be neglected if you do not cultivate some depth to your thinking.

HIGHLIGHTS FOR 1992—GEMINI

During 1992 much emphasis will be placed upon legacies, use of mutual funds and transformation-regeneration
of energies. Building and conserving are keywords here.
With both Uranus and Neptune accenting this area of your
life, it is obvious that what is new and untried—Uranus—
and your dreams and visions—Neptune—are calling for
recognition. Working with factual data is highly important. Dealing with realism is necessary for success. This
can be a most creative period, however, with the Capricorn element offering patience and perseverance to both
Uranus and Neptune.

Pluto will go retrograde February 25th accenting your
area of work-service-employment. Until Pluto is again direct on July 31st, it would not be wise to rock boats. Keep a
steady pace and work with routine and detail. Gemini is
quickly bored by detail and routine but during this Pluto
retrogression it is important to make these personality
changes. Pluto suggests introspection, making a value system through honest appraisals of your basic desires and
needs. Pluto can be a rich source of data and creativity, but
you need to permit it to surface first.

Uranus and Neptune both in Capricorn go retrograde
in April: Uranus on the 22nd and Neptune on the 20th.
Use caution regarding mutual assets, regeneration and inheritances. Plan, organize and investigate until Uranus
turns direct on September 24th and Neptune on September 28th. Then you may implement these desires successfully if you have worked with practical and sensible plans.

Saturn turns retrograde on May 28th affecting travel to
foreign countries, dealings with people from other cultures, educational opportunities and publishing. This
would not be a profitable time for travel to other lands or
for coming to definite decisions regarding the other areas
described above. If possible, wait until Saturn becomes direct on October 16th.

JANUARY

The 4th indicates potential benefits through a partner's assets and/or a legacy. Making practical use of mutual funds is important now. This can be an excellent period for making a turn-around, a "transformation" from the old to the new. On the 19th money, assets, investments and value systems come to the fore. Avoid confusing emotions with finances. Find other means of showing affection. Real estate, insurance, banking, foods, areas connected with nurturing are important to you. You need to feel good about your personal value system, and being service-oriented, find ways to be a giver with intelligent decisions. Jupiter is retrograde now affecting your home base. You may be feeling critical and objective. Imbalance between generosity, enthusiasm and optimism occurs with equally strong reactions of being analytical, expecting perfection and living with duties and responsibilities. You could start 1992 with a stimulating marriage, love union or business partnership. Someone original, outgoing and fun is evidenced. Your work site may need some investigation. Your value system appears to have deep, inner tendrils which may not appear on the surface.

FEBRUARY

Continuing the work situation from last month, Pluto turns retrograde on the 25th, signifying further intensity of introspection. There is need for recognition of things which you may have hidden or ignored, releasing of past habits no longer workable. Only you can make an honest appraisal of your needs in this part of your life. Until mid-month, travel plans to other lands, connections with people from different backgrounds, special training and psychic research can be progressive. The unexplored and untried hold fascination for you here. Attention continues in your area of legacies, regeneration and mutual funds. A slow but steady building influence is accented. There is potential success in visiting other countries and connections with various cultures especially strong on the 3rd and fulfillment on the 18th. After the 19th, romance is available at your career area. A loyal companion-worker or a friend may turn into a lover. Career combines emotional and creative satisfactions with past skills for profit and recognition. This can be a stimulating month with emphasis upon foreign travel, educational opportunities, career enrichments and emotional rewards. The past, the "tried and true" plus unexplored, innovative experiences await you.

MARCH

Career and public image receive accenting, beginning with the 4th and culminating on the 18th. You could work at home, planning and investigating with success now. Your career outlet evidences emotional satisfaction, as well as ambitions satisfied. Healing, counseling, teaching, music, photography, motion pictures are all highlighted now. Mercury goes retrograde on the 17th, suggesting caution in changes and travel. Postpone travel plans until April 9th when Mercury is again direct. Matters concerning friends and groups call for cautious responses. You need to find a balance between upstaging and appearing arrogant. Romance is connected with your career ambitions and someone who is intuitive, sensitive and affectionate. There is evidence of this being perhaps a "karmic tie" relationship. You could make an impulsive decision to travel to faraway places, as well as to make connections with people from differing cultures. Avoid being too quick to make choices; obtain realistic information before taking off into the blue. Practical planning can make these trips and experiences much more pleasant, though boring to implement.

APRIL

Uranus turns retrograde on the 22nd and Neptune on the 20th, both influencing regeneration, mutual funds and legacies. This is no period for action. Wait until Uranus becomes direct on September 24th and Neptune on the 28th. These are times for planning, visualizing, working with realistic information. Avoid feeling indecisive and stick with priority one before going on to the next. Mercury turns direct on the 9th, smoothing out relationships with friends and groups. Romance is a potential through meeting someone associated with organizations or friends. Avoid power plays with a romantic potential, as both of you need freedom. On the 3rd plans can be communicated to groups who may offer you leadership. These should culminate successfully by the 17th. Action and ambition thrive this month in the career and public image sector. Your ability to help offers emotional satisfaction. Your intuition is strong and studies connected with the occult can be interesting. After the 20th creativity in solitude can be profitable, combining beauty with practicality.

MAY

The past, family traditions, institutions, restrictions and what has been hidden are strongly accented this month. On the 2nd with the New Moon highlighting this area, your building-conserving instincts are highlighted. The entertainment field, interior design, fashion, teaching, writing, and publishing all come to the fore. You should be able to do much profitable work in solitude. A strong love of beauty, art and constructing practical works can be projected at this time. Music, dance, and any area where you express artistic talents are favorable. Romance can be sensational, mysterious and productive. The Full Moon on the 16th suggests employment intensities. You feel a part of the work-service you project now, proud and possessive. Jupiter becomes direct on the 5th, suggesting home matters lighten up. You may purchase a larger home, enlarge your current residence or pur-chase a vacation place, trailer, boat or second house. Saturn be-comes retrograde on the 28th highlighting your region of foreign travel, education, publishing and occult investigation. There may be restrictions here, a waiting period before you may implement your ideas. Until Saturn becomes direct on October 16th, it is wise to use caution before making decisions regarding this part of your life.

JUNE

You may find it difficult to go down just one path, as there ap-pear to be dual alternatives here. Travel and communications are accented now, and you may find yourself starting an interesting new chapter in this part of your life. Romance during this birth-day month appears versatile and flirtatious. It may be difficult to make choices, as you find more than one relationship appealing. The Full Moon on the 15th indicates consummation regarding the marriage, love union or business partnership sector. Someone ex-citing offers you a relationship situation which may or may not be made legal—neither of you seem to find this important. Friends and groups are active and offer you leadership positions. Your vi-tality is high now and you are feeling ambitious. After the 21st fi-nances are highlighted. You need to separate emotions and spending. Counseling, teaching and healing may seem to need monetary backing. However, you need to be objective when mak-ing these choices. You could cripple others by taking on respon-sibilities which do not belong to you. Use your head, investigate before shouldering duties which may be artificial.

JULY

Mercury goes retrograde on the 20th, slowing down your re-gion of relatives, communications and environment. There is need for you to keep a low profile and avoid appearing arrogant or domineering. You are a natural leader, but often are careless of accepting responsibility outwardly. Others may mistake your airy touch and wit for irresponsibility. The New Moon on the 7th accents lovers and children. Peaceable, pleasant cooperation is available but you must work with realities and not avoid neces-sary confrontations. You want to keep surface harmony, but it is not always a healthy attitude. Make your principles clear to lovers and children and stick to your guns. On the 14th fulfillment is a potential with an inheritance or a partner's assets. You find practi-

cal ways to use these funds. Pluto turns direct on the 31st affecting
your work-service-employment area. If you have done your
homework, Pluto has only goodies to shower upon you. Your
subconscious surfaces for choices and recognition. Romance
turns from a rather stable situation after the 14th to excitement,
passion and drama. Taking risks here can be exhilarating but
wearing. Continuing to be creative and productive away from the
public eye can be profitable this month. Be practical and persistent with creative efforts.

AUGUST

Mercury becomes direct on the 13th, highlighting communications, relatives and environment. As a family leader you may
need to make your position clear. You have the charisma and
sense of power to do this with ease. Public relations, acting, teaching, lecturing, or any area where you deal with others can be most
productive. Romance could appear on your very door step. You
need a secure and objective kind of home ambiance. Nothing too
outwardly emotional, but intellectually compatible. This is a positive month to project that new self-image and make a new beginning. You may feel scattered in time and energies and need a
change of pace for your highly-keyed nervous system. Try to get
away from the routine. With the New Moon connected with your
work site, ambition and prestige are important to you at this time.
On the 5th you could receive favorable notice and a deeper commitment. On the 13th, a trip to other countries, further training or
publishing are accented. Consummation of a previous plan can
now be effective. After the 23rd there is an accent upon home base
similar to that of your Venus emotions. You may work at home
now and/or use your home as a retreat from the draining effects
of the outer world.

SEPTEMBER

Until mid-month your home affairs continue in importance.
Research and analysis may be necessary in order to make plans
and organize. Then the emphasis moves toward areas connected
with children's interests and love affairs. Cooperation and harmony are desired, while anger and confrontations tend to be buried. A balance is necessary and what you have avoided discussing
in the past now surfaces for decisions. Indecision and procrastination create tension. Be honest with yourself and others. Uranus
goes direct on the 24th and Neptune on the 28th affecting regeneration of energies, mutual funds and inheritances. Your cautious
approach to these matters in the past can now be released and
some intelligent actions projected. Mutual respect, time for all
concerned and balance will be important factors in the love pic-

ture. Work and career matters move from beginnings on the 3rd to fulfillment on the 12th. Your intensity and ambition reaches toward nurturing and protective outlets. After the 12th Mars moves into your monetary and value system area. Try not to move too quickly or impulsively, investigate thoroughly before making financial commitments. Investments which are proven, stable and a necessity for the public good can be productive.

OCTOBER

Jupiter enters Libra on the 11th, adding further thrust to the lovers and children center of your life. Growth and expansion reflect the Jupiter vibratory influence. You may establish a partnership with a lover and/or a cooperative situation with children, with mutual satisfaction for all concerned. Saturn becomes direct on the 16th accenting trips to other lands, associations with people from different backgrounds, special education and publishing. Saturn is what you earn through cause and effect. Progressive and unusual circumstances may surround these trips or educational choices. New Age concepts and innovative methods blend with the Saturn grounding influences beneficially. You may learn while you enjoy. Ambition, prestige, favorable notice, promotions, new opportunities are evident. Many of the choices are up to you solely, as your inner desires are important. Romance is smouldering with intensity but also combined with the employment-service part of your life. The Full Moon on the 11th suggests fulfillment of leadership goals connected with organizations and groups. Action with finances and investment continues from last month. You have not yet completed these decisions and they need further attention and investigation.

NOVEMBER

Mercury goes retrograde on the 11th, suggesting that you postpone travel arrangements, check clarity in communications, and avoid signing important documents. Partnership questions indicate needed attention before commitment. Romance appears to be stimulating with a friend who can fly at the same altitude as you. However, slow down and think this through. You may just be excited by the holiday season and all the enchantments of illusion. Mars goes retrograde on the 29th so money, assets, and investments need caution and a slower pace. Impulsive action, grudges, anger and feelings of being "used" may need to be worked out. You may have confused finances and emotions. New ideas obtained through travel to foreign countries may be combined with creativity. Work done in solitude may produce interesting and sophisticated ideas. Progressive training adds value to work which is both practical and beautiful. Bringing visions and desires down to earth can be successful. After the 22nd your intense direction toward the work-employment region moves toward the marriage or love union potentials.

DECEMBER

The wedding or love commitment situation continues during the holidays and as the year ends, you may still be questioning this region of your life. Communications are open and direct with relationships. After the 22nd, you tend to be practical regarding partnerships. From high excitement of the past few months, you are now feeling more objective. Romance can be exotic and dramatic, making a comparison with marriage and enduring unions fairly uninteresting. Mental, emotional and physical freedom are important to you, as well as to your potential partner. Each needs lots of space and privacy. Career plans make interesting new opportunities as of the 2nd. New chapters and self-image may be projected with charisma as you look forward to a stimulating new year. Dualities and alternatives generally throw you and with so many opportunities you may need time away from the crowd to do some important "mulling." Finances continue to be indecisive. You would be wise to spend some time and investigative energies obtaining facts and coming to creative decisions, with your financial picture accented. A firm monetary-value system is a "must" before the new year approaches.

CANCER
June 22 to July 23

The element water symbolizes feelings, emotions, and desires. Cancer is the cardinal water sign, and thus represents this element at its most flowing and direct. You are a highly intuitive person, in touch with the deepest parts of your emotions, although not always consciously.

When you feel a bond with another person, you move instinctively to protect and nurture them. This is the motivation behind your famous tendency to "mother" people. When you feel safe and secure, you hold on for all you're worth to those people or projects you deem worthy of your support.

You retain and reflect the circumstances of your early upbringing, which can be positive or negative depending on how you were raised. Try not to become an emotional packrat; nurture the child within you and you will have much more energy to devote to your work and your loved ones.

You are an excellent manager, whether at work or in your home. This is because you feel strongly that there is a little piece of you in everything you touch. Your shrewd sense of the realities of any situation makes you a superior negotiator.

You face a unique challenge: how to express love and relatedness to other human beings without exposing your sensitive feelings to them. However, there are no guarantees in life, and in order to experience real closeness with others, you will have to risk a few emotional bumps and bruises. Let go of this urge to hide in your shell until it's "safe," and you will find, more often than not, that your deepest dreams of belonging and being loved have a surprising way of coming true.

HIGHLIGHTS OF 1992—CANCER

This new year heavily accents marriage, love unions
and/or business partnerships. Uranus and Neptune both
highlight this region, suggesting new, progressive ideas.
Neptune indicates intuition, a deep inner need for communication and dreams pertaining to past lives. Uranus
turns retrograde on April 22nd and Neptune on the 20th.
These are periods for deep introspection, for times of making balance sheets of your values. It would be wise not to
rock too many boats, with Uranus in this position. Neptune connotes procrastination and indecision. You may be
depressed or looking back sentimentally at the "good old
days," avoiding important connfrontations with current
facts. Cancer dislikes changes, and tends to avoid risks.
Repetition and keeping on with "what is" are important in
making you feel secure and stable. A lasting time-wise relationship is most appealing to the Cancer element. Uranus becomes direct again on September 24th and Neptune
on the 28th, taking some of the pressure off. Hopefully
during the retrogressions you have taken charge of these
areas in your life. If so, then the active, expansive and progressive Uranus offers you new and interesting paths,
more fulfilling and rewarding than the status quo. Neptune always indicates inner wisdom. It would be wise to
watch your diet during the retrograde times, being a water
sign, Cancer gains weight easily, especially the water and
fluids portion.

Pluto in Scorpio accents your sector of love affairs and
children. Pluto goes retrograde on February 25th until July
31st. Slow down, watch for reasons behind facades and beneath surfaces. Avoid manipulating others or being manipulated by them. Pluto is a subtle vibration, connected
with the subconscious, dreams and regeneration. Once it
is direct, you have a wealth of rich inner knowledge to project here.

JANUARY

As 1992 begins, your work-service region suggests emotional fulfillment through new and expansive opportunities. You may make changes, travel and/or deal much with the public. Romance may be met at the work site, with someone who is optimistic, fun and outgoing, offering you excitement and a sense of enthusiasm. Your region of love unions and marriage is going to be strongly highlighted all year, so you may just as well relax and face it. Potential learning opportunities will enter around partnerships, business as well as romantic. Action may be necessary here; your intellect focuses upon this part of your life, and both Neptune and Uranus are accenting it as well. The New Moon on the 4th suggests possibilities for research and dealing with realities in this area. On the 19th, you have a surge of energy suggesting fulfillment and capacity for presenting a new image. You may do this either by dragging your feet, or with understanding and excitement. Realize that this will make you a happier and more successful person in relationships. Jupiter is retrograde now until May 5th affecting your sector of relatives, environment and communications. Slow down here and play it cool.

FEBRUARY

Pluto goes retrograde the 25th, highlighting lovers and children until July 31st. There is much information behind the scenes. Your subconscious mind and dream symbols may tell you a lot. Watch actions and do some inner probing to discover your deepest desires. Be honest and confront factual data. Watch for mutual manipulations. Legacies, mutual funds and regeneration are highly accented. Until mid-month opportunities for latching on to progressive ideas can be helpful. Avoid being impulsive or impressed by avant garde people or concepts until proven. Romance tends to be linked with marriage and legalities and you could be considering action in this area. The New and Full Moons suggest further seesewing, progressive opportunities, ups and downs connected with mutual funds, a legacy which is hard to pin down plus indecision concerning changing your habits. Emphasis moves after the middle of the month to travel to foreign countries, probably by water, further education, publishing and dealings with people from different cultures. Older countries with much history, places which pull you intuitively, healing, the past and service-oriented outlets are all accented.

MARCH

Mercury turns retrograde on the 17th indicating it would be wise not to make career changes until it becomes direct again on April 9th. You could feel restricted during this retrogression as originality, action and ambition are running high. Wait for this period to pass before making demands or decisions. New opportunities are ahead. On the 4th, if you have not made that trip last month to other lands, the idea surfaces again for consideration. On the 18th you may decide, through communications with relatives and neighbors, to postpone it. Responsibilities may outweigh the value of the plan. Romace is a potential with someone mysterious, exotic, from a different culture or background with whom you feel a karmic tie. An inheritance continues its up and down vibration. Mutual assets need grounding and further investigation. You are responding to past feelings and ideas. History, family traditions, and occult studies take the limelight. This is a fine month to begin a new study, write, publish, or create actively in your own field of interest. Avoid over-indulgence and keep yourself busy. Try not to look back with sentimentality, and release old beliefs and reactions.

APRIL

This is the month when Neptune turns retrograde on the 20th and Uranus on the 22nd accenting your area of love unions, marriage and business partnerships. Uranus will be retrograde until September 24th and Neptune until the 28th. Make a schedule of time for solitude. Cancer dislikes confrontations or facing potentially unpleasant matters calling for decisions. You need to go within to discover your true values and desires in these parts of your present life. Take a look at the long-range picture and deal intelligently with cause and effect. After the 9th career matters surface for favorable notice. Progressive opportunities and positions of leadership can now be implemented successfully. Romance may be encountered at career level. Someone independent, active and intense is a possibility. Ambition and action can be mutually beneficial. The New Moon on the 3rd reinforces this situation, adding fuel to the Aries fire. Children and lovers need attention on the 17th. Avoid anger and manipulations. Passions run high but put the brakes on.

MAY

From the 2nd on, this month holds much entertainment and pleasure among friends and groups. Similar interests offer fulfillment among others of like concepts. Healing, counseling and helping those in need are appealing. The entertainment field in general holds satisfaction. Romance is present, with someone affectionate, stable and devoted to home and family. Jupiter goes direct on the 5th accenting relatives, environment and communications. Much of Jupiter's optimism and expansiveness can become grounded and materialized. Communications can be clear and precise, so that those around you know exactly what you mean. Editing, reporting, electronics, history, art and music criticism and fields where you may work alone are highlighted. Relatives and neighbors may appear critical of some of your ideas and desires. Ignore them! Saturn turns retrograde on the 28th indicating the need for using patience in the legacies, mutual funds and regeneration region of your life. Avoid trusting charming types with fast tongues. Check them out before making commitments. An inheritance tends to seesaw before landing. New Age concepts may prove helpful, offering progressive ideas for healing, change of psychic attitudes and release of past pains.

JUNE

With the New Moon on the 1st, this month suggests alternatives and dualities in behind-the-scenes matters. The past seems to have more than one message for you. You could begin some type of work which may call for interesting travel plans, probably by air. Combining creativity with public relations, associations for adding data to your sharp awareness can prove useful. Romance has a dual vibration, flirtatiousness and mystery both being encountered. After the 21st attention may be directed toward a new self-image. Although your sign can be slow to change, once you make a decision, you become quite fixed until it is achieved. Your compassion, and service-oriented personality may be presented in a most attractive new package. Showing some of your inner depth can bring much favorable attention your way. Career matters can be successfully projected this month. Your abilities, originality and leadership qualities are in the limelight. You may be offered a position of prestige, a raise or promotion and new opportunities. Trust yourself and take action. You communicate easily, knowing instinctively what others need and want to know.

JULY

This birthday month Mercury turns retrograde on the 29th signifying restraints and caution in finances and investments. Avoid extravagant spending. You may feel like "showing off," but this would not be advisable in the long run. Wait to spend until August 13th when Mercury will be direct again. Pluto becomes direct on the 31st lightening up relationships with children and lovers. If you have worked successfully with this Pluto influence in the past months, you should now have a rich source of data for helping you make intelligent decisions. Hidden matters in these

connections should be recognized and directed with positive results. Romance moves from a tender, emotional situation after the
14th to a more intense and active type of response. Avoid attempting to "buy" love or approval. You could be active now in building-conserving kinds of work for groups or organizations. You
have the capacity to combine beauty with practicality. The New
Moon on the 7th indicates pleasure, and social activities around
the home.

AUGUST

The money picture continues to be important through mid-
month. With Mercury direct on the 13th, some of the tension dissi-
pates. Learn to respect yourself as part of your value system experience. Romance could be encountered through relatives or
neighbors. Someone serious, responsible and intellectual is apparent. You may need to take the first step in forming a potential
relationship. Work which you can create in solitude, dealing with
more than one interest is indicated. Travel and change are accented. Try not to scatter time or energies. Watch to see that your
nervous system does not feel depleted. Diet is important too, so
don't eat when weary, angry or overly excited. You could be feeling "picky" when it comes to relationships with relatives now,
but try to use your sense of humor. Release past grudges and rigidities. Relax and don't expect so much from others.

SEPTEMBER

Both Uranus and Neptune become direct, Uranus on the 24th
and Neptune on the 28th. Marriage, love unions and business
partnerships feel less pressured. If you have been postponing a
commitment but have dealt with the messages from these planets,
this month could offer a lovely Autumn wedding ceremony. This
kind of relationship suggests mutual interests, building for similar goals and a basic, practical type of love response. After the 12th
much vitality and action are available for a new beginning. If you
have felt indecisive, it appears that you have made up your mind.
You feel comfortable in implementing past plans. Romance can be
pleasantly companionable. You may feel the need for some silence and privacy at home. This can be most helpful in recharging
your batteries and smoothing out your nervous system. Getting
near, on or around water is always relaxing.

OCTOBER

Love affairs and children are strongly accented. Intensity, jealousy, manipulation, and ambitions all surface at this time. Your
mind is clear and direct. You have the ability to see realities and to

confront important issues. Emotionally you respond the same way—right to the point. You are willing to give your love and efforts, but you also want to receive similar gifts from children and lovers. Mutual respect can be effective and successful. If too many rules and regulations are posed, rebellion, anger and manipulative behavior could result. Saturn turns direct the 16th and you may receive a long-term legacy, now past due. This can be a profitable time to work with mutual assets, and to transform the past. Your home base with the New Moon on the 3rd continues to offer security and a peaceful, comfortable environment. At Full Moon time on the 11th, career matters can take off with great vitality. Some of your ambitions may become actualities, if you use some force and executive ability. You could own your own business now, or have a successful personal profession.

NOVEMBER

Mercury becomes retrograde on the 11th, in your highly accented area of work-service-employment. It would be wise not to rock work situations until Mercury turns direct once more. You may find communications confused. This is not a successful period for travel plans. Changes at employment regions tend to be misunderstood. Romance can be good news, also at work site, stimulating, fun and companionable. You may spend some time profitably organizing your desires as to just where, how and when you wish to enlarge or change your employment situation. If you are happy there, just hang on, use patience, avoid signing important contracts or documents. Smile a lot—and keep your mouth closed! Mars also turns retrograde on the 29th emphasizing matters around that new self image. Don't push for events. Tone it down and use your charm and subtlety. Practical help and advice comes through friends and groups during the Full Moon of the 10th. Secure and caring people offer you assistance and give you favorable recognition for your talents. Continue releasing past habits and restrictive reactions.

DECEMBER

The old year is ending and excitement builds for the coming year's experiences. Progressive ideas and opportunities around your work area can be exciting. A new position, travel, change and rewards at your place of employment are indicated. On the 2nd you may be considering a visit to other countries, probably by water. With the Full Moon of the 9th, terminating or consummating indecisions can be productive. Romance is idealistic, unusual and sudden. Someone original, independent, and progressive appeals to you. New Age interests could be a bond between you. After the 22nd, you may be considering a holiday wedding or commitment. A former friend or companion becomes an enduring lover, stable and offering firm marital foundations. If already married, practical approaches and a mutual respect and need for stability can be established successfully. As this year ends you could put that best foot forward down the aisle. It is obvious there have been numerous learning opportunities this year, but undoubtedly you have come through with flying colors. That new start could be from the altar.

LEO
July 23 to August 23

Leo is the natural showman, entertainer, and royalty of the zodiac. Your innate charisma makes you fascinating to watch, and with effortless skill you attract friends and admirers around you.

You have a fantastic ability to take complete control of a situation where you are called upon to make an impression. This you do with style and flair. Even if you make a mistake, you do so with authority, and people are likely to be completely unaware that anything was amiss!

In love, nothing but the grandest of gestures will do. You are an extravagant lover, and you shower your partner with presents, physical affection, and words of endearment. You relate so strongly to tales of castles and kings that you may feel you have been born into the wrong time period. You desire the romance and adventure of those courtly days, and will do your utmost to make your life a reflection of those times.

The key to your success in life will be in your ability to have an unshakable faith in your self-worth. With this basic belief intact, you will always express your formidable talents in an effective way. But, if you somehow doubt your worthiness of the respect of others, something unfortunate happens. You become arrogant, overbearing, and demanding of attention. It's as if you are trying to convince others of something you don't believe but desperately wish to be true: your own significance. Relax, and "dance" with your power. Hold your charisma like a sparkling necklace instead of a ball and chain, and you will not fail to gain the love and respect of others.

HIGHLIGHTS OF 1992—LEO

Your work-service-employment sector will continue to be strongly accented. At times things will appear slow and restrictive. At others, you feel you are building firm foundations. There can be a rather seesawing motion. This swinging imbalance can affect your nervous system and energies unless you are aware of its purpose. Growth, progress and wisdom are the ultimate goals. Release outworn habits, customs and reactions. Try to go with this flow and enjoy the opportunities presented. Uranus and Neptune go retrograde in April, Uranus on the 22nd and Neptune on the 20th. Until Uranus moves direct on September 24th and Neptune on September 28th, you would be wise to be patient. No matter what the surface illusion appears to be, you *are* building stability, success, security and understanding.

Pluto turns retrograde from February 25th to July 31st, affecting your home sector. Pluto deals with the subconscious and dream symbols. What you have ignored or hidden around your home area now is calling for recognition. Introspection is necessary especially during the retrogression. Going deep within to make an honest value system assessment is of great priority. Take time, make a routine and be quiet, alone, relax and listen to your inner voice, your intuition. Watch for meanings in your dream symbols and appraise what is important to you and whether it is now present in your life.

Saturn will be retrograde from May 28th to October 16th highlighting marriage, love unions and/or business partnerships. These retrogressions suggest inaction, inner investigation and postponing of plans until Saturn is direct. Saturn deals with cause and effect and builds for enduring results.

JANUARY

As the new year begins, your region of work-service-employment is accented strongly. The New Moon emphasizes the importance of buildiing firm foundations. Enduring security and stability are also necessary. This can be a slow but sure vibration. Routine and detail are important. This may prove difficult for the fire of Leo, but your abilities and ambitions need this underpinning. Make sure you are clear and concise in speaking and/or writing. Romance is expansive and exciting. A person who enjoys life and has a fine sense of the ridiculous can enlarge your love situation. The Full Moon on the 19th suggests much successful creativity while you work in solitude. The past, family traditions, karmic or other worlds/lives/selves interest you. Releasing past losses can help you direct those energies toward more rewarding present outlets. Healing, food/drink, acting, composing, painting, sculpting, writing and various art forms are accented. Jupiter turns retrograde in Virgo indicating financial restrictions.

FEBRUARY

Pluto becomes retrograde on the 25th accenting the home. Until Pluto is again direct on July 31st, it is suggested that you do some deep probing of your honest desires in this part of your life. Pluto governs the subconscious dreams and what you have avoided recognizing. Try not to display or accept manipulative behavior. Until mid-month you may be contemplating a marriage, love union or business partnership with someone who is original, independent, and progressive. Communication on many levels will be important for any of these associations to be successful. If already wed, a new outlook can add maturity and interest to your relationship. Work continues to be most important and romance with a person who is practical and analytical can offer balance to your gregarious, ambitious and fiery nature. After the 19th, some of your vitality and actions turn away from work and move into the marriage and love union area. Finances continue to need a balanced attitude.

MARCH

With Mercury turning retrograde on the 17th, travel especially to foreign countries should be curtailed until it becomes direct on April 9th. You may feel rebellious and impatient with postponing travel, special training, a situation connected with publishing and other fields where you want to be active. Romance emphasizes a union with karmic ties, a former friend or lover and someone you relate to well on a soul level. Your region of transformation-regeneration suggests a turn-around in attitudes and desires from past to present. Mutual funds and assets need atten-

tion. Avoid confusing feelings and money. If you did not make a
commitment last month, you may still be actively considering it. If
wed now, a continual expansion of mutual interests and space
and respect is most important at this time. On the 18th a good hard
look at your money picture may offer practical means for investing. Deal only with financial realities. Real estate, banking, insurance, export-import, and the needs of the public are accented for
possible income areas. Health foods, hospitals, hospices, rest
homes and research laboratories are also accented for successful
investments of time, money and energies.

APRIL

Mercury turns direct on the 9th and that long trip you may
have postponed can be accomplished now. Foreign countries,
people from different cultures, education/training, publishing
and occult studies can be approached productively. Neptune
turns retrograde on the 20th and Uranus on the 22nd, accenting
your work-employment sector. Slowing down and using persistence toward ultimate goals are all important. Romance appears
exotic, dramatic and colorful. You could fall in love on that visit to
other lands, with someone original, fiery, active and ambitious.
Your region of legacies, mutual funds and regeneration takes on a
potential balance between sentiment and action. Listen to your intuition and then act. A legacy from an elderly person, an old
friend or from deep in the past is a possibility. Studying, attending
groups, lectures or seminars connected with psychic-occult subjects can be rewarding. Mysterious data can be obtained from
within. The Full Moon on the 17th emphasizes matters around
home. Time for honest appraisals of value systems and desires.

MAY

Your career area receives several strong thrusts this month.
Stabilizing and practical plans are building blocks toward fulfilled ambitions. Real estate, restaurants and bars, cruise ships
and resort hotels are all accented. The entertainment field is highlighted. Results may appear to be slow, but these are stable and
persistent vibrations. Romance appears connected with career affairs. Someone who is interested in home and family, who is passionate, caring and pleasure-loving is evident. Jupiter goes direct
on the 5th and your region of finances now can breathe a sigh of
relief. Although you still need to keep a balanced checkbook, you
can do some fun-spending. Saturn goes retrograde on the 28th affecting marriage, love unions and business relationships. Until
Saturn is direct again on October 16th, it would be wise to avoid
confrontations in those parts of your current life. Saturn deals
with cause and effect. You may feel restrained. Realize this is an

important learning opportunity for all concerned. A trip to other lands could be helpful.

JUNE

Friends, groups and organizations are accented this month. You will have many changes and alternatives to consider in this area. Travel and communications are highlighted, and your ability to be flexible will come in handy. You may find decisions hard to make, with so many choices. Romance is dualistic, flirtatious and indecisive. You could meet more than one attractive person, and find it hard to make a choice. You may need someone who can fly at the same altitude and communicate with you on many levels. This is an excellent period for you to do some creative work based upon intuitions. Writing a book or article on history, on family trees and/or backgrounds could be successful. Composing, painting or any arts and crafts fields could be profitable. A cook book or a "how-to" book regarding psychic-occult areas could also be successful. If you did not take that trip abroad last month, the idea may still be appealing. Joining a sports club, playing golf, tennis, swimming, enjoying a country club and social activities may help you expend vigorous energies in a productive way. Watch anger and tensions due to irritability and frustrations. Use that sense of humor.

JULY

Pluto turns direct on the 31st, lifting some of the intensity connected with your home situation. If you have spent some time delving within, made some honest appraisals, now can be a positive time for cooperation and mutual understanding. Pluto always works with important factors which have been hidden from conscious view. Mercury goes retrograde on the 14th, suggesting keeping a rather low profile with your usually dramatic image. Wait until August 13th when Mercury will be direct again. You could spend time and energy profitably making plans and visualizing just how you intend to project this interesting new image. After mid-month, romance becomes intense and active. Someone colorful and power-loving may interest you. Career matters are accented now, for practical, constructive methods. Through patience and perseverance, building opportunities are indicated as potentially rewarding. Past performances can blend your originality and ambition with a more down-to-earth outlook. The New Moon on the 7th suggests cooperation and harmony with relatives, environment and ease in communications. This would be an excellent time to use your charisma to inform those around you of some important desires. Be decisive and avoid attempting to please others.

AUGUST

With Mercury becoming direct on the 13th, the road toward new beginnings is open and broad. You may travel and/or try something new and exciting connected with the public. If you are dealing with legalities, your direct and accurate mentality can bring you successful conclusions. Romance takes on a more practical reaction, with someone who knows the meaning of a dollar. This individual will not be swept off his/her feet easily, but will watch actions and not merely words. Your money picture also takes on practicality. Purchasing things which have emotional meaning can be pleasureable. Giving gifts to show love also requires analysis. Friends, groups and organizations offer you numerous opportunities for change and potential travel. Communications can be productive; writing, teaching, lecturing, acting, sales, public relations and travel agencies are among those fields available to your talents. Avoid appearing dualistic or "flighty." Friends and groups which are talkative, born communicators may help you to waste time and energies, unless you concentrate on goals. Tying up loose ends at home is accented at New Moon time on the 5th. Final surges of data surface now, and everyone needs to make important long-range choices. Your birthday month suggests excitement, opportunities, clarification of past challenges and lots of fun.

SEPTEMBER

Your financial situation takes on strong accenting this month. It appears to be time for definite methods of saving and intelligent investments. Investigate and make critical appraisals before spending or investing. Make sure you receive monetary results in practical ways. After the 19th, some of the responsibility and/or restriction lifts and you may spend some of your pennies for fun once again. Uranus turns direct on the 24th and Neptune on the 28th affecting your region of work-service-employment. New, progressive concepts and methods can be successful. You may have opportunities connected with unusual businesses or New Age professions. Unexpected potentials appear, suggesting implementing your originality. Your intuition blends with practical approaches to work situations. Put some time aside each day for meditation. The arts, literature, music, psychic and occult matters as well as acting, motion pictures and photography are all accented. You have great empathy for the desires of the public. Romance may be met in your community or through relatives or neighbors. Communications are smooth and pleasant, as long as you appear to be cooperative and direct. A charming potential romance may hide some sub-surface challenges.

OCTOBER

Saturn becomes direct on the 16th, highlighting your region of love unions, marriage and business relationships. You may make a sudden decision regarding commitment. If already wed, this alliance takes on new, progressive tints. Each partner needs to feel free, to be original and not restricted. This partner has his/her rigid side and when confronted may react with tunnel-vision and stubbornness. This part of your current life will have its ups and downs but you won't be bored. Jupiter enters Libra on the 11th throwing influence toward your area of relatives, communications and environment. Things around you now lighten up and there is a more pleasant, peaceful ambiance. You may be able to find success through public appearances, acting, music, the law, arbitration and counseling. Romance appears close to home, adding further pleasure and mutual understanding of goals to a possible relationship. Someone who can be a partner as well as a lover is indicated. Action connected with the past, family, institutions, karmic reactions and emotional attitudes toward healing and nurturing are highlighted. Psychic and occult investigation may offer you feelings of security and stability. Some of the work/research in these areas can be directed toward helping those in pain or trouble. Watch diet intake, especially fluids.

NOVEMBER

On the 11th Mercury turns retrograde affecting your sector of lovers and children. Confusion in communications, rebellious attitudes and insistence upon freedom of action are all apparent. Excitement, lack of routine, a dislike of important detail investigation of facts all help add to this mutual confusion. Slow down and take time to be alone and quiet. Romance is impulsive, fun, entertaining but may be hard to pin down. Get away from it all with nature, sports, social/cultural activities or some kind of new training or educational interest. Play down emotions. Mars will be retrograde as of the 29th, indicating some importance in reviewing the past. Release anger, grief, loss or disillusionment. A period of inner cleansing, healing and regeneration is suggested. The tendency to hide negative emotions needs to be discarded. During the holidays, the question of marriage or union may arise again for decision. With the New Moon on the 2nd, you may take another look at this area.

DECEMBER

With 1992 closing out there is much excitement and optimism in many areas of your present life. Celebrations may be especially active and fun-oriented with lovers and children. You may find yourself teaching or writing children's stories and/or romance novels based on history and faraway places. Your intellect is honest and direct and communications-travel are now your "bag." The need for emotional cleansings of the past continues from last month. Be gentle with yourself, but hang in there and rid your ego of some negative hang-ups, so the new year will start on a happy, healthy basis. Romance and marriage/commitment is still in the offing, and there could be a Christmas ceremony. If you are already committed, then a new and more progressive relationship is a potential. At Full Moon time on the 9th, friends and groups are especially fun. You may have many invitations and find it hard to sort them all out. Visits to friends and with interesting, communicative groups bring you pleasure. Short trips and outings are accented. After the 22nd, some of the emphasis upon the area of children and lovers moves into your work-service region. With the new year in the wings, firm foundations and stable work conditions receive highlighting. Past successes help you receive recognition and practical rewards in this part of your life.

VIRGO
August 23 to September 23

You have a great need to be of service, to help out in any way you can to make a task or life easier for others. Unfortunately, in a culture where "the person who dies with the most toys wins," your attitude of cheerful generosity to your fellow human beings is sadly undervalued.

You are most brilliant when aiding the process of developing an idea or solving practical problems. Point a Virgo in the direction you want them to go, and they're off and running! You can dissect any challenge with surgical skill, plow like an icebreaker through a sea of detail, and implement solutions with ease.

In a romantic relationship, you may find it hard to find a compatible partner. Your heart burns as brightly as anyone's, but in a world where style is valued over substance, your quiet, dignified charm may be overlooked. The one who finally wins you will be lucky indeed, for there is nothing like the tangible comfort and the sympathetic ear that a Virgo devotes to a loved one as an island of ease and support in a sometimes unfeeling world.

You are the reliable one, the one who always shows up on time and gets the work done. You have little desire for the spotlight; you only want to be appreciated for the excellent work that you do. If appreciation is not forthcoming, you become depressed and hypercritical of yourself and others. But we are not in this life to be perfect—we are here to be complete. Don't take on the weight of the world—ask for the support and encouragement you need. With your capacity for self-sufficiency, your friends may have no idea that you need anything from them, and would be glad for the chance to finally show you how much you mean to them!

HIGHLIGHTS OF 1992—VIRGO

All during this year great emphasis will be upon children and lovers. There appear to be strong influences for making practical choices, for bringing into materialization your deep desires. Objective and analytical outlooks can be helpful. Watching actions and not responding with strong emotions is also suggested. You appear to have a need for enduring, stable, and conventional relationships. Firm foundations are important, a feeling of building for long-range goals. Both Uranus and Neptune are accenting this region, turning retrograde, Uranus on April 22nd and Neptune on the 20th. Uranus will be direct again on September 24th, and Neptune on the 28th. This period of retrogression suggests that you do some inner investigation of your needs. Uranus has a seesawing vibration, and you may at times feel your nervous system is highly keyed. Tensions and irritations may result, so that you find lovers and children "hard to pin down." A need to work with facts is part of your natural temperament and with Capricorn further accenting this reaction, you could appear too critical or analytical. Neptune further indicates indecision and procrastination. Neptune deals with drifting and dreaming, indulgences, drugs, psychic depressions and self-pity. To balance all of this, it would be wise for you to direct some of these influences toward creative work. New educational/training interests, projecting your talents toward fields which appeal to you, and using your fine intellect to expand your life are all suggested. You may need, to explore and to shift emotions and attention.

Pluto turns retrograde on February 25th relating to your sector of relatives, communications and environment. Pluto will be direct again on July 31st. Introspection, watching for meanings of dreams, meditation and time spent letting go of past garbage can be most rewarding.

JANUARY

Enormous accenting of relationships with children and lovers will continue all year. The thrust appears to be how to build and conserve these associations, with an enduring and mutually satisfying outcome. No longer do you enjoy being swept off your feet by the promises of a lover, nor the inattention of children. If you do not have offspring, perhaps you may teach, heal, counsel or just spend time around children. Whatever your personal situation the learning opportunity is pointed toward this sector of your current life. Virgo, being a service-oriented sign, suggests that some of your lovers may indeed be "children." Virgo loves to help and to offer tools so that others may help themselves. You have very strong feelings of duty and responsibility. Jupiter is retrograde until May 5th, suggesting that being too optimistic, not working with realities and accepting promises just won't work now. The imbalance may be difficult, leading to impatience, rebelliousness and confusion in communications. Working with the principle of cause and effect can be effective. On the 19th at Full Moon time friends and groups can offer compassion. Through giving service to others you place time and energies where they may be needed.

FEBRUARY

Pluto becomes retrograde from the 25th to July 31st affecting your area connected with relatives, communications and environment. Pluto deals with the subconscious, dream symbols, introspection and release of the past. It is obviously time to do some appraisal of what you wish to rid yourself of here. Letting go of old and tired customs and outlooks is important. After mid-February, a possible Valentine's Day wedding is suggested. Someone tender, compassionate, service-oriented is in the limelight here. Your work-service-employment region could take off into new and expansive areas. The unexpected, and the unusual are accented. Some type of progressive field offers you opportunity to use your innovative and individualistic skills in a totally new way. Third World countries, inventions, research labs, hostels, and any region where totality is important can be available.

MARCH

Mercury turns retrograde on the 17th until April 9th and affects legacies, mutual assets and regeneration of energies. There needs to be a slowing down and a relaxation from action. You may feel irritated and restricted during this retrogression but keep your sense of humor. Someone may be manipulating the inheritance and/or funds. Travel is not suggested, and communications need to be clear and direct. Avoid signing contracts, agreements or documents until Mercury is again direct. Romance, if not put into legal framework last month, still has your attention. An old friend, former lover or someone with whom you feel a soul-level tie is indicated. Both of you desire an enduring relationship. If you are already committed, then there is a gentle and almost mystic tie available to sweeten the association. Your work situation continues to be exciting and expansive. Action is now a potential, as you may have mulled over facts and come to a decision last month. After the 20th there is an added thrust to the challenges around legacy and mutual funds. You now take a more aggressive attitude here. Avoid anger or showing temper. Trust that you will receive your rewards when the time is right for all concerned.

APRIL

Neptune will go retrograde on the 20th and direct again on September 28th. Uranus goes retrograde on the 22nd and direct on September 24th. It is time to "cool it" in the strongly emphasized region of children and lovers. Times of retrogressions suggest that the positive use of the vibrations is to work with one's deepest self. This takes time, privacy and energy. Making a balance sheet of pros and cons can be helpful. Deal with facts and realities and drop emotional responses. Mercury is direct on the 9th, taking off restrictions and tensions surrounding legacy, mutual assets and regeneration challenges. Your abilities can be recognized and rewarded by an inheritance and/or the use of a partner's abundance. Your leadership and executive qualities are in the limelight. Romance is ardent, direct, impulsive and active, with someone who is fiery and independent. The subject of marriage seems to keep coming up. Action combined with emotion is indicated.

MAY

Travel to other countries, specialized education, publishing and dealings with people from different backgrounds are all accented. You may find it helpful to your own business/profession or skills and talents to make visits to the Middle East, the Orient or various lands connected with the colorful past. The entertainment field is on stage. Arts and crafts, music, acting, luxury items, art galleries, museums and restorations of historical sites are all interesting potentials. Food and drink, cruises, resort hotels, healing, and counseling are now indicated. A person who enjoys all of the good things in life, fond of mate and home, as well as an enduring alliance is a romantic possibility. Jupiter turns direct on the 5th, timing that new chapter and self-image for expansion and projection. Saturn turns retrograde on the 28th affecting work-service-employment. Until the 16th of October, you would be wise not to rock work boats or make big changes. Some progressive oportunities may need further research. Saturn deals only with facts and realities. Avoid charming but irresponsible people or ideas which are not truly grounded. Don't get caught up in someone else's dream which could become your nightmare.

JUNE

Your career reaches the limelight this month. You may be surprised at the various alternatives you will be offered. There are dualities present, some procrastination due to indecision and perhaps too many offers. Travel and communications are important. Combining business with pleasure, travel by air, getting your ideas out to the public can all be interesting and exciting. Connection with transportation, the media, writing, publishing, acting, sales and any area where you work with others is highlighted. Friends and groups offer you support and advice. However, avoid permitting anyone to hold you back due to their own rigidities and conventionalities. Some of them may have a dislike of risks or change and their reactions may not belong to you. Romance is flirtatious, dualistic and hard to pin down. You may even have more than one romantic interest. Finding progressive and explorative ways of implementing mutual assets can be rewarding. Originality and independence can be helpful toward reaching goals. You may start your own business or profession with the assistance of a partner's funds and/or a legacy. With the Full Moon of the 15th, your home could be an enjoyable place for social activities with stimulating people.

JULY

Mercury will be retrograde from the 20th to August 13th affecting family, the past, karma, other lives/selves, institutions and restrictions. This could be an excellent period for retreat from the busy world, for quiet and creativity. Working behind the scenes now rather than right out in the limelight can be productive. You could appear arrogant or pushy if you do not cool down and burn your fire in solitude. Romance has this same kind of mysterious, "away from it all" ambiance. After the 14th, passion, intensity and action can be expressed with depth. You may link up with someone who is successful, proud, gregarious and ambitious, a born leader and power lover. Pluto goes direct on the 31st releasing tensions and frustrations around communications, relatives and environment. Discarding the old, you now have more time and energy for positive reactions. Writing, research, healing, counseling and any area where you go right down to the core are acccented now for success. Critical analysis helps you deal with the previous actions of relatives and neighbors and replace the negatives with humor and positive attitudes.

AUGUST

Mercury moves direct on the 13th accenting creativity in work done in solitude. The past continues to hold fascination plus active results. History, restoration of museum and art gallery artifacts, family trees and research into ancient cultures are areas for you to enjoy. You could travel, gathering atmosphere responses and data. After the 23rd that new beginning and image can be presented in a practical, workable way. You have the ability to show your qualities of discrimination, elegance, precision and discretion successfully. Your career sector suggests further travel opportunities, communications accented and variety and flexibility highlighted. Changes and alternatives are available. Romance indicates a new outlook, someone of whom you are proud, who wants a lasting kind of relationship, based on mutual goals and interests. You have a strong desire for intellectual communication before you become interested physically. Bonding on many levels is of great importance to you when it comes to a love relationship. Mutual respect and similar tastes, a sharp wit and clear mentality also attract you.

SEPTEMBER

In this birthday month Uranus turns direct on the 24th and Neptune on the 28th. Your past efforts at cooperative understanding with lovers and chilren may now appear successful. It would be wise to continue to ground mutual respect and bonding through using factual realities among all concerned. Avoid any kind of attraction toward illusion. Your intuition and data gained through meditation and quiet times may now blend with practical action. Your new spiffy image continues to be effective and busy. In late September, attention focuses upon finances, assets, investments and values. You may reach a fine balance with sufficient fun-spending and savings. Romance is projected with this same type of influence. A cooperative and well-integrated relationship has strong potential. There tends to be much action, support and outlets for nurturing, service and assistance through friends and organizations. Orphanages, hostels, rest homes, animal shelters and work with the disadvantaged are accented. Your desire for giving practical service can now be fulfilled, with strong emotional rewards.

OCTOBER

On the 11th Jupiter enters your sector of money, assets, values and investments. This can be an upswing in this region, with a strong thrust of optimism and enthusiasm. Some purchases which lend beauty and interest to your life may now be bought for long lasting pleasure. Romance appears intense and passionate. Love attraction may be encountered through relatives or neighbors or at a community activity. Your intellect is calling for some challenges at this time. Ambitions and investigative skills combine, so that you could find rewards through research in progressive and unexplored fields. Your mind responds with intensity and action as does your romantic nature. Both need concentration and direction toward positive goals. Saturn turns direct on the 16th affecting your work-service area. It may feel as though a lid has been taken off, and you may now expand successfully. Your past performances and proven abilities assist you toward an intelligent work-service decision.

NOVEMBER

Your home sector comes in for much of the limelight this month. Mercury turns retrograde on the 11th, suggesting that communications may be garbled or confused or delayed until Mercury is again direct. Travel should be avoided, especially long-range trips or impulsive plans which look good at the time of the holidays. You may wish to expand your home territory, enlarge the present house, buy a trailer, boat or even second home. Romance has a stimulating effect, arriving at your door with enthusiasm and humor. A "fun person" is indicated, one who can help you expand and mature. Mars goes retrograde on the 29th affecting your region of friends, goals and groups. It would be wise not to spread your social activities too thinly at this season. Take care of those who appear overly dependent upon you. There may be avoidance of important confrontations, a pushing down of anger and grudges. Say what you mean when necessary and don't permit anyone to "use" you. Celebrate in your own fashion, without artificial guilt. On the 2nd your work-employment sector receives a new and progressive thrust of opportunity. Get the whole picture and don't make an impulsive decision. On the 10th people from different backgrounds or countries, publishing, special training and foreign travel are highlighted. Be practical and choose learning opportunities which are lasting and fulfilling.

DECEMBER

Some of your experiences are circling back to the beginning of 1992. The region of lovers and children returns for your final decision. Past research, data which is factual, choices based upon realities are all available for you to end much of this learning-maturing process. You understand your needs for stability, security, an enduring type of association, and you can at this time project it. You may be doing work at home, especially relating to communications, teaching, writing, reporting, sales, public relations or some type of public contact. Others may come to you for knowledge and assistance. Romance may be discovered at the work site with someone idealistic and original. This appears to be an unusual, unexpected and sudden attraction. Mars turns retrograde as of November 29th, and is still in that position. The suggestion that you deal objectively with friends and groups making demands upon your time, emotions and energies continues. Helping others to help themselves is a natural part of your skills. However, there is a point where others need to learn to walk by themselves and take on responsibilities. Try to keep a balance during the holidays between compassion and caring and permitting others to learn in their own fashion. The coming year seems to hold exciting and bountiful opportunities.

LIBRA
September 23 to October 23

Diplomat, romantic, artist. Libra is all these things, for you are ruled by Venus, the planet and goddess of beauty and attraction. You are in your element when your surroundings are both beautiful and harmonious. This is a necessity to your emotional and psychological well being. To be forced to cope with an ugly environment or rude individuals is an affront to you, and you will quickly disappear or disassociate yourself from such people or places.

This love of harmony makes you gracious and extremely social. An elegant and affable host, you know instinctively how to put your guests at ease. You have a well-balanced sense of things artistic, and you deeply appreciate fine art, excellent food, and the best of entertainment.

At times indecisive, you really are at your best in a team, with another person to bounce ideas off of and provide you with some motivation, which you sometimes lack. Be careful that your love of company does not become an obsession. Learn how to spend quality time alone with yourself. This helps you recharge your batteries and develop your relationship with yourself.

The "iron hand in the velvet glove" perhaps best describes your brilliance as a negotiator and diplomat. You never force another to go your way. You prefer to outline their options in such a way that your idea appears to be in their best interests! The other person may even end up thinking that it was their idea in the first place. This is also reflected in your skill at handling difficult people and situations. This you do with grace and ease, and your associates most likely turn to you to help set things straight in times of trouble and conflict.

HIGHLIGHTS OF 1992—LIBRA

Affairs related to your home are most important and lasting during 1992. This can be a productive time for settling in a safe and stable situation. You receive heavy influences during the year around your home. Neptune and Uranus are both posited here, with Uranus turning retrograde on April 22nd and Neptune on the 20th. These are periods, until Uranus is direct on September 24th and Neptune on the 28th, for slowing down and avoiding action. Uranus suggests erratic influences during its retrogression. Neptune indicates indecision, procrastination and possible self-indulgences. Neptune suggests your tendency to avoid important confrontations and realities. These can be profitable times for linking super-conscious self with conscious personality.

Pluto turns retrograde on February 25th until July 31st and affects your region of finances, assets, investments and values. Pluto cleanses, heals and transforms. Discard past failures, let go of anger or pain. Pluto can help you as it connects with your subconscious, dream symbols, and what you have buried or ignored. Transform the past with the help of this planet.

Your sector dealing with children and love affairs is also of importance this year. The indication here is of the need for a new concept, with mutual respect, and freedom for all concerned. Tensions and rebellion may be present, but the learning thrust suggests a more mature and progressive set of attitudes.

JANUARY

As 1992 opens, home base is strongly accented. The indication is that now is the time to establish a stable and secure home. The New Moon of the 4th suggests that you need to work with factual data and realistic expectations. Working with the pros and cons of how you want your home to be is important. Your sign is especially sensitive to surroundings and environment, so plan to implement your tastes. You may also work at home, using your talents and skills most productively. With the Full Moon of the 19th, career affairs take the limelight. Emotional satisfactions are indicated. Counseling, nurturing, feeding, offering help to all the disadvantaged and those in trouble can be fulfilling. Romance available through relatives and your community appears optimistic, fun, enthusiastic and companionable. Someone who is a lover of life is eager to help you expand your horizons in many ways. Saturn is highlighting the region of lovers and children with much seesawing motion. Highs and lows occur this month, and often tensions and irritations erupt. Duties and old habits fight with the desire for freedom, You seem caught in the middle here. Get away from the scene from time to time, and keep your sense of humor.

FEBRUARY

Pluto turns retrograde on the 25th affecting money, assets, investments and values. Until this planet is again direct on July 31st, you would be wise to avoid making changes or taking important actions. Pluto deals with your subconscious, the meaning of dreams, meditation and introspection. It is time now to decide what is important to you, as your working value system. Making an honest appraisal of your needs/desires is necessary. Releasing outworn habits and customs is also important. Let go of financial fears or misconceptions. Romance is connected with home base, with a stable, persistent lover. He/she could arrive at your front door. Lovers and children continue with the seesawing learning experiences. This could be difficult for your nervous system. Laugh and refuse to play games. After mid-month the work-service-employment sector is accented. Helping others, giving service and working with psychic-occult matters can be fulfilling. Your employment picture helps you offset some of the children-lovers difficulties. Put your time and energies of your work toward rewards now.

MARCH

This Spring month emphasizes your work-service-employment sector. Work which is healing, helpful, nurturing and with emotional impact is highlighted. You could do fine work connected with hospitals, orphanages, animal shelters, the homeless and hostels and rest homes. Psychic-occult data can also be productive. Your empathy and sensitivity in whatever your chosen field is recognized. Acting, motion pictures, photography, music, literature and psychic phenomenon are also potential areas of output. Romance may be found at the work site. This is a tender gentle and karmic touch, a non-abrasive encounter. A former friend could become a lover. Mercury goes retrograde on the 17th connected with your sector of marriage, love unions and/or business relationships. It would be wise to postpone any decisions in these associations until April 9th when Mercury is again direct. Avoid signing important documents after the 17th. Travel should also be avoided during the retrogression, and keep communications clear. The region of lovers and children is still an up and down situation. Action may be called for during March, but frictions and demands, irresponsible behavior and rebellions still need cooling. Keep your own inner peace.

APRIL

After the 9th your marriage, love union and business relationship sector is active. A new start with someone who is a leader, an explorer, executive type is suggested. Ambitious, fiery and passionate also describe him/her. If already wed or committed, a potential for stimulation, expansion and something new and exciting can be projected in the relationship. There is much possible action and growth available in these associations. Your work region indicates rewards and recognition for your good work in the past. Your caring and service-oriented attitudes may result in raises, promotions and prestige. Neptune goes retrograde on the 20th and Uranus on the 22nd accenting home. Avoid decisions or action until they are direct again. Make your plans and visualize the ultimate desired outcome. Work only with realities, with facts and investigated, provable data. You are working for enduring effects. Perhaps you may feel restricted, duty-bound and overly-responsible during this period, but go with it. Balance routine with fun and social pleasures. Realize you are building an important foundation and enjoy the ride.

MAY

This is a grand month for the practical implementation of changes of habit and outlooks. New ways of using time and energies can help you achieve goals easily. A partner's assets may be used for mutual benefit. You could receive a handsome legacy. This can be a building-conserving month. Your creativity is high and you have the talent for combining beauty with practicality. Romance is available with someone stable but charming, dedicated to family. The entertainment field could offer you opportunities. Acting, singing, or design and fashion can be outlets currently. Jupiter moves direct on the 5th releasing tensions and repressions regarding the past, family, karmic ties, restrictions and institutions. If you have done some investigation, you are ready to expand these parts of your life profitably. Working with persistence and routine plus enthusiasm and optimism helps you reach your aims harmoniously. Saturn goes retrograde on the 28th, so that irritations and misunderstandings arise in the love affairs-children area. Ultimately, this learning experience leads toward maturity and progressive attitudes.

JUNE

A summer vacation is a strong possibility, particularly by air travel. Faraway lands, foreign people and backgrounds may appeal to you at this time. You could have a learning opportunity to go with the fun. Publishing is accented, as well as special educational opportunities and training in a new field of interest. Romance has a flirtatious, dualistic tinge allied with exotic cultures. Travel and communications are strongly highlighted and you could write, teach or lecture once you have made an interesting and colorful journey. More than one romantic alternative is indicated. Career matters offer emotional rewards for work well done. Psychic studies can be fulfilling as well as service-oriented fields. You have a natural empathy for the needs/desires of the public. Marriage, love relationships or business partnerships continue to be active. Avoid impulsive behavior in this area of your life. Finances continue a restrictive suggestion. Your inner self may have messages for you through dream symbols or meditation. Listen and watch for these, as they come from deep, inner desires and data. Your money picture and value system concepts need balancing.

JULY

Friends and groups may offer you a big surprise this month recognizing your abilities and putting you center stage. You could find rewards through joining organizations connected with worldwide needs, large corporations, legal activities connected with politics. After mid-month, romance may be encountered with a successful, powerful and colorful individual. Mercury turns retrograde on the 20th, indicating time for cooling much communicative or travel activity. With all this attention, be cautious about appearing arrogant or pushy. Wait until Mercury turns direct on August 13th to implement travel plans. Pluto turns direct and much of the intensity previously felt concerning finances and assets is lifted. Hopefully you have done your homework and now are more assured about your true values. Some of the discarding and releasing accomplished to date leaves room for happier, more successful results in the financial picture. The New Moon of the 7th suggests positive timing for presenting a new image. Full Moon time on the 14th suggests practical renovations at home for lasting effects.

AUGUST

As Mercury becomes direct on the 13th, previous travel arrangements and communications can now be manifested profitably. Fun vacation time is available to you now. You may accompany a group or friend to exciting, dramatic places. Countries with artistic cultures appeal to you at this time. Romance is quiet even mysterious and with a touch of something hidden. You require an intelligent and practical partner. There may be a tendency to be critical and analytical. A second influence emphasizes travel to other countries, meetings with people from different backgrounds, special education, publishing and psychic-occult matters. This complex vibration adds fuel to the travel fever you may be experiencing. Travel, probably by air, to more than one area is also accented. You could visit places which offer you background for work which you incorporate successfully later. Learning languages and relating to a variety of people and situations can also be rewarding. Special training, especially related to communications, is also highlighted. Occult psychic studies, investigation and seminars, lectures and meetings can be appealing.

SEPTEMBER

Uranus becomes direct on the 24th and Neptune on the 28th, toning down the seesawing motion of Uranus and the procrastination and indecision attributed to Neptune. You may latch on to the vibrations at your home base and project them creatively. This is a persistent building influence, and a fine balance between progressive and original and emotional and visionary. Music, dance, the arts, literature, psychic-occult affairs and anything which is creative plus original can be successful. Tying your desires down to earth can be fulfilling. Romance has a sense of a new start. Someone similar to you, with mutual goals and pleasures, who can be charming and cooperative is available. A companion on many levels of understanding can offer broad horizons in love. After the 12th, career matters take on further emphasis. Emotional satisfaction through service-oriented output is high. Action plus empathy points you toward realistic career goals. There is ease and harmony as you receive recognition and rewards, without climbing the ladder. Your good work of the past now has this satisfying effect. The New Moon of the 3rd accents money values and investments. Work with realistic facts only. Oil, engineering, mining, healing, research labs and investigative fields are all areas to be given attention.

OCTOBER

Jupiter on the 11th adds optimism and enthusiasm to your region of a new image and beginning. Don't project impulsively or without planning, however. You need not risk or speculate, if you have organized your desires. Act with trust and integrity. Your money picture continues being highlighted this birthday month. It is on your mind, connected with romance and even your outer personality. Assets and values may also suggest your personal skills and talents. Your subconscious, dreams, meditation data and the time and energy left from discarding the past can all be helpful. Saturn becomes direct on the 15th affecting love affairs and children's interests. New, unusual and progressive mutual understandings can now be implemented with success. Freedom of expression and action, as well as ideals and unconditional love can be beneficial. Avoid accepting or engaging in rebellious attitudes, thumbing of noses at responsibilities or becoming erratic-eccentric. Career continues to offer not only emotional rewards but added duties which can be fulfilling. Creativity plus action and intuition combine now for a fully-rounded career experience.

NOVEMBER

Relatives, communications and your environment take on strong emphasis this month. During the holidays, you can enjoy lots of fun and excitement among these areas of our current life. There is a thrust of pleasurable communications and progressive attitudes. Mercury, however, turns retrograde in this region on the 11th. This intimates postponing travel. Make sure communications are clear and concise. Avoid signing important contracts, agreements or documents. You may tend to make impulsive choices now, but need to be cautious about details and the "fine print." Think before you speak or write. Romance is active, fun, and opens fascinating new possibilities. Someone who is witty but caring, friendly yet passionate is on stage now. There may be potential changes, different outlooks and associations in your community which offer exhilarating challenges. Mars goes retrograde on the 29th affecting career matters. It would be wise to just settle in for a while and avoid changes or decisions here. Your previous emotional responses need objectivity. Don't get involved in the affairs of others. Try to separate feelings and career actions. The Full Moon of the 10th suggests a legacy and/or abundant use of mutual assets in constructive ways.

DECEMBER

As 1992 winds down you may shake your head and hope the new year will offer less confusion, challenges and changes. The holidays may be spent productively at home, rather than in travel. A love affair and children's affairs now appear to be more mature and beneficial to all. If you have no offspring, the word "children" may be read as "personal creativity." It seems this sector which has been so upsetting and a strong learning challenge now offers successful outcome. The slowing down and balancing act connected with career continues. Wait and check out data before coming to conclusions. With this year ending, special educational opportunities, training, publishing and occult matters are accented. You may find it difficult to make decisions. It would be wise to do some investigation, work with pros and cons and then take a progressive step forward. Much maturity and inner security have undoubtedly been achieved. As the old year disappears, you envision triumphs and much happiness in the one approaching.

Scorpio is ruled by the planet Pluto. This influence makes you a person of extremes, with deep passions, much intensity, and an attraction to things mysterious. There is very little middle ground with you in your emotional responses to people or ideas. You also have an extraordinary ability to hide your feelings and motives from others. Only those who know you well, or the very observant, can tell what you are thinking or doing most of the time.

You are a survivor, with tremendous will and inner resources to draw upon in trying times. You also lend your formidable strength to your loved ones in time of need. Again and again, you attract challenging life experiences to you to constantly test your ability to cope with life. You are a law unto yourself. This suits you just fine, but others may not agree with the independent view. If you aren't careful, you may find you have gained a reputation for being ruthless.

More than any other sign, you require some emotional outlet. Take care not to repress your feelings; otherwise they can turn against you, breaking out uncontrollably or eating away at your soul from within. To be healthy, a balanced person must acknowledge their emotions, and then let them go. Finding a positive expression for your feelings through work or art is a good way to prevent yourself from stagnating.

You seek answers to the mysteries of life. In loving another person deeply, and with the entire fiber of your being, you may find some of those answers. In love, we human beings get a taste of what it is like to be divine, and the ecstasy that you experience with your lover is perhaps the perfect vehicle for your passion.

HIGHLIGHTS OF 1992— SCORPIO

Your planetary ruler, Pluto, goes retrograde on February 25th until July 31st. This accents your sector connected with new beginnings and new self-image. Pluto connects with subconscious infomation which can be a rich source of important information. Introspection, dreams, what you have hidden from the conscious mind now surface for decisions. During this retrogression, discard old pains, angers and passions. It is time now to face these challenges. Pluto suggests that letting go of old and no longer viable customs and habits offers you healed energies for growth.

Your region of relatives, communications and environment is also strongly accented all during 1992. Uranus turns retrograde on April 22nd and Neptune on the 20th. Until Uranus is direct again on September 24th and Neptune on the 28th, relaxing and personal analysis are necessary. Uranus offers original and innovative ideas to be blended with your methods of communication and how you appear in the community. Neptune connotes intuition, psychic-occult matters, visions and dreams. It is also allied with the arts, music, literature, motion pictures, TV, photography and creativity in numerous fields.

The ultimate learning opportunity for these two vibratory influences is to be practical, persistent and build for enduring values. Uranus has an up and down vibration which can affect your nervous system. Use your sense of humor. Neptune connotes indulgences, drugs, alcohol, sex, food/drink and manipulations, indecision and procrastination.

JANUARY

1992 opens with strong emphasis on relatives, communications and environment. With the New Moon on the 4th, there are several influences accenting this sector of your life. All of those ambitions, dreams and inner desires have the potential for practical implementation. Work only with facts and realities and avoid wishful dreaming. You have the type of mentality which may criticize, analyze, dissect, investigate and make realistic conclusions. You need to always avoid using manipulation. Romance has a totally different vibration currently, one of fun, wit, excitement, impulse and ardor. Someone who lifts you from the depths of duties and responsibilities can be a real treasure. Jupiter is retrograde, accenting your sector of friends and groups. This is a service-oriented influence, objective and practical, not colorful at all. Routine and discretion are important. You receive rewards and recognition for work well done.

FEBRUARY

Pluto turns retrograde on the 25th emphasizing new beginnings and self-image. Wait to act until July 31st when Pluto becomes direct once more. What you have hidden or ignored in the past now suggests it is time for choices and decisions. Dreams, meditation, and introspection are important at this time. Releasing past pain, trouble, anger and old customs and habits is necessary before you can attain successful results. Make honest appraisals of your values and inner desires. Visualize and organize until July 31st and then ... project and implement. Romance may be discovered through relatives or at community activities. Someone practical, realistic with a desire for a stable and enduring relationship is indicated. Your home also comes in for highlighting now. You could be creating original and progressive products from there. Progressive ideas can be stimulating. You may want to make important and different changes in your foundation spot. Think it through, investigate realities before you make a decision. Check people and situations out accurately and precisely.

MARCH

Mercury turns retrograde from the 17th until April 9th affecting your work-service-employment region. This position suggests that you avoid appearing domineering or overly ambitious. Your leadership qualities are basic to your nature, but currently you need to play it cool. Continue to be original and independent but keep a low profile until Mercury is direct again. If communications have clarity and practicality, you will be heard and rewarded. Romance has a tender, gentle ambiance this month. Love affairs and children may offer emotional fulfillment and support.

A tie with someone of a karmic type is indicated. This has a soothing quality with a lasting, caring vibration. On the Full Moon of
the 18th friends and organizations underwrite a foundation for
some of your projected ideas. Investigation, working with facts
and precision can be successful. Those who "can do" offer you assistance. Home base continues to be a place for new and progressive creative opportunities. You need to keep concentration and
direction toward goals. Services combined with friendships and
groups have practical underpinnings, giving others tools to help
themselves in down-to-earth ways. Your rewards here are of an
inner, quiet kind.

APRIL

Mercury turns direct on the 9th, suggesting communications,
changes and travel enter the picture. Your mentality and ways of
expressing yourself are direct, clear and to the point. Your capaci-
ties for leadership, executive talent and exploratory goals may be
consummated successfully. Romance has this same active ambiance, with someone vital, passionate, intense and fond of winning. You could meet a love partner at the work place. Avoid
power plays however. This could become a no-win situation unless there is respect and lots of space. Uranus turns retrograde on
the 22nd and Neptune on the 20th, affecting relatives, communications and environment. These periods, until Uranus becomes
direct on September 24th and Neptune on the 28th, indicate a
slowing down and relaxation of these areas. Work for lasting results, accept responsibilities and work with routine and detail. Be
cautious about impulsive decisions, confusion in communications and a seesawing effect. Indecisive behavior, self-indulgence
and periods of self-pity may be suggested. Keep a sense of humor.
Support and empathy come from lovers and children at this time.

MAY

From the New Moon on the 2nd through this Spring month,
marriage, love unions and/or business relationships are strongly
accented. The desire for stability, security and endurance in this
sector of your present life is highlighted. The partner here suggests the need for mutual goals and methods, for achievement for
mate and family. While this is a loving, pleasurable vibration, it is
also a practical, common sense one. This relationship influence
suggests beauty, passion along with down-to-earth realities.
Friends and groups appear supportive and active. However
avoid any type of manipulation or jealousy. Jupiter turns direct
on the 5th influencing the expansion and stabilizing of your associations with organizations, groups and friends. You will receive
those "just rewards" for past accomplishments. Saturn will be ret-

rograde from May 28th until Uctober 16th. This position accents your home base situation. Changes, originality, explorations in what is new are all apparent. You may want to make a change in residence. Unusual people may reach your front door, offering innovative ideas. These are times for working through investigation with realities and facts.

JUNE

This month accents a legacy, mutual assets and regeneration of time and energies through discarding the past. Dualities, changes and communications are highlighted. Travel and changes of pace may open up fields of interest contributing to these parts of your life. An inheritance may need to be divided and/or you may receive more than one. Mutual funds need direction and combining of methods for beneficial results. Writing, teaching, lecturing, sales, public relations, journalism or any area where you travel, meet all kinds of people and situations are available. Avoid scattering of time and energies. Love takes on a similar reflection of these influences. You may find it hard to have just one romance in your life. The choices appear difficult for an enduring relationship. This month could be a successful one for foreign travel, connections with people from other cultures, special education and publishing. Trips especially around, near or on water appear relaxing. Work matters continue their upswing, with new opportunities for self-employment. Originality, executive and leadership qualities all come in now for recognition and rewards. The money picture indicates risks but stimulating opportunities if you do some investigation first.

JULY

Matters concerning your career take center stage this month. Your ambitions are strong, your public image colorful, even dramatic. After mid-month, you desire the limelight. However, be cautious here, with Mercury becoming retrograde on the 20th, influencing travel, change, communications and intellect. Think before you speak or write. Be direct, but not offensive. Your abilities will be apparent, especially in connections with the public. Romance can be passionate and intense available at the career level. Someone ambitious and vigorous is on the scene. You may feel pride in their accomplishments but try not to be jealous or possessive. Mutual regard for originality and space is important. Pluto goes direct on the 31st suggesting potential success in implementing a new beginning and image. Hopefully in the past months you have discarded much of the old garbage. It is now time to combine what you have learned from your subconscious, dreams and meditation with conscious action.

AUGUST

Mercury turns direct on the 13th so the brakes on your career sector are off now. Emphasis continues in this region, and you could combine an interesting vacation for business and fun. Prestige, a raise, bonus, promotion or a new and expansive opportunity are all in the limelight. Romance may be discovered among friends and groups. A person who is conventional, intellectual, analytical and objective is indicated. It may be up to you to furnish the intensity and start of a relationship but it would be based upon stable and enduring mutual goals. You could receive a legacy which you might have to split with another, or project mutual assets in more than one direction. Writing, publishing, teaching, lecturing, communications of all kinds, plus travel and change are also in the cards this month. The New Moon on the 5th adds fuel to the fire when it comes to making a new chapter in your present life. If you have worked successfully with the Pluto influences, you should have riches to add to your former personality. Earning your place at the top, fulfilling inner ambitions offers you opportunities to bring desires into practical implementation.

SEPTEMBER

Groups, organizations and friends are supportive of your plans for analyzed and well-researched projects. Proven data, people who are strongly service-oriented and persistent efforts all receive tribute. Your mentality has a concise and sharp vibratory influence. Uranus becomes direct on the 24th and Neptune on the 28th lifting some of the restraints and tensions from situations with relatives, the environment and communications. You may experience a strong sense of relief in these areas. Past frustrations connected with duties and responsibilities disappear. You could now experience opportunities for freer expression and projection of some of those past desires. Letting go of artificial guilts with relatives and community can be a positive transformation. Romance is mysterious and idealistic. Someone charming, cooperative, a better lover than mate or parent is significant. Vacation plans or a trip to another land offer emotional and creative opportunities. Publishing, education and psychic-occult matters are also fulfilling. With New Moon of the 12th children and lovers appear supportive and empathetic. Avoid permitting them, however, to be overly dependent or manipulative.

OCTOBER

Saturn becomes direct on the 16th, releasing tensions or strain around home base. Some of your progressive plans may easily be implemented. Originality, invention, New Age interests and the unexplored are areas where you may work at home. Concepts stirring around in your mind in the past may currently be expressed. If you have dismissed those charismatic characters from your home, new, interesting and stimulating people may now enter. Remember the importance of timing. Jupiter on the 11th accents your region of the past, other lives/selves, karma, work done in solitude, institutions, and restrictions. There is an excellent opportunity for expansion. You could balance out work and creativity with success. Romance is vigorous, intense and new. Love appears with a different look. This is an opportune month for you to project ambitions, to use energies and time constructively. You could find new ways of directing your intellect and emotional nature, so that both mind and feelings are enriched. Be cautious about coming on too strong.

NOVEMBER

During your birthday month, finances, assets, investments and your value system are being accented. Mercury goes retrograde on the 11th, suggesting caution and research before making decisions. This is not the best time for travel, and you should be careful in signing agreements, documents or contracts. It is important that before you link up with someone stimulating and fun romantically, that you do some investigation. Make sure your material situation is not a base for the relationship. Impulsive and passionate choices may not have the enduring value you desire. Communications, travel and change are highlighted for emotional rewards. Recognition and prestige bring you fulfillment on many levels. Keeping sufficient energy and vitality directed toward the unexplored must be balanced with caution and analysis. The New Moon on the 2nd affects home base, suggesting potential new challenges. Illusions need to be dissipated and actualities well grounded for mutual benefit. Around the 10th the question of a stable and secure marriage, love union and/or business relationship is up for grabs. This could be a loving, practical and enduring kind of association. However, there are also indications of stubborness and rigidities.

DECEMBER

Your monetary picture continues in importance during this holiday season. Avoid emotional or impulsive spending, or trying to make an impression with finances. Celebrating at home will be more beneficial than travel, which could become confusing and wearing. Home base can be exciting, progressive and have sufficient originality and fun for all concerned, especially if each member is honest and open. Hosting social activities can be pleasureable. Romance is unusual, exotic and challenging. Mars turns retrograde and affects foreign travel. Trips appear to be un-

rewarding this month. As the year winds down, love affairs and
children's interests are highlighted. An old friend or former lover
now offers empathy and tenderness. The grounding, materialization and projection of your dreams and desires can be seen far off
now. Your talents for working well with facts and realities
through research can suggest future success.

SAGITTARIUS
November 23 to December 22

You are a light-hearted traveller of life. You feel that we are only sure of this one shot at life, and you are going to give your best effort to enjoying the time allotted to you. A gypsy at heart, you are the one who is likely to drop everything at a moment's notice to take off for adventures and parts unknown. Only the lightest touch can tame your soul.

Your symbol is the centaur. These mythological creatures—half human and half horse—were famed warriors and healers. As this symbol may suggest, you have an almost religious devotion to the sanctity of the human spirit. Your unflagging commitment to freedom and a fair shake for all makes you a spirited fighter for the liberation of all beings. However, sometimes you can be over-zealous and forget that tact and consideration for peoples' feelings are as necessary to motivate others as your irresistible, fiery will.

In a romantic relationship, you frustrate and fascinate by turns. You absolutely reserve the right to emotional sovereignty, and once a person tries manipulation games with you, you're gone. But you will always stay with the person who allows you the room to be yourself. To this partner you give of yourself wholeheartedly with warmth and devotion.

Sometimes you play the clown, complete with pratfalls and facepaint. At other times, your human half is in control, and then you are busy debating the philosophical questions of the ages. Your broadness of vision at these times is staggering. Either way, your friends and associates can definitely count on you to provide stimulating and diverting company!

HIGHLIGHTS OF 1992—SAGITTARIUS

All during this year, the most important and lasting emphasis is upon your region of finances, values, assets and investments. This should be a period for you to ground your money situation in a practical, stable way. Uranus turns retrograde on April 22nd and Neptune on the 20th, both affecting this part of your life. Uranus will be direct again September 24th and Neptune on the 28th. During these retrogressions, you would be wise to re-search every potential opportunity regarding money chal-lenges. These are periods to plan and organize but not take action. Once these planets are again direct, then imple-ment those dreams. You could buy into provable bonds, real estate, work financially with institutions, pay off your home and car, see your insurances are profitable, etc.

Pluto going retrograde on February 25th until July 31st affects your past, family traditions, other selves or lives, and restricting habits and concepts. These all need dis-carding, as they are no longer viable. Direct these released and transformed energies toward new and progressive goals.

Saturn affects your region of relatives, communications and environment, turning retrograde on May 5th and di-rect on October 16th. These can be constructive times to work with critical analysis and cause and effect. Build for a stable, enduring lifestyle in these areas. Avoid impulsive or rebellious behavior. Direct communications with clar-ity and be progressive, but practical.

JANUARY

Beginning the new year with accenting money, value system and assets, you might as well realize these challenges will continue well over the total year. This learning opportunity suggests growth and a maturing attitude toward money and values. You need to "put your money where your mouth is," both with finances and actions. Your intellect appears steadier than ever before, more able to handle facts and realities with patience and perservence. You handle investigation proof and data well. Writing, teaching, lecturing on "how to" skills can be successful. Putting your talents into practical channels helps you add to your basic income. Romance is stimulating, startling and even "out of this world." You are attracted to someone new and original. This relationship can be mutually exhilarating and pleasurable. Jupiter is retrograde until May 5th affecting career and public image. Don't make big changes, impulsive decisions or feel rebellious. It is necessary to flow with rules, regulations and precedent.

FEBRUARY

Your area of communications, relatives and environment is highlighted. Unusual and progressive opportunities are suggested. Teaching, writing, publishing, acting, sales, public relations, the media and travel are evident. You may meet people who have outlooks that are new to you. Stimulation of thought and action in community activities could result. Romance stabilizes, offering a more practical relationship than last month. You could see serious value in this association, with enduring results. Pluto turns retrograde on the 25th until July 31st, accenting the past, family history, other lives, restrictions and institutions. These are periods helpful in obtaining wisdom through dreams, meditation and introspection. It is time to rid yourself of past garbage and regenerate these energies toward more productive goals. Probing deep within and making honest appraisals are important. Listen to your intuition. It can be a valuable companion and teacher. You go ahead more successfully when you proceed slowly and with caution.

MARCH

Your sector of love affairs and children comes in for much attention this month. Mercury turns retrograde from the 17th until April 9th. You may find it hard to control your temper. Tensions and frustrations appear, as everyone wants to be the leader. Power plays may surface, and anger run hot. Don't permit yourself to be manipulated or buckle down to the desires of those in the picture. This is not a productive time for travel or making changes. See that communications are clear and avoid signing important documents until April 9th. Romance can be a comfort to offset these aforementioned tensions. Someone close has a soothing and tender effect on you. A type of "karmic link" is indicated here as well. Home base can be a refuge from difficulties. Listen to dreams and wisdom from psychic-occult studies. At the Full Moon of the 18th, you may receive some favorable recognition at the career level. Taking progressive action in your environment can also be a productive outlet for some of the challenges now encountered with children and/or lover. This region tends to clear up after the 20th when you put your foot down. Equal rights for all is a potential slogan here. Freedom and leadership need to be balanced by responsibilities and service.0

APRIL

Neptune turns retrograde from the 20th until September 28th and Uranus from the 22nd until September 24th. These planets accent money, assets, investments and values. A fine balance needs to be kept between dreams and realities. This is an up and down vibration, progressive innovative and active. Find interesting ways to add to your financial picture, if this is important. If not, you may wish to use your talents creatively, rather than working with the money picture. Mercury is direct on the 9th highlighting the region of lovers and children. Communications should be direct and honest. Each person may be original and individualistic, but need to pay his or her own way. The principle of creating one's own reality can be projected successfully at this time. Romance is ardent and idealistic. A lover and/or children may appreciate you and your principles and show their affection and loyality. It may be time for offspring to be on their own. This may also apply to a lover. At home you may want to add beautiful, harmonious and pleasurable artifacts to your environment. Psychic books, groups with similar interests, classes -lessons-seminars may all be held with "soul mates" of similar interests.

MAY

Jupiter turns direct on the 5th affecting your career and public image region. Past patience and following regulations now indicate prestige and favor which you have earned. Your service-oriented causes return for practical, enduring effects. Your career matters should be stabilized and secure. Saturn turns retrograde on the 28th until October 16th. This indicates slowing down and flowing with situations regarding relatives, communications and environment. Duties and responsibilities, the elderly, family be-

liefs and community restrictions can be irritating. You want to try
the new and innovative now but feel held back. It would be wise
to get away from it all to "baby" yourself from time to time. Try to
see the funny side. There are several accents surrounding your
work-service-employment sector. This is a grounding and materializing influence. Romance which is secure, passionate, pleasure-loving yet practical may be met at the work site. Arts and
crafts, healing, theatre, music, cruises, resort hotels, restaurants
and bars, hospitals, hostels and animal shelters all come in for attention workwise. Giving service and the type of employment
where you are emotionally satisfied can be fulfilling. Work and
love appear in excellent balance.

JUNE

A June wedding is a possibility. Someone who can fly at the
same altitude as you, a born communicator and fun type is highlighted. A pal, a companion, a wit and communicator is indicated
for relationship. This could be a love union or a business partnership, as well as marriage. If already wed, open communications
become fun, mutual learning-training in new fields may bring
both partners into more stimulating contact. Travel can be en-
lightening. A legacy and mutual funds suggest emotional fulfillment. You may receive an inheritance. Psychic-occult research
can be strongly productive. Regeneration of energies may result
through the turning around of past responses. Feelings at "gut
level" are accurate and compassionate. Healing can be transmit-
ted with empathy. Emotional assets are important. Giving and re-
ceiving appear as one. The Full Moon of the 15th indicates a successful new start and image. A field or interest which exhilarates
you may currently become your next goal. Travel, studies and
educational opportunities contribute drama and color to your desired new image.

JULY

Pluto turns direct on the 31st releasing much of the tension
and intensity around your region of the past, family beliefs, institutions and restrictions. You should be a wiser, more competent
and happier person. Pluto probes at deep inner levels often with a
volcanic intensity. This calls for recognition of what is old and
outworn. Old hurts, hates, angers and griefs which have been discarded now disappear from your life. People and situations "go
into the light," as you have worked within previously. You perhaps have learned that Pluto holds a rich source of creative data
and knowledge. Mercury goes retrograde on the 20th affecting
your region of foreign travel, connections with people from other

backgrounds or cultures, publishing, psychic-occult research and special training. Your desire for heading the top of the ladder needs relaxing at this time. Wait until Mercury is direct on August 13th before taking action. Communications need clarity, so think before speaking or writing. After mid-month romance turns dramatic and is connected with faraway places. You may obtain emotional satisfaction through creativity associated with famous places or historical cultures. Extend your educational background. Legal, political, corporate or theatrical fields can be both fun and profitable this month.

AUGUST

With Mercury direct on the 13th, this could be a fun vacation month, especially in out of the way areas of the world. Regions where you can either be outdoors with nature or among the "rich and famous" are indicated. Romance appears around your work place, with someone reserved, elegant, intellectual and conventional. She/he may be work-oriented as well. Duties and responsibilities will be important. The love union, marriage or business partnership question arises again. You may still be flirting with a commitment. After the 23rd, there is further action in your career sector, combined with a romantic aspect. Some of your ambitions and drive for recognition are now balanced with discrimination, investigative abilities and persistence. You do not balk so hard at routine and detail, understanding their necessity for success here. The needs of the public, hospitals, hospices, animal shelters, research laboratories, health food stores, office machines and historical restorations, art galleries and museums offer outlets for your creative skills.

SEPTEMBER

Uranus goes direct on the 24th and Neptune on the 28th accenting your money picture. Past restraints now appear lessened. You may begin to implement practical, researched ideas about assets and investments with success. Self-indulgence, indecision and procrastination are dissipating. Your intuition is strongly accurate now and creativity moves from emotional levels toward productive outlets. Matters connected with worldwide or planetary challenges are accented for investment and/or value service. Oil, water, drugs, alcohol, and addictions have a meaningful thrust. These may not be personal, but suggest a type of work you may join. Music, acting, literature, motion pictures, TV and photography, are also highlighted for investment purposes. These "investments" and "assets" also pertain to your skills and talents, as well as finances. Career affairs continue their routine pace from last month. Daily practical and persistent efforts will bring slow but sure results. Romance is available through friends and groups. Mutual goals and interests can be a bond. After mid-September, mutual funds appear active and vigorous. You may discover ways to benefit all concerned here. Follow that intuition in this region, as your emotions are right on target.

OCTOBER

Saturn goes direct on the 16th helping to ease restrictions around communications, environment and relatives. You receive what you have done over the past now with strong accuracy. Progressive community efforts and activities balance out well with facts and research. This is a building influence. You may have earned a firm place among relatives and in the environment. On the 11th Jupiter accents the area of friends and organizations. Social pleasure and activities are accented this month. Your charisma and ability for arbitration can put you in the limelight. Romance is passionate and mysterious. There is something illusive and hidden which can be exciting. Your intellect joins with the romance vibration, suggesting that your mind is stimulated by these same responses. Someone who has great, possibly manipulative charm is indicated. You could be creatively productive working in solitude. Psychic-occult matters are strongly evident. What you learn through inner probing, periods of quiet as well as studies can be profitable. Going beyond, beneath, below and behind in retrospective periods can be strongly and richly rewarding. Counseling, healing and personal analysis can be tools for maturing with wisdom and understanding. Avoid drugs, alcohol indulgences, manipulative behavior or jealousy.

NOVEMBER

What is new and untried is accented. Mercury goes retrograde on the 11th, however, suggesting caution in travel, changes and communications. This is not the best time for visit or travel. Communications also need to be kept clear of confusion. Watch that active tongue and try to think accurately before you speak or write. A new romantic attachment is allied with this new chapter in your life. Someone like you, in that he/she loves changes, exploration, travel and having fun. This can be a pleasureable relationship, each needing much freedom. Commitment may be postponed, and present enjoyment a priority now. Mars goes retrograde on the 29th, suggesting restrictions on mutual funds and the delay of a legacy. Confusion and emotional turmoil around an inheritance is also a potential. Perhaps family issues are confusing and overly-emotional. Your work-service-employment region on the Full

Moon of the 10th comes in for practical rewards. Raises, bonuses, promotions or recognition are all indicated. The slow but sure routine is working successfully. There is still, until the 22nd, a bit of cleaning up regarding dismissal of past habits and problems. A type of hang over early in the month suggests you may need a post-graduate course here. So, spend more time on these matters and then enjoy a real Thanksgiving.

DECEMBER

Stimulation and excitement surface as you visualize and plan for a new chapter and image. The coming year suggests an upward motion for higher flight. Expansion, exploration, maturing and action are all strongly accented. You may reach out with trust toward the new. Romance may be encountered among relatives or environment now. Someone original and even eccentric may appeal to you. Opportunities in the community are of an innovative nature. Working with new concepts, ideals and actions pointed toward the well-being of everyone is goal one currently. The legacy and mutual funds situation continues to be delayed and confused. Home base offers empathy and understanding. You feel the warmth and comfort of safety and love here. Your home may also during the holidays give compassion, healing, comfort and assistance to those in need. Building, conserving and implementing your beliefs and talents brings in next year with serenity and exhilaration.

CAPRICORN
December 22 to January 21

Capricorn is a sign with much ambition, and you have a good eye for practical concerns and long-term gain. You have the abilities to make an excellent administrator or executive, and you are able to work for long periods of time alone, and without encouragement. What you crave most is the respect and honor of your peers—to be thought of as an individual of "consequence."

Along with the respect of others, you also want the trappings of success. The leather briefcase and the beautiful home are tangible hallmarks of both your worth and the affluent life you can work so hard to secure.

You give your heart, but never very easily. You have a fear of opening up and being vulnerable to others. Human emotion is both unpredictable and uncontrollable. Being a practical earth sign, you like to run smoothly, and love has a way of turning life upside down. You sometimes feel insecure, too, and you cover this up with a mask of indifference. But when you feel relaxed, either with your beloved or with one or two close friends, then your wonderful, dry wit comes through. Off comes your mask and you reveal yourself to be a warm, strong, and earthy lover or friend.

You are able to undergo prolonged periods of material or emotional privation if you have your eye on a worthwhile goal. Watch out that you don't become hardened by your work ethic. More than any other sign in the zodiac, a Capricorn needs to take time off and just play. If you can't seem to "find the time," then go ahead and write it down on your schedule! Without the balance and light heart that play provides, you may become hard and cynical, with little appetite to enjoy the fruits of all your hard work.

HIGHLIGHTS OF
1992—CAPRICORN

This appears to be your year. Emphasis is strongly on your region of a new self image and new beginnings. It is time for you to express your talents in open, practical ways. Neptune in this area goes retrograde from April 20th to September 28th and Uranus from April 22nd to September 24th. These are periods to slow down and work from within. This vibration is of cause and effect. Slow, sure, cautious always wins the race ultimately. It would be wise to use the retrogressions for inner probing as to your deep desires. Uranus suggests erratic influences, although potentially progressive and innovative, Neptune connotes indecision. It also deals negatively with drugs, alcohol, depressions and self-pity. In positive implementation of these influences, Uranus indicates what is new and unexplored. Neptune indicates the arts, literature, motion pictures, TV, psychic-occult affairs and beauty. How one uses these potentials is his/her responsibility and freedom of choice. Once these planets are again in direct position, then you may project desires and visualizations for practical effects.

Pluto will be retrograde from February 25th to July 31st affecting your region of friends, groups and organizations. Pluto indicates timing for introspection. Ridding yourself of past hurts and angers here offers you healthy energies for regeneration and progressive results.

Saturn is retrograde from May 28th to October 16th highlighting finances, assets, investments and values. These are times to be cautious, to research and work only with factual realities. Wait until Saturn is direct before making plans for investment.

JANUARY

New chapters and image are possible now, and projecting your talents attractively are open opportunities. With the new month of the 4th, these plans may be successfully organized and implemented. Your intellect is sharp, decisive, and analytical. You see behind facades and beneath surfaces, and work well with facts. Your vitality appears well grounded, with strong persistence. This really is a time to go for all those desires you have been mulling over previously. Romance is stimulating and fun with someone who is a lover of life. This could be a person you have known in the past, who surprises you with emotional reactions now. Jupiter turns retrograde affecting your sector of foreign travel, special training, publishing and psychic studies. This is not a positive time for travel and communications need great clarity to avoid confusion. Until Jupiter becomes direct on May 5th, you tend to have a critical, restrictive outlook in this area. Wait until then, as these situations lighten up and you feel more optimistic. The Full Moon of the 19th suggests questions regarding marriage, love unions and business partnerships. Avoid being overly-emotional, or giving or accepting manipulative behavior.

FEBRUARY

On the 25th Pluto turns retrograde until July 31st highlighting friends, groups and organizations. These are periods for inner investigation, for letting go of what is no longer important in these areas. Old habits and customs, beliefs and concepts need probing. The releasing of energies for more profitable goals here is necessary. Your financial picture is strongly accented with seesawing motion until mid-month when your intuition is clear and direct. Your mentality can be scattered, with many alternatives all needing research. People with charm may offer "pie in the sky" money opportunities. Wait and research before spending or investing. Caution with the budget is ultimately rewarding. Mutual goals and methods may be bonds between you. Relatives, communications and environment offer support and empathy for your goals. These who are older and wiser may offer advice. Listen to your intuition. Creativity in the arts, painting, sculpting, acting, music, literature and psychic knowledge can be appealing and constructive.

MARCH

Mercury turns retrograde on March 17th, putting emphasis upon your region of home base. Communications and travel should be kept in holding positions. Avoid impulsive choices or speaking before you think things through. Temper, power plays and quick decisions can get you into hot water. Visualize and organize until Mercury is direct on April 9th. Be creative but inactive on a conscious, busy level. Romance appears through relatives or community activities with someone who may be a former friend or lover. There is a deep feeling of karma in this relationship. Your financial situation needs balancing. Continue work with realities, avoid charming but irresponsible people and hard to pin down offers. Your nervous system may be highly keyed currently and you need changes of pace. Get outdoors, exercise, enjoy some social and cultural activities. Your vitality needs balancing between relaxation and enriching, progressive possibilities. You may feel on a mental emotional seesaw at this time. Take the wide, long-range view.

APRIL

This month both Neptune and Uranus turn retrograde. Neptune on the 20th until September 28th and Uranus on the 22nd until September 24th. You may feel restricted during this period. However, this can be a productive time for making lasting, practical plans. Mercury turning direct on the 9th lightens matters around home base. Past tensions and irritations cool off and members at home begin to project their individuality successfully. With this emphasis, power plays do not work. Mutual respect and lots of space are necessary. Romance appears right at your door, active, passionate and vital. Someone headstrong but colorful, ambitious and warm is accented for potential relationship. You may accomplish some type of creative work at home this month. Being independent, having your own business is one of your desires. Emotional satisfaction through the combination of putting your monogram upon your products and working with beauty and art bring great results. The New Moon on the 3rd adds further emphasis to this part of your life, so the fire and drive of these influences may help you reach the top of the ladder easily. Avoid appearing domineering.

MAY

Children and love affairs take the stage this month. There appear mutual desires for enduring, affectionate and practical relationships. Putting down roots, bonding with love and mutual interests are also highlighted. There is a need, however, to avoid stubborness and tunnel-vision. Confrontations which are unpleasant fail. Everyone needs to feel safe and secure. All of you connected in these situations have a deep need for lasting unions based on mate, home and family. The entertainment field may call to you. Acting, music, cruises, resort hotels, restaurants and bars and all luxuries bring pleasure. Other practical creative outlets can be healing, hospitals, hospices, animal shelters, orphanages, and any region where the disadvantaged and those in trouble need assistance. Saturn turns retrograde on the 28th affecting your money picture, until October 16th. You will find it important to live within your means and stick to your budget during these times. Save and put away your money and asset opportunities until Saturn is again direct. Jupiter is direct as of the 5th, and this may be a pleasant time for travel to other lands, meetings with people from different cultures, a new course of study, publishing and occult-psychic matters. You may combine business with pleasure in your travel plans. The study of art restorations, museums, historical sites, cultural artifacts or any kind of investigative work can blend harmoniously with travel.

JUNE

Your work-service-employment sector is accented this month. You may have more than one alternative, finding it difficult to choose. Communications, sales, public relations, travel, the media, and any field connected with the public are accented. You may need to use caution in scattering time and energies. Consummating one goal before starting another is suggested. Romance is flirtations, dualistic and fun. You may have more than one type of relationship as a potential. Someone who is witty, active, changeable, travelled and communicative is indicated. You may be giving attention mentally to commitments, such as marriage, love unions and/or business relationships. There seem to be conflicts between emotional needs for stability and security and desire for freedom and lack of responsibilities. If already wed, support, emotional companionship, feelings of safety and enduring bonds are accented now. Depressions, manipulative behavior or resisting change are to be avoided. The Full Moon of the 15th suggests original work done in solitude, perhaps writing, creative art, or whatever your personal field of expression accents. A new, original type of home is also in the offing. Unexplored areas offer challenges from your previous home base.

JULY

Pluto goes direct on the 31st lessening tensions and irritations around your sector of groups, friends and organizations. By now you should have arrived at some progressive decisions. Former customs, habits, concepts, people and reactions need introspection. What you have hidden or ignored calls for recognition and decision. Mercury goes retrograde on the 20th slowing down travel and communications, until August 13th. A legacy may be delayed now and the use of mutual funds postponed for action. Be cautious in using manipulation or power plays here. Relax and wait for more successful timing. After mid-July romance appears

in this region with someone ardent, ambitious, fiery and vital.
There can be stubborness and rigidities between you. Praise and
affection work much better than confrontations. Your area of
work-service becomes more stable and enjoyable. You feel a more
enduring kind of relationship possible. Be careful about taking
stands as rules and regulations result in rebellion. The Full Moon
of the 14th suggests full speed ahead for new beginnings.

AUGUST

With Mercury direct on the 13th, a legacy may arrive more
abundant and generous than expected. This could be a fun vacation month, featuring dramatic and colorful people and/or
places. You may receive recognition, a bonus, raise or promotion
plus profitable use of mutual assets. Romance appears in other
countries, perhaps with someone who has status, and is somewhat cautious and reserved. You may find it necessary to make
the first move toward a relationship. Work alternatives are dualistic, more than one potential offer indicated. Avoid impulsive
changes. Communications and travel are accented. You may
work successfully with the media, writing, teaching, acting, editing, sales, the public in general and travel in any form. Watch for
emotional and financial confusion and erratic behavior on the Full
Moon of the 13th. After the 23rd, there is further emphasis upon
foreign travel, special training and occult-psychic matters. Travel
for business with pleasure is accented. You may be offered a
learning opportunity allied with travel plans. Education available
in other countries is also a potential. This is an analytical, objective
and discriminating vibration. Avoid, being overly critical of these
opportunities.

SEPTEMBER

This is the month when both Uranus and Neptune turn direct,
Uranus on the 24th and Neptune on the 28th. Your region of new
beginnings and self-image are released from past restrictions.
These can be excellent times for going ahead with former plans.
Presenting your talents attractively can be most productive. After
mid-month career and public image are highlighted. A balance
between pleasurable working conditions and romance is possible. Your intellect is able to deal sucessfully with the law, politics,
arbitration, counseling, and decision-making. Creativity in the
fields of fashion design, interior decorating, modeling and theatrical areas can offer success. After the 12th, marriage, business or
love partnerships have strong emotional appeal. Home, mate,
family and a stable association are important currently. You could
make a sudden, impulsive choice based on the desire for an enduring union. If you are already committed, then there may be

swings of emotional responses. Avoid manipulation and erratic feelings.

OCTOBER

Jupiter enters your career region on the 11th, adding further optimism, action and enthusiasm to last month's emphasis here. Expansion and progressive opportunities are indicated. You may receive offers for a better position, recognition, raises and an upswing in your public image. Saturn turns direct on the 16th lightening your sector associated with money, assets, investments and values. Past restrictions concerning your money picture are currently eased. If you have worked with facts, you should now be in a position to make intelligent decisions about finances. Worldwide interests, New Age challenges and unexplored vistas are available for investments. These are true not only of money, but your talents and skills. Friends and groups may offer you a position of leadership and prestige. Romance appears also in this part of your life. Try not to be jealous or possessive. This person can be powerful, ambitious, dramatic and colorful and/or manipulative, domineering and self-indulgent. If already wed, emotional challenges are still in place for choices.

NOVEMBER

This can be a most interesting and stimulating month. Mercury goes retrograde on the 11th, cautioning travel and communications decisions. Avoid signing important documents and postpone travel. Unexplored, expansive and enthusiastic vibrations are accenting your region of the past, work done in solitude, karmic and family ties and institutions and restrictions. Romance is also based here currently, with someone who is humorous, vital, a lover of life and pleasure. This part of your present life suggests that work in quiet introspection, releasing of past griefs, angers, losses and habits can be productive. New horizons are potentials. Your creativity combines wisdom and knowledge with teaching, writing, editing, healing and lecturing. Mars goes retrograde on the 29th affecting marriage, love and business partnerships. It would be wise to use caution and check with your deepest emotions for an honest appraisal of your needs. If already committed, try not to be rigid or stubborn about healthy changes.

DECEMBER

Stimulating, creative work done in quiet still continues its positive influence. Your intellect is direct, open, sharp and vibrant. You may even feel prophetic at times. A progressive, exciting thrust is apparent in your mentality. After the 22nd that new chapter and image may be projected successfully. With the holidays present this month, finances, assets and values are accented. It would be wise to keep a balance between emotional spending and caution. Romance appears on the scene allied with financial challenges. Someone progressive, original and active is suggested. The relationship is strongly idealistic. With the New Moon of the 2nd, relatives and community activities can be fun. The past sentimental sweetness helps the bonding. You may discover some progressive outlets for use of assets and investments. Third World countries and problems, unexplored regions, cleaning up the environment and allied situations offer new uses for your money and value system. Your dreams and visions may be well implemented in the coming year.

AQUARIUS
January 21 to February 20

Genius or eccentric? Aquarius can be both, and neither, and these conditions can exist at the same time! Allow me to explain. An Aquarius can at one moment expound at length on quantum physics or the latest discoveries of extra-terrestrial life. In the next moment, they can forget their own address. Your unconventionality may shock or startle others, but what you wish to do is shake people out of their complacency.

Since you are an air sign, you are sociable and friendly, with a great interest in exchanging ideas with others. In this "Age of Aquarius," you embody your humanitarian gift to humankind, an extraordinary ability to envision the best that human beings are capable of.

You bring fun and excitement to your romantic relationships. You always manage to bring the new and unexpected to share with your lover. With your originality, you are able to make the best of most situations you encounter. A deep respect of personal limits brings with it an ability to work out relationship problems and to hang in there with your partner for the long haul.

At your visionary best, you live and breathe the spirit of equality. But do you actually practice it? The domain of human emotions may puzzle you, because where human hearts are concerned, reason and rationality have little sway. In the abstract realm of ideas you are indeed a genius, but you can be dumbfounded that others may not see the whole picture as you do. Have patience with your associates; they may take some time to catch up to your enlightened view of the world.

HIGHLIGHTS OF
1992—AQUARIUS

The major accenting of the new year, which will continue to flow all through 1992, emphasizes matters connected with the past, family traditions, other selves/lives, institutions, work done in solitude and restrictions. Attempting to find meaning and practical knowledge can be important. Neptune will turn retrograde from April 20th to September 28th and Uranus from April 22nd to the 24th of September. During this time investigation and research can be rewarding. These vibrations connect with the principle of cause and effect, so that what you have done in the past now returns. These can be creative periods for making plans, organizing and testing. Under situations the influence of Uranus and people arrive and disappear with equal rapidity. Your nervous system may feel very "geared up," so you will need periods of relaxation. Neptune connects with procrastination, indecision, drugs, alcohol and depression in its negative thrust. Music, the arts, literature, your intuition and the study of occult-psychic matters may be dealt with successfully. Once these two planets turn direct, your inner processes of investigation and decision making may be materialized effectively.

Pluto goes retrograde from February 25th to July 31st highlighting career and public image. Pluto indicates ridding yourself of what is no longer viable. Letting go of past hurts, angers, customs, outlooks and reactions can be necessary.

Saturn will be retrograde from May 28th to October 16th, putting the limelight on new beginnings and image. Here you need to work only with realities, patience, humor and persistence. Investigate and test and then take that big step with confidence.

JANUARY

As 1992 opens the spotlight is on your region of the past, family history, institutions, restrictions, other lives/selves and work done in solitude. Reviewing these parts of your life may bring much important data to the surface, for either discarding or projecting in progressive ways. Jupiter is retrograde affecting a legacy, use of mutual funds and regeneration of energies. Until May 5th when Jupiter will be direct, caution and discretion are important. An inheritance may be blocked and mutual assets may not be fluid now. Once Jupiter is direct, then an upswing in enthusiasm and action will be accented. The legacy may appear with more abundance than you expected. Mutual funds become loosened and practical investments are indicated. Romance is stimulating and optimistic, available through groups or friends. Someone original, independent and progressive may appeal to you. You may have opportunities for travel, combining an unexplored area with business needs. Communications can be rewarding. Groups and organizations with exciting new ideas offer you interesting changes of pace. Broader horizons and alternatives are suggested.

FEBRUARY

That new beginning and image are in the forefront. It is past time to step out and be innovative and original. Some of the inner you wants recognition and a different physical projection. After mid-month, finances, investments, assets and your value system are accented. Interests connected with water, oil, gas, shipping, export-import, ocean travel, psychic-occult fields, and arts and crafts take center stage. You would be wise to listen to your intuition but avoid getting emotions entangled with money. Don't permit dependents to lean on you. They are not your financial responsibility. Help them help themselves in other ways than loans or financial gifts. Romance after the 19th meshes with money and values. Pluto turns retrograde from the 25th until July 31st affecting career. Slow down, do some strong introspection and watch meanings from dream symbols and meditation. Rid yourself of angers or griefs, and project energies toward progressive, mature goals. Until the 31st, avoid taking outer action. Discard outworn reactions and lighten your past career burdens through a new, freer, but practical set of ambitions.

MARCH

Your region of relatives, communications and environment is being affected by Mercury turning retrograde on the 17th until April 9th. Avoid making big changes or trips. Avoid signing important documents or agreements until Mercury is direct once

more. Keep your temper cool and don't push. You may be feeling
rebellious, misunderstood by these around you. Make plans for
your goals and organize, but wait for making important choices
or actions. Romance is supportive, sweet and empathetic. You
may find someone of great value now, with strong "soul mate"
ties between you. Your money picture and assets appear fluid.
This could be an excellent month for projecting the new chapter
and image previously mentioned. You are feeling vital and excited by this new beginning image possibility. Trust yourself and
put your originality and innovative talents on stage. The Full
Moon on the 18th accents legacy, mutual funds and regeneration.
You may find ample emotional influences around these areas of
your present life. Be objective and discreet. Make a critical analysis based on factual information. You would be wise to make investments which have a natural ability for success, such as the
needs of the public.

APRIL

This is the month that both Neptune and Uranus go retrograde, Uranus from the 22nd to September 24th and Neptune
from April 20th to the 28th of September. Relax and do some active investigation and organization. Your region of the past, family traditions, institutions, restrictions and work done in solitude
is being accented. It is time to sort out the old and outworn. This
can be a maturing-growing period but it is also one of erratic motion. Use your humor and keep a steady course until these planets
are direct. Romance appears ardent, demonstrative and active. It
may be encountered among relatives or community activities. A
person who is a leader, vital, and ambitious is accented. You may
make an impulsive commitment. Try not to project power plays.
Your money picture tends to take off rapidly. Keep control of finances and values. Don't combine emotions with money. Avoid
manipulations or dependencies.

MAY

Your home base is out in front this month. You may work at
home with successful results. This could be a favorable time for
adding beauty and basic practical additions to your home, painting, new construction, decorating, or adding more land to the
original residential area. Romance appears steady and secure
with affection, family and mate important. You may meet someone right at the front door who is interested in an enduring, loving
commitment. You may also be hosting entertainment and social
activities at your home. Combining professional interests with
entertaining could be fun and productive. Your vitality and leadership abilities accent the sector connected with communications,

relatives and environment. Communications are active, direct, open and vigorous. Politics, the law, a new line of business, the military, engineering, or any unexplored field can bring you success. Saturn goes retrograde on the 28th, suggesting you slow down and avoid decisions regarding the new beginning and image until October 16th.

JUNE

Children and love affairs hog the limelight this month. There are dualistic and changeable alternatives which may be confusing. A flirtatious, fun-loving, witty and companionable influence is indicated. Romance is flexible, with much freedom and space necessary. Communications and travel are highlighted and your personal creativity could be enriching. Teaching, healing, writing, painting, design, fashion, sales or any field where the public is involved can be outlets for satisfactory results. Say what you mean in these areas of your current life. Speak up and out so your meanings are clear. Then listen to the others concerned. Mutual desires can be communicated with humor and ease. Your work-service-employment sector is highlighted, suggesting that empathy, healing, counseling and helping those in need are open for potential success. There are some other areas which also can be interesting employment ideas: music, acting, painting, sculpting, arts and crafts, and helping your community. Spending time on, near or around water can have a relaxing, soothing effect. There is a need to have time and quiet for yourself to keep a positive balance.

JULY

Marriage, love unions and/or business partnerships receive much attention now. You may be feeling impulsive, rushing toward a decision with ardor. If already wed, you may find some new ways of firing up romance. Mercury turns retrograde on the 20th, suggesting quieting down, thinking things over realistically and postponing actions until Mercury is direct on August 13th. A love partnership suggests power plays. While this relationship may be fun, passionate, colorful and dramatic, you would be prudent to wait and test before August 13th. If already committed, use humor and patience and do some inner research about the value of the partnership. Pluto turns direct on the 31st lessening the restraints upon the career sector. You should now have a clear awareness of what is important and how to achieve your goals. Your ambitions are high, and reaching the top of the ladder is a potential. Avoid appearing arrogant or possessive, jealous or manipulative. Keep all cards on the table and work for mutual beneficial results. Home base offers stability, pleasure and comfort.

AUGUST

With Mercury becoming direct on the 13th, marriage, business or love union relationships are accented. You have the ability to work successfully with communications and to see with clarity. This could be a fine month for honeymoon or travel among the "rich and famous." Children and love affairs take on a more objective outlook. You may find the areas of teaching, writing, lecturing, sales and public relations attractive. Humor and intellectual "travel" can be fun, opening up larger vistas for your leisure time. You may have more than one path of expression, with this dualistic vibration. Romance is discreet and objective. A stable, practical and mutually respectful arrangement is indicated. The use of a partner's assets needs investigation before projection. Real estate, counseling, art galleries, museums and historical sites all come in now for a mix of emotional and financial rewards, based on practical efforts. The New Moon of the 5th accents career ambitions off to a potential new start. Favorable recognition offers you higher status.

SEPTEMBER

Uranus goes direct on the 24th with Neptune on the 28th affecting your region of the past, psychic studies, family, institutions and restrictions. Previous research, planning and organizing can be projected with successful results. All the introspection and interpretation of dream symbols now mesh for new directing. Practical, down-to-earth goals and grounded, materialized aims are now at the starting gate. The wealth of the past now may be pointed toward the present with excellent effects. After midmonth your region of foreign travel, connections with people from different backgrounds, psychic-occult interests, publishing and special training are all highlighted. You could combine pleasure and business in a trip to other countries. You may also begin a new course of study-training effectively. In romance, someone from a different country/culture appears exotic, cooperative and full of charisma. Your area of work-service-employment may take off rapidly with new and unexplored opportunities. Real estate, children, the disadvantaged, restaurants and bars, counseling, music, acting and any area connected with nurturing and the emotions of the public are highlighted. You have a need to find some fulfillment in your work-service.

OCTOBER

Career matters and public image are strongly accented. Your ambitions have an intensity, and you feel well equipped for success. Your intellect is sharp, accurate, investigative and critical. You get right to the major points, based upon factual data. You know how to communicate with clarity and originality. Romance and emotional fulfillment are available in the career region. Someone intense, ambitious, fond of leadership and prestige is highlighted. You may either have mutual goals and methods, or jealousy and competition. Jupiter enters Libra on the 11th, putting the limelight on foreign travel, people from other backgrounds, publishing, education and psychic studies. This could be a profitable period for making a trip to other lands. You could make associations which, along with being pleasurable, contribute to your professional goals. Saturn turns direct on the 16th suggesting a new image may now be projected productively. Originality, worldwide interests and all space age interests surface for your use. You may obtain new and progressive data through travel or research. The materializing and grounding of your visions and dreams may be accomplished satisfactorily at this time.

NOVEMBER

Friends, groups and organizations indicate exciting and stimulating opportunities. The unexplored, faraway and different are accented at this time. Mercury goes retrograde on the 11th, suggesting that changes or travel would not be wise this month. There is a need to think before you talk or write. Impulsive action should be avoided. Communications need to be made clear, open and direct. During the holidays, fun and variety may be found among friends and groups. New ideas with people who are both progressive and service-oriented offer you opportunities for using your originality and skills. Romance is also discovered in this area, with someone who is a freedom-lover, fond of pleasure, travel, change and worldwide events. This may be a stimulating and colorful potential relationship, but both of you avoid responsibilities which may tie you down. Mars becomes retrograde on the 29th affecting your work-service-employment area. Your emotions tend to be confused with your work output, so avoid responding with your feelings. Try to be objective and remain cool. This is not a productive time to make changes. The Full Moon on the 10th indicates pleasure, hospitality and love at home.

DECEMBER

The work-service-employment region remains in the same static position. Take the attention off of this part of your life and turn it toward pleasures and fun with friends and groups. This is a fine time to write, teach, lecture, or communicate in any creative fashion. Romance appears to be new, different, changeable and somewhat erratic. There is an up and down swing here. This can be an idealistic but strongly intellectual kind of relationship. After the 22nd attention is placed upon the past. Take from it what is rich and important and discard the rest. With the New Moon of the 2nd, your money picture appears fluid. Best avoid over-spending. Your empathy and compassion can be the most benefi-cial presents possible. Lovers and children can be witty and fun, although hard to pin down for that "definite maybe." There is charisma here, but avoidance of duties and responsibilities as well. With the new year approaching, you step out with exhilara-tion and many fascinating plans for the successful future.

PISCES
February 20 to March 21

Pisces is the mystic of the zodiac. You are deeply religious, although not always in the orthodox sense of the word. As a mystic, you have an intense longing for some other reality, something both more magical and more elusive than the mundane, 9-to-5 world that we live in. You know on a gut level that all the frustrations and attractions of the world are actually an illusion. The Hindus call this illusion "maya," and at your best you live in the world but manage to maintain a sense of detachment so that this maya does not affect you too deeply.

Because you lack clear boundaries about what is "real," you may develop problems coping with the structure of day-to-day living. It is as if the whole concept of being limited by time and space becomes intensely irritating to you. Generally speaking, you have more important things on your mind.

One of these is falling in love. You are an incurable romantic. You came into this world a lover, and you will most likely leave this world a lover. Unfortunately, you tend to fall in love not with a flesh-and-blood person, but with your own projections. You also have a tendency to become bored with a relationship quickly. Still, if your lover can hold on lightly and provide the necessary romance and mystery, you will give unreservedly of your passion.

You have boundless imagination. All things are possible with you. Your symbol is the two fishes, swimming in opposite directions. This means you have the ability to transcend any limits and live in the heights, or depths, of which a soul is capable. You could live quite comfortably in heaven or hell. The key is either realm lies within.

HIGHLIGHTS OF 1992—PISCES

This new year will emphasize matters connected with friends, groups, organizations and goals. These can be fine periods for the practical implementation of common sense output. Many of your dreams and visions can be projected successfully. People who have "know how," the ones who sell, produce, act as agents and get your talents out before the public eye are accented. If you have been holding back, friends and groups offer you outlets. Public needs are important. Working with realities is necessary for success. It is time to buckle down and create workable items which are ultimately profitable. This influence also extends to making firm founfations with friends and organizations. It is time to put down roots in this region of your life.

Pluto turns retrograde from February 25th to July 31st affecting your sector of travel to foreign lands, dealings with people from different cultures/backgrounds, publishing, special education and psychic-occult affairs. These retrogressive periods are calling for you to let go of past habits, customs, angers and pains no longer viable. Your value system here is of importance.

Uranus will be retrograde from April 22nd to September 24th and Neptune from April 20th to September 28th. These planets indicate slowing down, keeping a balance among friends and groups. Action should be shelved until these vibrations are again direct.

Saturn in Aquarius goes retrograde from May 28th to October 16th accenting the past, family tradition, institutions, restrictions and past lives/selves. Letting go of all negatives and keeping what is helpful can enrich this year.

JANUARY

The necessity for building firm foundations with groups and friends is accented strongly. It would be wise to research and be practical when it comes to your decisions here. Organizations which deal with needs, with implementation of down-to-earth assistance attract your talents. With the New Moon of the 4th, this influence continues throughout 1992. Your mentality currently has enormous reserves of patience, persistence and analytical power. Romance is ardent, intense, fun and active. You may meet someone progressive, a traveler-explorer, needing liberty and space. The relationship could emerge at your career site. Short trips are accented, combining fun with business purposes. New opportunities, favorable recognition and emotional satisfaction are all apparent. Jupiter is retrograde in your region of marriage, love unions and/or business partnerships until May 5th. You need to use caution and reserve in this area during this period. Avoid impulsive decisions or being swept off your feet. Saturn accents your sector of the past, family, karma, other lives/selves, institutions and restrictions. A balance needs to be kept between feeling original and progressive, yet tied to past habits and concepts.

FEBRUARY

Pluto goes retrograde from the 25th to July 31st highlighting your area of travel to other countries, connections with people from other cultures, publishing, psychic-occult studies, special education and training opportunities. Pluto suggests periods of introspection, meditation and working with your inner value system. Make a balance sheet of pros and cons, then watch for the meaning of dream symbols and data received through silence and solitude. Ridding yourself of old, outworn ideas and customs opens up a cleansing-healing-transforming experience. Romance may be discovered among friends and groups with someone seeking a secure, stable and enduring relationship. After midmonth, emphasis appears in the region of new beginnings and self-image. Listen to your intuition. What you have assimilated from the past may now be packaged and used for sympathetic compassion. Your service-oriented vibration here indicates the need to show love and receive it, especially on a healing basis. Your intellect and communicative skills move from attention on the past to a new potential chapter and image. There is a softening, a fluidity and gentleness apparent here. The erratic past influence has slowed down, becoming more balanced now. You appear to have removed some barriers.

MARCH

During this birthday month finances, investments, assets and your value system are accented. Mercury goes retrograde from the 17th until April 9th, suggesting slowing down and playing your money situation cautiously. Avoid being impulsive and wait until Mercury is direct. Try to take the long-range view and don't react with temper or impatience now. Travel and communications are affected by this influence. Trips should lie postponed and take care in signing documents, agreements or contracts. Romance is new, sweet and feels like an old friend or lover at depth. As you are working with a new image, so too may this person be attempting to change. There can be mutual support, with similarities of outlooks and understanding. The Full Moon of the 18th suggests a cautious and practical attitude toward marriage, love union or business commitment. There is security and stability in this area. This is a positive time to diffuse from past successes those causes which have brought rewarding effects. Perhaps they may need some restoration or refurbishing. As your birthday period continues you are growing from the past into an enriching future-present potential.

APRIL

Mercury goes direct on the 9th releasing some tensions and restrictions regarding your money picture. New, explorative and active potentials are indicated. You may implement your own business or profession at this time. There is much activity regarding not only your finances and assets, but your values as well. Your personal skills and talents are ready for positions of leadership and executive recognition. Romance is bright and vigorous with someone who is individualistic, ambitious and forceful. Mutual space and respect is necessary for a successful relationship. Uranus goes retrograde from the 22nd until September 24th and Neptune from the 20th to September 28th. These positions accent your region of friends, groups and organizations. Work with routine and responsibility during these retrogressions. Build foundations and use practical, realistic methods toward goals. This Spring month could begin the blooming and blossoming of that new chapter and self-image.

MAY

This month's vibrations accent relatives, communications and environment. You may have interesting and pleasurable social activities. Romance may be encountered; stable, loving, enduring and companionable in potential. Your intellect and methods of communication may be slow but are steady and sure. You tend to delve deeply, work with factual data and then make your decisions. Relatives may find you more "fixed" in your opinions and actions than previously. This is a building vibration, suggestive of making foundations which are lasting and firm. The arts, painting, sculpting, theatre, music, food, healing and service-oriented fields can be inspirational and rewarding. Jupiter becomes direct on the 5th, releasing past restrictions upon marriage, love unions and business partnerships. Your past caution and working with realities pays off now. Your decisions in these areas are currently based upon practical, factual knowledge. Saturn becomes retrograde on the 28th accenting the past, family, other lives/selves, institutions and restrictions. You feel the need for changes of pace and for balancing your nervous system. Get away from routine from time to time. Listen to wisdom from within and avoid irresponsible but charming people.

JUNE

Home base is in the spotlight this summer month. With the New Moon of the 1st, there is a dualistic, changeable influence. You may feel like traveling, purchasing a second vacation home, a boat or trailer or adding to your present residence. You may also work from home base, writing, teaching, editing, composing. Romance appears at the front door with someone charming, witty, fun and at times scattered and unfocussed. Your financial situation has much activity, drive and ambition. You would be wise to obtain facts before making monetary decisions. You are eager to start a new business/profession, and while enthusiasm and optimism are strong, make sure you have firm underpinnings of reality. Much of your attention currently is on children and lovers. There is a combination of deep emotional attachment and equally strong rigidities. Manipulations may have an undercurrent here, despite harmonious facades. Avoid mutual dependencies in this part of your present life.

JULY

Your work-service-employment region is strongly accented now. Your ambitions are strong, and your desire for recognition and positions of leadership suggest rewards. Mercury turns retrograde on the 20th, suggesting a slowing down. This is not a profitable time to take trips. Wait until Mercury is direct on August 13th. Communications need clarity, avoiding delays or confusions. Try not to appear domineering, jealous or aggressive. After the 14th, romance becomes fiery and ardent. You may meet someone dramatic, colorful and as ambitious as you currently. Emotional fulfillments are possible through the entertainment field, law, politics, public relations, sales, large corporations, banking and worldwide challenges. Pluto turns direct on the 31st,

lessening the restrictive effect around travel to foreign countries,
dealings with people from different backgrounds, special educational opportunities, publishing and psychic-occult matters. If
you have worked with introspection, meditation, watched dream
symbols and probed your subconscious, now can be a fertile period for responding to any or all of the experiences described
above. You may add greatly to your creativity by either travel to
lands which hold a rich source of wisdom or by studying/train-
ing in integrating your inner and outer selves. Avoid upsets with
relatives or neighbors. Make sure communications are up-to-date
and clear.

AUGUST

Mercury going direct on the 13th takes the brakes off your
work-service-employment sector. You may travel for business
and fun, receive a raise, bonus, or new progressive opportunity.
Appearing before the public can gain you favorable recognition.
Your charisma and vitality are high. Romance may turn into commitment at this time. After being analytical and investigating
background, desires and mutual goals, a lasting relationship
could materialize. If already committed, further security and mutual aims can be implemented in practical ways. The question of
another residence or getaway place arises. You may feel the need
to enjoy a change of pace, social fun and short trips for new vibrations. On the New Moon of the 5th, faraway places may have a
strong pull. Delving into occult data can be enriching, and your
subconscious a source of creativity. Travel to areas such as the
Orient, the Near East and places near, on or around water can be
profitable. A new educational-training program needs investigation before decisions are clear. Publishing is a potential opportunity, especially work based on occult data, music, healing or mystery.

SEPTEMBER

Your attention may be on marriage or love unions. This is a
cautious and conventional influence, based upon practical approaches. If already wed or committed, mutual goals and understanding can be a deep bond. Uranus turns direct on the 24th and
Neptune on the 28th accenting friends, groups and organizations.
Progressive ideas and visions may now be implemented successfully. Emotions are calmed, and procrastination and indecision
lifted. Friends and groups can be helpful, especially in building-
conserving situations. Foundations appear firm. After mid-
month attention is highlighted upon a legacy, mutual assets and
regeneration of energies. You may receive an inheritance of much
beauty and history. There is also potential harmony in decisions

around the use of mutual funds. Cooperation and equality in partnership is accented. Balancing out work and play is important. Romance is in this section of your life, with someone of great attractiveness and charisma. He/she may have problems, however, being a people pleaser and indecisive. Communications connected with the law, politics, arbitration and counseling are also strongly within these vibratory influences.

OCTOBER

Jupiter enters your legacy, mutual assets and regeneration area. This indicates optimism, abundance and expansion, so if you did not receive that inheritance in September, you should receive it now. The mutual funds situation should be generous. An active thrust surrounds the regeneration of energies area, so that balance and harmony are easily attained. Saturn turns direct on the 16th. The dismissal of no longer viable beliefs or customs can be effective. Cleansing-healing-transformation based on a practical set of values is potentially available. This could be a lovely season for a trip abroad, as well as publishing, dealings with people from other cultures, and the study of occult-psychic matters. Some of your ambitions and vitality can be consummated in this sector now. Romance appears intense, forceful and even exotic. Someone colorful, powerful, active and dramatic is indicated. Investigation of past cultures, going beneath surfaces and behind national facades can be helpful to your creativity. Research, archeolgy, oceanography, history, and occult wisdom call out for pleasurable opportunities for growth.

NOVEMBER

Your career and public image sector takes off at a very high speed this month. You may travel, receive offers for progressive and stimulating opportunities and/or receive raises and bonuses now. Mercury goes retrograde on the 11th suggesting caution with travel and communications. Take care in what you sign, and say exactly what you mean. There is a great deal of enthusiasm and activity here, but don't get carried away. Romance has this same influence, with a person who is exhilarating, witty and always ready to travel or make changes. Your intellect and creativity appear pointed toward the public. Writing, teaching, lecturing, the entertainment field, sales, public relations, travel agencies and your own business are accented for successful projection. Avoid impulsive decisions and think over all offers carefully before making choices. Mars goes retrograde on the 29th accenting children and lovers. There is a seesawing motion between wanting to take action and avoiding changes or risks. Emotional relationships suggest the need for honesty and clarity. Manipulation, dependence, refusal to change and rigidities of the status quo all need a shake-up, but not right now.

DECEMBER

With the New Moon of the 2nd that new chapter and image are demanding recognition and projection. Show yourself as you really are, and discard the masks. Your career sector continues to be highlighted for changes, expansion and new opportunities. Communications can be witty, original and sharply to the point. Creativity blends with progressive methods of relating to the public. Your individuality comes through loud and clear. Romance appears allied to the past. A former friend/lover may offer exciting and innovative ideas about the potential relationship which is mainly intellectual, communicative, with a strong idealistic streak. It may also tend to be unrealistic, but romantic. Children and lovers continue to fight change. Avoid manipulative behavior. Permit yourself and others to be themselves. As 1992 completes its influence, home is the best place to be. Entertaining can be fun with guests who are intelligently communicative and witty. The new year suggests an enriching, maturing and firm foundation.

Professional Chart Readings From Llewellyn

There are many types of charts and different ways to use astrological information. Llewellyn offers a wide variety of services which can help you with specific needs. Read through the descriptions that follow to help you choose the right service. All of our readings are done by professional astrologers.

If you have never had a chart reading done before, we suggest that you order the Complete Natal or Detailed Natal service. We encourage informative letters with your request so that our astrologers can address your needs more specifically. All information is held strictly confidential.

Be sure to give accurate and complete birth data: exact time (a.m. or p.m.), date, year, city, county, country of birth. Check your birth certificate. *Accuracy of birth data is important.* Please include your order with the form on the last page or mail to the address that follows the descriptions. For a complete list of Llewellyn's Astrological Services, write for a free copy of the *New Times* or check the box on the order form.

Personalized Astrology Readings

APSO3-119 Simple Natal: This gives you the maximum benefit. It is a computer-calculated chart print-out that is designed and programmed by Matrix. It has all of the trimmings, including aspects, midpoints, Chiron and a glossary of symbols. We use Tropical/Placidus unless you state otherwise. $5.00

APSO3-101 Complete Natal: Our most thorough reading. It not only gives you the computer chart and detailed reading, but also interpretation of the trends shown in your chart for the coming year. It is activated by transits and focuses on any issue you specify. $125.00

APSO3-102 Detailed Natal: Complete natal chart plus interpretation with the focus on one specific question as stated by you. Learn about aspects of your chart and what they mean to you. $65.00

APSO3-105 Progressed Chart With Transits: Use this reading to understand the evolution of your personal power. Provides interpretation of present and future conditions for a year's time with a special focus as stated by you. Include descriptive letter. $85.00

APSO3-108 Vocational Guidance: Natal chart plus interpretation focusing on your career. Give details of work history (résumé) and outline of training and talents. Find your calling with this chart. $50.00

APSO3-118 Child Guidance: Avoid traumas by knowing what your child needs. Great for newborns, baby showers or Christmas. $60.00

APSO3-109 Relocation Reading: Find out what areas are best financially, romantically or for success. Specify up to three cities at least 100 miles apart for our analysis of their potential for you in terms of specific goals, or we will recommend three general areas according to your interests. Your present location may be one of the three. Describe what you are looking for in moving. $75.00

APSO3-110 Horary Chart: Gives the answer to any specific question. This is divination at its best! Should you marry? Will you get a new job soon? Give precise time of writing letter. $50.00

APSO3-503 Personality Profile Horoscope: Our most popular reading! This ten-part reading gives you a complete look at how the planets affect you. It is an excellent way to become acquainted with astrology and to learn about yourself. Very reasonable price! $50.00

APSO3-114 Compatibility Reading: Determines compatibility of two people in an existing relationship. Give birth data for both. $75.00

HOW TO ORDER
Send all birth date information and payment to:
Llewellyn's Personal Services
P.O. Box 64383-467, St. Paul, MN 55164-0383
Allow 4-6 weeks for delivery.

Astrological Services Order Form

**Complete order form with accurate birth data
plus your full name for all services.**

Service name and number_____

Full name (1st person)_____

Time_____ ☐ a.m. ☐ p.m. Date_____ Year_____

Birthplace (city, county, state, country) _____

_____

Full name (2nd person)_____

Time_____ ☐ a.m. ☐ p.m. Date_____ Year_____

Birthplace (city, county, state, country)_____

_____

Astro knowledge: ☐ Novice ☐ Student ☐ Advanced

Include letter with questions on separate sheet of paper.

Name_____

Address_____

City_____ State_____ Zip_____

Make check or money order payable to Llewellyn
Publications, or charge ($15 minimum):
☐ Visa ☐ MasterCard ☐ American Express

Account Number_____ Expiration Date_____

Day Phone_____ Signature_____

☐ **Yes!** Send me my **FREE** copy of the *New Times*!

Mail this form and payment to:
Llewellyn's Personal Services, P.O. Box 64383-467
St. Paul, MN 55164-0383. Allow 4-6 weeks for delivery.

Full Circle
A Song of Ecology and Earthen Spirituality

Full Circle combines visionary art with rhythmic lyrics and essay into a cohesive message for personal empowerment and planetary healing. It successfully integrates spirituality and politics while focusing on our global predicament. It offers spiritual activism as a cure for despair and shows how you can awaken your primal self. *Full Circle* unleashes the spirits of an endangered planet to roam the corridors of the wildest imagination. Order your copy today!

Full Circle, 192 pp., $12.95, L347

The Complete Handbook of Natural Healing

The Complete Handbook of Natural Healing explains how to prepare a variety of natural remedies in your home. With this easy-to-read guide you'll be able to heal yourself and your family of many minor ailments. Author Marcia Starck gives an introduction to the roots of disease, tips on staying healthy, and suggestions on a more complete diet. No home should be without this natural remedy handbook, so order your copy today!

The Complete Handbook of Natural Healing
384 pp., $12.95, L742

The New A To Z Horoscope Maker and Delineator

This is a completely revised and up-dated version of the standard text-book and reference guide on astrological techniques. Written by astrologer Llewellyn George, it features a dictionary of astrological terms, sections on every type of astrology and tons of information for the beginner. It is useful for those seriously interested in constructing horoscopes.

The New A to Z Horoscope Maker and Delineator
592 pp., $12.95, L264

To order please use order form on last page.

Astrology For the Millions

Written in an enjoyable, easy-to-understand style, *Astrology for the Millions* enables you to cast a complete, professional horoscope without complex mathematical calculations. Author Grant Lewi takes you beyond the basic natal chart and adds to the planetary aspects and basic Sun-Moon combinations. He gives key interpretations for all the planets in the signs, plus the tables necessary for locating them easily in your chart. This book also enables you to project your chart ten years into the future. Order today!

Astrology for the Millions, 408 pp., $12.95, L438

The Healing Herbs of the Zodiac

This is a charming little book jam packed with herbal knowledge. Natural herbal remedies are presented for ailments associated with the signs of the zodiac. For example, Aries is connected with the head and face. Under the Aries chapter, cayenne mixed with sage is a remedy for nervous headaches. This book also suggests remedies when dealing with specific inter-planetary actions. More than 70 herbs are covered, and the black and white drawings will help you with identifications. Pocket-sized.

The Healing Herbs of the Zodiac, 63 pp., $2.95, L486

Charms Spells and Formulas

Charms, Spells and Formulas shows you how to make and use Gris Gris Bags, Herb Candles, Doll Magic, Incense, Oils and Powders. Written by Ray Malgrough, it can be used to gain love, protection, prosperity, good luck and prophetic dreams. It is a practical guide to simple folk magic involving the lore of Louisiana Hoodoo, New Orleans Voodoo and other southern traditions. *Charms, Spells and Formulas* is as enjoyable as it is practical. Order today!

Charms Spells & Formulas, 171 pp., $6.95, L501

To order please use order form on last page.

Horary Astrology
The History and Practice of Astro-Divination

This guide by Anthony Louis is for the intermediate astrologer and gives information on the art of astrological divination. It's the best method for getting answers to questions of personal concern: Where are my keys? Will the house burn down? Will I ever have children?plus countless others. The basic premise behind horary astrology is that a question, like a person, comes into the world at a particular significant moment. Discover horary astrology today!

Horary Astrology, 500 pp., $18.95, L394

Financial Astrology

Financial Astrology, edited by Joan McEvers, shows you how to use astrology for financial success. It includes charts of successful, famous investors. It also discusses how natal charts can be interpreted to find out if your success is in commodities, real estate, precious metals, or another area. *Financial Astrology* gives new insights into the cycles techniques of financial wizard W.D. Gann. This is volume three of Llewellyn's ongoing New World Astrology Series. Send for your copy today!

Financial Astrology, 368 pp., $14.95, L382

Prediction In Astrology
A Master Volume of Technique and Practice

Prediction In Astrology is the most instructive and comprehensive book ever written about prediction in mundane astrology—the astrology of nations and celestial phenomena. Master astrologer Noel Tyl shares the most comprehensive overview of Solar Arc theory and practice ever written in the English language. He also examines the developments of the Mid-East war, and extends insights into the next millennium.

Prediction In Astrology, 400 pp., $18.95, L814

To order please use order form on last page.

SUPER DISCOUNTS ON
LLEWELLYN DATEBOOKS AND CALENDARS!

Llewellyn offers several ways to save money on our great line of almanacs and calendars. With a four-year subscription you receive your books as soon as they are published. The price remains the same for four years even if there is a price increase! Llewellyn pays postage and handling as well. *Buy any 2 subscriptions and take $2.00 off! Buy 3 and take $3.00 off! Buy 4 and take an additional $5.00 off!*

Subscriptions (4 years, 1993-1996)

☐	Astrological Calendar	$39.80
☐	Sun Sign Book	$19.80
☐	Moon Sign Book	$19.80
☐	Daily Planetary Guide	$27.80

Order *by the dozen* and save 40%! Sell them to your friends or give them as gifts. Llewellyn pays all postage and handling on quantity orders.

Quantity Orders: 40% OFF

1992	1993		
☐	☐	Astrological Calendar	$71.64
☐	☐	Sun Sign Book	$35.64
☐	☐	Moon Sign Book	$35.64
☐	☐	Daily Planetary Guide	$50.04
☐	☐	Magickal Almanac	$71.64

Include $1.50 for orders under $10.00 and $3.00 for orders over $10.00. We pay postage for all orders over $50.00.

Single copies of Llewellyn's Almanacs and Calendars

1992	1993		
☐	☐	Astrological Calendar	$9.95
☐	☐	Sun Sign Book	$4.95
☐	☐	Moon Sign Book	$4.95
☐	☐	Daily Planetary Guide	$6.95
☐	☐	Magickal Almanac	$9.95
☐		Goddess Book of Days	$12.95
☐		The Goddess Calendar	$9.95

Please use order form on last page.

LLEWELLYN ORDER FORM
LLEWELLYN PUBLICATIONS
P.O. Box 64383-467, St. Paul, MN 55164-0383

You may use this form to order any of the Llewellyn books or services listed in this publication.

Give Title, Author, Order Number and Price.

_____

_____

_____

_____

_____

_____

_____

Shipping & Handling: We ship U.P.S. when possible. Include $1.50 for orders under $10.00 and $3.00 for orders over $10.00. Llewellyn pays postage for all orders over $50.00. Please give street address.

Credit Card Orders: (minimum $15.00) call 1-800-THE-MOON (U.S.A. & Canada), during regular business hours, Monday through Friday. Other questions please call (612) 291-1970. You may mail in your charge order:

☐ **Visa** ☐ **Master Card** ☐ **American Express**

Account No. _____

Exp. Date _____ Phone _____

Signature _____

Name _____

Address _____

City _____ State _____ Zip _____

☐ Yes! Please send me your free catalog!